SHORT CUTS
for busy dressmakers

SHORT CUTS
for busy dressmakers

Ann Ladbury

Clothes designed by Janet Palmer
Illustrations by Jil Shipley

B.T. Batsford Ltd, London

Acknowledgment

I would like to thank Bernina sewing machines for their help with ideas and the preparation of samples of stitches.

First published 1980

ISBN 0 7134 1811 7
Set by Tek-Art Limited
Printed by The Anchor Press Ltd
Tiptree, Essex
for the publishers B.T. Batsford Ltd,
4 Fitzhardinge Street, London W1H 0AH

Contents

Introduction

This book is really about saving time; about how to sew successfully but yet not spend too long on it.

Why are we in a hurry? Why do we want to produce things in less time than it once took? Because our whole existence and the framework of life is different. More activities are open to us and we want to take part in many of them. Not long ago the chance to play various sports or to attend social functions and entertainments was open to relatively few. So our time has to be re-allocated but not I hope at the expense of such an enjoyable and economical activity as sewing.

Everyone, from time to time, wants something in a hurry. Even I, steeped in the craft and its traditions, have to choose a pattern that is easy, fabric that won't be any trouble, and avoid lengthy processes when I am short of time and need an outfit quickly. And how I bless such things as Wundaweb and Velcro to help me. I have chosen processes for the book that make good practical use of the aids available to us and I have packed in lots of tips too. The contents are confined to processes of two kinds: those that are quick to do and those that can be time-consuming but cannot always be avoided. For the latter I have described how I work them in a quick, easy way.

There are a number of reasons besides lack of time for which short cuts in sewing are sought. I hope one of them is not a desire to lower standards. Not only is that obviously undesirable and very short-sighted, but it is unnecessary. Taking a short cut or using an aid or a gadget does not have to equate with inferior results — all the things I suggest in this book make for excellent results.

Where the following reasons for adopting short cuts are concerned, it is in all cases a very good thing to take advantage of a quicker or easier method.

Limited skill

With all crafts it is necessary to practise in order to be skilful. If you haven't done very much sewing or if the things you have made have been spaced out in time you should avoid complicated processes and styles. You may reach the limit of your interest in pursuing the craft, but happily, fashion is such that it is easy to be well clad without having to make classic outfits.

Loss of interest

If your sewing takes a long time and you don't seem to be getting anywhere, it is easy to lose interest. Quick, successful results that you can wear will encourage you to go on.

Lack of confidence

Your confidence may have been sapped earlier by mistakes at school, by a mother who can make anything or you may just be the sort who is not relaxed with practical things. Adjust your approach to consider the few actions you need to take in order to make something, not the many; consider also the little time it will take if you adopt some short cuts.

Lack of experience

Limited sewing experience means limited knowledge of handling different fabrics; making a range of simple garments is a quick way to increase your knowledge.

All the designs in Part Two provide you with the chance to increase your skill and confidence while making things to wear. Choose from the fabrics suggested and use the processes in Part One and you can't go wrong.

PART ONE
Processes & techniques

General tips

Use a medium to large machine stitch, not a small one.

If the fabric wrinkles or puckers when you begin machining, put a piece of tissue paper or old pattern pieces underneath.

Avoid fabrics like checks that take a long time to lay out and prepare.

Plain fabrics show every stitch and seam line; small prints and patterns are easier.

Avoid processes where you went wrong last time. Practise those when you have plenty of time.

It is actually quicker to use the iron on each process as you work. When complete, the garment needs only a quick press.

Always have the iron out when sewing.

Don't hurry the pressing. An extra 20 seconds spent now is worth 2 minutes of frustration later.

Think of the iron as a sewing aid; use it before you stitch as well as afterwards.

Avoid close-fitting styles; they will take longer to fit.

It is easier to make a top and skirt, if you have fitting problems, than a dress.

When attaching wide braid press it in position with strips of Wundaweb which do not need to be tacked and which make it firmer.

Attach braid or ribbon with one row of machine stitching down the centre.

Choose loose styles drawn in with a belt, elastic, etc.

If you choose fabric that frays, make sure you have a bottle of Fray-Check by you as you sew.

When using pile fabrics or those with a one-way pattern, mark a chalk arrow on the wrong side of each piece after cutting out, so that you will see clearly the direction in which to stitch.

Eliminate clearing up — spread an old sheet, piece of plastic or even newspapers on the floor round the machine and working area to catch the bits.

Jersey and knits are easy to sew provided you choose the correct processes.

Where appropriate choose border fabrics or those with ready-hemmed edges to save time.

Needlecord and cotton velveteen are not difficult to sew, contrary to general opinion.

Velvets with woven backing and deep pile are very difficult to sew.

Velour is easy to sew.

Panne velvet is not difficult to sew.

Buy white cotton fringing and dye it any colour.

Buy white or écru crochet edgings and inserts and dye any colour.

Buy two silky dressing gown girdles in different colours and twist to make into a belt.

Remember that most fabrics need to be softened with steam in order to press them properly.

Instead of pinning down a pattern, place a couple of things on it to weight it while you chalk round the edge. Remove pattern to cut out.

If threads slip and elude you, lick your fingers for a better grip.

When stitching a bias seam use a slight zig-zag stitch to keep the 'give' in the seam.

Reinforce the top of a slit seam by placing a folded piece of ribbon or tape under the final few machine stitches.

When applying binding ease it on round concave edges but stretch it to go round convex curves.

Twill weave braid — the sort without a selvedge — is a good substitute for binding.

If you are stitching to a V, start at the point and stitch outwards; return to the point and stitch the other side.

1 Pockets

If you don't want to omit pockets completely either because you need them or because they form part of a style feature, choose one of the following types.

POCKETS FOR USE

Vertical seam pocket

This is the easiest type of pocket to make; it is not visible and you can use it. The seam pocket can be added to any garment and placed in any convenient position. Its only disadvantage is that it can become floppy and wrinkled but this is overcome by using interfacing to keep it flat.

The pocket bag is an oval shape angled from a straight vertical edge 22 cm long. If you have to cut your own, draw round your hand to obtain the right shape and size.

Cut out once in soft iron-on Vilene and twice in fabric for each pocket. If the fabric is bulky cut one piece in cotton lawn, nylon jersey or lining fabric.

Press the interfacing to the wrong side of a piece of fabric (not the lining piece). This is the back section of the pocket.

Fig 1.1

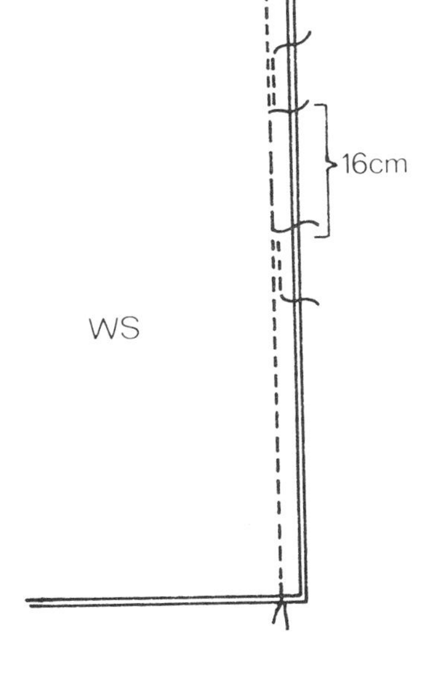

On the garment mark the pocket opening in the seam 16 cm in length. Machine the seam from hem to lower chalk mark and from the upper mark to the top of the garment, reversing the stitching to fasten off at each end of the pocket opening. Adjust the machine to the longest stitch and machine the length of the pocket opening. Press the seams open (fig 1.1).

Place the back pocket bag to seam allowance of back of garment, with right sides together, and machine, taking no more than 5 mm seam allowance (fig 1.2).

Fig 1.2

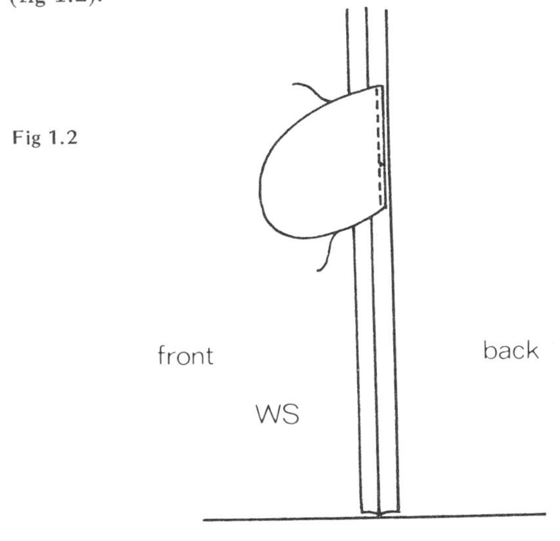

Attach the front pocket (it may be lining) to the front in the same way. Press open the seams.

Re-press the back pocket so that it extends towards the front of the garment and lies on top of the front pocket piece. Snip the seam allowance on the back of the garment level with the end of the pocket, at the top and bottom. Neaten the edges of the garment seams.

Pin the pocket pieces together, inserting the pins well within the outer edge. Using tailor's chalk, mark the shape of the bag, drawing a line from the seam at the top of the pocket opening, round the outer edge and finishing at the garment seam. Machine on this line.

Remove pins. Trim the edges to 5 mm and zig-zag over the two edges to neaten (fig 1.3).

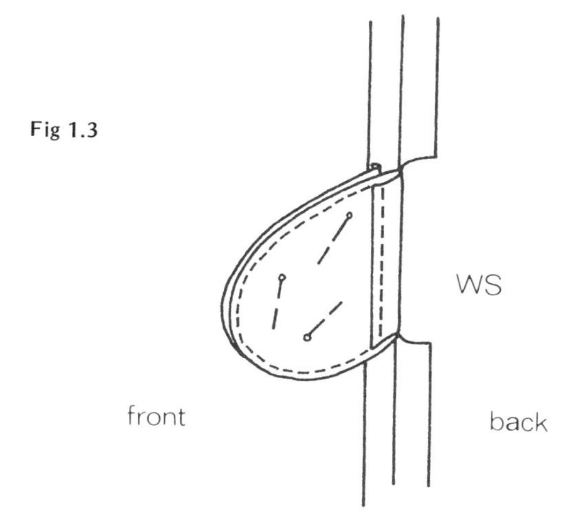

Fig 1.3

Cut a piece of Wundaweb 12 cm long and slip it under the pocket at the front. Push it into the fold at the seam between the garment and the pocket to hold the pocket in position. Press well to melt the adhesive. Remove the large machine stitches in the seam (fig 1.4).

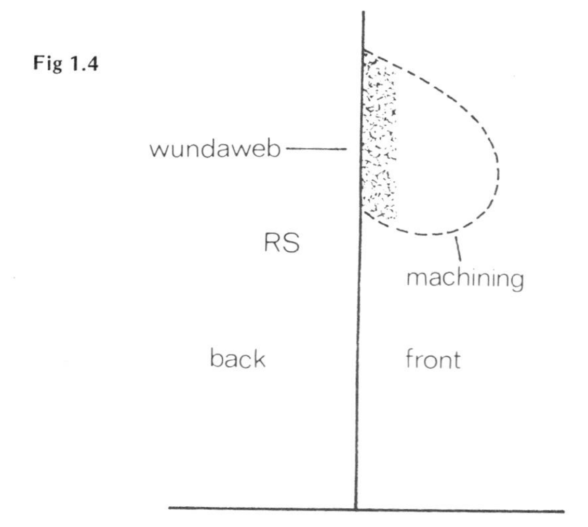

Fig 1.4

TIP If you want to make a feature of the pocket, baste it to the garment, draw a chalk line on the right side within the edge of the pocket and machine.

Horizontal seam pocket

If you have a yoke seam on a shirt, jacket, skirt or trousers, a pocket can easily be inserted. Begin by cutting a piece of Vilene exactly to the size of the bag. This will vary according to the position of the garment. Pin it to the right side of the garment and trim to size, making sure the edges will not interfere with processes to be worked later. This is the pattern.

Cut one piece of lining fabric the same size as the Vilene but adding 1 cm seam allowance all round. Cut a piece of garment fabric but make it 3 cm deeper than the lining. Cut a piece of soft iron-on Vilene the same size as the fabric and press it to the wrong side (fig 1.5).

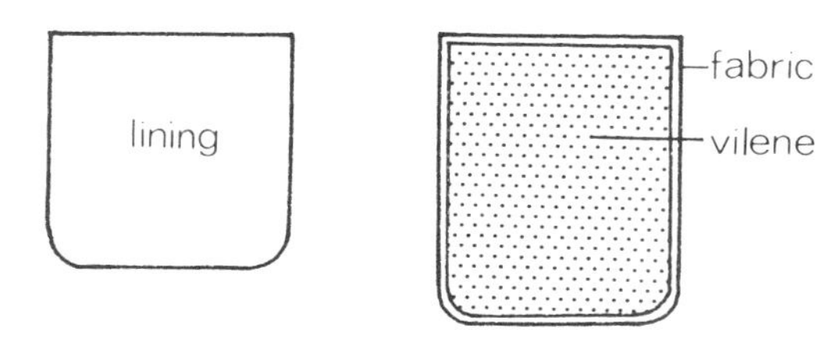

Fig 1.5

Stitch the garment yoke seam but leave a gap where the pocket is to go. The gap should be the width of the original Vilene pattern. Alter your machine to its biggest stitch and stitch across the pocket opening. Press the seam open, neaten the edges and add top stitching if you wish (fig 1.6).

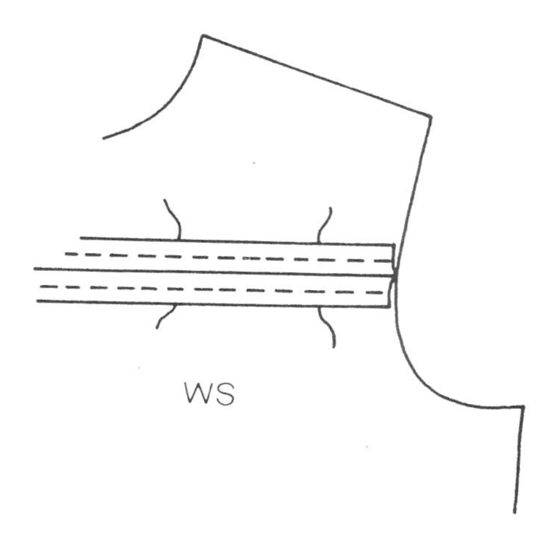

Fig 1.6

On the wrong side put the piece of pocket lining to the lower yoke seam allowance with right sides together. Machine 3 mm from the edge. Press so that the pocket lining hangs down (fig 1.7).

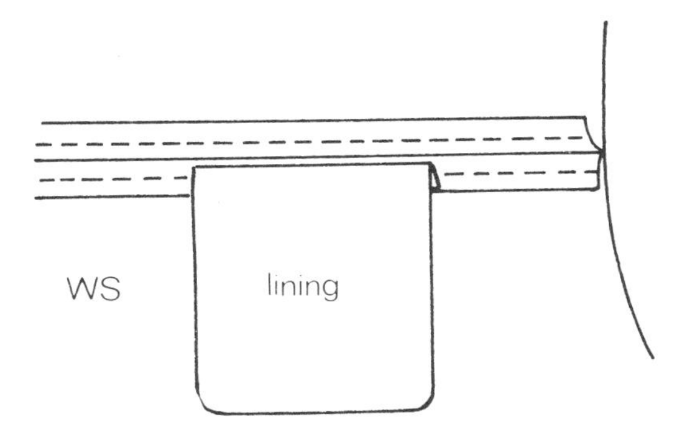

Fig 1.7

Put the interfaced fabric right-side down on top of the first piece with the edge level with the edge of the upper seam allowance on the yoke. Machine the two together 3 mm from the edge. Neaten the pocket edge by working zig-zag stitch over both edges (fig 1.8).

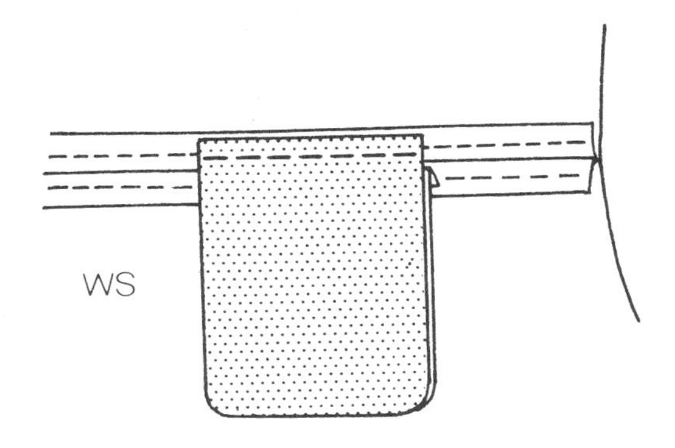

Fig 1.8

Pin the pieces of pocket bag together. Mark the size and shape of the pocket with tailor's chalk or with pencil if chalk is not visible on the Vilene. Machine round the bag, trim the turnings to 5 mm and neaten both edges together. Where the bag crosses the yoke seam, herringbone the edges of the bag to the seam allowances. Remove pins, press well and remove the large machine stitches in the seam (fig 1.9).

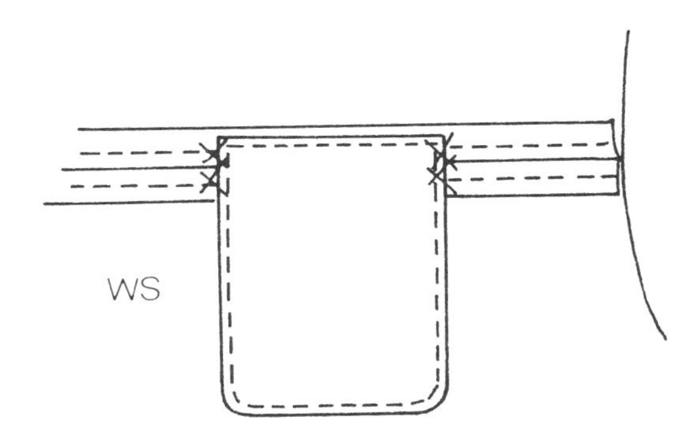

Fig 1.9

Patch pocket

This is mainly decorative with limited functional use, simply because things make it bulge. Decide on the best size and position by cutting a piece of Vilene and pinning it on the garment in various places and at different angles, trimming the Vilene until you are satisfied. This is the pattern.

Cut a piece of soft iron-on Vilene 4 cm deeper than the experimental pocket. Cut a piece of fabric the same size. Cut one more piece 4 cm shorter than the Vilene. These three pieces will make one pocket. If the fabric is bulky cut the smaller piece from cotton lawn, lining material or nylon jersey (fig 1.10).

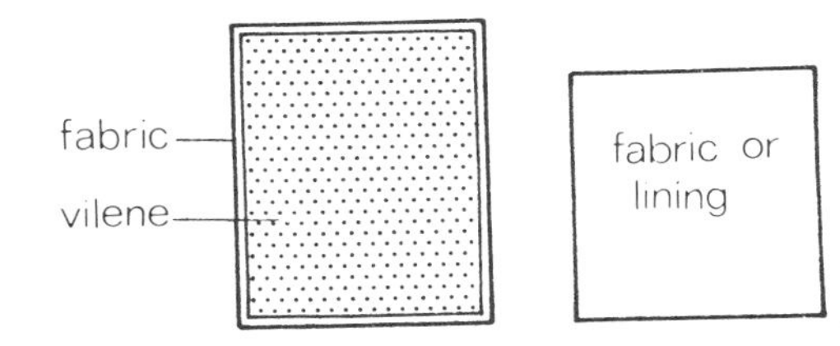

Fig 1.10

Place the lining piece to pocket piece right sides together with top edges level and machine, taking 5 mm seam allowance. Press the turnings open if both layers are fabric, press towards lining if the smaller piece is made of lighter fabric (fig 1.11).

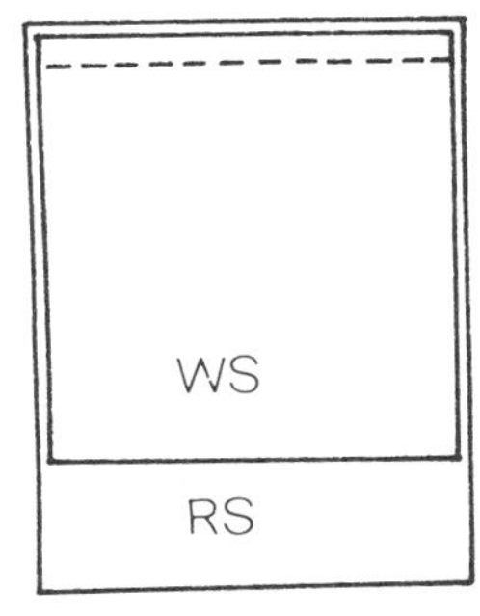

Fig 1.11

Bring the three raw edges of pocket and lining together, insert pins round the outside, well within the outer edges. The lining is smaller than the pocket so you will have to force the edges to meet (fig 1.12).

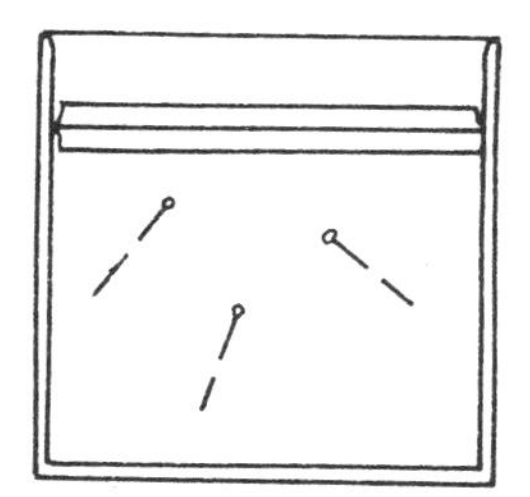
Fig 1.12

Using tailor's chalk and a ruler, chalk a line on which to stitch. Mark a gap 4 cm long in one side through which to turn the pocket. If the pocket has curved corners use the paper pattern, or original Vilene pocket, as a guide to marking accurate pairs of curves.

Machine all three sides, reversing at the top and at each side of the gap (fig 1.13).

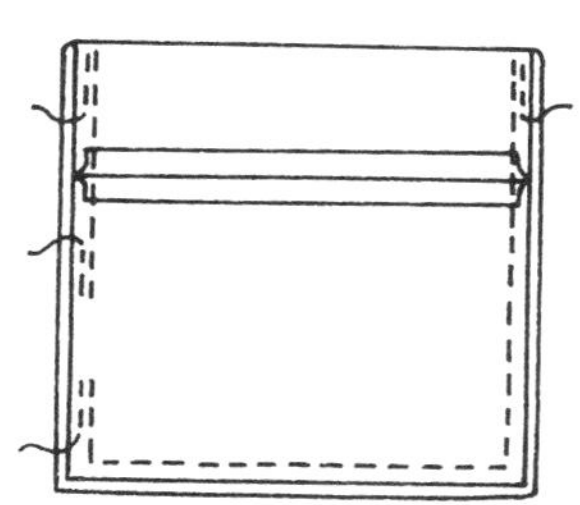
Fig 1.13

Remove pins. Trim raw edges to 3 mm and cut off the corners. Press the stitching flat. Push the pocket through the gap and turn it right-side out. Roll the corners and edges and press the edge from the lining side. Press the raw edges inwards at the gap.

Edge stitch all round the outer edge of the pocket. Machine again across the top 2 cm down from the top edge. Press (fig 1.14).

Fig 1.14

Place pocket in position on the right side of the garment, anchor with two pins. Baste the pocket across the top and then round the other three sides. Do not remove the pins.

Machine, starting at the edge level with the lower row of machining, stitch at an angle up to the top of the pocket, swivel the work, stitch along the top for three stitches, swivel and stitch round the pocket parallel with the edge. At the second corner repeat the triangle (fig 1.15).

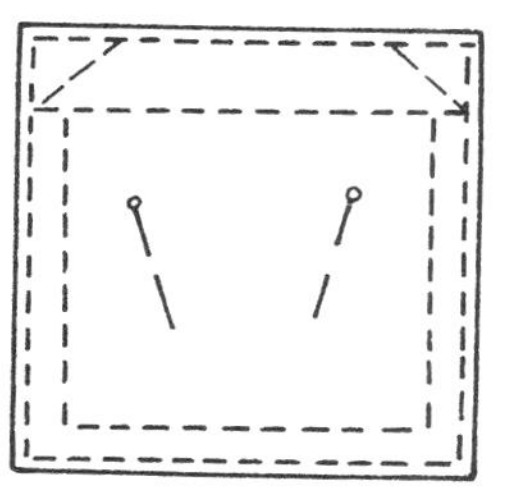
Fig 1.15

Remove pins and basting. Fasten off machine ends. Press well on both right *and wrong* sides of pocket.

TIPS Edge stitch the pocket and leave your machine set on that stitch; don't do any more sewing before stitching the pocket in position. This will ensure two rows of identical stitching.

When making the strengthening triangles at the top of the pocket count the stitches as you work the first one and make the second corner identical.

Double patch pocket

If you require two patch pockets, one above the other, the quickest way to do them is to make one and divide it with machine stitching.

Cut a piece of fabric the width of the lower pocket and long enough to extend from the top pocket position right down to the base of the lower pocket. Add 3 cm hem allowance at the top and 1.5 cm round the other sides.

Neaten round all four sides. Turn in the top edge 3 cm and press. Slip a piece of Wundaweb under the edge and press well. Machine on the edge across the top and again 2 cm below and parallel (fig 1.16).

Turn in and tack the other three sides of the pocket. Tack and press. At the edge that will be nearest to the side seam slip a strip of Wundaweb, cut to 1 cm wide, under the edge and press. The strip should be about 18 cm in length (fig 1.17).

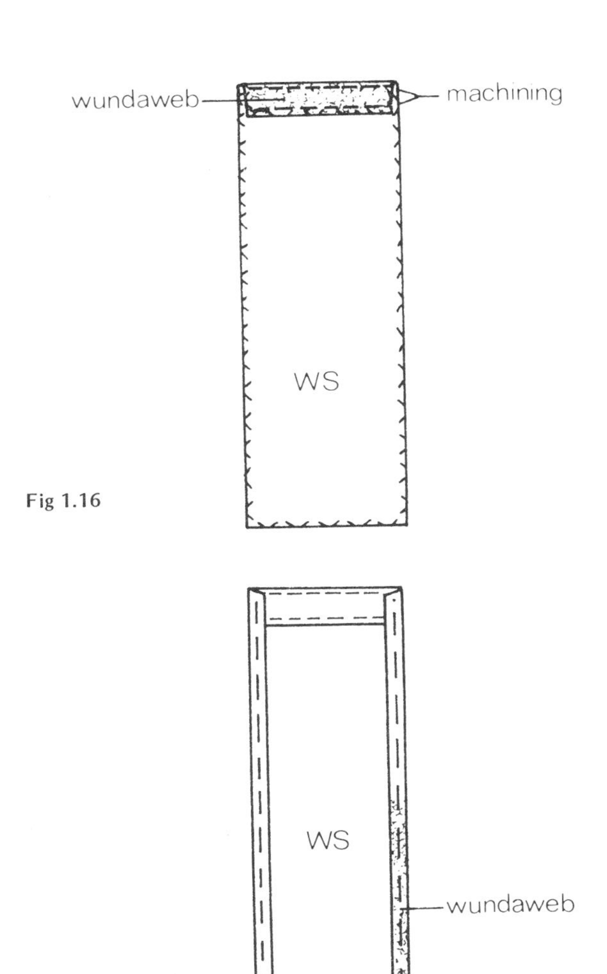

Fig 1.16

Fig 1.17

Place the pocket on the right side of the garment and pin in position. Baste across the top and round all edges. Machine in place all round but leaving a space of 12 cm where the Wundaweb has been

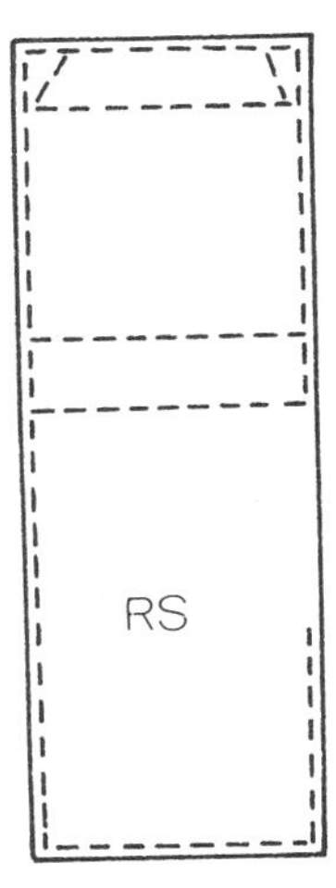

Fig 1.18

inserted. Stitch up from the corner for 6-8 cm then stop. Start again 12 cm above and continue to the top. Stitch triangles at the top corners as described for the previous patch pocket (fig 1.18).

Using tailor's chalk, rule two parallel lines across the pocket, one to mark the base of the top pocket, the other to mark the top of the lower pocket. Machine on these lines. Fasten off all ends of machining. Remove pins and tacking and press well on both sides (fig 1.19).

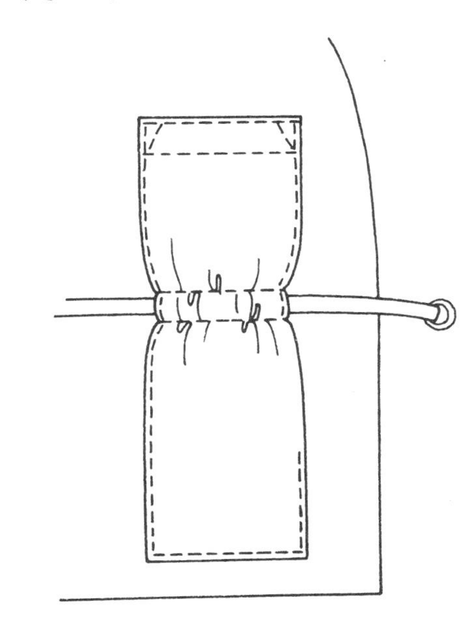

Fig 1.19

TIP If the garment has a belt, make a slot for it by stitching the parallel lines described above at waist level. Mark these lines before attaching the pocket to the garment and do not stitch across the ends of the belt slot.

POCKETS FOR DECORATION

Pockets which involve cutting the fabric take a long time to do properly. If you want the effect that a flap or a welt provides make them purely decorative.

Cut a piece of Vilene to the shape of a flap or welt and pin it to the garment in various positions, trimming it until you are satisfied. This is the pattern.

Flap

Cut a piece of soft iron-on Vilene to size allowing 1 cm seam allowance all round. Cut two pieces of fabric the same size, or, if the fabric is bulky, cut one piece in lining fabric. Trim 2 mm off the outer edges of the lining or under piece of the flap. Press the Vilene to the wrong side of the outer piece (fig 1.20).

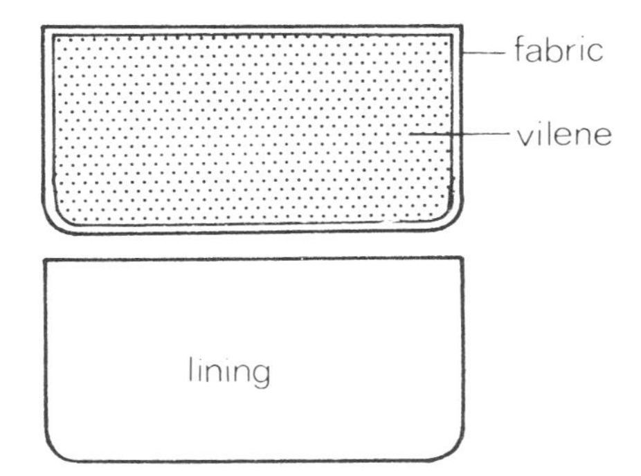

Fig 1.20

Place flap and lining right sides together making the edges meet. Tack together. Machine across the ends and along the bottom, taking 1 cm seam allowance. Chalk a line on which to stitch, especially if the flap has rounded corners (fig 1.21). Remove

Fig 1.21

tackings and trim turnings to 5 mm and cut off the corners or snip the curves. Turn flap right-side out and roll edges. Press on both sides. Baste along the flap to hold the layers together. The flap will be slightly curled inwards due to the fact that the lining was smaller (fig 1.22).

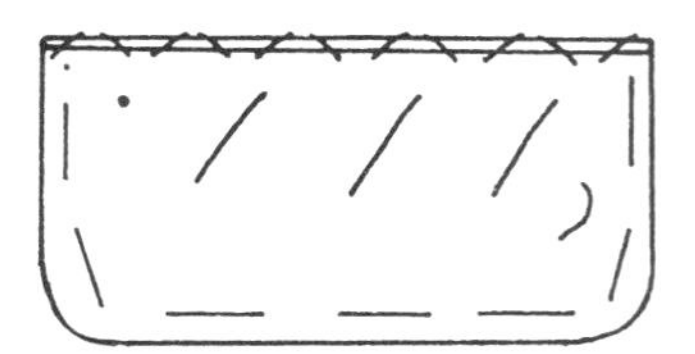

Fig 1.22

Trim the raw edges at the top of the flap to 3 mm and neaten the edges together. Press.

Place the flap on the garment upside-down and right-side down with the neatened edge in what will be the position for the top of the flap. Baste to the garment. Machine flap to garment, placing the stitching 3 mm in from the neatened edge. Remove tacking, roll flap down so that it is right-side up and tack firmly below the join. Press well and stitch by machine or hand 5 mm below the join. Press again (fig 1.23).

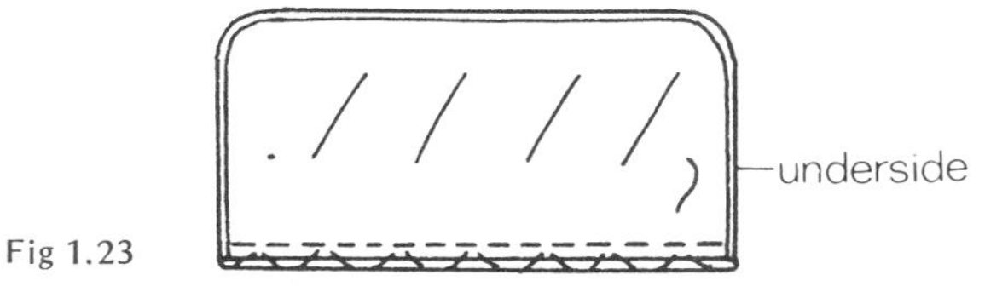

Fig 1.23

Finish by sewing a button through the centre of the flap and the garment, or insert a metal-capped press stud (fig 1.24).

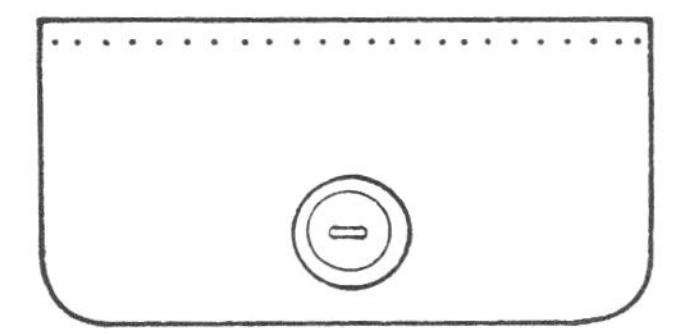

Fig 1.24

Welt

A welt is a rectangle, usually fairly narrow. Using an experimental welt cut in Vilene, cut a piece of fabric double the width plus 1 cm seam allowance all round. Cut a piece of soft iron-on interfacing the same size and press it to the wrong side of the fabric (fig 1.25).

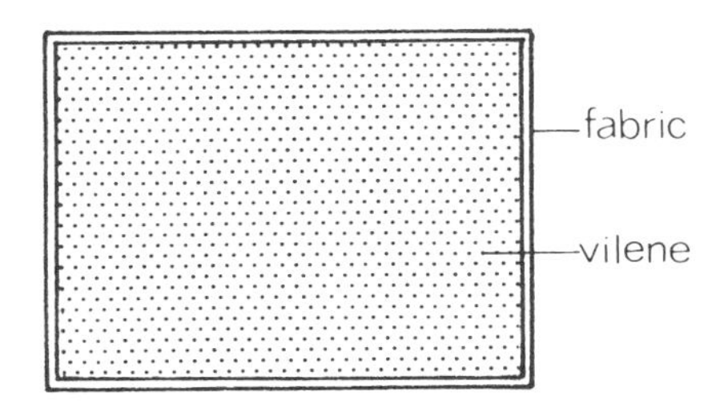

Fig 1.25

Trim a little off the ends of the welt at an angle, starting halfway along the side and graduating to 2 mm at the raw edge of the welt (fig 1.26).

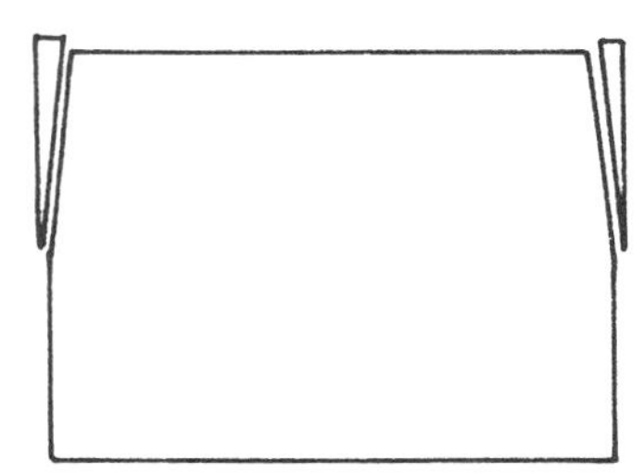

Fig 1.26

Fold welt right sides together, make the ends meet and pin. Machine across the ends taking a 1 cm turning. Trim edges to 5 mm and cut off the corners (fig 1.27).

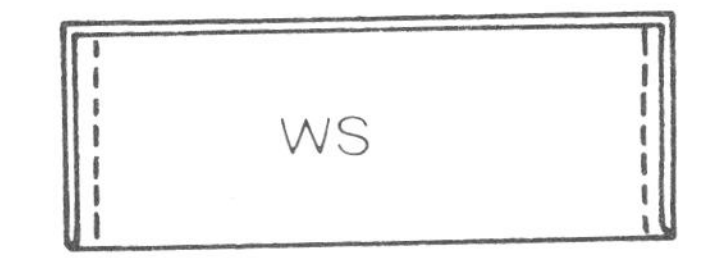

Fig 1.27

Turn welt right-side out and roll the ends. Press. Baste across the welt to hold the layers together. The welt will be slightly curled. Trim raw edges to 3 mm and neaten (fig 1.28).

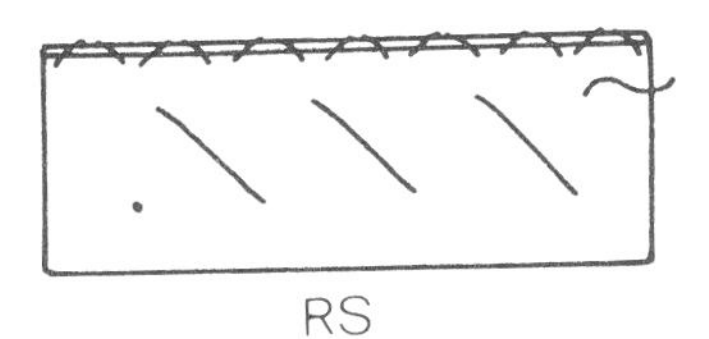

Fig 1.28

Pin welt in position on the garment with right-side down and below the position it will be in when finished. The neatened edge should be at the top. Tack to the garment. Machine along the welt 3 mm below the edge. Remove tackings (fig 1.29).

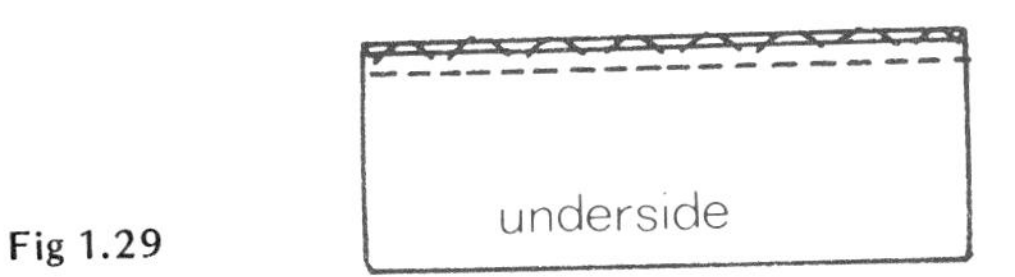

Fig 1.29

Roll welt over so that it is right-side up. Tack welt to the garment just above the join, tack the top edge and tack across the ends. Slip stitch the welt ends to the garment by hand, then machine across the ends 4 mm from the edge and along the bottom 4 mm above the join (fig 1.30).

Fig 1.30

TIPS When attaching the flap or welt to the garment, begin machining at the centre and stitch to the end, turn and stitch to the far end, turn and stitch back to the middle. This prevents movement of the flap as you stitch.

When you machine don't stitch right to the end, stop and turn 2 mm before the end. This prevents the stitching from showing when the flap is folded into position.

Use Fold-a-Band inside the welt; the edges give you an accurate stitching line. Cut it to size, press to wrong side of fabric and cut out adding 1 cm seam allowance all round.

2 Waist finishes and belts

The choice of waist finish depends mainly on the design of the outfit. If the waist will be covered choose one of the quick finishes as follows.

ELASTIC PETERSHAM

When making skirts from knit fabric omit the zip and darts. Finish the waist edge of the skirt with zig-zag stitch. Measure elastic petersham round your waist and cut, allowing 2 cm to overlap. Lap one end over the other end, machine in a square to hold firmly.

Divide the petersham and the top of the skirt into four. Use pins to mark the skirt, but with dots made with felt pen on the petersham.

Place one edge of the petersham on the right side of the skirt, overlapping by 1 cm. Match up the four marks and pin. Have the petersham to the right and insert the pins with the heads to the right (fig 2.1).

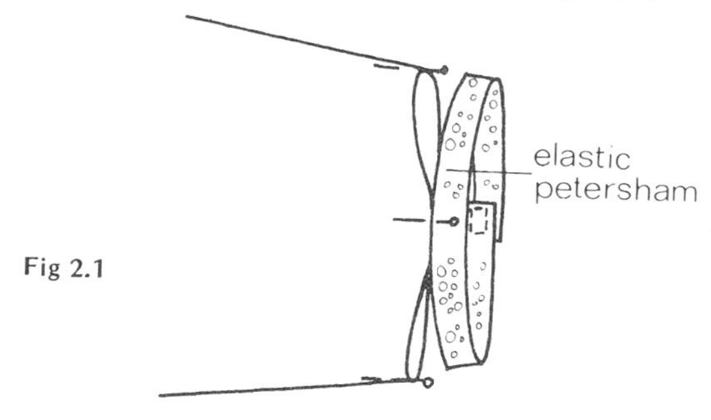

Fig 2.1

Set the machine to a zig-zag stitch, begin by reversing for four stitches for strength, sew forward for four stitches then start to stretch the petersham to fit the fabric as you stitch. Remove the pins as you reach them.

Tuck the petersham into the top of the skirt and press the edge.

ELASTIC IN A CASING

If the style is suitable and the fabric light in weight the waist can be drawn in with elastic, a much quicker process than gathering the fabric into a waistband.

Fig 2.2

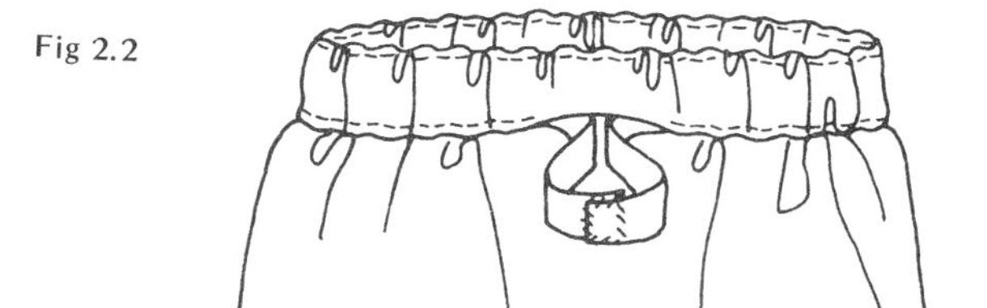

Use elastic that is at least 2 cm or more wide and when cutting out the skirt, extend the pattern at the waist by twice the width of the elastic plus 1 cm. Complete the remainder of the skirt. Turn over a hem at the waist of the skirt slightly wider than the elastic, turning under the raw edge and machining it down. Leave a gap in the stitching 2 cm long for threading the elastic. In addition machine along the top edge of the skirt.

Measure the elastic round your waist, allow 2 cm to join it and cut. Sew the eye of an elastic threader to the end of the elastic and thread it through the casing.

Pull out the ends, overlap them and join by hemming securely in a square (fig 2.2).

> **TIP** Prevent the elastic from twisting as you thread it by pinning across the elastic at intervals as you pull it through. After it is in place arrange the gathering equally on the elastic and then back stitch or machine across the elastic at each side seam (fig 2.3).

Fig 2.3

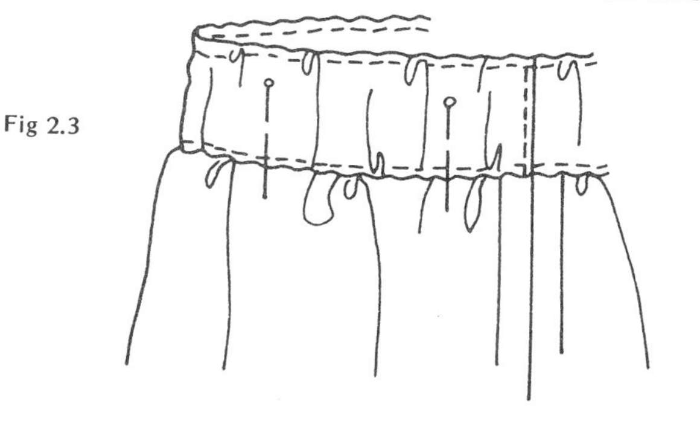

PETERSHAM

Complete the seams, darts and zip of a skirt or trousers. Measure petersham round your waist, slip the two parts of a metal clasp on the ends, fold back and pin each end of petersham so that it fits exactly when fastened. Take it off and trim the surplus ends, leaving 2 cm. Machine in a square with a zig-zag stitch beside the clasp.

Neaten the top of the skirt or trousers with zig-zag stitch. Place the edge of the petersham on to the right side of the fabric. Begin by pinning the two sections of clasp beside the zip so that they are level with the opening, then pin across the petersham at intervals round the waist. Have the petersham and the heads of the pins to the right. Remember that the petersham is at this stage upside down. If you are using curved petersham it is the convex edge that is pinned to the garment.

Work zig-zag stitch over the edge of the petersham, finishing off firmly at each end (fig 2.4). Tuck the petersham inside the skirt and press.

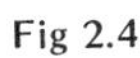

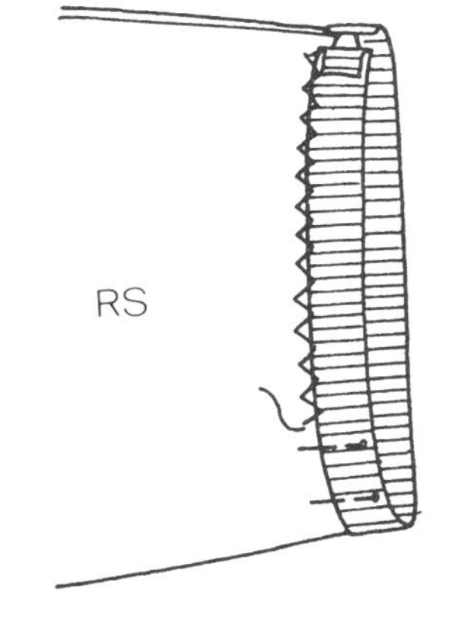

Fig 2.4

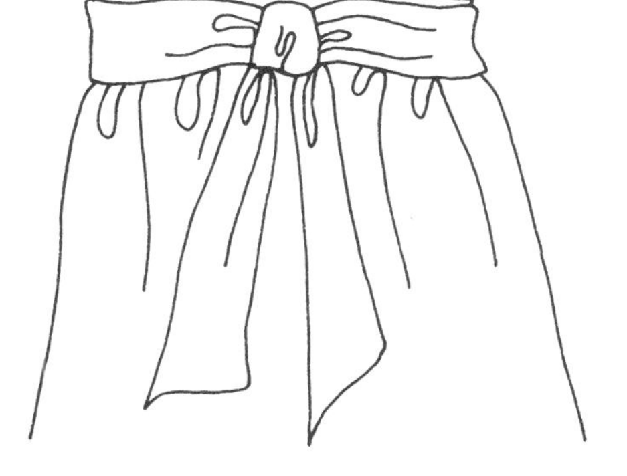

Fig 2.5

WAISTBANDS

Making and attaching a waistband is time-consuming because a precisely even width has to be established and also it has to fit exactly.

> **TIPS** Measure the waistband stiffening round your waist, allow 10 cm overlap and cut. Make the waistband that length and make the trousers or skirt fit the band when you attach it.
>
> Having attached the waistband, if you find it loose snip the fabric on the inside of the band at the sides and insert a piece of elastic petersham. Pull it up to reduce the back waist and stitch the ends firmly by machining a rectangle right through the band.
>
> When making a full light-weight skirt, save time in fitting by cutting extra-long ends to the waistband (or sew ties on afterwards) adding a metre to each side of the zip. In wear the skirt is fastened then the ties are wrapped round the top and tied or buckled to size. This is also an attractive cover-up if you have inserted elastic in the top of a gathered skirt (fig 2.5).

Stiffening a waistband

There are two quick ways of stiffening a waistband.

Cut a length of petersham or waistbanding to your waist size plus 10 cm for overlapping. Place this on the wrong side of a piece of fabric, arranging it on the straight grain, and, putting a length of Wundaweb between the stiffening and the fabric, press it in position. Turn the fabric and banding over so that you can press again thoroughly from the fabric side in order to melt the Wundaweb.

Cut out the waistband fabric, allowing a seam allowance along one edge and both ends. On the other edge allow the width of the stiffening plus a seam allowance (fig 2.6).

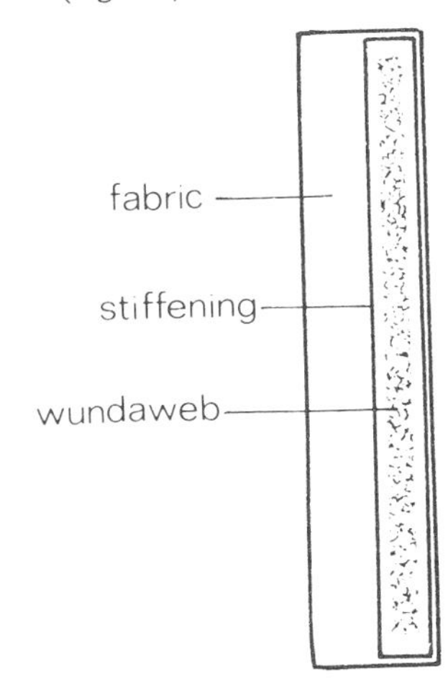

Fig 2.6

The other method is to cut a piece of fabric on the straight grain to the width of Fold-a-Band plus two seam allowances, and long enough to fit your waist plus 10 cm for overlapping. Press firm iron-on Vilene to the wrong side of the fabric. On top of that, as a stitching guide, press a piece of Fold-a-Band. Align it centrally. Note that it should be only the exact size of your waist plus overlap and no seam allowances are included.

TIP A wide seam allowance is not necessary on a waistband and in fact it hampers the process of attaching it. Allow only 5 mm all round, or a little more on a thick or fraying fabric.

Attaching the waistband

Mark with chalk the 10 cm overlap at the end of the waistband. Hold the skirt or trousers *wrong*-side out and pin the overlap point on the band to match the zip or opening on the back edge of the skirt. Pin the other end to match the front edge, leaving a seam allowance extending. Pin at intervals between matching the waistband and skirt-edge seam allowances. The seam allowance on the waistband is indicated by the edge of the petersham or Fold-a-Band. Insert the pins vertically. Tack the band to the garment, making the stitching just beside the edge of the petersham or Fold-a-Band. Remove the pins. Machine on the tacking. Remove the tacking (fig 2.7).

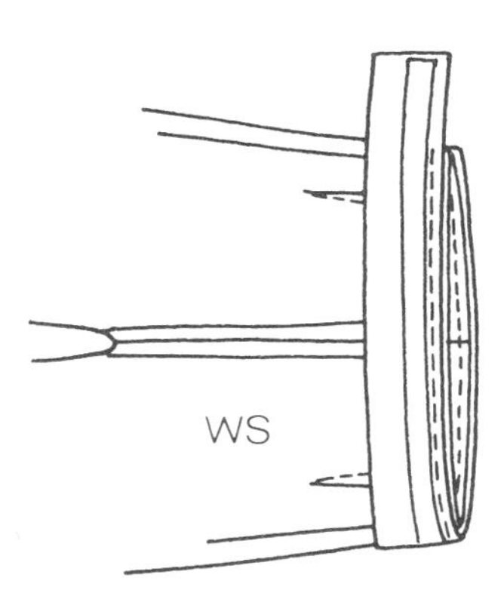

Fig 2.7

TIP Make it easier to turn the band over by stitching a little way from the edge of petersham, allowing 1 mm for fine fabrics, 2 mm for heavier ones.

Trim the seam allowances to 3 mm. Fold band up and press on both sides, pressing the turnings up into the band. Also press all other raw edges over on to the stiffening. This includes the two ends and sides of the extension.

Fold the band in half, either along the edge of the petersham or along the perforations in the Fold-a-Band and press, then bring the edge down on to the right side of the garment. Tuck under the raw edge so that it just covers the stitching. Pin vertically. Pin the overlap so that all edges meet. Tack all round pinned edges. Remove the pins. Press the band.

Work a row of machining all round the band with the right side uppermost. The stitching should be an even 2 mm inside the edge all round so that it catches in the petersham as well as the fabric edges. Use a straight stitch, the blind him stitch or an open embroidery stitch. Remove tackings. Press. Attach fastenings (fig 2.8).

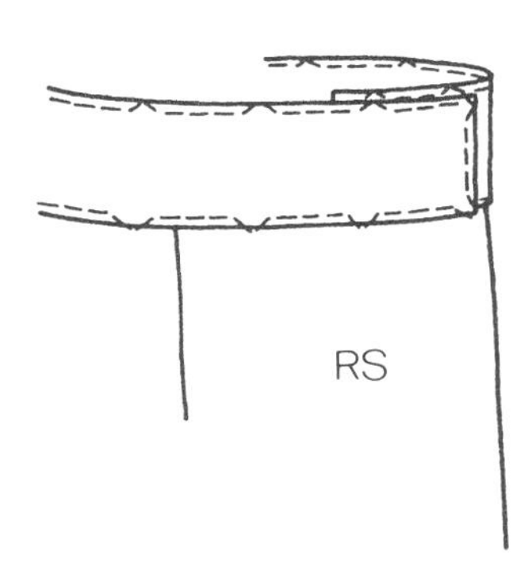

Fig 2.8

Waistband with ties

Press Fold-a-Band to the wrong side of a strip of fabric that is waist size plus enough to pass round the waist again and tie or buckle. Cut the band with a seam allowance all round beyond the Fold-a-Band. Attach the waistband to the skirt as described above but leaving two extensions at the top of the zip. Machine all round. No fastenings are needed.

WAIST OF A ONE-PIECE DRESS

If a one-piece dress is to have a belt added it helps to draw the waist in first with elastic. This gathering not only marks the waist but it holds it in position in wear so that the dress will not ride up. It also keeps the gathers evenly round the waist. The belt is worn on top.

Use a length of elastic petersham cut to fit your waist plus 2 cm. Cut a piece of fabric, on the bias if woven, 1 cm wider than the elastic and long enough to fit on the dress all round the waist.

Using a length of curved petersham fastened round your waist on top of the dress, insert pins in the dress, blousing it if you wish, level with the lower edge of the petersham. Take off the dress and check that the pins lie in an even curve. Run a row of tacking round the dress on the pins. Remove the pins.

Work zig-zag stitch along each side of the strip or casing of fabric. Turn in one end by 1 cm and place it over the centre back seam of the dress or, if there is a zip, beside it. Machine the casing to the wrong side of the dress. Have the lower edge of the casing just over the marked line and use a decorative stitch. Zig-zag stitch is satisfactory but serpentine or another open stitch looks better on the right side of the dress. On reaching the other end turn under the end of the casing to meet the first end, or beside the zip. Stitch along both sides.

Thread the elastic through the casing, overlap it by 1 cm and join by hand or machine (fig 2.9).

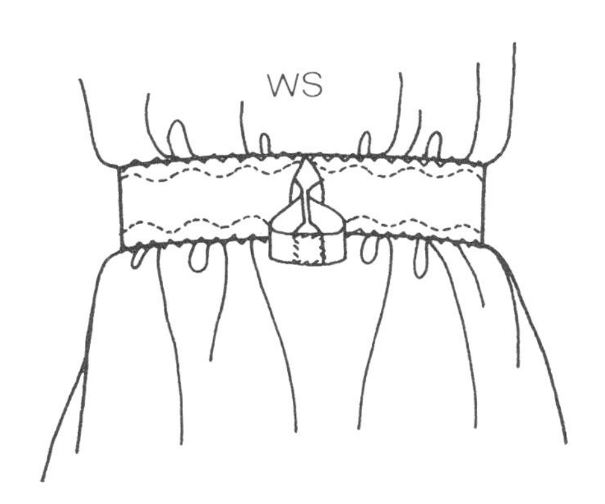

Fig 2.9

QUICK BELT

Cut a length of Fusabelta of suitable width, to the required length. The amount left for fastening will vary according to the method of fastening but if you use a buckle or a detachable clasp, as described below, add 15 cm for fastening.

Cut a length of fabric on the straight grain equal in length to the Fusabelta but 2 cm wider. Place the fabric wrong-side up on the pressing board, place the Fusabelta adhesive side down. Fold in the side of the fabric and tuck it under the backing flap. Press slowly using only the toe of the iron and making sure the fabric does not wrinkle. Turn the belt and press again.

Neaten each end of the belt by working zig-zag stitch over the edge. Thread the ends through the clasp, attach a piece of Velcro to hold the ends back. Hem the hooked, scratchy side to the back of the belt and the soft side to the ends of the belt. This allows it to be let out if necessary. The pieces of Velcro should be 4 cm long. Use whichever width of Velcro fits the belt. Using two pieces of Velcro enables you to detach the clasp and use it on other belts (fig 2.10).

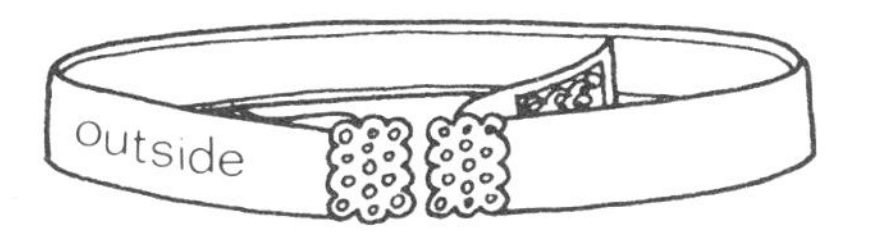

Fig 2.10

WIDE BELT

This is only satisfactory when made in firm crisp fabrics including suede and leather. Cut two pieces of fabric 8 cm wide and long enough to fit your waist plus 15 cm to fasten. Note that if using suede or leather cut only one piece and turn a single hem all round. Place the pieces of fabric right-sides together. Stitch round the outside taking 3 cm turnings, making each end narrower as shown. Slope the stitching to make the ends only 3 cm wide to prevent them from being visible when fastened. Leave a gap of 5 cm in one side. Press the stitching and turn the belt right-side out through the gap. Fold in the edges along the gap and press the belt, rolling out all the edges carefully. Either slip stitch the gap to close it or machine all round the belt on the edge.

Thread one end of the belt through a large plastic or wooden ring, fold back and hem the end. Pass the belt round your waist, thread the other end through the ring towards the inside and establish the fastening position. Sew a 4 cm length of Velcro to that end to fasten it to the back of the belt (fig 2.11).

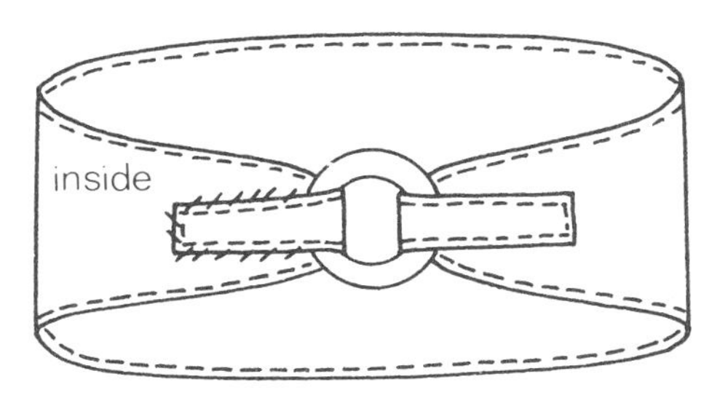

Fig 2.11

EASY FITTING BELT

Cut three long pices of fabric 2-3 cm wide. Fold in one side by 5 mm and press. Fold the other side over twice until the two folds are together. Machine down each side of the strip. Make the three pieces in the same way and press them. Put the strips side by side and machine across them 5 mm from the end. Pin this stitched end to your ironing surface and plait the strips loosely, keeping them flat. At the far end stitch across the ends to hold them together (fig 2.12). Neaten both ends with zig-zag stitch and pass through a clasp hemming the ends down firmly with the belt adjusted to fit.

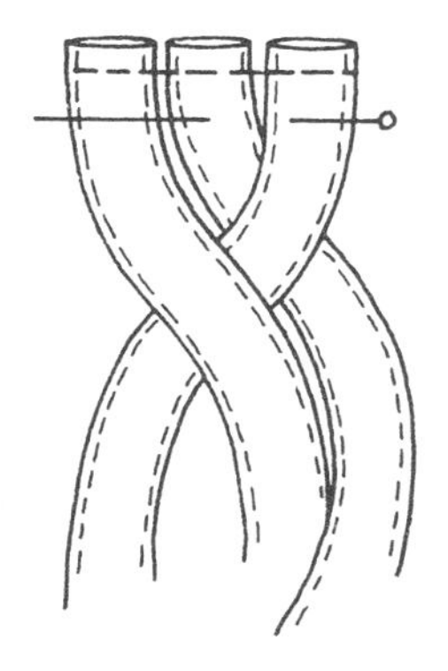

Fig 2.12

The ease in the plait provides comfort and room for expansion.

The ends may be held back with Velcro if the clasp is to be used on other belts.

STRAIGHT TIE BELT

Cut a length of Fold-a-Band to the length required, i.e. to pass round the waist once or twice and knot or tie in a bow. Press the Fold-a-Band to the wrong side of fabric, on the straight or on the cross. Cut out round the Fold-a-Band, allowing 3 mm seam allowance. Fold the belt right-sides together and pin with the raw edges and the pin heads to the right. Machine across the end and along the side, removing pins as you reach them, and stitching just off the edge of the Fold-a-Band. Leave a 4 cm gap in the stitching. Press the stitching (fig 2.13). Trim off the corners of the belt and turn it right-side out through the gap. Roll the edges and press carefully with the toe of the iron. Turn in the raw edges at the gap and press. Either machine all round the belt or slip stitch the folds together to close the gap.

Fig 2.13

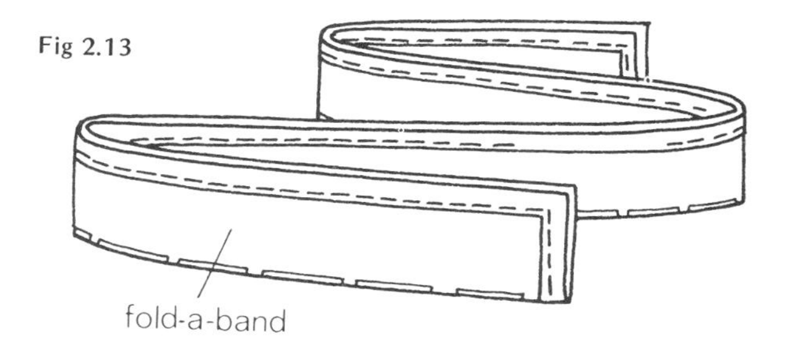

QUICK SASH

This is suitable to be made in any fine fabric such as voile, chiffon and light-weight jersey.

Cut strips of fabric on the cross 8-10 cm wide. Join the pieces to make the strip long enough to pass round your waist and tie. Leave the ends cut at an angle of 45°. Finish the edge of the sash in one of two ways. Either use the hemming foot and roll a narrow straight or shell edge hem or set your machine to satin stitch and feed the fabric edge under the needle right-side up, turning under the edge a little and stretching it as much as possible. This produces an attractive fluted edge, more fluted on jersey than on woven fabric (fig 2.14).

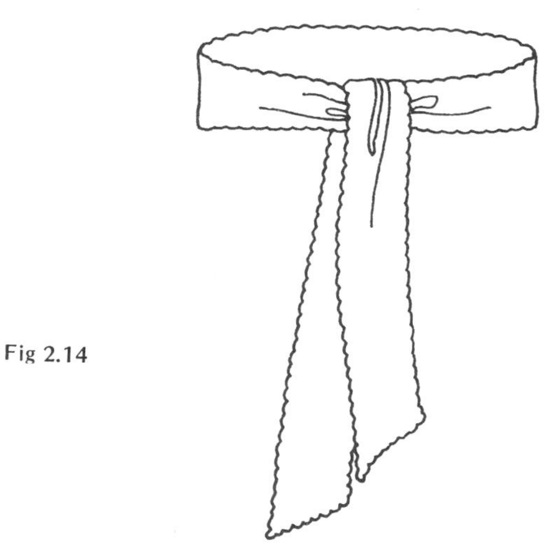

Fig 2.14

KNOTTED TUBE

Cut strips of fabric on the bias 2 cm wide, or wider if you wish, long enough to pass round your waist and tie, and also add an extra 10 cm or so for knotting. Fold the fabric right-sides together and machine 3 mm from the raw edges. Use a slight zig-zag stitch to allow the fabric to stretch and use Drima thread to ensure that the thread does not break later.

Turn the tube right-side out. Slip a rouleau turner into the end and sew the eye to the turnings. Ease the turner through the tube and pull it out. Cut off the rouleau turner and trim the ends of the tube. Push the ends in a little way and knot them. Knot the tube at intervals all the way along, although it can be used as it is (fig 2.15).

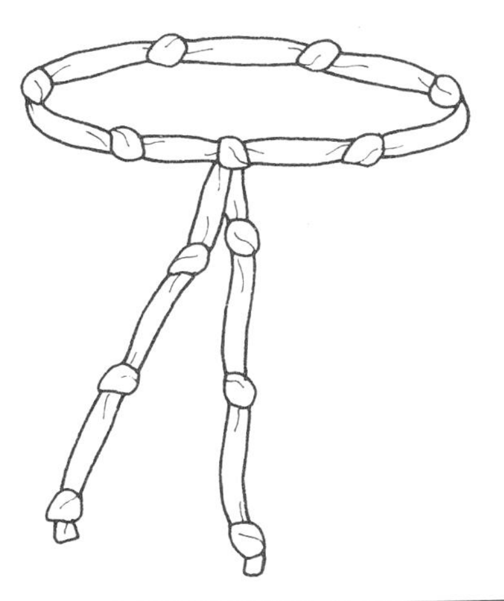

Fig 2.15

> **TIP** If pieces of fabric have to be joined for the belt, make the joins at an angle, whether the fabric is on the cross or straight grain.

BELT LOOPS

The quickest way to make belt loops is to make a length of rouleau as described above but cutting the fabric 1 cm wide if it is light-weight.

Cut loops twice the width of the belt plus 3 mm for ease and 1 cm for the ends. Snip the stitching of the side seams or other seams, slip the ends into the seam, turn to the wrong side of the garment and re-stitch the seam to catch the loop ends (fig 2.16).

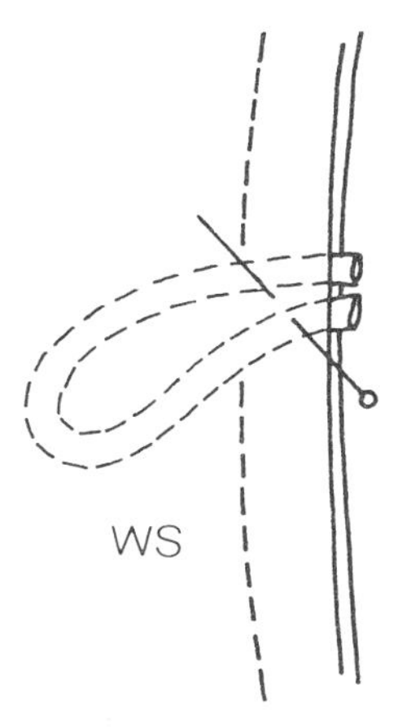

Fig 2.16

When putting loops on the waistband of a skirt or trousers, slip the ends under the waistband before doing the final stitching. Press the loops up over the band. If you wish to stitch them down work a bar tack through the loops to hold (fig 2.17).

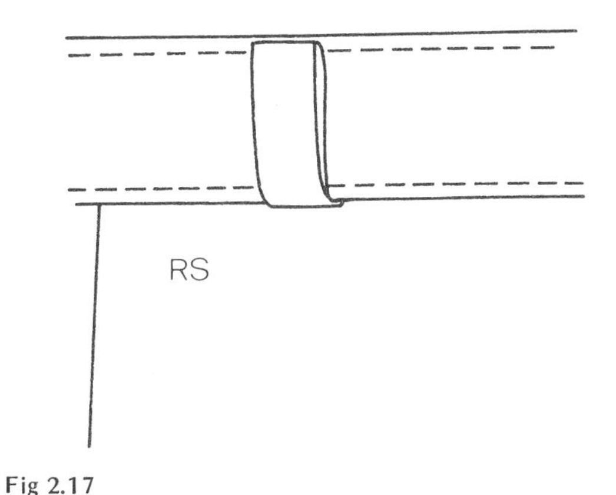

Fig 2.17

3 Sleeves

Choosing styles featuring deep armholes, raglan or kimono shapes or dropped shoulder lines will make the fitting and sewing much easier. Nevertheless construction will be quicker and less liable to error if you remember the following.

RAGLAN SLEEVE

Any design with seams running from under-arm to neckline.

The raglan edges of both sleeve and bodice are on the bias and will stretch very easily. It is partly this tendency to give which makes the raglan comfortable to wear, so whilst you want to retain this property, at the same time make sure the edges are not stretched before being joined together — never lift by the top of the sleeves or bodice.

Join bodice and sleeve under-arm seams before setting sleeve to armhole. If the style shows gathers along the top of the bodice or sleeve, a dart in the top of the sleeve, or even a seam running from neck to wrist on the outside of the arm (as often found in coats), leave the process until after stitching the raglan seams.

Place right-side sleeve to right-side bodice, matching the under-arm seams. Insert one pin vertically with its head outside the edges of the fabric.

Bring neck edges of seam together so that they meet at the fitting line, not necessarily at the edge of the fabric. Pin at that point.

Tack from neck edge to under-arm and turn the work over to tack the other side from neck edge to under-arm. There is often some ease to distribute on one edge of the seam, or you may have stretched one edge inadvertantly. If so, insert a few pins across the seam before tacking and take small stitches over them. If the edge is very full or badly stretched and the fabric will respond to shrinking then steam it gently after pinning, but before stitching. Remove all pins except the one at the under-arm. Machine the seam.

Alternatively the tacking may be omitted for speed, more pins inserted across the seam and the seam machined by stitching over the pins or removing them when approached. If you do not tack the seam stitch from under-arm to neck, turn work over and stitch the second section from under-arm to neck (fig 3.1).

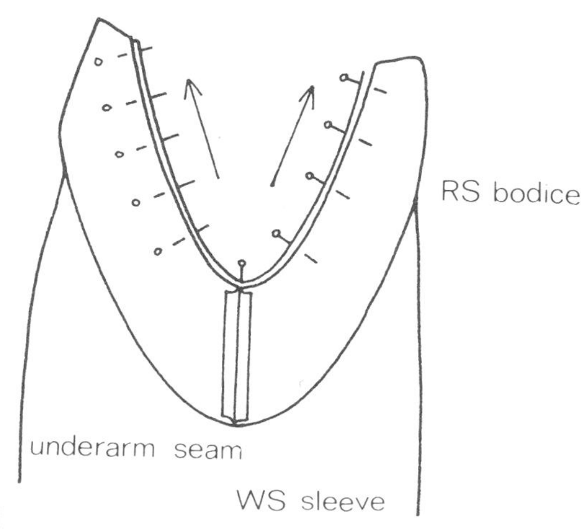

Fig 3.1

TIPS Make sure pins are uppermost when machining.

Make sure pin heads are to the right and off the edge of the fabric and out of the way of the foot.

Stitch with a slight zig-zag stitch, set at about the first division on the dial, to retain the give in the seam. If you cannot zig-zag, stretch the fabric slightly.

Neaten both raw edges together after trimming. The seam should stand upright under the arm but be pressed towards the bodice along the straight sections up to the neck.

If making welt or top-stitched raglan seams, work the top stitching now.

Never snip the turnings of raglan seams; the bias property makes it quite unecessary and apart from weakening the seam, the position of the snips is visible on the outside of the garment because they cause a slight wobble or bend in the seam.

KIMONO SLEEVE

An old-fashioned term used to describe any style where the sleeve and bodice are cut in one piece.

Stitch and finish shoulder seams. The correct direction for stitching is from the neck down the outside of the arm to the wrist or hem of the sleeve. The lower part of the seam is very much on the bias, so take care not to stretch the fabric.

Some designs omit a shoulder join, cutting the sleeve and bodice pattern to a fold. This produces a very loose fit and is normally confined to casual clothes such as robes and caftans, and to short-sleeved shirts and blouses.

Join the under-arm seam by placing back and front right-sides together. Match the under-arm curve and pin. Place sleeve hems together and pin.

Tack from hem to under-arm, turn work and tack from sleeve hem to under-arm. Remove pins and machine the seam (fig 3.2).

Fig 3.2

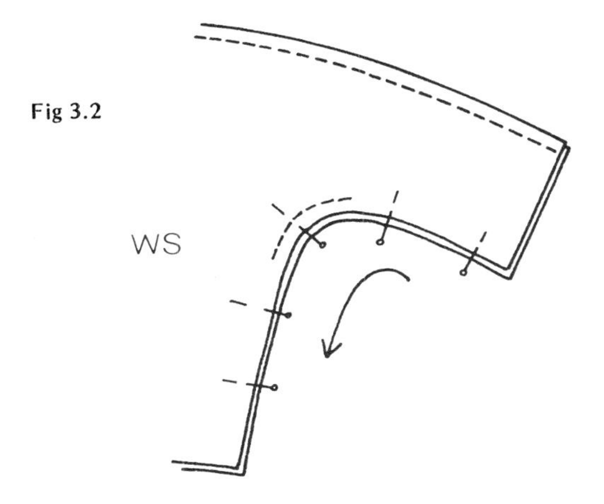

Alternatively insert more pins across the seam and machine over them, omitting the tacking stage.

With both methods, stitch a second time round the pronounced curve of the under-arm, placing the second row of stitching precisely beside the first. If the fabric is loosely woven reinforce it by placing a piece of folded bias binding or a piece of folded bias fabric on the seam before working the second row of stitching.

Press the seam open, using only the toe of the iron to press round the under-arm curve.

Neaten the raw edges. Snip the seam edges three or four times round the under-arm curve at intervals of about 1.5 cm. These cut edges may have to be neatened on badly fraying fabric although there will be no strain on them apart from abrasion in wear and washing.

Occasionally kimono sleeves are cut high under the arm for a closer fit, but as this restricts movement additional room has to be provided by inserting a gusset. It may be triangular or diamond-shaped. The easiest and strongest way to attach a gusset is to turn in all edges and press.

After stitching under-arm seams place gusset wrong-side down to right-side under-arm, tack in position and machine round the outer edge with a small straight or zig-zag stitch. On the wrong side the raw edges may be neatened (fig 3.3).

Fig 3.3

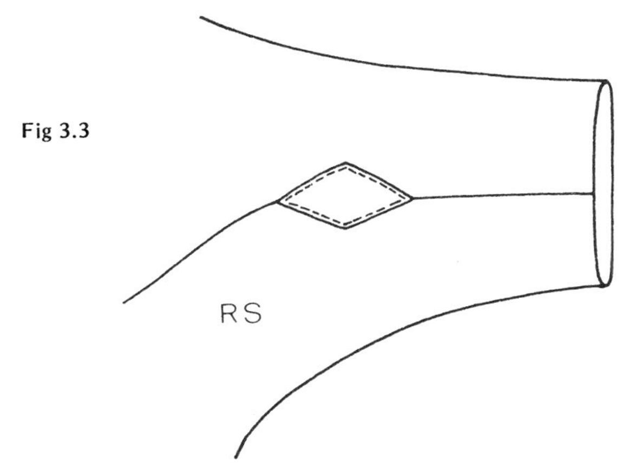

TIPS When snipping turnings do not cut the bias reinforcement.

Snip at an angle to the seam — the snips are then slightly longer.

Kimono sleeves are liable to strain at the weak point under the arm so do not anchor the garment at the waist with belt loops, etc. If the garment is a dress with a waist join, make it fit loosely.

Jersey fabric will be less likely to split than woven.

DROPPED-SHOULDER SLEEVE

The main feature is a seam line below the shoulder bone and because this restricts movement the garment usually has a low armhole. The bodice has a straight or only slightly shaped armhole and the sleeve has a flattened sleeve head. Men's shirts are really drop-shouldered.

Set the sleeve to the bodice armhole before joining the side or under-arm seams. Complete any shoulder or yoke seams and then place sleeve to armhole right-sides together, matching the central sleeve-head point to the shoulder seam or a mark indicating the position of the shoulder seam. Insert a pin across the seam. Lift the fabric, hold with the sleeve uppermost and continue pinning from that point down to the under-arm (fig 3.4).

Fig 3.4

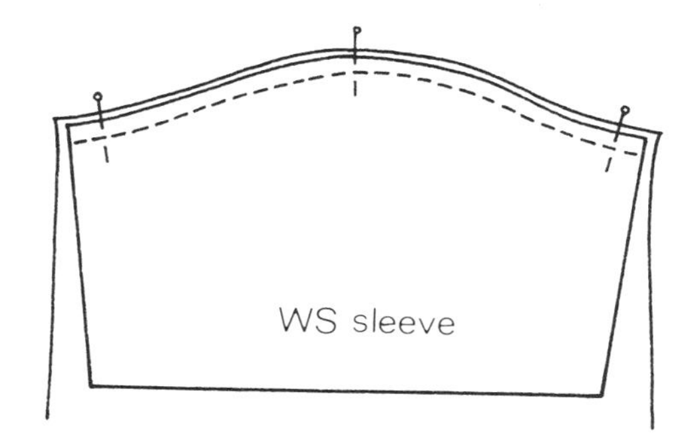

Repeat on the other side of the sleeve head.

Tack, remove pins and machine, stitching with the sleeve uppermost.

Alternatively the tacking may be omitted and the seam stitched over the pins.

Press the seam towards the sleeve. Neaten raw edges or work a welt seam or machine fell seam.

Complete the sleeve and under-arm seam. Begin by pinning the under-arm seams together. Tack and stitch from there to the hemline, turn work over and stitch from under-arm seam to sleeve hem.

TIPS Never snip the seam allowances. Even if the under-arm is slightly shaped there will be sufficient give for it to lie flat.

Always press as for an open seam first in order to ensure a good line on the right side, even if the seam is to be completed by another method.

Never insert shoulder pads. They would be placed on the natural shoulder and would therefore make it appear that you were wearing a badly fitting set-in sleeve. If the dropped-shoulder line does not look right on you, let out the garment seam allowance to its maximum, so that the seam comes further down your arm.

SET-IN SLEEVE

The seam is positioned exactly over the shoulder bone at the front, and at the back it runs in a vertical line. This sleeve must always be tacked into the armhole and fitted in order to find the correct position for the sleeve.

The sleeve head is curved in a pronounced convex shape, the armhole edge is fairly straight for about three-quarters of its length before it follows a deep concave shape for the under-arm.

There are no short cuts when making this conventional style of sleeve but I have a foolproof way of handling it so that the setting-in of the sleeve is easy.

Begin by making up the entire garment and also the sleeves. Delay the insertion of the sleeves in order to make it the final process.

With both right-sides out of garment and sleeve place the sleeve seam to the garment side seam right-sides together and pin.

The two raw edges are similar in shape and will fit together easily so, without stretching, hold the under-arm sections of the sleeve and garment together and tack. The amount that can be tacked at this stage will be about 8 cm on each side of the seam. Fasten off the tacking (fig 3.5).

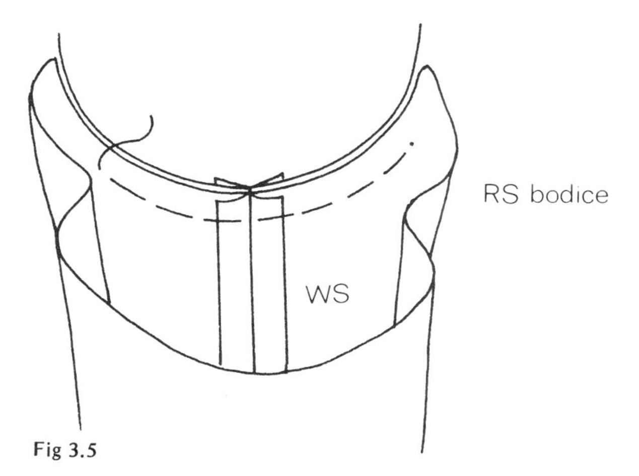

Fig 3.5

The shape of the sleeve head is so different from that of the top of the armhole that it should be held carefully. The sleeve is bigger than the armhole to provide room for movement and this excess fabric in the sleeve must be controlled.

Put your hand inside the garment and take hold of the sleeve head and the top of the garment armhole, at the shoulder seam. Holding the two together, pull them through the neckline and then flip them both over so that the sleeve is lying on top of the armhole but the edges are still together. Do not pull the whole of the sleeve through and do not turn the garment inside out; rather use the remainder of the garment as a cushion with which to support the sleeve.

Put the central sleeve-head point to the shoulder seam (or shoulder point if there is no seam). Insert one pin across the seam. Move your hand to support one side of the sleeve head between this pin and the end of the tacking. Spread out your fingers under the two edges and pin. Start by inserting one pin in the centre of the area, then pin in the middle of each smaller area and so on. Continue putting in pins to divide up the ease into smaller and smaller bulges. Any large amount of ease left undivided will form a pleat when stitched (fig 3.6).

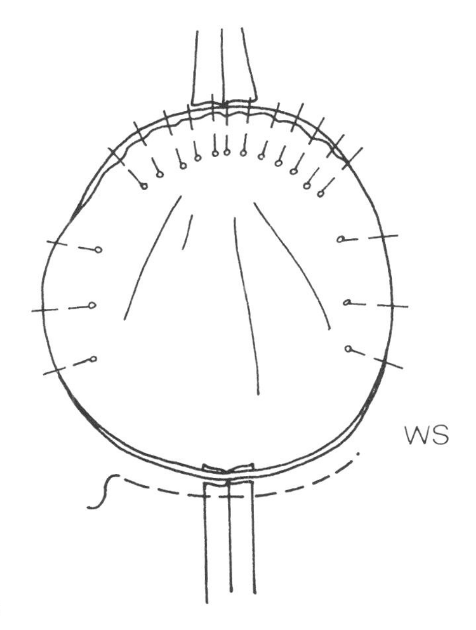

Fig 3.6

Move to the other side of the sleeve head and pin in the same way.

When distributing this ease remember that the most should go to the front of the shoulder seam to provide room for the shoulder bone that protrudes. There should be a little ease over the top and to the back of the shoulder seam but none down the straight part of the back armhole because most people are almost hollow at that point.

Turn garment so that sleeve is right-side out and see how it hangs. Adjust pins if you can detect any obvious bulges of fullness.

Tack the sleeve head with small stitches. Insert the needle under a pin, remove the pin and complete the stitch, insert the needle under the next pin and so on. This ensures that the ease stays put. Fasten off the tacking (fig 3.7).

Try on the garment. If the shoulder seam is too long and the sleeve needs lifting, mark a new line while it is on you, with tailor's chalk. Take off the

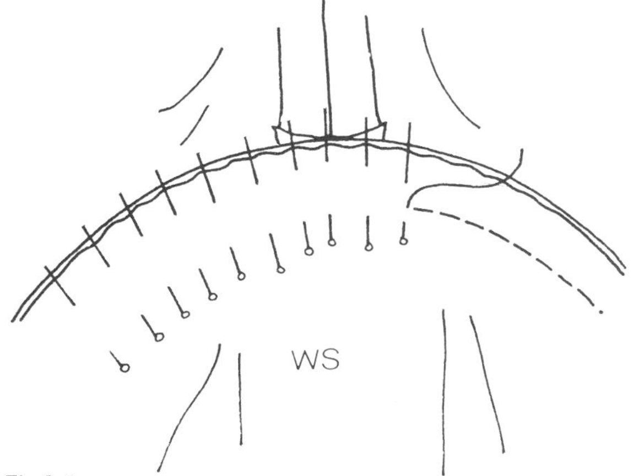

Fig 3.7

garment, remove the tacking from the sleeve head only, trim the surplus fabric from the armhole in a smooth line, leaving 1.5 cm seam allowance.

Re-pin the sleeve head, tack and try on again.

Stitch the sleeves into the armholes. Use a medium-size stitch, work with sleeve uppermost and machine very slowly beside the tacking stitches. If any part of the sleeve head begins to form a wrinkle, stop, use a pin to flatten it or snip the next tacking stitch and proceed.

Remove tackings and trim the turnings to 1 cm before neatening them together.

Press from the right side with the turnings facing towards the sleeve to support the sleeve head.

TIPS Never use a gathering thread in a plain sleeve; it makes it impossible to achieve a smooth sleeve head.

Never cut off the sleeve head if it seems too full; persevere. It is only correct manipulation which is required.

If you have sloping shoulders and always have difficulty in avoiding a droopy look, pop shoulder pads in to support the sleeves.

If you are putting a zip in the side seam, stitch the seam to the point at the base of the zip position, leaving it open at the shoulder end. Put in the zip with the slider at the seam allowance level. Work a bar tack to hold together the folded edges at the top of the zip and set in the sleeve, stitching above the zip (fig 3.8).

When making puff sleeves insert a gathering thread over the sleeve head but hold the sleeve and manipulate it in the same way as described for a plain sleeve.

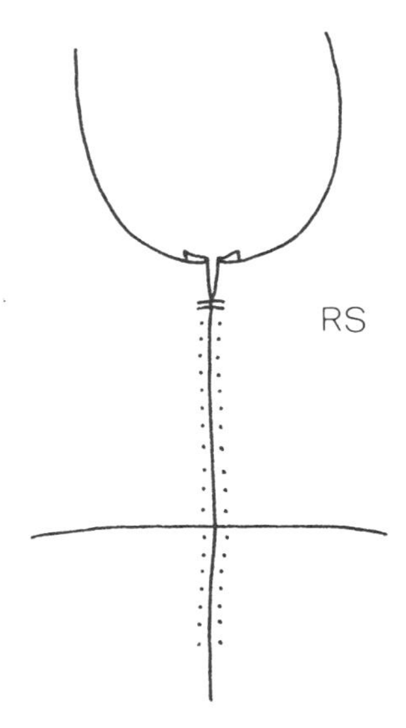

Fig 3.8

SHORT SLEEVES

Machined hem

This is quicker than hand sewing but in addition it is stronger. It is important to avoid the impression that you machined the sleeve hem in order to save time by working two rows of stitching, one at the hem edge and one at the sleeve edge. You can therefore make it look attractive if the stitch is zig-zag or a decorative machine stitch.

It is further improved if you lengthen the sleeve when cutting out in order to allow for a finished hem of at least 3 cm.

If the fabric is reversible, e.g. plain polyester/cotton, work machine fell seams on the garment and turn the hem over to the right side to finish it, giving a cuff effect (fig 3.9).

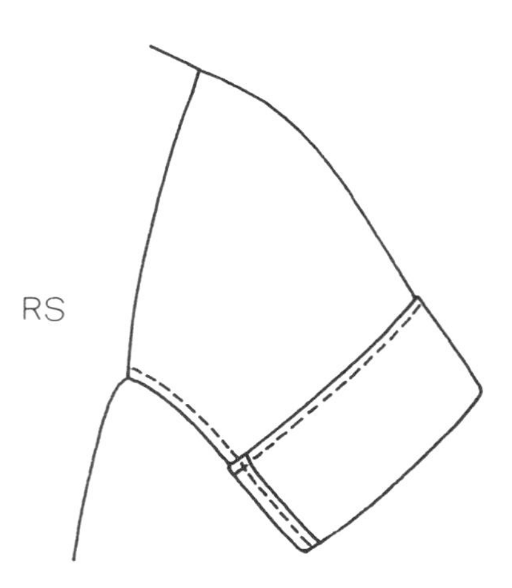

Fig 3.9

> **TIP** Begin and end machine stitching at the under-arm seam.

Wundaweb hem

Allow for a hem exactly 4 cm in depth, adding extra when cutting out or shortening the sleeve if necessary. After stitching the seam, neaten the raw edge at the bottom of the sleeve.

Turn it up to the right side to exactly 4 cm and press the folded edge. This is best done by sliding the sleeve on to the sleeve board and holding an adjustable marker set to the correct measurement, while pressing and moving the sleeve round.

Cut a length of Wundaweb long enough to go round the sleeve plus 4 cm overlap. Slip this under the hem edge, making sure the edge of the Wundaweb strip is exactly in the fold. Overlap the ends. Make sure the Wundaweb is hidden, then pull the sleeve outwards, holding fabric only. This avoids tightening of the hem by the adhesive.

Press the hem using a hot iron and damp cloth. Press only the depth of the hem, not over the neatened edge. Press several times in each place to ensure that the adhesive has completely melted.

> **TIPS** Use the iron sideways, i.e. parallel with the hem edge, to avoid pressing over the neatened edge.
>
> Do not turn a deep hem on fine fabric such as voile, and do not use Wundaweb on fine fabric.

Turn-back cuff

Add a cuff or replace a separate cuff as follows. When cutting out extend the length of the sleeve so that it measures 28 cm from under-arm to hem. Straighten the sleeve seam edges if they slope inwards.

Stitch sleeve seam and neaten lower edge of sleeve. Fold hem 10 cm deep to wrong side of sleeve and press. Place a length of Fold-a-Band on the wrong side with the central holes exactly over the pressed crease. Press in position. Re-fold the sleeve hem.

Fold sleeve hem over to the right side to form a cuff, turning up 5.5 cm and pressing. Insert a few pins vertically to hold it back.

Turn sleeve wrong-side out. Slip a length of Wundaweb under the neatened edge of the hem. Make sure it is completely concealed. Press once only, using a hot iron and damp cloth (fig 3.10).

Fig 3.10

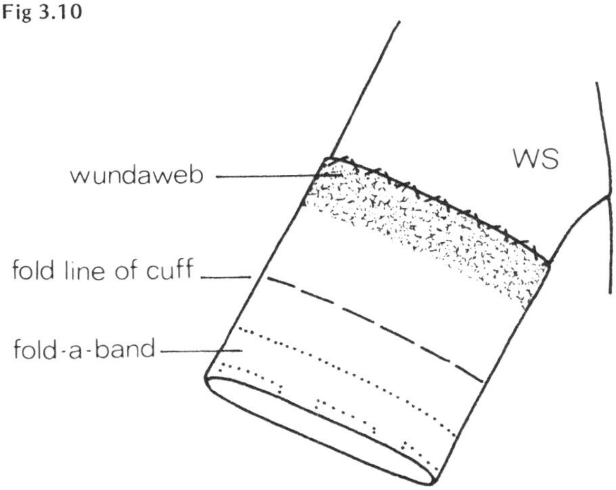

wundaweb
fold line of cuff
fold-a-band
WS

Fig 3.11

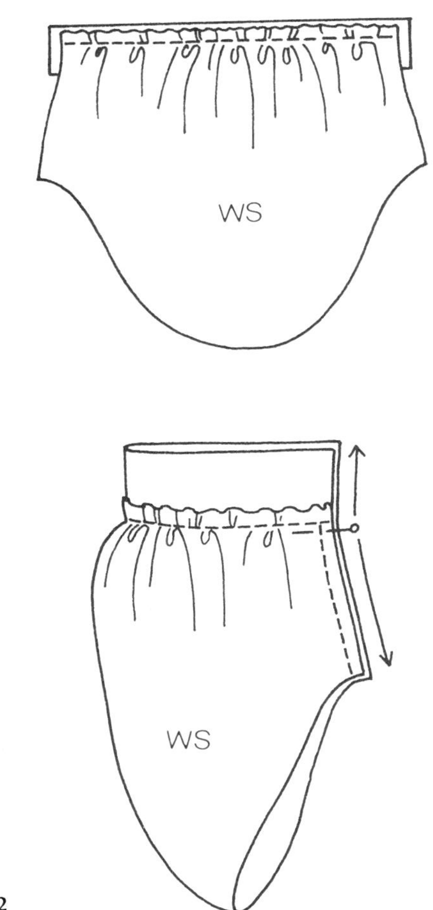

Fig 3.12

Remove the pins and unfold the cuff. Press the hem containing the Wundaweb until the adhesive has completely melted. Where the hem crosses the under-arm, work a few herringbone stitches.

Fold the cuff back into position and press.

> **TIPS** Position the join of the Fold-a-Band at the under-arm seam.
>
> If the fabric is soft or floppy, work a bar tack between the cuff and the sleeve at the under-arm seam.

Gathered into band

Check that the band is the correct length to fit the top of the arm. Attach interfacing to wrong side if needed.

Insert gathering thread along lower edge of sleeve, starting and finishing 3 cm from the sleeve edge.

Fold the band and the sleeve to find the centre and mark each with tailor's chalk.

Place the band to the sleeve, right-sides together and edges together. Match the centre points and pin. Bring each end of the band to the edge of the sleeve and pin. Pull up the gathering thread and wind the end round a pin. Distribute the gathers so that rather more of the ease appears at the centre of the sleeve and less at the ends near the under-arm. Pin all the way along and tack. Remove pins (fig 3.11).

Machine with gathers uppermost. Remove tacking thread and gathering thread. Trim the raw edges to 3 mm wide. Turn sleeve right-side up and press so that the turnings lie towards the band. Press only the band, do not flatten the gathers.

Fold sleeve right-sides together, pin across the seam where the band joins the sleeve, keeping turnings in position. Machine from the band join to the under-arm, remove the pin, turn the sleeve over and machine across the band. Press the seam open and neaten the raw edges (fig 3.12).

Trim down the turnings within the band to 3 mm.

With the sleeve right-side out, fold the band over and crease, insert a couple of pins and press the fold carefully.

Turn sleeve wrong-side out. Turn under the raw edge, bringing the fold down on to the machine stitching. Tack and remove pins.

Complete the band either by hemming by hand, working a stitch in each machine stitch, or if you prefer to machine it, bring the fold down further to cover the machining, tack and stitch from the right side. Use a straight stitch or a small zig-zag or, if suitable, machine embroidery stitch. Two rows can be worked, one on each edge of the sleeve band (fig 3.13).

Fig 3.13

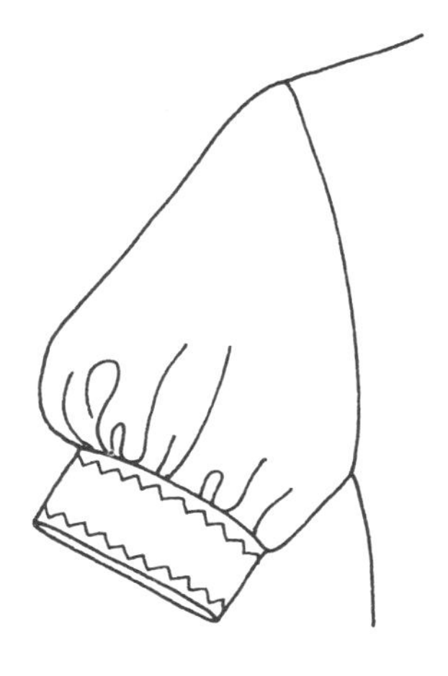

TIP Cut the sleeve band to take Fold-a-Band and the central fold position is easy to find.

Double sleeve

A plain short sleeve can be made more quickly from two layers of fabric. In addition it is easier and firmer to handle, and, subsequently, creases less in wear and in washing. If the fabric is medium- to heavy-weight or thick, use lining fabric, cotton or polyester and cotton lawn, or nylon jersey.

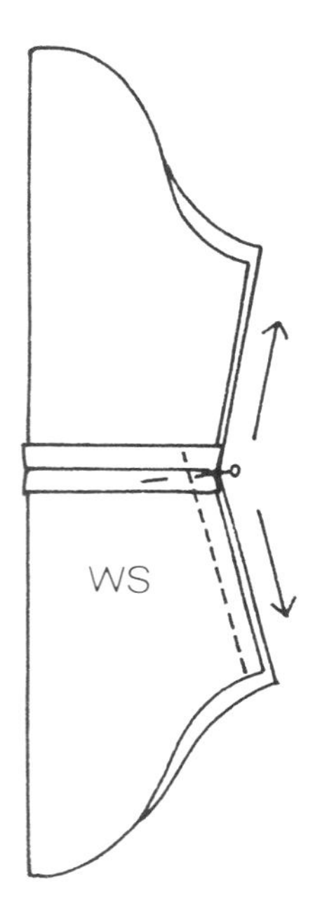

Fig 3.14

Cut out sleeves twice in fabric, or once in fabric and once in lining material. Allow only 1 cm hem along the lower edges, not the hem allowed on the pattern. Place them right sides together in pairs, each sleeve against its under sleeve.

Machine along the lower edge, taking 1 cm turning. Press the join open.

Fold sleeves right-sides together, matching under-arm seam edges. Insert one pin across the seam with pin head extending beyond the raw edges of the fabric (fig 3.14).

Machine the under-arm seam, taking 1.5 cm or whatever seam allowance there is. Start just before the pin and stitch to the end. Remove the pin, turn the sleeve over and machine from the seam to the raw edges.

Trim the seam edges to 1 cm; snip turnings above and below the join. Press the seam open.

With sleeve wrong-side outwards, roll the lining or inner sleeve over the outer one so that it is on the outside. Hold the lower edge of the sleeve, roll the inner sleeve towards you to reveal 1 mm or so of outer sleeve. Slide it on to the sleeve board and press, revolving the sleeve in order to press all round (fig 3.15).

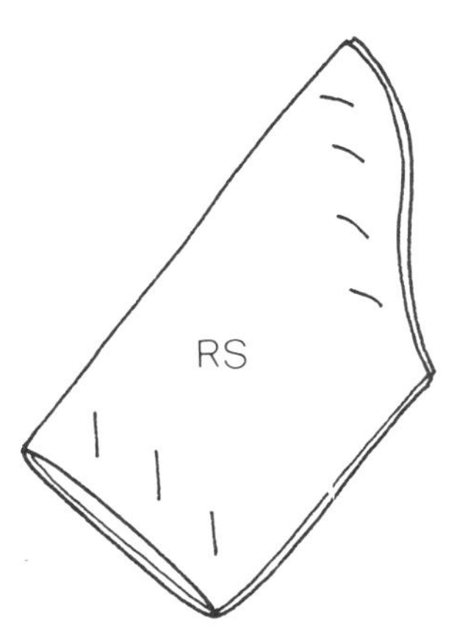

Fig 3.15

Turn sleeve right-side out and baste round the lower edge. Baste round sleeve head to hold the two layers together.

Set the sleeve in as one layer.

TIPS When making a lined garment make the sleeves like this but set in only the outer sleeve, using the edge of the lining to neaten the armhole join.

If the lining is not a good match prevent any possibility of it showing in wear by working a row of machining round the lower edge of the sleeve a little way from the edge in order to make sleeve look decorative.

This method can also be used for long sleeves that are full at the wrist. Contrasting colours can be used with effect especially for evening wear in light-weight fabrics. Do not line long-fitted sleeves in this way because it is not possible to allow the ease needed in the lining.

LONG SLEEVES

Some of these finishes are also suitable for full short sleeves

Gathered at wrist

Elastic

Stitch the sleeve seam. Make sure the sleeve is the correct length, allowing 5 mm for a hem to take elastic 3 mm wide.

Neaten the raw edge and turn it up 1 cm. Press all round. Machine on the folded edge from the right side with a small zig-zag or decorative stitch. Note that the width of the stitch should be no more than 2 on the machine dial.

Turn sleeve wrong-side out and insert pins at intervals across the hem to hold it up. Using the same machine stitch as before, work round the sleeve just below the neatened edge. Fasten off the end of the machining leaving a 5 mm gap in the stitching.

Measure elastic round your wrist and cut, allowing 1 cm for joining. Thread through the sleeve, join by oversewing firmly (fig 3.16).

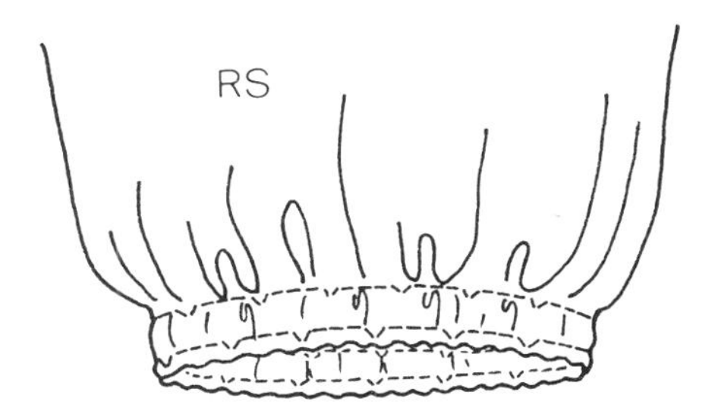

Fig 3.16

An alternative method is to use shirring elastic on the machine spool for stitching the hem instead of inserting elastic later. A third row of shirring may be needed between the two rows to ensure sufficient grip.

Elastic with frilled edge

Cut out the sleeves sufficiently long to allow for the frilled edge plus 1 cm for the hem. Depending on the fabric, allow between 2 and 3 cm for the frill but no more than 4 cm or it will extend beyond the thumb joint.

Stitch the sleeve seam. Turn a narrow hem round the lower edge and machine with a straight, zig-zag or embroidery stitch.

With sleeve wrong-side out measure the frill depth from the hem and mark round with tailor's chalk.

Cut strips of fabric on the cross 1.5 cm wide, to take elastic 8 mm wide. Work a small zig-zag stitch along each side. Place strip wrong-side down to wrong side sleeve with one edge on the chalk mark. Tack down the centre to attach it to the sleeve. Leave a slit for inserting the elastic by turning in both ends of the strip so that the folded edges meet. Press. Machine along each edge of the strip with a small zig-zag or embroidery stitch (fig 3.17).

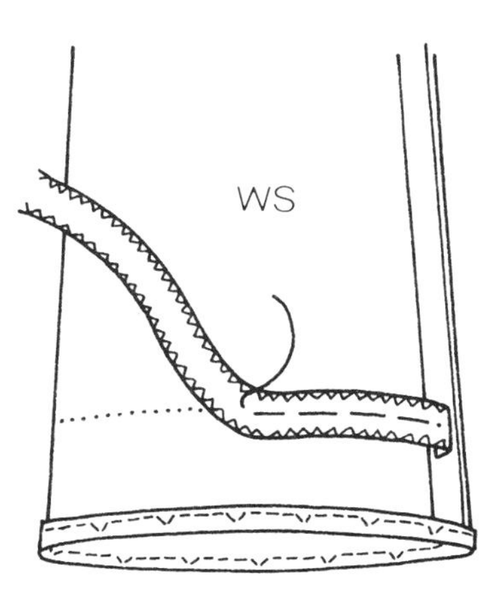

Fig 3.17

Measure elastic round your wrist and cut, allowing 1 cm to join. Thread through slot and join by oversewing firmly.

Alternatively put shirring elastic on the machine spool and work three or five rows of shirring round the sleeve. Begin by marking up a chalk line on the right side of the sleeve and work the stitching from that side. On completing one circuit do not end the stitching but lift the machine foot and move the work slightly to one side (the width of one prong of the foot), lower the foot and work the next row.

Instead of shirring elastic use narrow conventional elastic cut to fit your wrist plus 1 cm to overlap. Mark the position with tailor's chalk on the wrong side of the sleeve. Set your machine to a medium width zig-zag (about Mark 2½ on the dial). Slip the elastic over the wrong side of the sleeve and put under the machine foot, anchor the elastic by reversing for a couple of stitches, then stitch forward but stretch the elastic as much as possible as you stitch. Obviously you must use up all the fabric as you machine. If you have not operated this particular technique before, it helps to practise to see just how much you can stretch the elastic (fig 3.18).

It also helps to use soft elastic (which is made from a single flat strip of latex covered with viscose yarn) because it stretches more than elastic made of several cores.

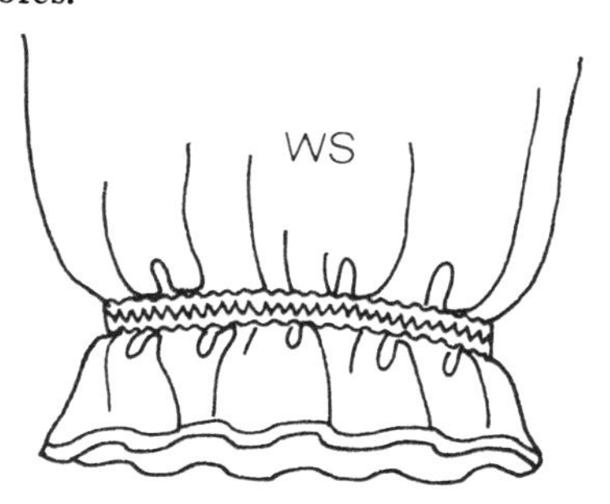

Fig 3.18

If the lower edge of sleeve is straight or almost straight, the frilled edge can be double. Cut the sleeves long enough to allow twice the frill depth in addition to the basic length plus 3 cm for the elastic. After stitching the sleeve seam neaten the lower raw edge. Turn up and press a fold to form the lower edge of the frill. Work a row of basting round the sleeve above this fold to hold the surplus fabric in position. With sleeve wrong-side up work two rows of small-size zig-zag stitch, one just inside the neatened raw edge, the other 1 cm away. Leave a gap in one of them and thread elastic through (fig 3.19).

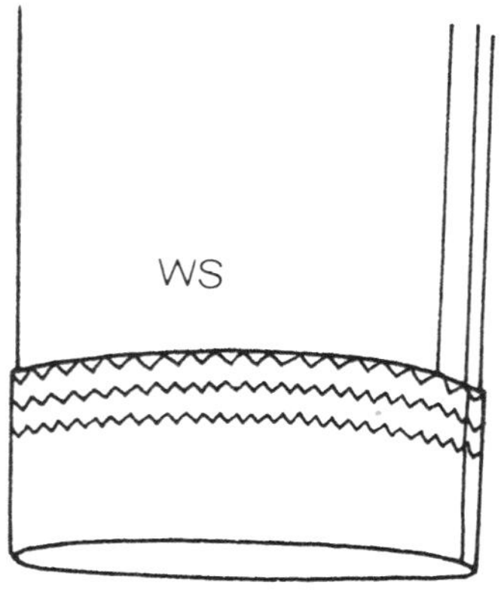

Fig 3.19

Prepare the sleeve as above but work rows of shirring instead of inserting conventional elastic. Work from the right side, having put a guide line in tailor's chalk for the first row. As the fabric is double you may need six or seven rows of shirring to obtain sufficient grip.

Band with frill

Cut the sleeves to the exact length plus enough to allow for a frilled edge, but do not plan for a deep frill. Cut two strips of fabric 4 cm wide. The strip should be long enough to pass over your hand plus 3 cm for seam allowance. Turn in and press a 1 cm turning along each side. Insert a gathering thread across the sleeve at frill depth. Mark the centre of the sleeve and band (fig 3.20).

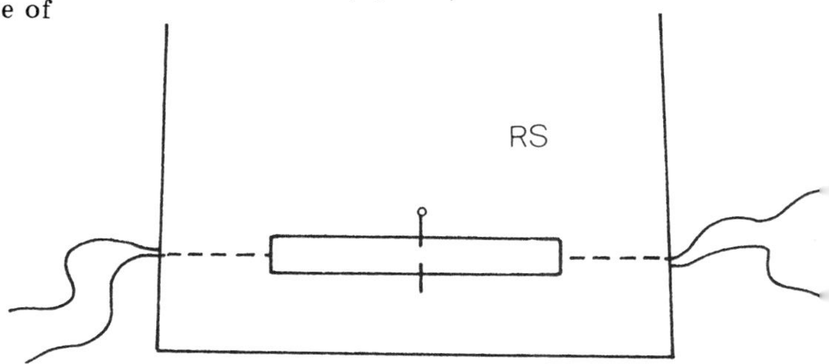

Fig 3.20

Place wrong-side band to right-side sleeve, matching centre marks and pinning the ends of the strips to the sleeve edges.

Pull up the gathering thread, even out the gathers but avoid having any within 2 cm of the sides of the sleeves. Tack the strip to the sleeve. Attach the strip to the sleeve by working a straight or zig-zag stitch along each edge.

Remove tacking. Fold sleeve right-sides together and stitch the seam. Turn up a narrow hem round the lower edge of the sleeve (fig 3.21).

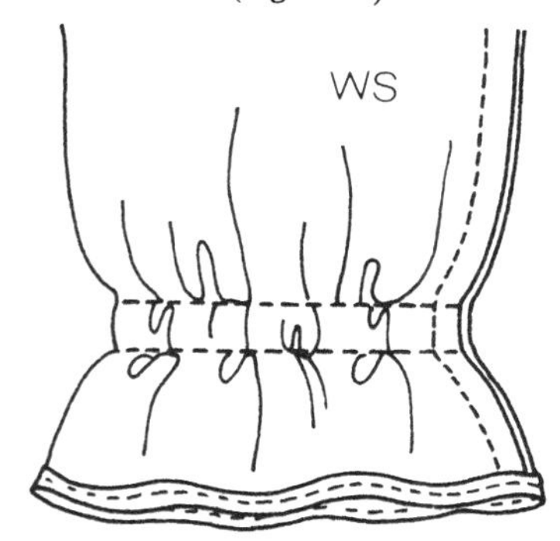

Fig 3.21

The above method gives a loose fit at the wrist. For a tighter fit cut the bands to fit your wrist, allowing 3 cm for turning in the ends.

Stitch the sleeve seam, leaving 6 cm open at the wrist. Neaten the seam and press open. Turn up a narrow hem round the bottom of the sleeve, stitch by hand or machine.

Turn in and press 1 cm along each side of the band. Insert a gathering thread in the sleeve. Place the strip wrong-side down to right-side sleeve, matching centres. Turn in ends of band and pin beside the opening. Pull up the gathers evenly across the sleeve. Tack the band to the sleeve, tacking across the ends as well as along the sides. Machine all round the band with a straight or zig-zag machine stitch.

Fasten the wrist opening by making a worked loop on the band at the front of the sleeve and sew a button to the back. When fastened, the band should meet edge to edge (fig 3.22).

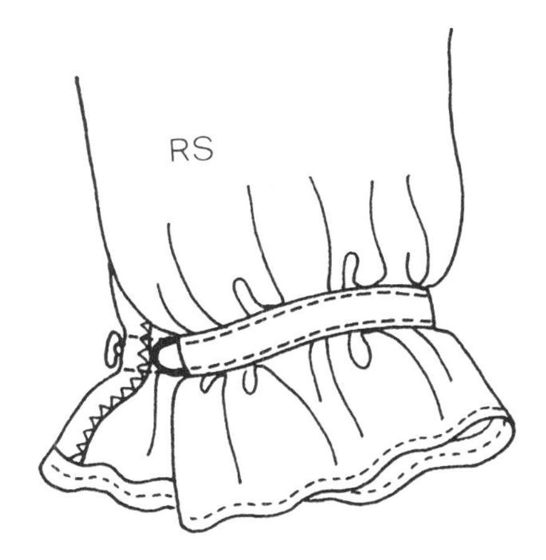

Fig 3.22

> **TIPS** Sleeves with elastic in the wrist will ride up unless additional length is allowed. Cut sleeves at least 6 cm longer than required; they look nicer anyway if puffed up a little.
>
> Begin and end bands, crossway strips, elastic, etc., at the under-arm seam so that joins are not visible.
>
> Elastic seems to become tighter as the day wears on so to avoid this make sure it is long enough. Pin it round your wrist and wear it for ten minutes or so before cutting it to size.
>
> It is essential to use synthetic thread, e.g. Drima, with elastic and shirring elastic since cotton thread may break under the strain.

With cuffs

Jersey cuff

The cuff can be either made from fabric or you can use cuff ribbing, or you can knit your own ribbing. Ribbing that you buy is already tubular. If you knit your own, knit it the required depth and sew it up, making sure it will slip over your hand.

To make fabric cuffs, cut strips of jersey fabric across the width of the fabric to provide maximum stretch. The width should be at least 9 cm for a narrow cuff, allowing 1 cm on each edge for attaching to the sleeve. The cuff should be long enough to slip over your hand when joined. Make it fairly tight. Join the cuff with a slight zig-zag stitch. Trim the edges and press open, or, if the fabric curls up, press to one side (fig 3.23).

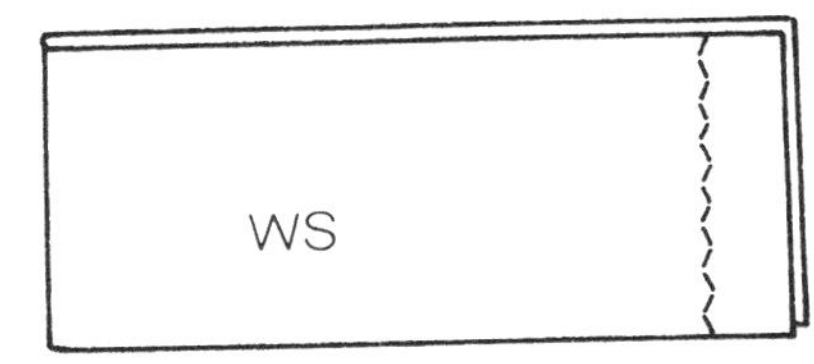

Fig 3.23

Fold the cuff with wrong-sides together and press. Note that fabric cuffs and purchased ribbing are folded double to attach, but hand-knitted ones should be single in order to avoid excessive bulk.

Join the sleeve seam and neaten. Insert a gathering thread round the lower edge of the sleeve. Slip the sleeve, wrong-side out, over the cuff. Pin at four equidistant points. Seams must be together. Pull up the gathering thread until the sleeve fits the cuff, *when the cuff is extended to its maximum size by stretching.* Insert additional pins with the pin heads extending beyond the raw edge of the fabric. Slip this assembly over the free arm of your machine or, if you have a flat-bed model, turn so that it is cuff-side outwards and slide it under the machine foot. Attach sleeve to cuff with a zig-zag stitch set at No. 1 on the dial. As you sew, stretch the cuff as much as possible, removing the pins as you come to them. Remove the gathering thread. Trim the raw edges to 5 mm and neaten all together with a zig-zag stitch (figs 3.24 and 3.25).

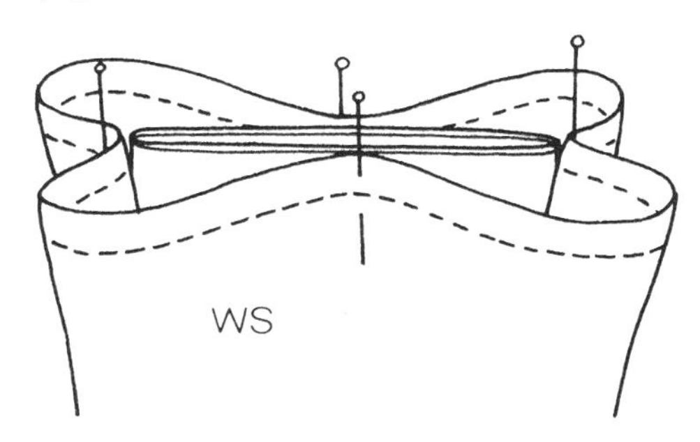

Fig 3.24

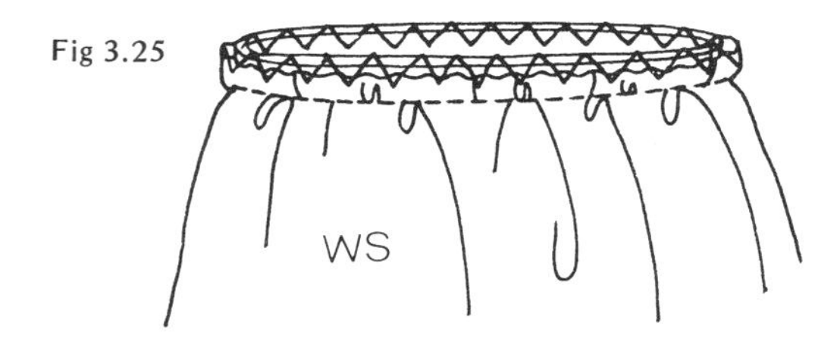

Fig 3.25

Wrap cuff

Use this method with woven fabrics and those that require interfacing (fig 3.26).

Use the cuff pattern provided in your pattern and cut out and attach the interfacing. Alternatively if you have no pattern, cut strips of Fold-a-Band adhesive-side down to wrong-side fabric with central holes exactly on the straight grain. Press to adhere. Cut out allowing 1 cm seam allowance all round the outer edge of the Fold-a-Band.

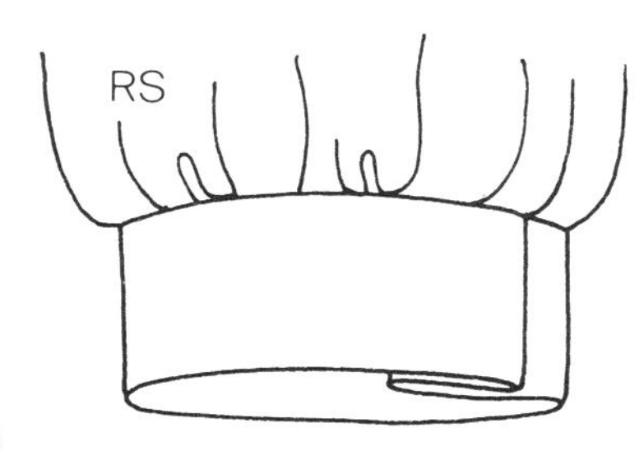

Fig 3.26

Fold cuff right-sides together and machine across the end to join, taking 1 cm turning. Press open and trim the edges down to 5 mm. Stitch and neaten the sleeve seam. Insert a gathering thread across the lower edge.

Hold cuff right-side outwards and slip the sleeve over it with right side against the cuff. Pin the seams together and pin at three other points, spacing the pins out equally. Pull up the gathering thread until the sleeve fits the cuff. Wind the end of the thread round a pin and distribute the gathers at a point 2 cm from the seam, towards the back of the sleeve so that it is free from gathers. This is where the cuff will wrap. Tack the sleeve to the cuff.

Machine round the sleeve with gathers uppermost. Remove tackings and gathering thread and trim the turnings down to 5 mm. Turn sleeve right-side out and press the join so that the turnings lie towards the cuff. Do not press over the gathers.

Turn the sleeve wrong-side out, fold the cuff over in half (Fold-a-Band will automatically crease at the centre) and press the crease. Turn under the raw edge of the cuff to fall on the machine stitching. Insert pins vertically and hem into the machine stitches, or tack the fold to cover the machining completely and machine the cuff from the right side, just below the join. If you do this, work a matching row of machining near the lower edge (fig 3.27).

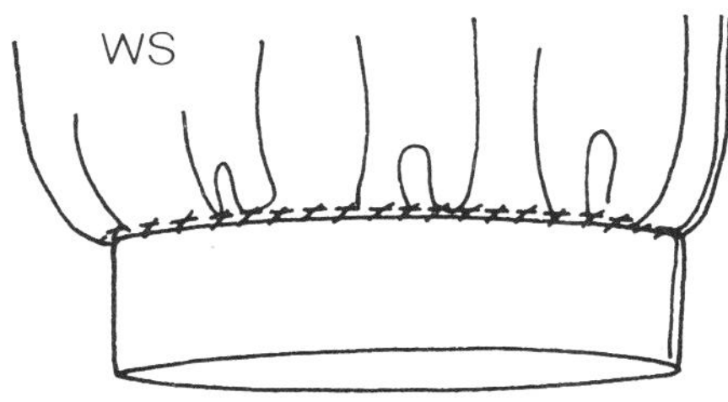

Fig 3.27

Put the sleeve on, wrap the cuff over to fit, where the flat area comes, and mark the size of the wrap with pins. Take off the sleeve.

Attach fastenings. Choose between hemming a narrow strip of Velcro in position and attaching two press studs. When fastened, the cuff must fit the wrist comfortably. For decoration, buttons may be sewn on the outside (fig 3.28).

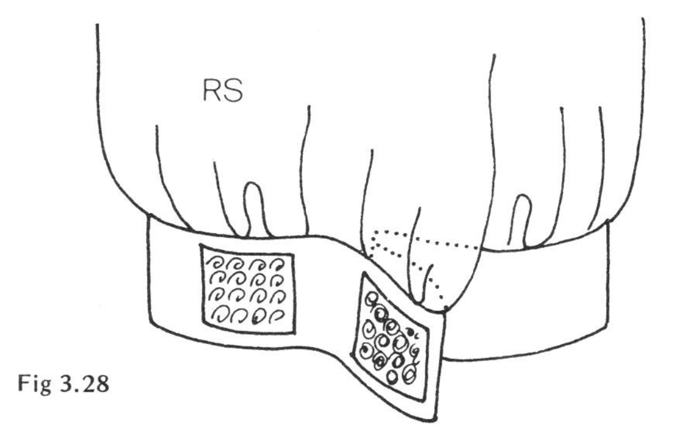

Fig 3.28

With opening and cuff

The position of a sleeve opening is marked on the pattern. If you wish to make the opening in that position mark that position on the fabric and cut.

With wrong side towards you roll a tiny hem along the cut edges, hemming by hand as you roll it. Half way along, stop and make a small horizontal snip at the top of the cut, making a snip on each side of the cut. This enables you to roll the hem evenly to the top. Hem the second side. Press. Fold the sleeve with right sides together and pin to hold the rolled edges of the opening together. Pin at the top of the opening and 3 cm beyond it. Place under the machine and stitch from the top of the opening, level with the edge of the rolled hem, to the folded edge, stopping just below the pin at the 3 cm point. The stitching should slope gradually as for a dart (fig 3.29).

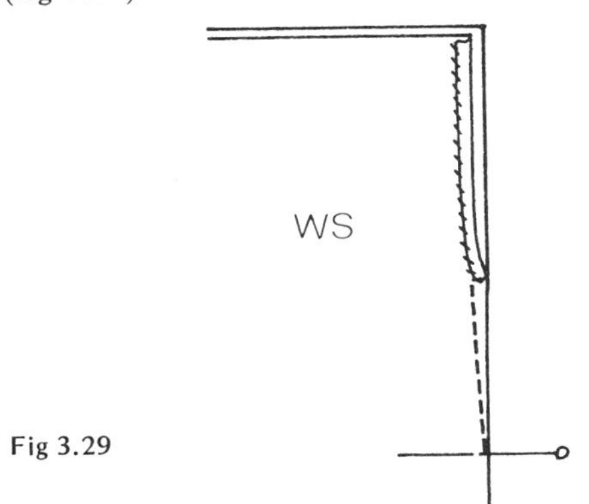

Fig 3.29

Press this little dart flat so that the fabric lies equally on each side of the opening. Finish by working herringbone stitch over the raw edge and make a bar tack to hold the two hemmed edges together at the top. Stitch the sleeve seam.

Alternatively the opening in the sleeve can be left in the under-arm seam and the cuff fastened at that position with one button and buttonhole or a press stud.

Stitch the sleeve seam, leaving 7 cm open at the wrist. Press the seam open and neaten the edges. Cut strips of Wundaweb 8 cm long and 1 cm wide, slip them under the neatened edges beside the slit and press well with a hot iron and a damp cloth (fig 3.30).

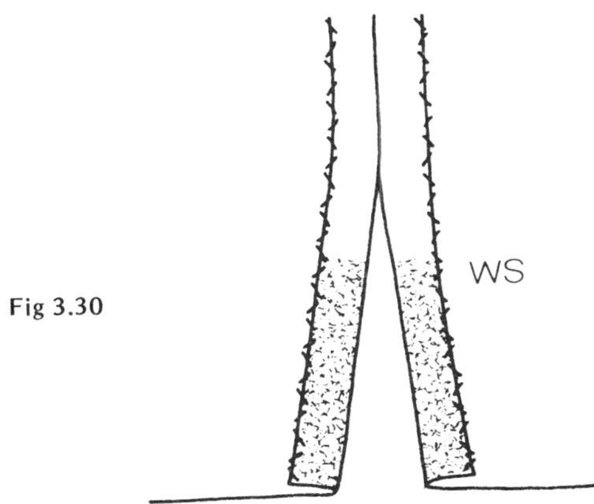

Fig 3.30

Make the cuff for both types of opening by cutting out in fabric, using the pattern provided and attach interfacing, or if you have no pattern, press strips of Fold-a-Band on to the wrong side of your fabric and cut out allowing 1 cm turning round the outer edge. The cuff should be 21 cm long without turnings, or, your wrist measurement plus 5 cm ease and 2-5 cm overlap plus turnings.

Fold cuff wrong-sides together and machine across the ends. Trim edges and corners. Turn cuff right-side out and press (fig 3.31). If you wish to top stitch the ends and lower edge do it now.

Fig 3.31

Baste along the cuff to hold the two layers together.

Place cuff to right-side sleeve with ends of the cuff level with the edges of the opening. Pin. Pull up gathers or insert tucks if it is a shirt-style sleeve. Tack cuff to sleeve and machine. Remove tacking stitches and gathering thread. Trim raw edges to 5 mm and neaten all together with zig-zag stitch. Press the turnings down towards the cuff (fig 3.32).

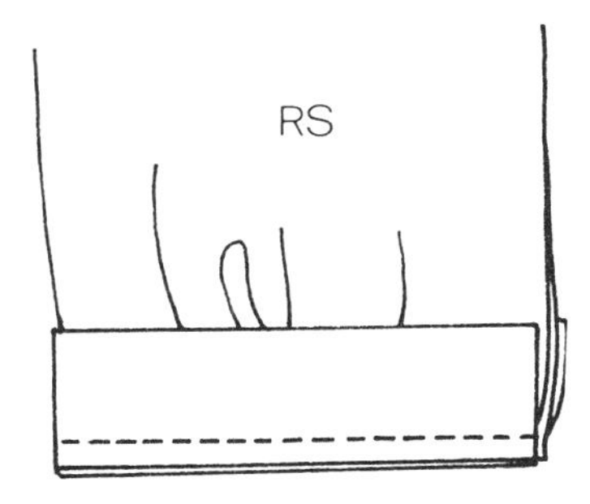

Fig 3.32

Attach fastenings so that the cuff overlaps to fit when fastened. Use a button and buttonhole, a narrow strip of Velcro, button snaps, metal studs or press studs.

TIP If it worries you that the join might show at the end of the cuff, make a corner at the buttonhole end when you first stitch the ends. Turn cuff right-side out including the corner, snip the turnings at the end of the machine stitching and attach the cuff as described but making sure this overlap corner is located at the front of the sleeve (fig 3.33).

For a quick sleeve opening, measure about a quarter of the way along the wrist edge of the sleeve, on the back of the sleeve, and make two snips in the edge 1-1½ cm apart. Cut a small piece of Wundaweb and press back the fabric with it underneath. Make and attach the cuff (fig 3.34).

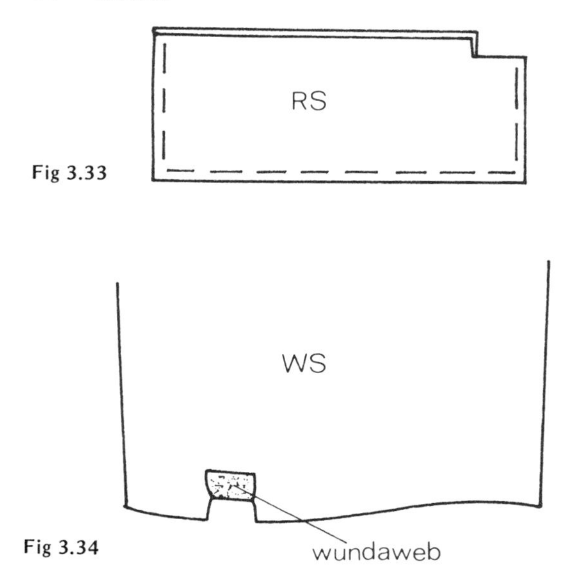

Fig 3.33

Fig 3.34

With strap

A long sleeve of normal width can be decorated and also reduced in width by a strap.

Cut two pieces of Fold-a-Band 20 cm long and trim one end of each to a point. Press these to the wrong side of a piece of fabric. Cut out round the outside, leaving 1 cm seam allowances. Fold straps right-sides together, pin, and machine round the point and down the long side, just off the edge of the interfacing (fig 3.35). Trim the turnings. Cut off the point. Using a rouleau turner, turn straps right-side out. Roll the edges and press.

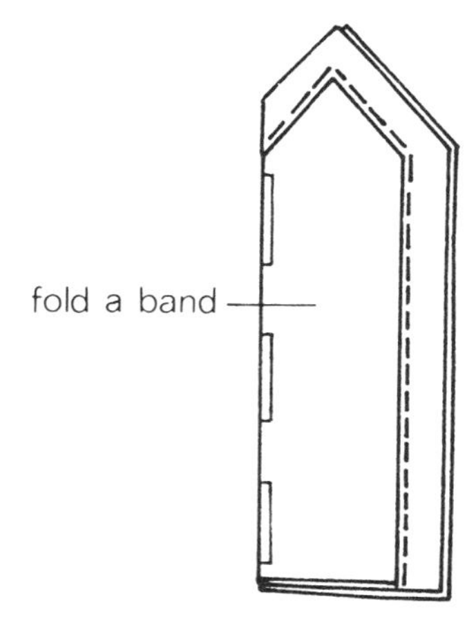

Fig 3.35

Place straps against the back edge of the sleeve 10 cm above the hemline on the right side. The strap must extend across the sleeve. Hold it in place with a piece of Sellotape. Fold sleeve right-sides together and machine the seam. Press it open and neaten the edges including the edges of the straps. Turn sleeve right-side out and press strap towards the front of the sleeve (fig 3.36).

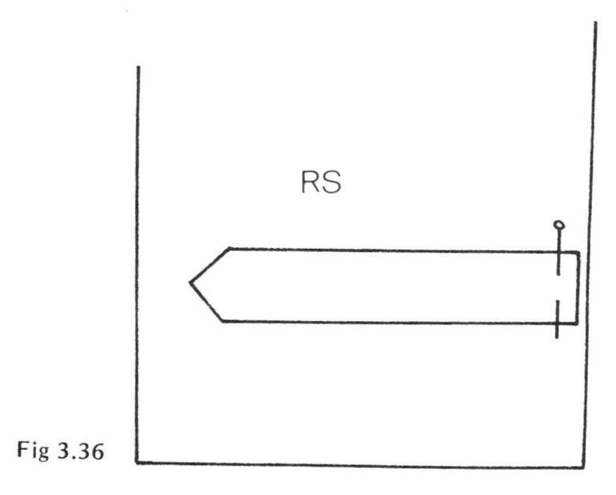

Fig 3.36

Turn up the sleeve hems. Bring straps across sleeves, gathering the sleeve a little and sew a button through the point of the strap and the sleeve (fig 3.37).

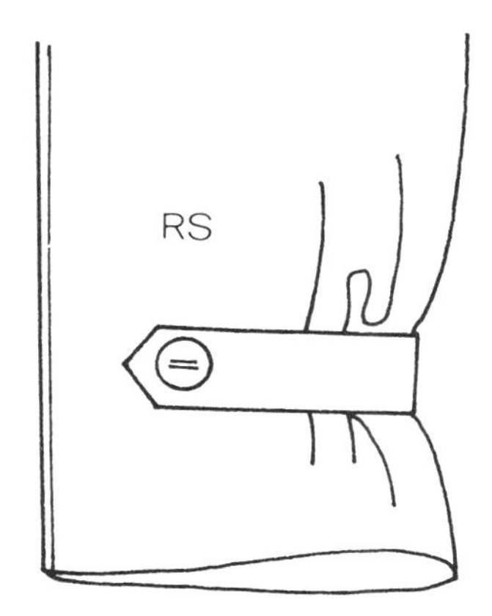

Fig 3.37

An alternative sleeve strap can be made by making two straps 30 cm long for each sleeve. Place one on each edge of the sleeve and anchor. Stitch the seam, turn up the hem. Bring the straps over the sleeve and tie (fig 3.38).

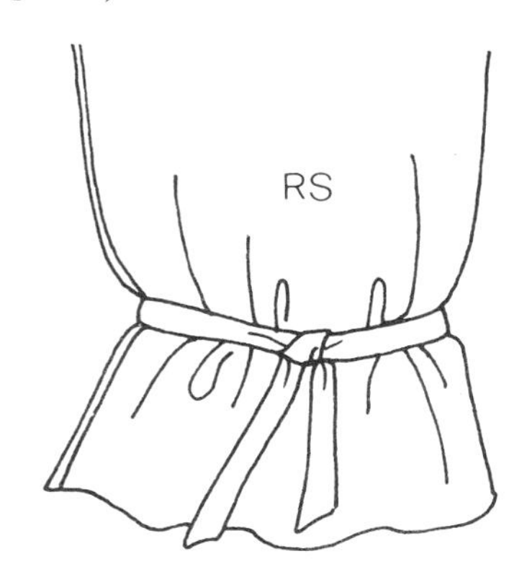

Fig 3.38

4 Necklines and collars

NECKLINES

Necklines may be faced or bound, as described in the chapters containing those processes, but they have to have an opening as well which may contain a zip.

Bound and tied

Round necklines may be finished with a narrow binding as described in chapter 10 *Edges and hems*. The garment is often gathered into the binding. The ties may be made by leaving long extensions of crossway fabric to be machined or hemmed when the neck binding is finished. Alternatively ties of ribbon, cord or crochet may be inserted into the ends of the neckline binding (fig 4.1).

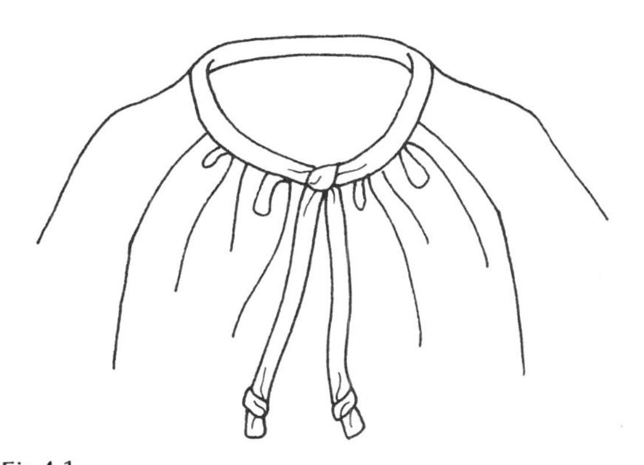

Fig 4.1

> **TIP** Thread beads on to the ends of the ties; sew in place or tie a knot in the tie.

The slit opening below the ties may be made in one of the following ways.

Straight bound opening

Chalk a line on the right side of the garment to indicate the position of the opening.

Cut two crossway strips of fabric the length of this line plus 1 cm, and 2 cm wide. Place the strips on the right side of the garment, right-side down with the raw edges meeting on the chalk line. Pin (fig 4.2).

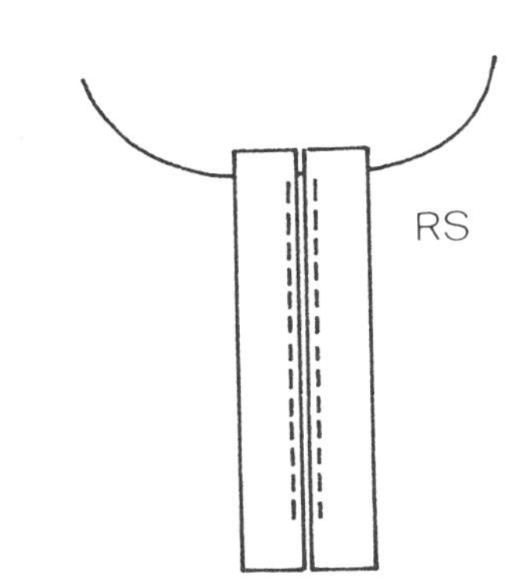

Fig 4.2

Machine 3 mm from each raw edge, fastening off each row of stitching at the base. The two rows must be parallel and the same length.

Turn the work over and cut the garment fabric between the rows of stitching. Snip to within 1 cm of the bottom before cutting out at an angle to the ends of the two rows of stitching (fig 4.3).

Use the toe of the iron to press over the strips.

Fold the raw edge of each strip over twice, bringing the fold to cover the machine stitches. Tack and press.

Turn the work over and machine from the right side, stitching exactly in the dent formed

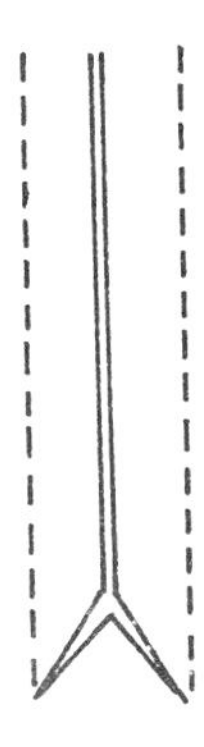

Fig 4.3

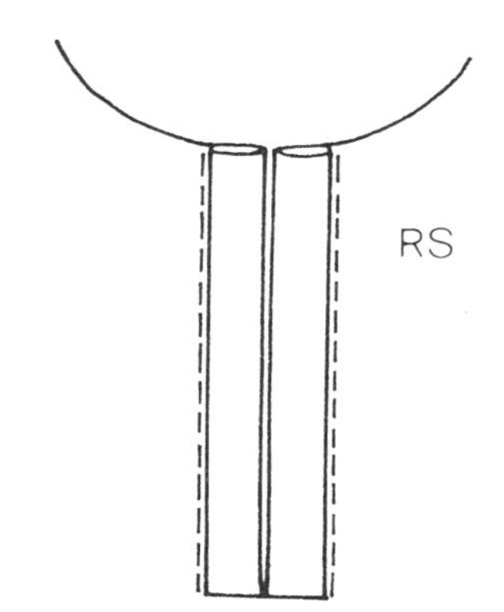

Fig 4.4

by the strip. Fasten off at the lower end (fig 4.4).

Fold the bindings down on to the lower part of the garment so that the triangle cut earlier stands upright. Insert a pin across the bindings to hold them together and machine across the base of the triangle, attaching the strips (fig 4.5).

Fold the opening back and press.

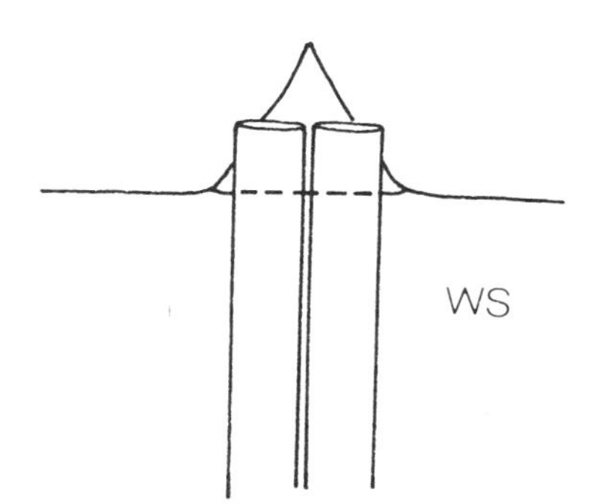

Fig 4.5

> **TIP** If the fabric frays easily press a small square of Bondaweb to the wrong side of the garment at the end of the chalk line, before you start.

V bound opening

Mark the length of the opening on the right side of the garment. Cut a crossway strip of fabric 2 cm wide and twice the length of the opening.

Cut the opening, cutting a V 2 cm wide at the top. Place the strip right-side down to the right side of the garment and pin. Have the raw edges level at the top of the V but gradually reduce the turning taken on the garment until, at the base of the V, you take only a couple of threads. Tack, then turn the work over so that the garment is uppermost and machine. It helps to open out the V as straight as possible. Take a 3 cm turning all the way along the crossway strip (fig 4.6).

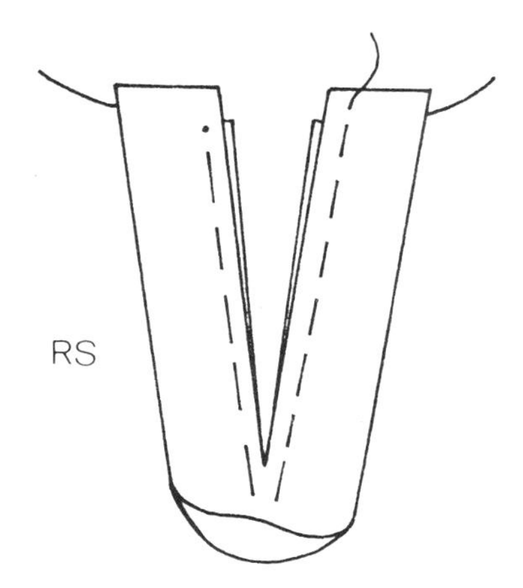

Fig 4.6

Use the toe of the iron to press the strip outwards. Fold its raw edge over twice so that it covers the machine stitches. Pin across the strip and tack. Remove the pins. Turn the work right-side up and machine in the well which is formed by the strip or hem on the wrong side (figs 4.7 and 4.8).

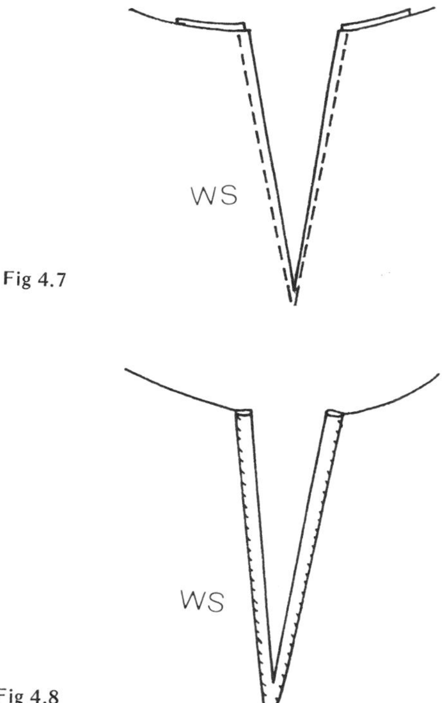

Fig 4.7

Fig 4.8

> **TIPS** If the fabric frays easily press a small square of Bondaweb to the wrong side of the fabric at the base of the marked opening, before cutting it.
>
> Use a small machine stitch to attach the crossway strip, especially at the base of the V.

Strap opening

For speed and accuracy use Fold-a-Band inside the strap. It serves as an interfacing as well as being a guide to stitching straight. Adapt the strap width indicated on the pattern to the width of the Fold-a-Band.

Mark the position and length of the opening on the right side with chalk.

On the wrong side press a small rectangle of Bondaweb to cover the bottom of the opening. Peel off the paper (fig 4.9).

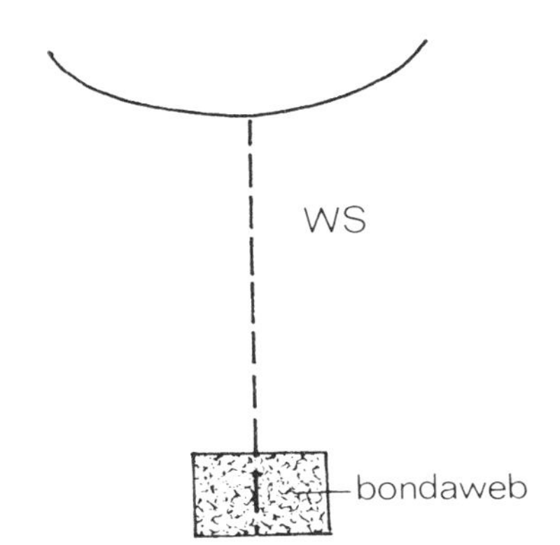

Fig 4.9

Cut two pieces of Fold-a-Band the length of the opening, shaping the top to a curve the same shape as the garment at the neck. The pattern may be used as a guide.

Press the strips on to the wrong side of fabric with one edge exactly on the straight grain. Cut out round the Fold-a-Band, leaving 1.5 cm seam allowance all round.

Place the strips right-side down to the right side of the garment with the two raw edges meeting close together over the chalk mark. Tack the strips down. Machine, using the edge of the Fold-a-Band as a guide. Start at the bottom on each side, working to the neck edge each time to make two parallel rows of stitching equal in length (fig 4.10).

Trim the band edge down to 3 mm.

Turn the garment over and cut between the rows of stitching to within 3 cm of the bottom. From there cut out at an angle to the ends of the stitching (fig 4.11).

Using the toe of the iron press the bands over.

Finish the band on the right-hand side by turning it up across the bottom, fold it on the centre of the Fold-a-Band and tack. Turn under the raw edge of the band and tack. Hem down the fold and slip stitch across the bottom, or machine all round close to the edge (fig 4.12).

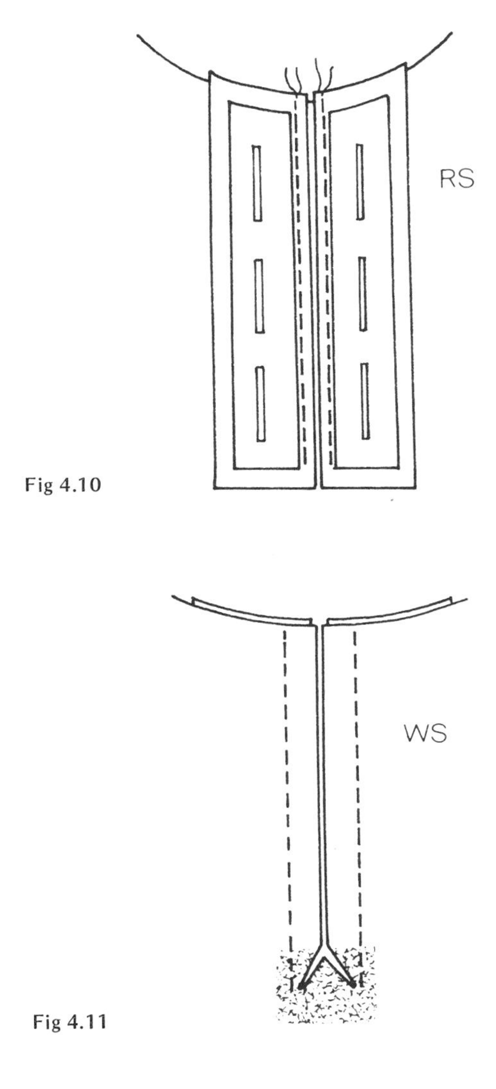

Fig 4.10

Fig 4.11

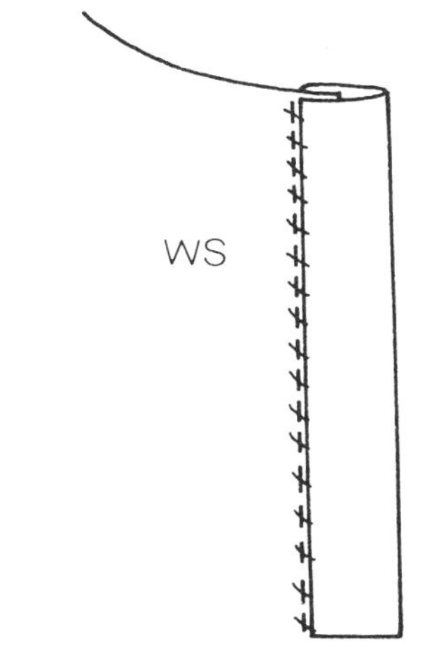

Fig 4.12

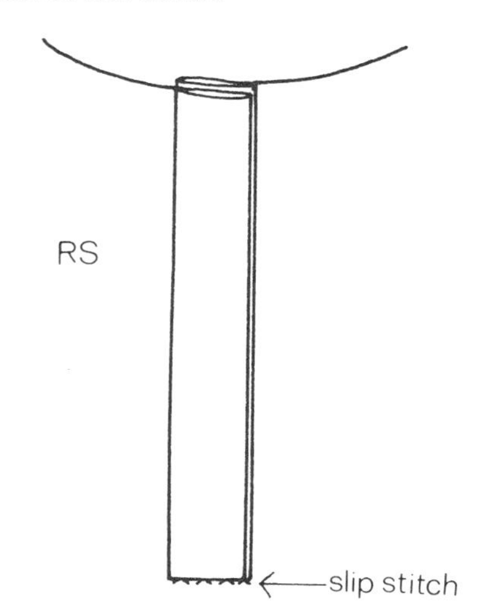

Fig 4.13

Work any buttonholes now.

Pin the band in position over the triangle of fabric at the base of the opening and slip stitch it in place by hand (fig. 4.13).

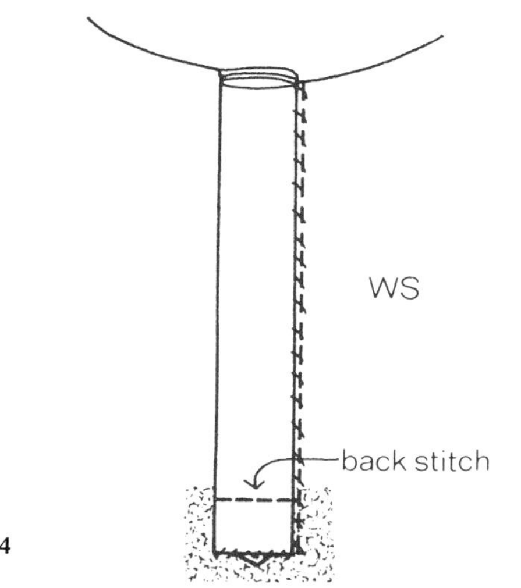

Fig 4.14

Complete the left band by hemming down the length. At the base trim the raw edges down to 3 mm, neaten and hold in place under the other band with a few back stitches (fig 4.14).

TIPS If the pattern provides a piece that combines the strap with a neck facing, still use Fold-a-Band, attaching it to the wrong side of the facing at the centre-front edge.

Even it the garment has a strap opening that extends to the hemline, still use Fold-a-Band, both as a guide and as an interfacing.

Seam opening

If there is a seam and the opening can be left there, construct an open seam, leaving the top unstitched, neaten the edges and hold the turnings back with a very narrow strip of Wundaweb. Allow the Wundaweb to extend beyond the base of the slit of the opening (fig 4.15).

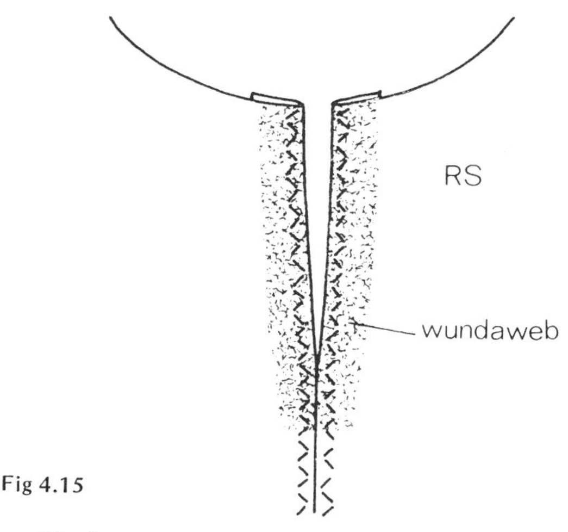

Fig 4.15

Work a straight, zig-zag or decorative stitch down each edge between 3 and 5 mm from the edge. The stitching may be continued down beside the actual seam too.

Faced opening

A method of making a slit opening where there is no seam. It is more often used in wrists of long sleeves rather than in an obvious position such as the centre front, although it could be used at the centre back of a neckline. Do not use on transparent fabrics as the facings will show.

The opening has a weak spot at the base but this can be strengthened if the opening is made as follows.

Decide on how long the opening needs to be without strain when putting on the garment and mark the line with chalk on the wrong side. Cut a rectangle of fabric on the straight grain 5 cm wide and 3 cm longer than the opening. Press a strip of Bondaweb down the centre 4 cm wide and peel off the paper backing. If the fabric frays neaten the two long edges and one of the shorter ones.

Place the rectangle right-side down to the right side of the garment with the centre over the line of the opening. Attach with a couple of pins (fig 4.16).

With the garment wrong-side up machine 2-3 mm beside the chalk line, work to a point at the base and stitch up the other side 2-3 mm from the chalk.

Cut between the two rows and snip right into

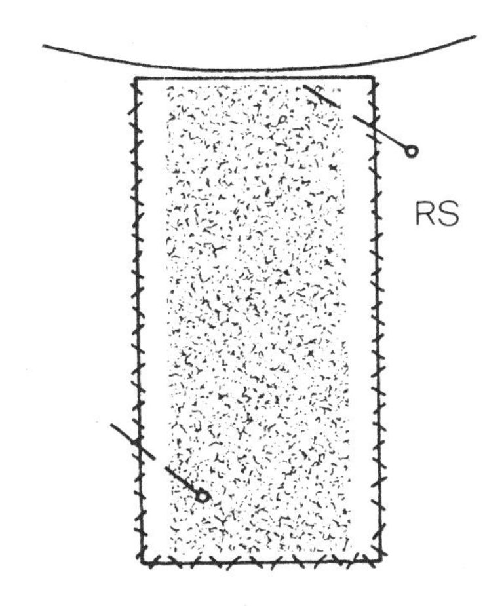

Fig 4.16

the point. Roll the facing completely to the wrong side, press the edge with your fingers, tack if the fabric is springy, then press from the right side. The Bondaweb will not only hold the rectangle in place during wear but will help prevent fraying at the weak base (figs 4.17 and 4.18).

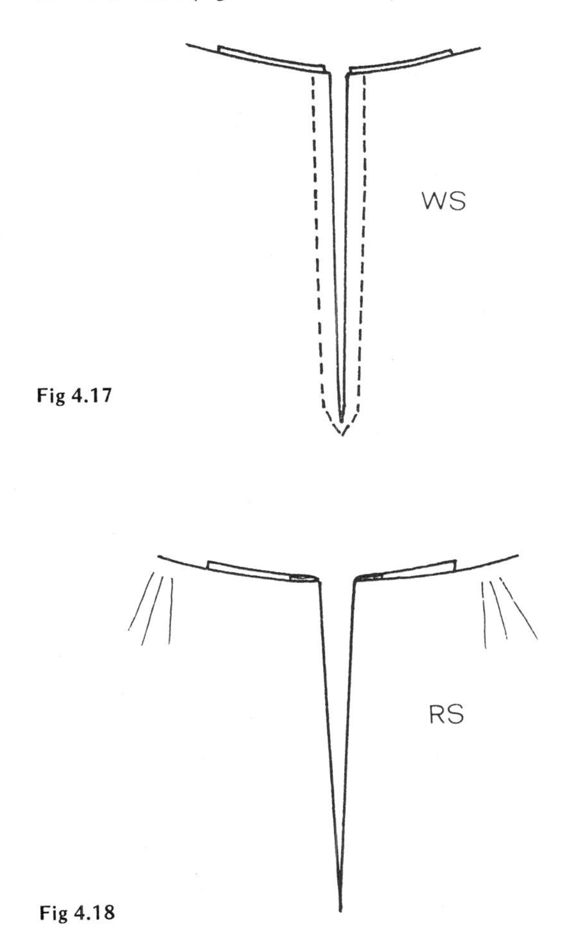

Fig 4.17

Fig 4.18

COLLARS

Collars are made from double fabric; the ones that are quickest to cut and construct are those made from a piece of fabric that is folded.

Most collars need some interfacing in them.

The conventional methods of attaching are time-consuming, so short cuts can be taken in joining the collar to the neckline, employing methods that are often used in ready-made clothes.

Even though these ways of attaching are quick to do there are several points to remember in order to ensure good results.

Trim down the seam allowance on the neckline of the garment to 1 cm. This makes it easier to handle.

Mark the centre back and centre front of the neckline — one may be marked already by a zip or other opening.

Pin the collar to the neckline, inserting the pins across the seam, matching centre back and centre front points.

If there is any ease in the collar it should be arranged approximately where the shoulder seams fall.

Bias roll

The collar is a rectangle of fabric cut on the cross, the exact length of the garment's neckline and four times as wide as the finished effect. It is usually fastened at the back above a zip.

Cut a strip of light or soft iron-on Vilene and press it to one edge of the collar. The Vilene should be less than a quarter of the width of the rectangle (fig 4.19).

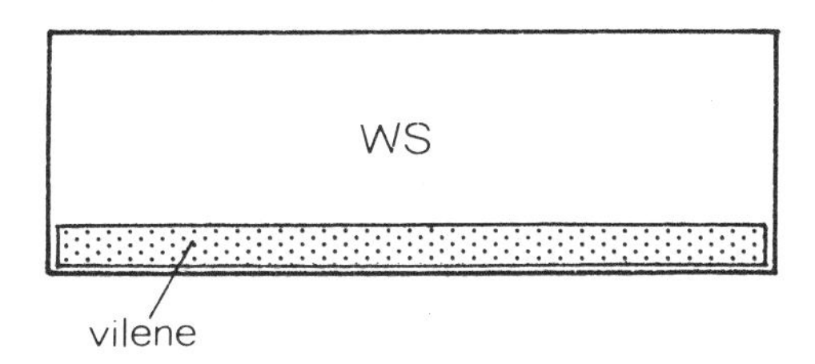

Fig 4.19

On the garment, fold back the centre front or back seam allowance or facing on to the right side and pin. Fold the collar wrong-side together and machine across the ends. Trim the turnings and turn the corners right-side out. Press. Fold the collar and press a crease to mark the centre front. Place collar to neck edge with the interfaced edge against the garment. Pin the centre front; pin the ends of the collar at the centre back on top of the turned-back facing. Pin at intervals in between. Tack and machine from end to end. Trim the turnings to 5 mm and zig-zag to neaten. Press the seam down into the garment and the collar up, fold the facings to the wrong side. Press. Allow the collar to roll over (figs 4.20, 4.21 and 4.22).

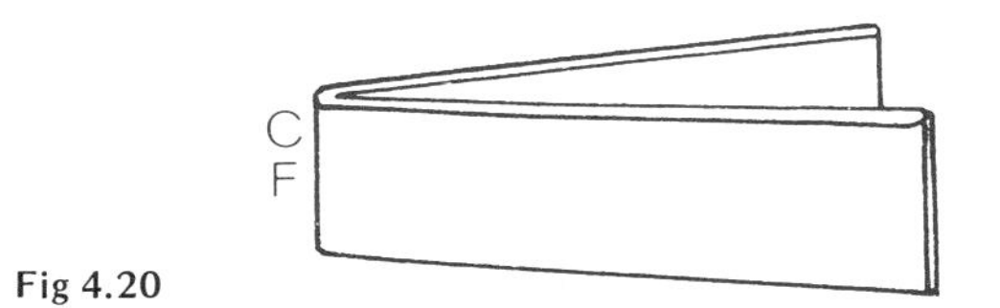

Fig 4.20

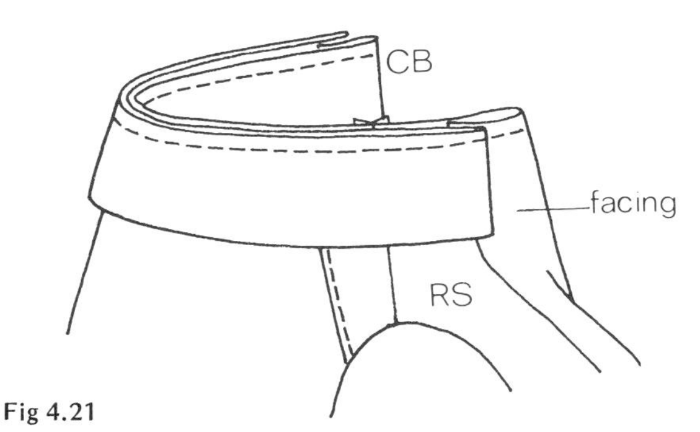

Fig 4.21

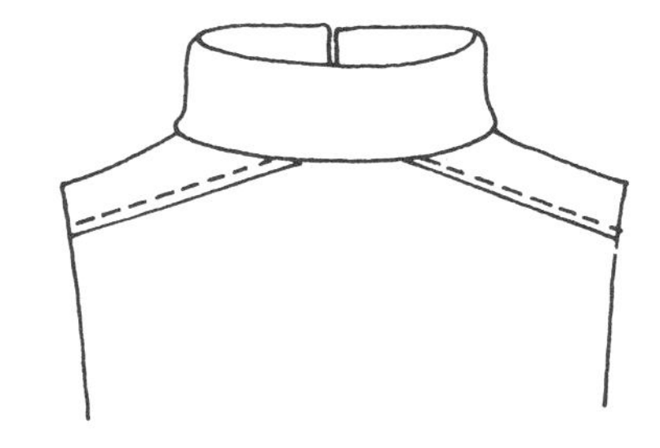

Fig 4.22

Bias finish and tie

The collar is a long piece of bias fabric that fits the neck edge of the garment but with ends long enough to tie at the front. The width can be twice the finished collar width or if you want it to roll, four times the width. Pieces of fabric may have to be joined to make a piece long enough. Make sure the join falls at the centre back.

Measure the length of the neck edge of the garment, cut a piece of iron-on Vilene to the same length and 1 cm less in width than the stand of the collar. Press it to one edge of the bias fabric, in the centre (fig 4.23).

Fig 4.23

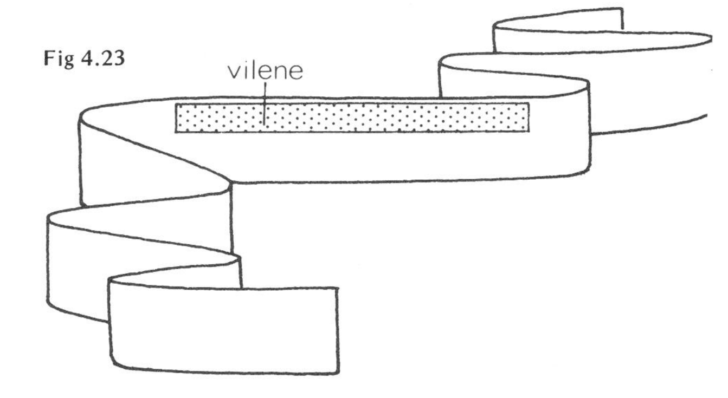

On the garment, fold the front facing on to the right side and pin. Measure the distance from the fold at the edge back to the centre front — usually 1-2 cm, depending on the width of the facing. Fold the bias piece with right sides together and machine across each end and along the edge, leaving a gap in the middle equal to the size of the neckline on the garment, minus the distance measured across the facing (fig 4.24).

Fig 4.24

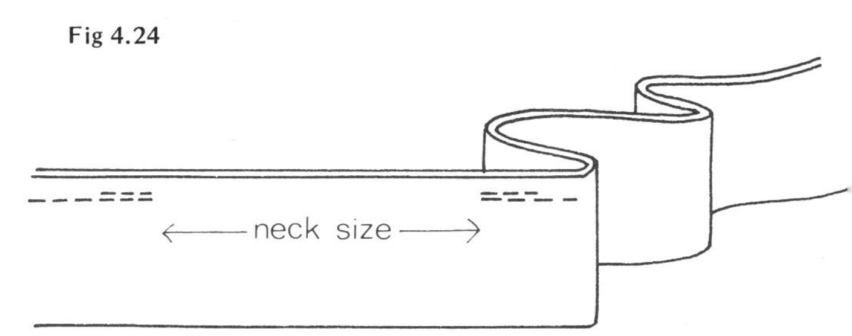

Trim the turnings and turn the tie ends right-side out and press. Snip the turnings at the ends of the stitching. Match the centre back to the centre back of the garment and pin.

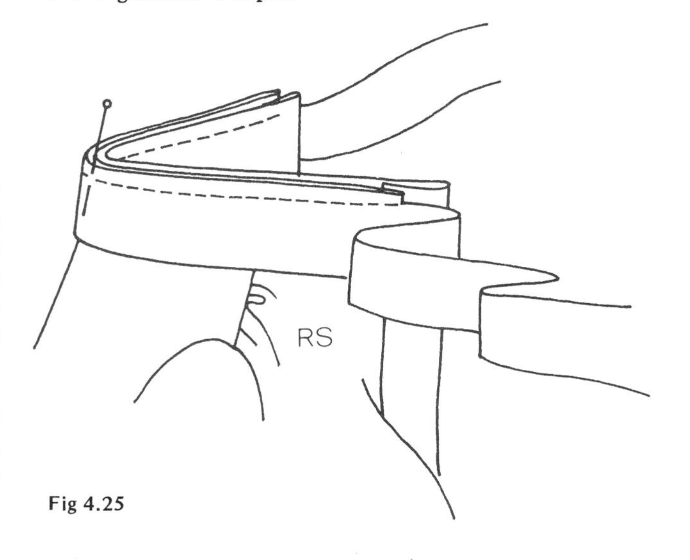

Fig 4.25

Bring the ends of the neck section to the centre front on top of the facing and pin. Pin at intervals. Tack and machine from end to end (fig 4.25). Trim the turnings to 5 mm and zig-zag to neaten. Fold the facings on to the wrong side. Press the neck join down into the garment.

Cowl

The collar is a very wide piece of bias fabric with one edge attached to the neck of the garment. A cowl is usually attached to a low neck so an opening in the collar is unnecessary although there is sometimes a zip in the back of a dress below the cowl. Very successful in jersey fabric.

Fold the collar and join with a narrow seam. Turn a narrow hem along one edge, machine, hand sew or hold with Wundaweb (fig 4.26).

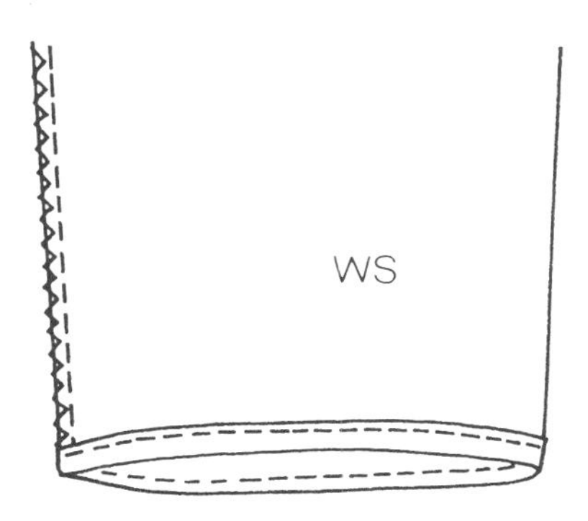

Fig 4.26

Place collar to neckline with the right side to the wrong side of the garment. Match the seam to the centre back and match the centre fronts. Pin at intervals. Tack and machine. Trim the turnings to 5 mm and zig-zag to neaten. Press the join down on to the garment (fig 4.27). Fold collar down.

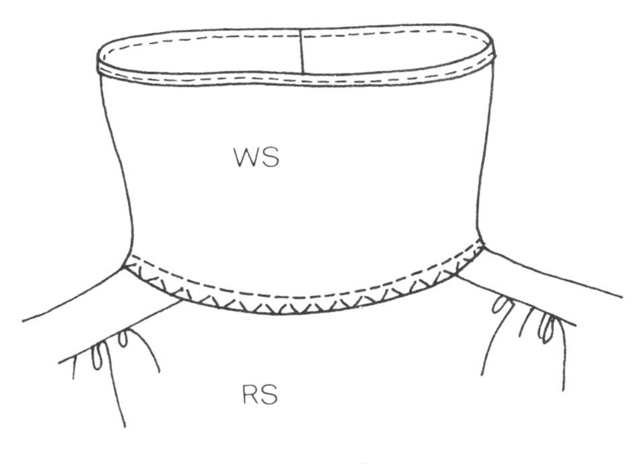

Fig 4.27

Fold-down collar

This type of collar, e.g. shirt collar, may be a rectangle of fabric folded at the outer edge, or it may be shaped, in which case the collar is cut in two pieces and joined at the outer edge.

Single layer method

With a folded collar cut iron-on Vilene the same size and press it to the wrong side of the fabric. Mark the centre back of the collar (fig 4.28).

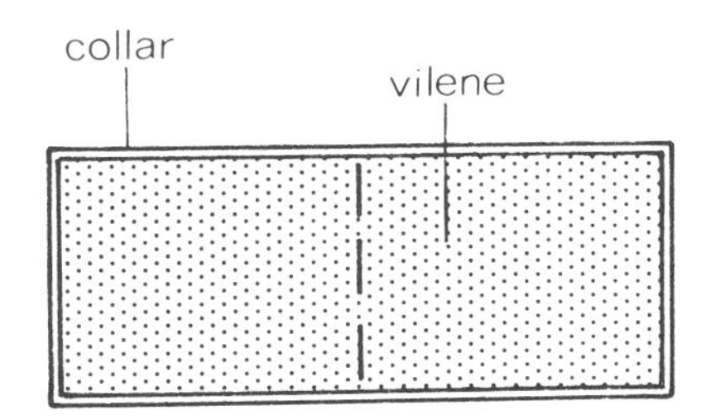

Fig 4.28

Place the right side of the collar to the wrong side of the neck, match the seam allowances and centre back marks. Pin and tack. Machine across the neck but leave the seam allowance free at the centre front. There may already be a zip in position so the stitching will cross the top of the zip and the seam allowance of the collar will extend beyond that (fig 4.29).

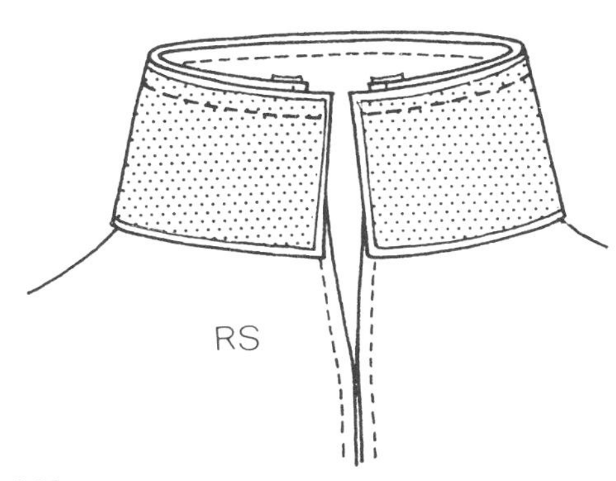

Fig 4.29

Trim the turnings, snip every 5 mm right up to the machining and press the seam open and then into the collar.

Stitch the collar ends. Either fold the collar right-sides together, stitch across the ends, trim and turn through, or, fold the collar wrong-sides together, turn in the edges to meet each other, and slip stitch. The second method is more accurate and easier to do (fig 4.30).

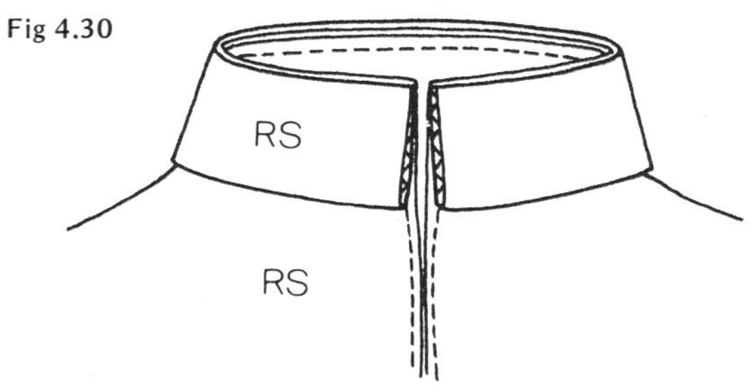

Fig 4.30

Roll the collar into the position it will take up in wear and work a row of diagonal basting along it through both layers. Trim the remaining raw edge of the collar so that only 5 mm extends beyond the row of machine. Turn under the raw edge to cover the stitching and tack. Finish by hemming or machining on the edge (fig 4.31).

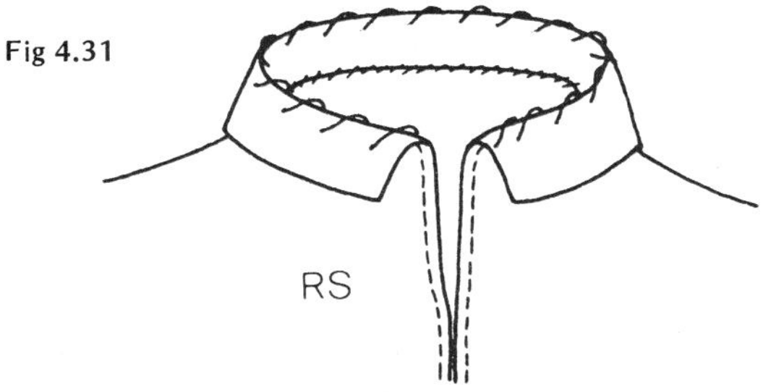

Fig 4.31

Double layer method

If the collar is in two pieces begin by trimming 2 mm from all edges of one piece. Attach iron-on interfacing to the wrong side; this is the under collar.

> **TIP** For a crisp shirt collar also attach iron-on Vilene to the top collar. Transparent Vilene is usually suitable.

Place top collar and under collar right-sides together, tack and machine round the outer edge. Make the raw edges meet and stitch with the top collar uppermost, taking the original seam allowance. The under collar is smaller in order that the collar rolls correctly. Trim the seam allowances, snip the outer edge turnings, cut off the corners and turn the collar right-side out. Roll the edges well and press. Edge stitch the collar if you wish. Bring the raw edges together at the neck and tack together (figs 4.32 and 4.33).

Attach to the neckline in the same way as the bias

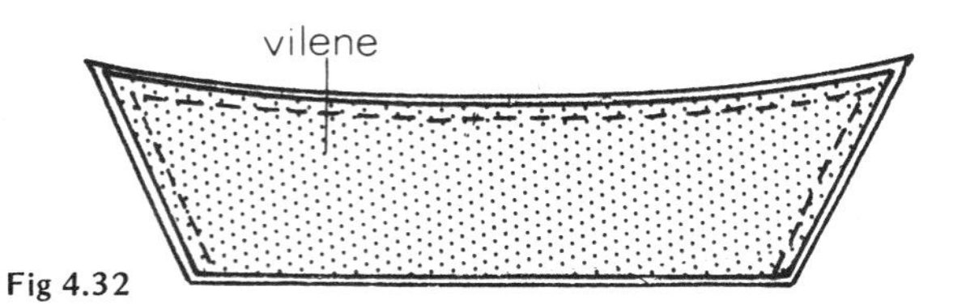

Fig 4.32

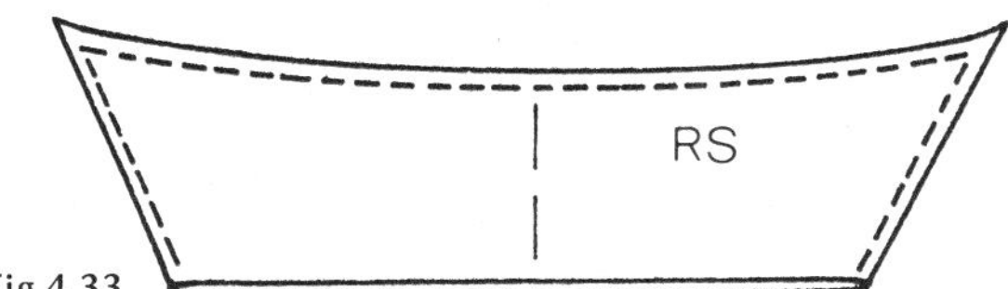

Fig 4.33

roll, folding the facings back on to the right side of the garment first.

Alternatively, when joining the collar pieces, stitch only to the seam allowance at the centre front corners. Turn and press the collar and attach by the single layer method described for the one-piece collar. Edge stitching can be added after the collar has been attached (fig 4.34).

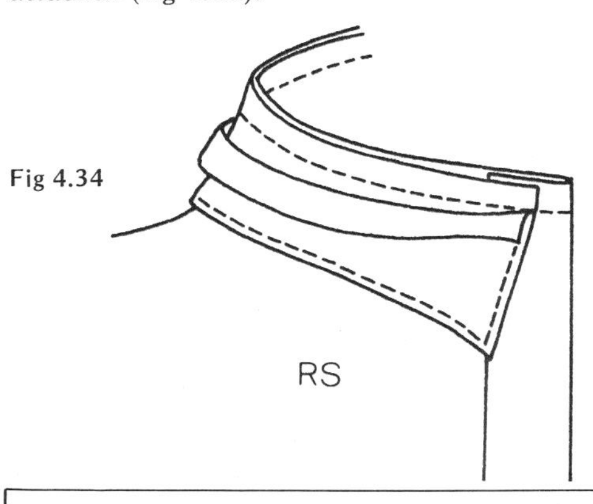

Fig 4.34

> **TIPS** It is easier to attach the collar soon after working the shoulder seams because you can arrange the neckline flat on the table to pin the collar.
>
> Save time by pinning the collar to the garment neckline to see that it is the right length. If too long unpin and trim a little off each end of the collar. Proceed to interface and attach.
>
> If the collar meets edge to edge at the centre back, hold the two edges together with a small piece of Velcro. Hem one piece extending from the collar, the other piece under the edge it meets (fig 4.35).

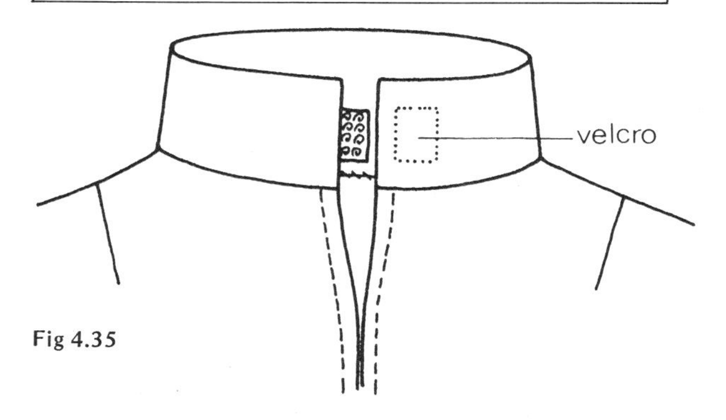

Fig 4.35

5 Machine stitching

As stitches are the means of holding the fabric together, if you take any short cuts by using big stitches or by not fastening off thread ends securely, it will in the end be time wasted, not saved. However, with hand sewing it helps to know which are the most useful stitches to learn and perfect, and where machining is concerned there are plenty of tips to help make sure that what you do is right the first time and will not need unpicking.

Obviously the greatest saving of time comes with making maximum use of the sewing machine. A certain amount can be done with a straight stitch but to have the choice of operations offered by a swing needle machine speeds up the sewing a great deal. With a fully automatic machine your whole approach to garment construction should alter. Sometimes people say that they feel they won't need embroidery stitches anyway, but a number of those stitches can be brought into beneficial use. If you vary the width and length, use them for different purposes, put different stitches together, and regard them as variations rather than embroidery, you will see how versatile they are.

The machine can be used for two kinds of stitching apart from decorative embroidery and repairs: temporary and permanent.

TEMPORARY STITCHING

There are three main temporary stitches, all inserted to hold fabric in position until a permanent stitch replaces them.

Tailor tacking

Use for marking seam allowances, etc. Work the stitching beside the edge of the paper pattern after cutting out, but before removing the pattern. Make sure there are no pins near the edges of the pattern. If the pattern has seam allowances, the edge of the paper should be folded back to 2 mm beyond the fitting line.

As this method of marking inserts a lot of tufts of thread and they have to be removed later, confine its use to areas where long seams require marking rather than points or corners. Insert a No. 80 needle and then attach the tailor tacking foot to the machine; thread with Atlas tacking thread. Set the zig-zag width to No 2. Set the stitch length on 4. Before stitching loosen the top tension, remembering to return it to the correct position after stitching. Take the top thread through the foot and then fit it into the slot and pull it out to the left to start. Stitch. The thread is lifted over the central bar of the foot, forming big loops. After stitching part the layers of fabric and nip the threads (fig 5.1).

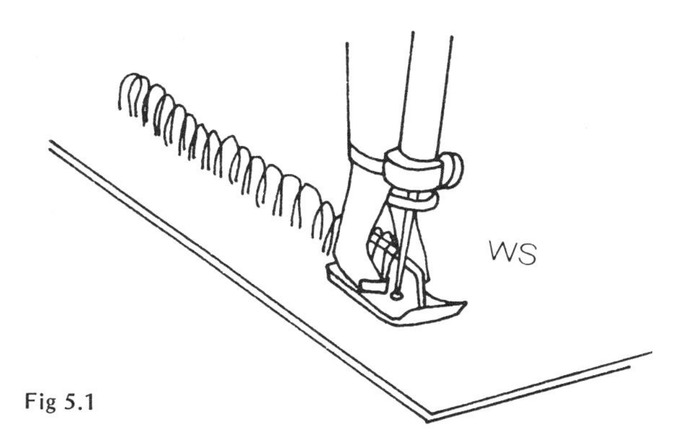

Fig 5.1

Basting

This is also called machine basting or tacking.

Insert the needle with two eyes, the Magic Needle, and the zig-zag foot. Thread the machine with Atlas tacking thread and thread the upper eye.

Set the zig-zag width to maximum (4) and the length to 2½ or 3. Move the needle to the far left position and set the automatic pattern lever to blind stitch (fig 5.2).

Place pieces of fabric with right sides together and pin across the seam. Place the fabric under the foot, and if the stitching is to withstand the strain of fitting reverse at the start but with the width of stitch set on 0, then set to No. 4 to baste. Hold the fabric fairly taut in front and behind the foot, removing the pins as you approach them. The stitching forms on the left of the foot where the needle is positioned.

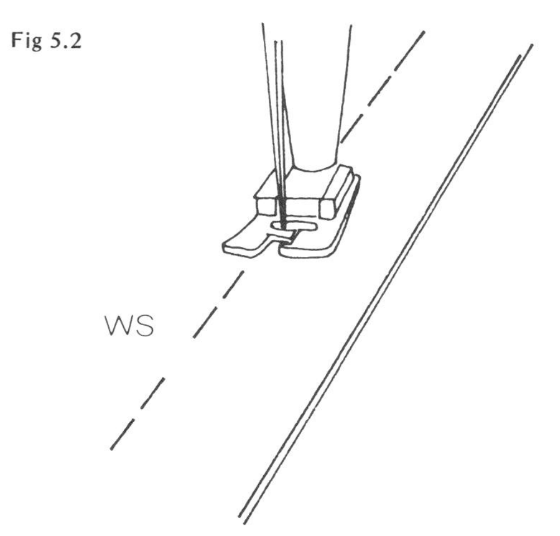

Fig 5.2

Work permanent stitching beside the basting nearer the raw edges.

When ready to remove the basting, snip the reversing at both ends, take hold of the spool thread and ease gently out.

Large straight stitch

A quick way of inserting a gathering thread, a method of marking a line and also a useful stitch for holding fabric together for fitting if your machine doesn't adapt to basting.

Thread the machine in the usual way with normal sewing thread. Adjust to the biggest stitch the machine will make. Leave reasonably long ends of thread when starting and finishing so that there is plenty to grasp when the time comes for removing the stitches. If you are doing a lot of big stitching it is worth spending a moment threading the machine with thread of a contrasting colour to make it easy to distinguish it after permanent stitching has been put in. Do not stitch too close to the raw edges of woven fabric or they will fray when you remove the thread (fig 5.3).

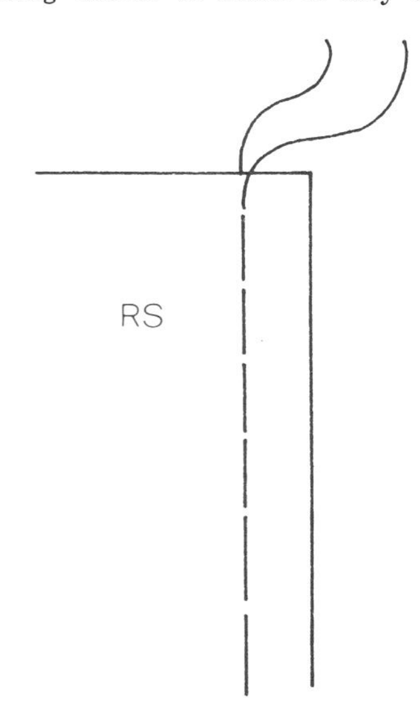

Fig 5.3

When marking or inserting a thread for pulling up, work with the right side of the fabric uppermost. When you remove the thread, pick up the spool thread, the one on the wrong side, and it will pull out easily.

When used as a temporary holding stitch work the permanent stitch just beside it so that removal of the large stitch is easy (fig 5.4).

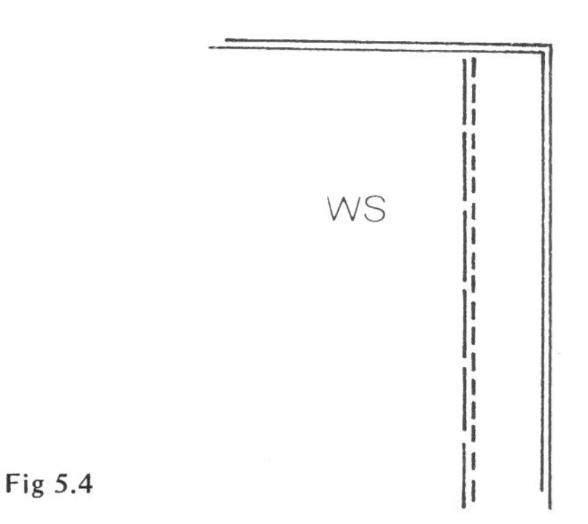

Fig 5.4

PERMANENT STITCHING

Unlike temporary machining, permanent stitches must be exactly the right size for fabric, the correct type of stitch must be selected and it must be accurately placed and the thread ends securely finished off.

Select the stitch and try it out on a double piece of fabric. Adjust the machine setting until the stitch looks satisfactory on the fabric on both sides. Unless there is something wrong with the machine the stitch will always hold the layers of fabric together satisfactorily.

The tension should not need adjusting except sometimes on exceptionally heavy or fine fabrics, although the best machines have an in-built tension adjustment that works automatically.

It is vital to use the correct type and size of machine needle. Fine needles are now used much more than previously. Fabrics are constructed and finished in a variety of ways and keeping a selection of all the needles available ensures good results. It is often only by trying the stitch that it is possible to determine which needle is best. The needle should slide easily into the fabric without breaking its construction and without noise. The ordinary sharp pointed needle is satisfactory for use on woven fabrics but some jersey fabrics made from synthetic fibres are so closely knitted that the needle cannot penetrate properly. This means that the top and bottom threads cannot lock together and so a stitch is not formed. The solution is to use a ball-pointed needle. As its name implies it is round instead of sharp and it eases its way between the loops of knitting. The principle is similar to that of the rounded point of a knitting needle that slides easily in use; if a sharp pointed needle were used it would not slip so easily between stitches (fig 5.5).

Fig 5.5

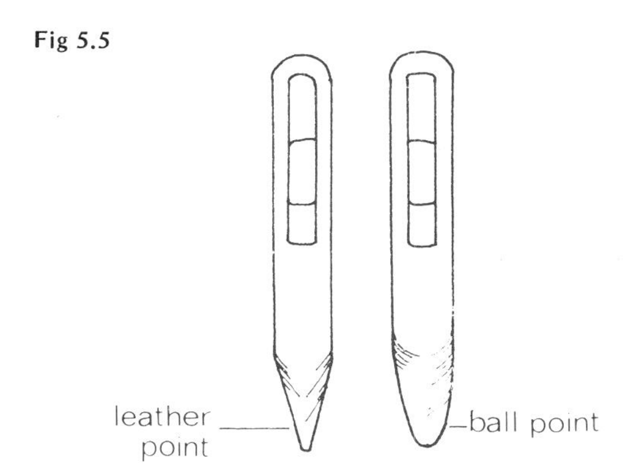

Leather, suede and plastic should be sewn with a spear-pointed machine needle. It has a very sharp three-sided cutting point that makes a small slit in the fabric. An ordinary needle might stitch satisfactorily but the point would force round holes in the material which would be weak and liable to tear with thread movement whereas the cut edges made by the spear close up round the thread and grip it, preventing movement.

The chart on page 48 is a guide to the size and type of needle required for various fabrics, but remember to try out a row of machining first on spare fabric before working on the garment. It saves time in the long run. If the stitching disturbs the weave or makes holes, use a finer needle. If the machine makes a noise or the needle makes a popping or bumping sound use a finer needle. If the machine fails to form a stitch change to a ball-point needle. If the fabric wrinkles place a piece of tissue or fine typing paper under the fabric before stitching. If there seems something radically wrong with the stitching, unthread the machine and start again, checking the threading procedure in your instruction book. If the threads tangle or knot at the start of stitching, remove the spool plate and spool and clean out fluff beneath with a small brush.

Starting and finishing

Always have the needle at its highest point when inserting and removing fabric.

Make sure the fabric is right under the foot at the start.

Lower the foot and turn the wheel to lower the needle into the fabric before starting to stitch. To anchor the threads reverse for two stitches before going forwards.

At the end of a row of stitching stop just before the raw edge or it may wrinkle, reverse for two stitches and remove the fabric after raising the needle.

Always remove the fabric towards the back so that the thread runs against the foot otherwise the needle may bend or break.

The cutter blade is situated at the back of the foot so use it to quickly cut the threads. Cut off close to the fabric but leave ends of 10 cm on the machine. With the work and your hands still in this position behind the foot quickly turn the fabric round and cut the thread ends that were left at the start of the seam. This is quicker than searching for them later.

TIP If you cannot reverse on your machine or you do not wish to have the double stitching, drop a spot of Fray-Check liquid on to the thread ends.

Straight stitch

The stitch should appear similar on both sides of the fabric. Never use a very small stitch even on fine fabrics as it tends to compress the fabric. The best stitch is the one that appears to lie on the surface and yet can be seen locked between the two layers when the fabric is parted. A stitch that is too long will cause wrinkling and will not hold the layers together.

Zig-zag stitch

A very slight zig-zag stitch should be used for seams on jersey fabrics and others with give, including lacy or open weaves. The dial should be moved so that it is only just off 0 and the resulting stitch should look like a straight stitch. If it doesn't then you have gone too far on the dial.

A wider zig-zag is used for working over raw edges but keep the width to the minimum or it appears ugly. A very wide stitch is no more effective than a narrow one. Keep the stitch short in length too, but not so close that it forms a firm ridge.

A good zig-zag stitch is one that looks neat, with the proportion of the length to width set so that the stitch is effective but flat. As it is often worked on a single layer of fabric, the right and wrong sides of the stitching may not be exactly alike in appearance.

Sizes of machine needle and stitch

Fabric	*Stitch size*	*Needle*
Barathea	Medium-large	90 (14)
Batiste	Small	70-90 (11-14)
Bedford cord	Medium-large	100 (16)
Bonded fabrics	Large	90 (14)
Bouclé	Medium-large	90 (14)
Brocade	Medium	70-90 (11-14)
Calico	Medium	90 (14)
Camel cloth	Large	100 (16)
Challis	Medium	70 (11)
Chambray	Medium	79-90 (11-14)
Cheesecloth	Medium	70 (11)
Chenille	Large	100 (16)
Chiffon	Small	70 (11)
Cire	Small-medium	70 (11)
Corduroy	Medium-large	90 (14)
Crêpe	Medium	70-90 (11-14)
Damask	Medium	90 (14)
Denim	Medium-large	90 (14)
Doeskin	Medium-large	90 (14)
Donegal	Medium-large	90-100 (14-16)
Drill	Large	110 (18)
Duck	Large	100 (16)
Dupion	Medium	70 (11)
Duvetyn	Medium	90 (14)
Faced cloth	Medium-large	90 (14)
Faille	Medium	70 (11)
Felt	Large	90 (14)
Fur fabric	Large	100-110 (16-18)
Gabardine	Large	100-110 (16-18)
Georgette	Small	70 (11)
Gingham	Medium	70 (11)
Grosgrain	Medium	70 (11)
Habutai	Medium	70 (11)
Harris Tweed	Large	100 (16)
Jersey	Medium, slight zig-zag	70 (11)
Knit	Large, slight zig-zag	90 (14)
Lace	Medium	70-90 (11-14)
Lamé	Medium	70 (11)
Lawn	Small	70 (11)
Lurex	Medium	70 (11)
Madras	Medium	70 (11)
Moire	Medium	70 (11)
Mungo	Medium	90 (14)
Muslin	Small	70 (11)
Needlecord	Medium	70 (11)
Ninon	Medium	70 (11)
Ombre	Medium-large	70 (11) Ball-point if necessary
Organdie	Small	70 (11)
Panne	Medium	70 (11)
Percale	Medium	70 (11)
Plisse	Medium	(70 (11)
Polyester/Cotton	Medium-large	70-90 (11-14)
Poplin	Medium	70 (11)
PVC	Large	90 (14)
Reversible cloth	Large	100-110 (16-18)
Sailcloth	Medium-large	90 (14)
Sateen	Medium	90 (14)
Satin	Small-medium	70-90 (11-14)
Seersucker	Medium	70 (11)
Shantung	Medium	70-90 (11-14)
Stretch towelling	Medium, slight zig-zag	90 (14)
Suede cloth	Medium, slight zig-zag	90 (14)
Surah	Medium	70 (11)
Taffeta	Medium-large	70 (11)
Ticking	Large	100 (16)
Towelling	Large	90 (14)
Tweed	Large	100 (16)
Velvet	Medium-large	70 (11)
Velveteen	Medium-large	90 (14)
Voile	Small-medium	70 (11)
Winceyette	Medium	90 (14)

Fig 5.6

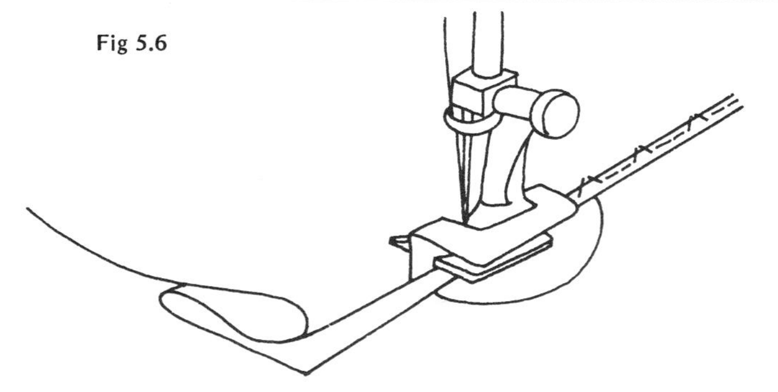

Combination stitches

Some stitches combine the straight and zig-zag movement. Select from these according to the effect you want.

The blind hem stitch makes four straight stitches followed by one zig-zag to the left. When used to fix a hem, set the zig-zag quite wide so that it catches the fold of fabric each time, but if used for decoration or on seam edges keep it narrow for neatness (fig 5.6).

The universal stitch that stitches and neatens

jersey fabrics makes one straight stitch followed by a movement to one side, another straight stitch and so on. Fabric can be lapped and stitched twice. In addition to stitching two edges in the usual way it can also be used for decoration and for seam raw edges. The overlock stitch makes two straight stitches before making one zig-zag to the right. A third stretch stitch makes four small zig-zags followed by two wider ones. This is used for open seams on stretchy fabrics (figs 5.7, 5.8 and 5.9).

Another combination stitch, the running or serpentine, is a straight stitch that runs from side to side. An attractive decoration for narrow hems and also useful for seam turnings (fig 5.10).

With all the above stitches keep the stitch length short.

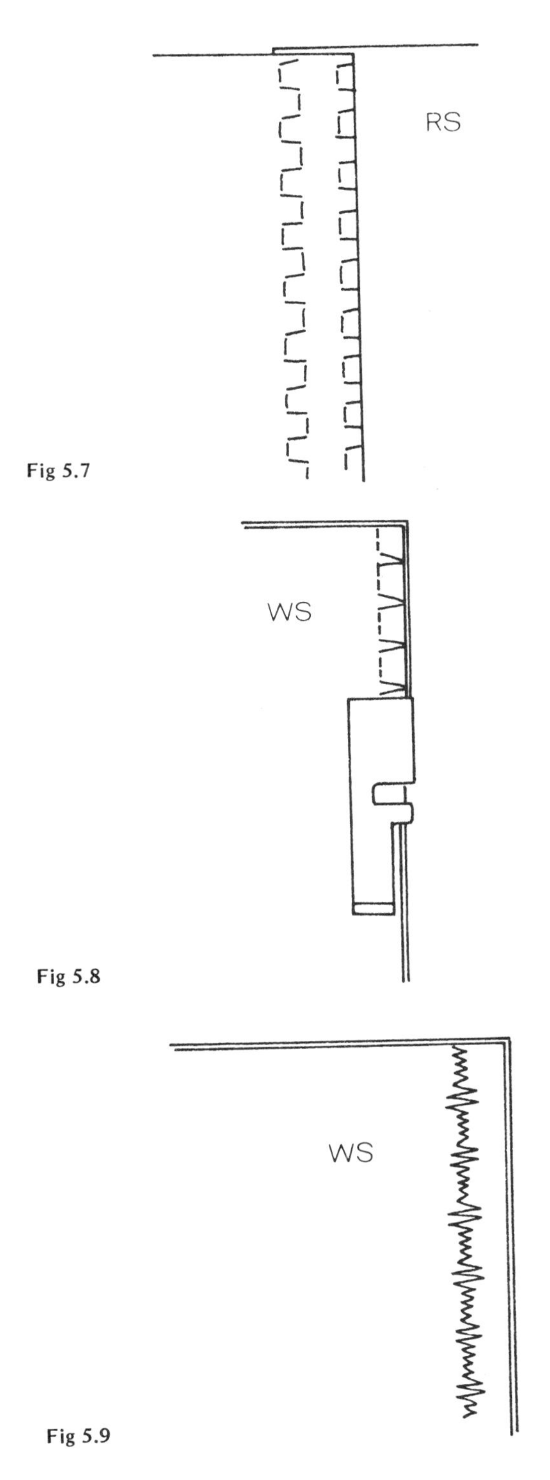

Fig 5.7

Fig 5.8

Fig 5.9

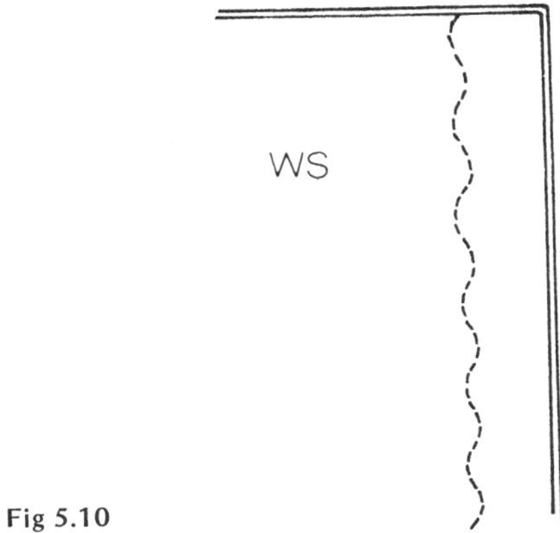

Fig 5.10

TIP If a stretch seam flutes, feed an extra thread in under the foot. The thread is removed after the seam has been pressed (fig 5.11).

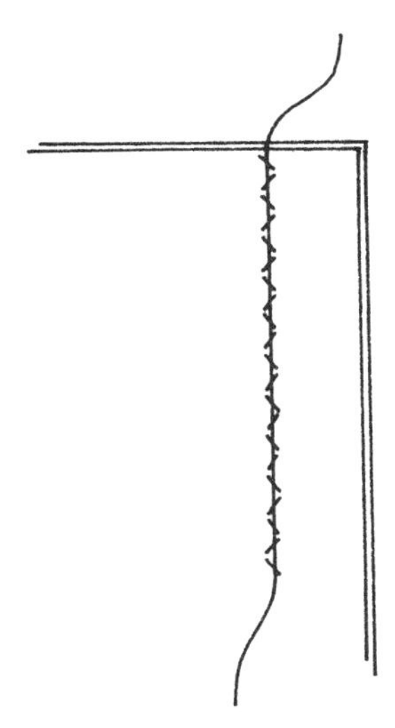

Fig 5.11

Satin stitch

Use the embroidery foot which has a wide, deep groove under the base, or, for buttonholes, use the buttonhole foot.

For satin stitch or any of the close embroidery stitches set the stitch length indicator on the line above 0, set the stitch width as required between 1 and 4. When using normal sewing thread, the satin stitch may appear too close and the fabric may not move, in which case move the stitch length indicator further from 0. Test the stitch on fabric first, putting a piece of paper underneath when working on a single layer of fabric (fig 5.12).

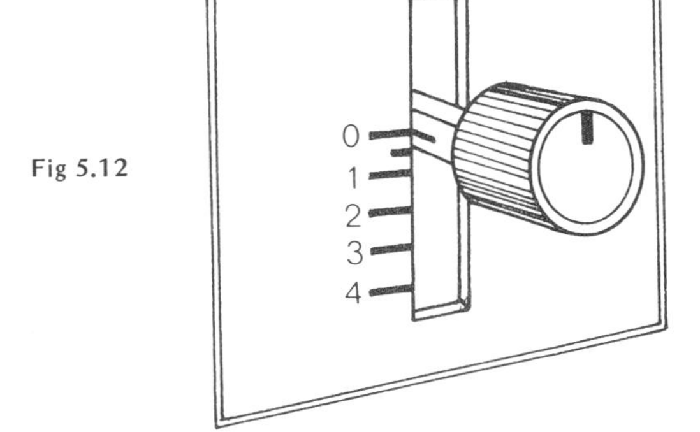

Fig 5.12

Top stitching

Effective decorative stitching can be added by using a straight, zig-zag or embroidery stitch. Adjust the length and width of the stitch according to the type of fabric.

A slightly heavier straight or zig-zag stitch can be made by using two reels of thread on the top of the macine. Use the right size needle for the fabric and place a reel of thread on each spindle on top of the machine. Thread both ends of thread through the machine in the usual way, one at a time, and thread both through the eye of the needle. Set to a medium length stitch and sew (fig 5.13).

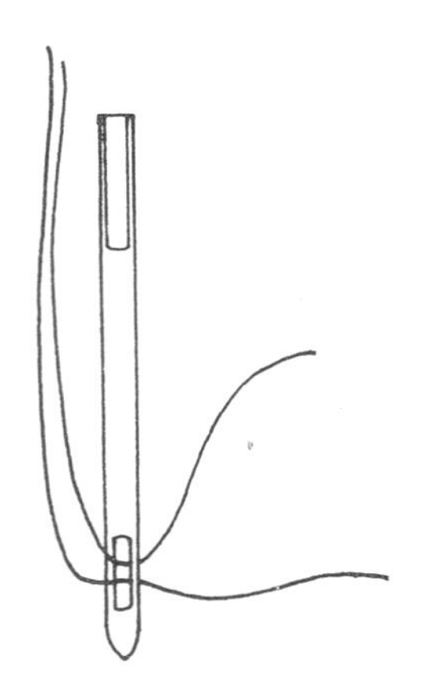

Fig 5.13

The double or twin needle can also be used for decorative stitching, producing shaded effects when used on very fine fabrics, a double row of stitching with a slight raised effect on opaque fabrics. Two different coloured threads can be used on the machine.

Insert the needle and thread into the machine making sure you pass the threads one each side of the tension disc but together through all the other points until you reach the needle. Insert the spool and machine in the usual way with the needle in the central position (fig 5.14).

A medium length straight stitch is very effective but so too are some of the zig-zag stitches such as the blind stitch.

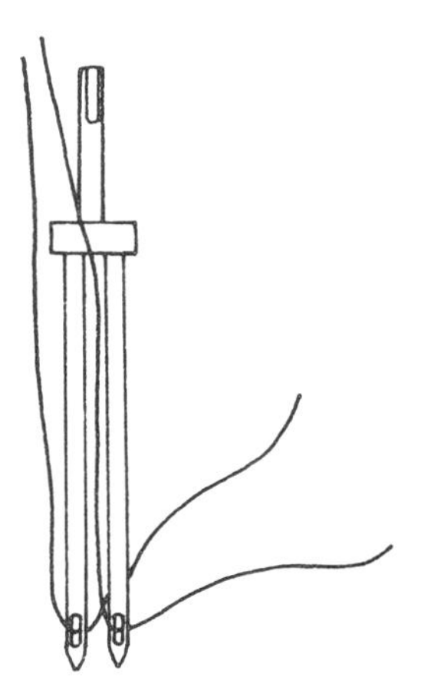

Fig 5.14

Another effective way of working decorative stitching is to work any of the zig-zag stitches or embroidery stitches to emphasise seams, edges, etc. Choose a stitch that is suitable for the type of fabric and the garment.

TIPS Contrasting colours of threads show up so it takes longer to get neat results; it is quicker to use matching thread.

Always top stitch from the right side of the garment.

Try to work through the same number of layers throughout to get the same effect.

Keep straight by using a groove or edge of the foot as a guide. Or use the grooves marked on the needle plate. If stitching further from the edge than this stick a piece of Sellotape across the machine base and use the edge as a guide (fig 5.15).

One way of working two parallel rows of top stitching is to move the needle position for the second row, but keep the foot in the same place on the fabric as for the first row (fig 5.16).

Get into the habit of removing the spool case and cover regularly to brush out fluff. It accumulates quickly because synthetic fibres and threads tend to shred and ball together. This can jam the machine if you leave it there.

Put one drop of oil in the spool socket regularly and one spot occasionally on the other moving parts you can see. If you use the machine a lot do this once a week.

Use a new needle every couple of garments; some fabrics, particularly synthetic knits, blunt the needle very quickly and it will damage the fabric, even fail to form a stitch.

If you put a special type of needle in the machine and you have to leave off for a while, write the size and type of needle on a piece of paper and leave it under the foot to remind you.

Also, when you have given the machine a thorough oiling, leave yourself a message under the foot to remind you to clean off surplus oil when you come back, before putting fabric under the machine.

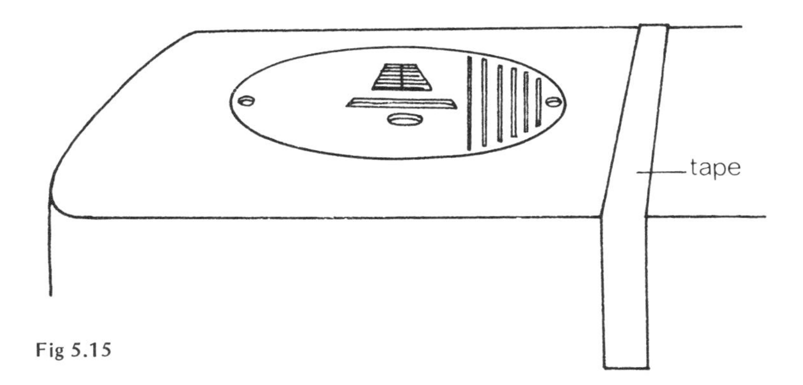

Fig 5.15

Unpicking machine stitches

If you reversed at the end, now snip the stitches, pulling open the two layers of fabric apart. On reaching the single line of stitching, lift one thread with a pin, undoing about four or five stitches until you can take hold of the thread.

Hole the end of thread very firmly and tug with a sharp movement, pulling back along the stitching. The thread will break some one or two centimetres further along the line. Turn the fabric over and pick up the other thread. It will still be slightly stuck to the fabric but it is loose. Hold the end firmly and tug it back along the stitching to break the thread. Continue in this way.

Press the fabric to close up the machine holes.

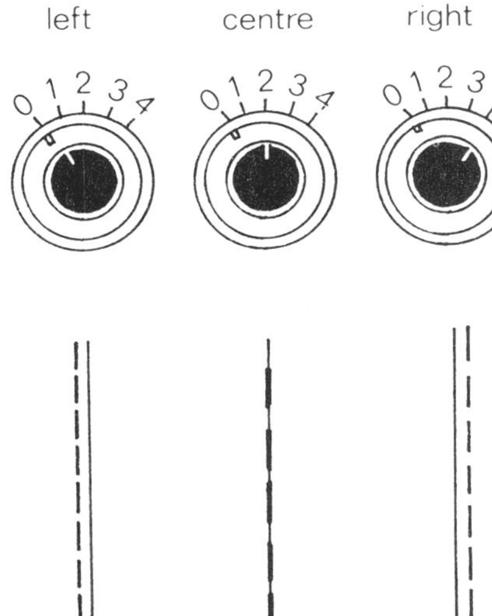

Fig 5.16

6 Some more machining ideas

Use your machine as much as you can for both functional and decorative processes. Explore the benefits that imaginative use of the basic stitches will bring. Accustom yourself to changing from straight to zig-zag, become familiar with the type of stitch that results from different setting, stitch lengths and widths so that you eliminate errors and reduce experimenting to the minimum.

Although I have made suggestions about thread and about stitch size in the machine finishes that follow, remember that both needle and stitch size must be suitable for the particular fabric that you are using. Where I have referred to 'normal sewing thread' this means the thread you are using to construct the garment, e.g. Drima.

FINE EDGING

This is suitable for all light-weight fabrics, both knitted and woven.

Prepare machine
Ordinary foot
Anchor Machine Embroidery thread No. 30 or normal sewing thread
Stitch length: ½ — ¾
Zig-zag: 1½

Trim the garment edge to 1 cm longer than needed. Turn under the 1 cm and press or tack (fig 6.1).

Fig 6.1

Place under the machine right-side up and work the machining over the folded edge. Fasten off. Cut off thread ends and carefully trim away the surplus fabric on the wrong side.

This finish is particularly useful on the edges of frills, lingerie and blouse hems (no risk of hem showing through skirt).

LACE EDGE

This is a lace extension for lingerie etc.

To attach lace edging to jersey fabric:
Prepare machine
Ordinary foot
Anchor Machine Embroidery or normal sewing thread
Stitch length: ½ — ¾
Zig-zag: 1½ — 2

Mark the position on the garment for placing the straight edge of the lace, or trim the garment edge to length plus 1 cm. With the right-side up, position the lace and zig-zag over the edge. On the wrong side trim away the surplus fabric close to the stitching (fig 6.2).

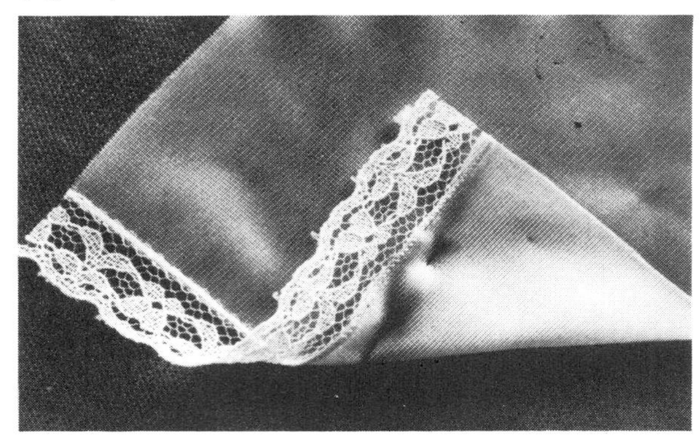

Fig 6.2

On woven fabrics set the machine for straight stitch, length 2. Mark the position for the lace or trim the edge. Place the edge of the lace in position on the right side and work the stitch evenly just within the outer edge of the lace. Fold the raw edge back on the wrong side, pulling against the stitching and press or tack and press (fig 6.3).

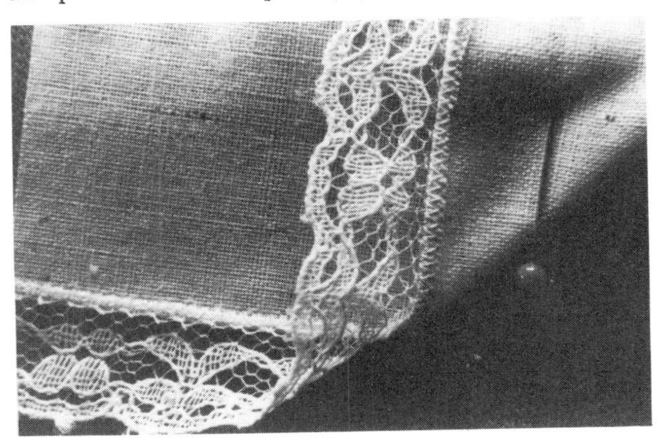

Fig 6.3

Set the machine to stitch length ½-¾; zig-zag 1½ and work this over the edge of the lace.

TIP This is a good method to use when adding lace to a collar. Place the collar pieces wrong sides together, with interfacing between, attach lace to outer edge as described (fig 6.4).

Fig 6.4

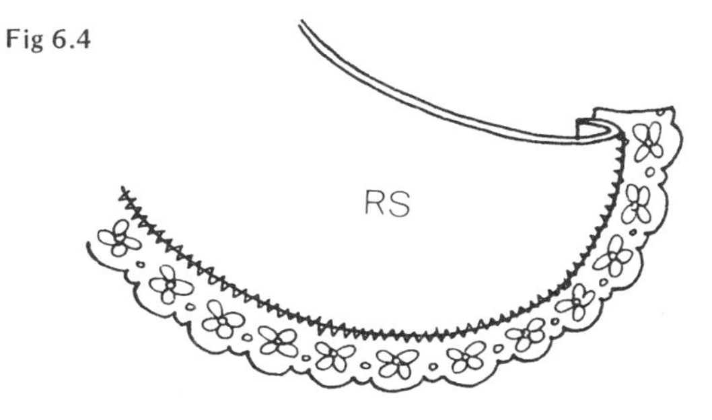

SHELL HEM

Use on soft fine fabrics. Fold under the edge of the fabric and press or tack and press.

Prepare machine
Zig-zag foot
Blind hem stitch setting
Normal sewing thread
Stitch length: 1½
Zig-zag: 4

Insert fabric under the foot with the fold to the left and right side up. Work the stitch so that when the needle moves to the left it misses the fabric (fig 6.5).

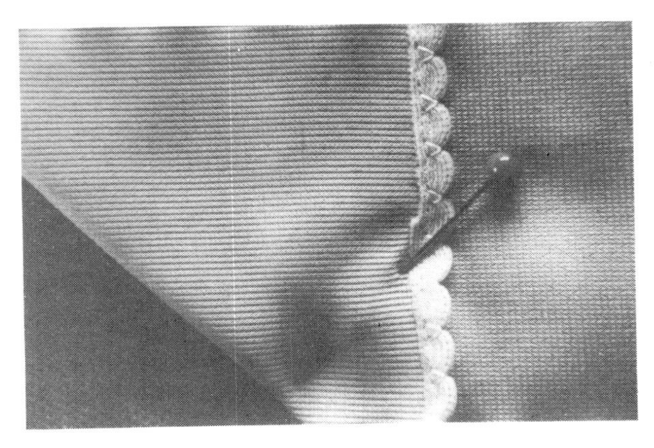

Fig 6.5

Work a second row of stitching, this time zig-zag, stitch length 1½ and zig-zag ½, about 5 mm inside the blind stitch. On the wrong side, trim away the surplus fabric close to the zig-zag.

SHELL TUCKS

Fold the fabric right-side out and press where the tuck is to be.

Prepare machine
Zig-zag foot
Blind hem stitch setting
Anchor Machine Embroidery thread
Stitch length: 1½
Zig-zag: 4

Place fabric under the foot with the fold to the left. Work the blind hem stitch so that the needle misses the fabric fold when it moves to the left.

Using an adjustable marker press another crease in the fabric parallel with the first, work a second tuck, and so on until you have sufficient. Press tucks flat.

TIPS Work the tucks on a piece of fabric before cutting out the garment piece.

Make the tucks exactly on the straight grain.

SCALLOPS

Prepare machine
Satin stitch foot
Automatic pattern: scallop
Anchor Machine Embroidery thread
Paper under the fabric
Stitch length: satin stitch
Zig-zag: 3 — 4

Trim the fabric edge to 1 cm longer than needed. Place fabric on paper and under the foot. Work the stitch parallel with the trimmed edge (fig 6.6).

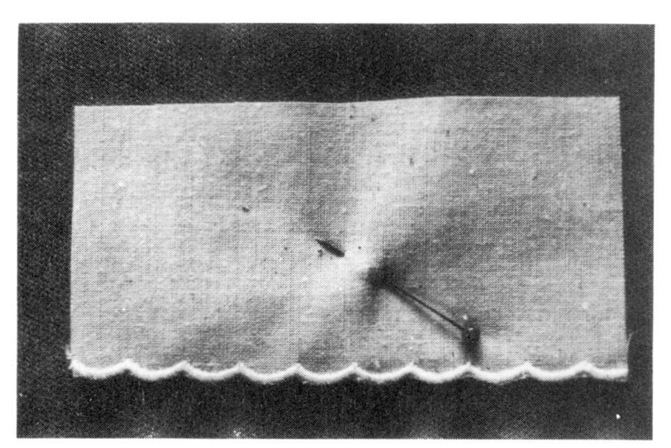

Fig 6.6

Tear away the paper. Trim away surplus fabric on the wrong side, close to the scallops.

TIP A firmer edge can be produced by feeding crochet cotton No. 10 under the foot. Feed it down through the bar on the front of the machine. Make sure the needle passes at either side of the cotton as it zig-zags.

LOOP SCALLOPS

Attach to a finished garment edge, e.g. hemmed or faced. Set the machine as above and work with paper under the fabric. Position the fabric so that the needle catches the fabric edge when the far left point of the stitch pattern is reached (fig 6.7).

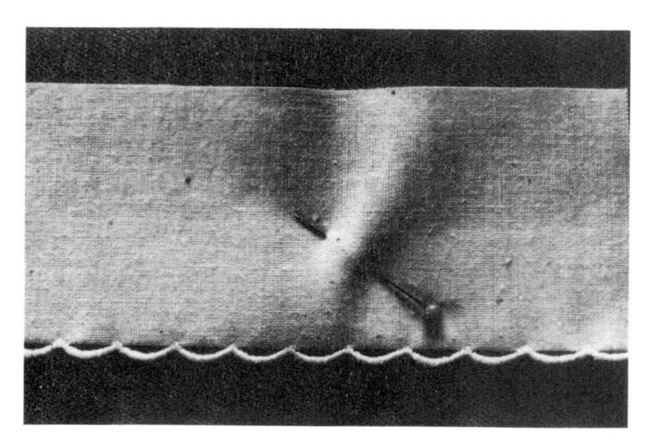

Fig 6.7

TIP Make tucks with looped edges. Fold and press the fabric where the tuck is to be. Work the scallop loops on the edge. Work a row of straight stitching the width of the foot away. Press the tuck to one side. Fold and press the fabric for the next tuck and so on.

CORDED HEM

Use on any medium or heavy fabric. It can be worked at any distance from the edge but if the garment is shaped keep the hem fairly narrow.

Prepare machine
Satin stitch foot
Anchor Machine Embroidery thread or normal sewing thread
Soft Embroidery Cotton in contrasting colour
Stitch length: ½ — ¾
Zig-zag: 1½

Decide on the depth you want the hem, turn up once and press, allow 1½ cm more and trim away the surplus on the wrong side.

Attach the measuring bar to the foot and adjust it to the hem depth decided upon. Place fabric under the foot, right side up, and work the zig-zag stitch, feeding the embroidery cotton under it (fig 6.8) or work through the hole.

On the wrong side trim away the surplus fabric close to the stitching.

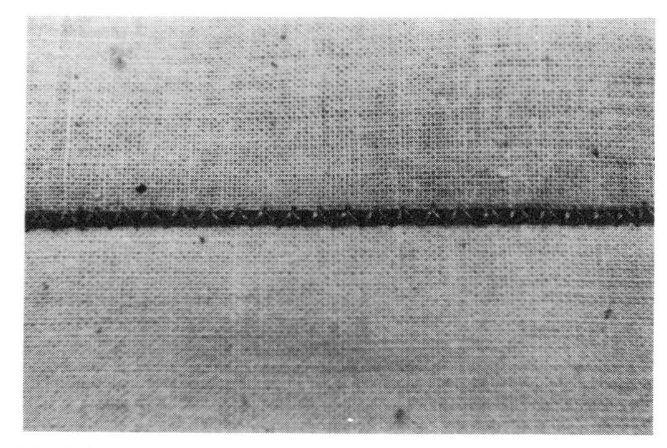

Fig 6.8

TIP Unpick a section of one seam of the garment, turn up the hem and work the corded hem. Re-stitch the seam, catching in the ends of embroidery cotton. This avoids an unsightly join (fig 6.9).

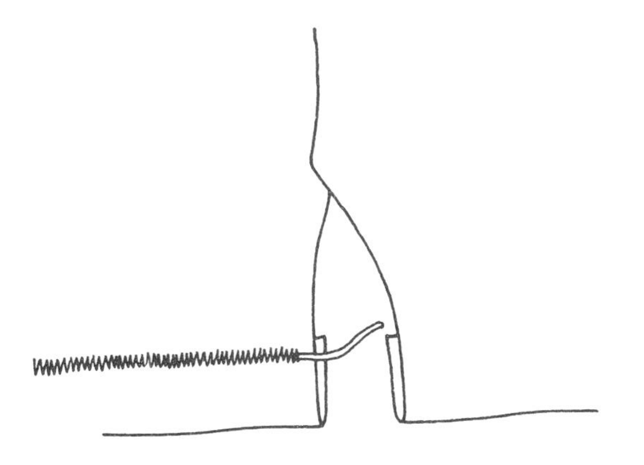

Fig 6.9

PIPED EFFECT

Use this as an alternative to piping or top stitching to emphasise an edge or a style feature.

If worked on a hem prepare it as for corded hem. If a style feature, finish the edge first, e.g. facing.

Prepare machine
Satin stitch foot
Machine Embroidery Thread
Soft cotton embroidery thread to match or tone
Stitch length: satin stitch
Zig-zag: 1½

Work in the same way as for corded hem but the satin stitch covers the embroidery cotton entirely (fig 6.10).

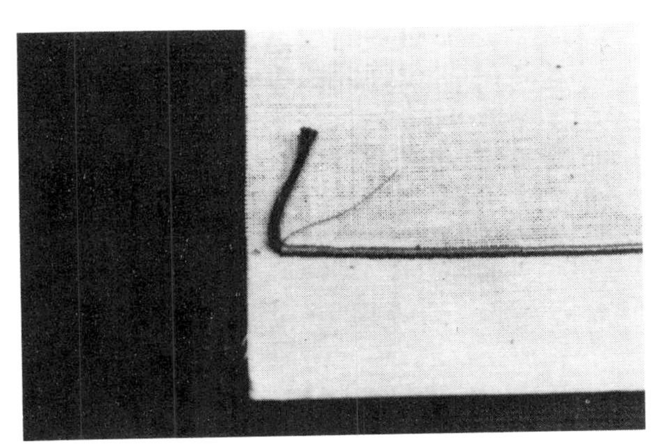

Fig 6.10

DUAL-COLOUR HEM

Use on fine fabrics. Use two different thread colours. If the fabric is printed choose two of the main colours of the print. Work parallel with any finished edge, e.g. faced or hemmed.

Prepare machine
Ordinary sewing foot
Normal sewing thread in two colours
Twin needle
Automatic pattern: blind stitch
Stitch length: ¾ — 1
Zig-zag: 2

Place the fabric under the foot right-side up and stitch parallel with the finished edge (fig 6.11).

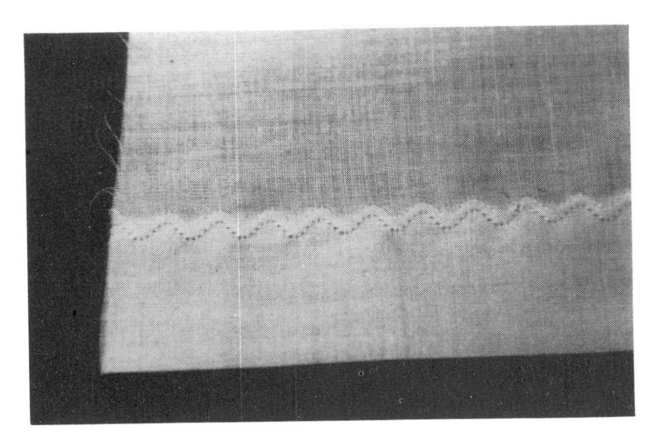

Fig 6.11

BRAID EFFECTS

Machine stitches in various colours can be added to the edges of plain ribbon or petersham ribbon. The simple stitches such as blind stitch can be used in a single or twin needle, stitching on each edge of the ribbon and also, if desired, added off the edge of the ribbon (fig 6.12).

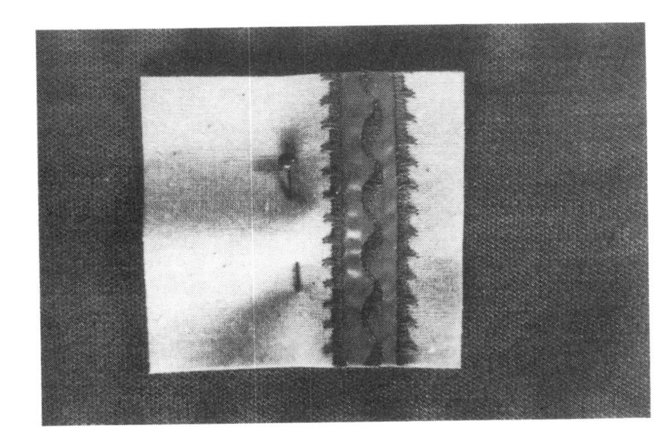

Fig 6.12

If you use an automatic embroidery pattern choose one that does not necessarily require to be matched equally on both sides of the ribbon. Some of the larger patterns must be matched but it takes a long time to perfect the technique of doing it. It is easier to choose a smaller pattern, or a different one for each side. If, when you have worked the pattern, you feel it would be advisable to separate the two rows more, then work a third stitch, preferably an open one, down the centre (fig 6.13).

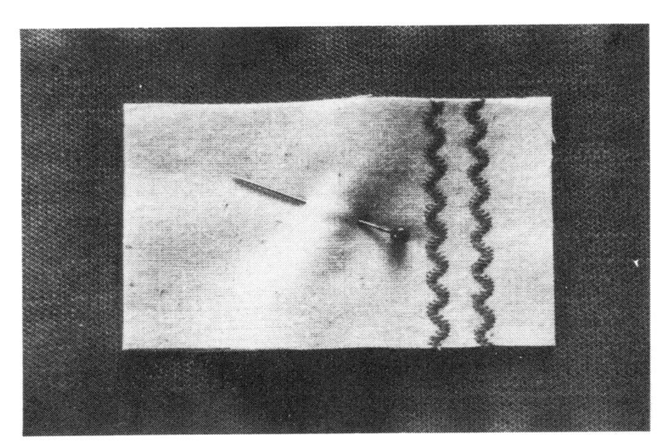

Fig 6.13

TIP If you have to make a false hem use the serpentine stitch. Butt together the raw edges of the garment and hem fabric, place a narrow strip of interfacing beneath the stitch with centre of foot over join. Work another row of stitching either side of the join. Trim away surplus interfacing. Finish the hem (fig 6.14).

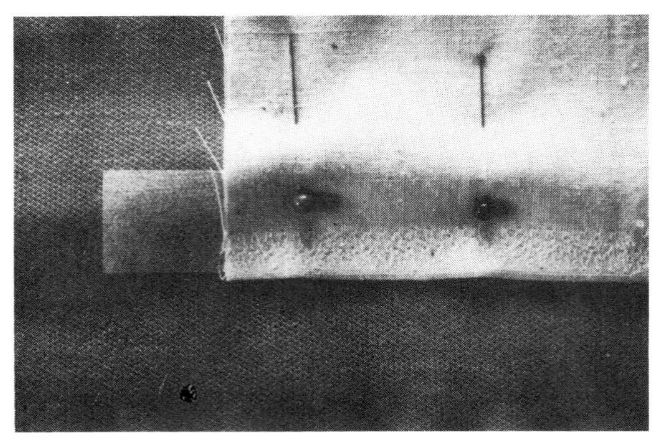

Fig 6.14

7 Seams and darts

SEAMS

Save time by using as few seams as possible. Straight pattern edges can often be pinned together before being placed on the fabric to eliminate a seam. It cannot be done with shaped seams and it should not be done if the seam is likely to be needed for fitting.

If your pattern provides a front and back yoke, place the two together at the shoulder seam and eliminate that seam (fig 7.1).

Front and back skirt pattern pieces can be cut to a fold instead of a seam (fig 7.2).

A straight or loose dress with a centre front seam or buttoned front, can be cut without side seams (fig 7.3).

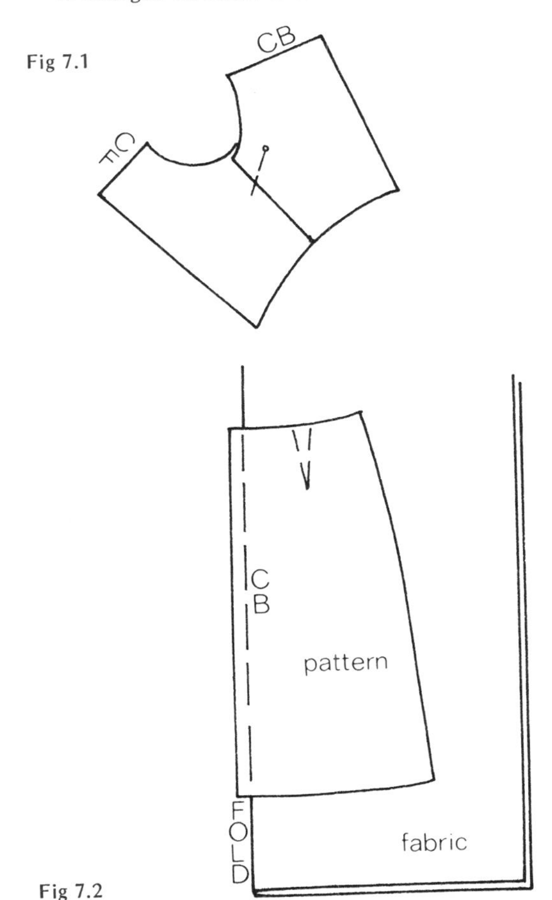

Fig 7.1

Fig 7.2

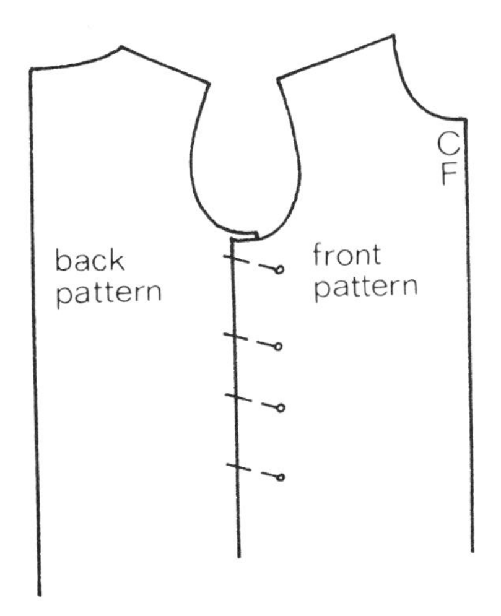

Fig 7.3

There are many more possibilities which you will discover for yourself.

Eliminating seams will alter the grain position on the garment, often making the seams that are left very much on the bias. Take care with these seams, taking note of the following points and it will not be a problem. If you are using a striped, checked or line-pattern fabric be sure that the design will be at an acceptable angle on the remaining seam before you eliminate seams.

Basic seam

Place the two pieces of fabric with the right sides together. Lift the upper layer and move it without stretching until the raw edges are together. Match up each end before settling the area between. Swivel the fabric until the seam edges are lying vertically in front of you with the wider part of the garment farthest from you.

Nearly all seams are on the bias of the fabric and it is important to stitch them in the correct direction. If you work from the widest part up to the narrow, wrinkling can be avoided and the garment seams will handle better. This last point is not so important in short seams but it is vital in long ones on dresses and skirts.

Arrange the fabric and insert pins across the seam from right to left. Use a pin about every 10-15 cms on plain fabric or one that requires no matching. Prepare as many seams as possible for machining at one time. By placing them as described there is little movement and handling so that fraying and stretching are kept to the minimum (fig 7.4).

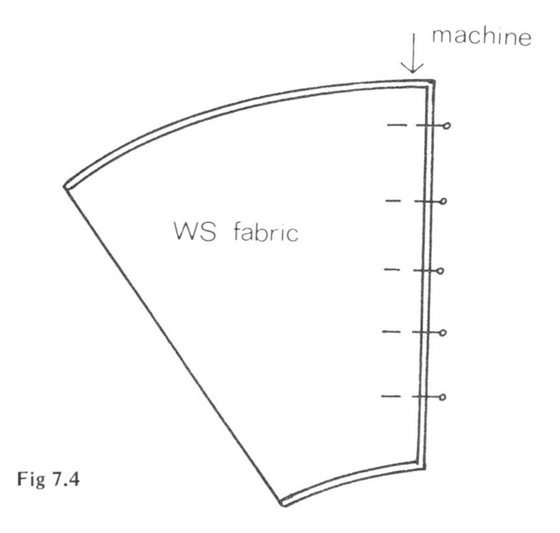

Fig 7.4

Hold the fabric flat and take it to the machine. Insert the seam under the foot, lower the foot and stitch forward for two or three stitches. Reverse for two stitches and stitch forwards. Too much reversing produces a rigid end to the seam that is difficult to press but a couple of stitches will fall within the seam allowances.

The bias edge will tend to 'give' slightly as the foot travels over the fabric. Allow the fabric to 'give' in this way. Do not stretch it as it goes into the machine but do not push it either. Use synthetic thread such as Drima in order to provide 'give' to match the seam. Remove the pins as you reach them.

When sewing on any fabric that has 'give', stitch with a very slight zig-zag stitch to ensure that there is enough stretch in the seam to compensate for the bias edge and the type of fabric. This applies to any knit fabric of any type and those of lace construction. Set the zig-zag dial to ¼.

On reaching the end of the seam stop before the raw edge appears and reverse for two stitches before removing the fabric.

TIP You can save time later by cutting off all thread ends now. Use the cutter on your machine or small scissors and cut ends close to the fabric.

For check fabric or matching patterns, insert every pin very carefully, picking up a small amount of fabric exactly on the seam line. As you insert the pin make sure it is exactly on a main part of the design and check the underneath layer to ensure that the pin picks up the same part of the design. When you stitch, sew over these pins, slowly, to ensure that the fabric does not move (fig 7.5).

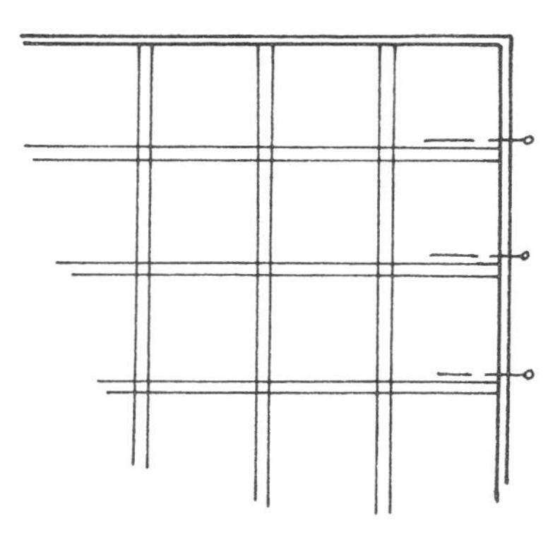

Fig 7.5

Pressing

Place the seam flat and press the stitching, then open out the fabric and arrange it on the sleeve board wrong-side up, having the hem or widest part to the right. Run the iron along the fabric with its side pressing against the line of stitching. Pull the fabric at intervals on each side of the seam to make sure that the join itself is flat against the board. Run the iron along beside it on the second side.

Using the toe of the iron, open the seam turnings. Help it by opening the turnings with the fingers of your left hand and pressing each part as you open it. Return to the right hand end and press again but using the iron flat.

By pressing in the same direction as you stitched you will avoid bubbling beside the seam.

Complete the pressing by turning the fabric over to press the right side and to remove any wrinkles you may find. Return to the wrong side and press again.

TIP When pressing any pile fabric or one with a raised surface place a piece of spare fabric on the sleeve board, right-side up, and press the fabric on it with its right-side down to cushion the pile. When pressing the right side, place the spare fabric on top, pile down, before putting the damp muslin on top of that. This applies to towelling, velour, plush velvet and crêpe.

Finishing

The raw edges of the seam need neatening. This is not only to prevent fraying but also to prevent the turnings from curling up and causing a ridge.

If the fabric frays place the edge under the machine foot right-side up, turn under the edge a little and stitch with a straight stitch on the edge or a small zig-zag over the edge.

If the fabric frays but is not light enough in weight to turn under, work a medium-width short zig-zag stitch over the edge. This stitch should be small and close otherwise the fibres will still fray out between stitches. In addition, a large stitch will make the edge curl over (fig 7.6).

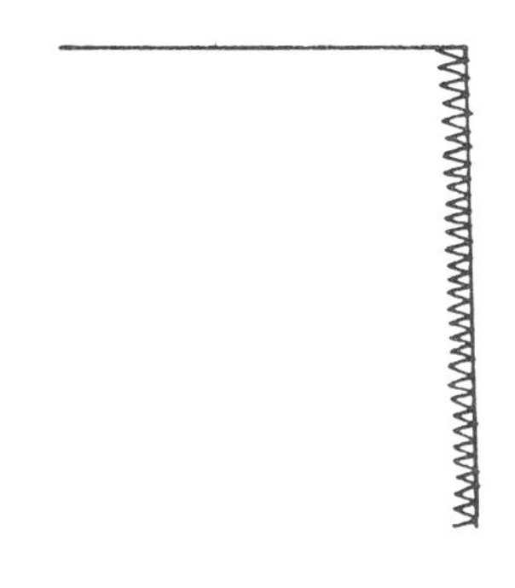
Fig 7.6

On jersey or knit fabrics work the blind hem stitch or the serpentine stitch along the edge to stabilise it (fig 7.7).

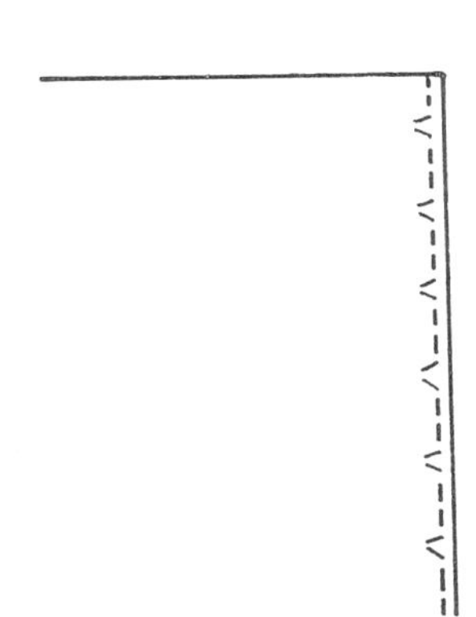
Fig 7.7

If your machine does only a straight stitch then work that on the turning 3 mm within the raw edge. It will not prevent fraying but it will stop it from going too far.

Press all seams lightly after finishing.

TIPS Whatever method of finishing you choose always stitch in the same direction, that is, from wide to narrow part of the garment.

Seams in synthetic jersey often wrinkle, especially near the hem of a skirt. Press the seam then pin the wrinkled section wrong-side up to the sleeve board. Put a pin at each end, stretching the seam. Cut a length of Wundaweb lengthwise into three and slip these pieces under the seam allowances. Press well with a hot iron and a damp muslin cloth. Allow to cool, unpin (fig 7.8).

Jersey seams running across the body must be stabilised to prevent them stretching. Cut pieces of ribbon or seam binding to the length of the seam copied from the pattern, include in the seam stitching or zig-zag to the turnings afterwards (fig 7.9).

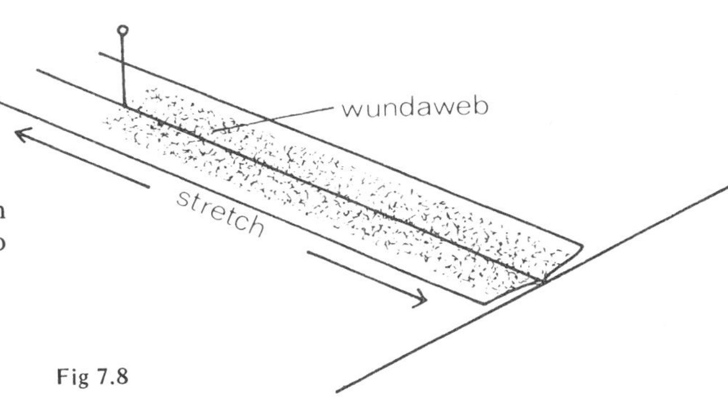

Fig 7.8

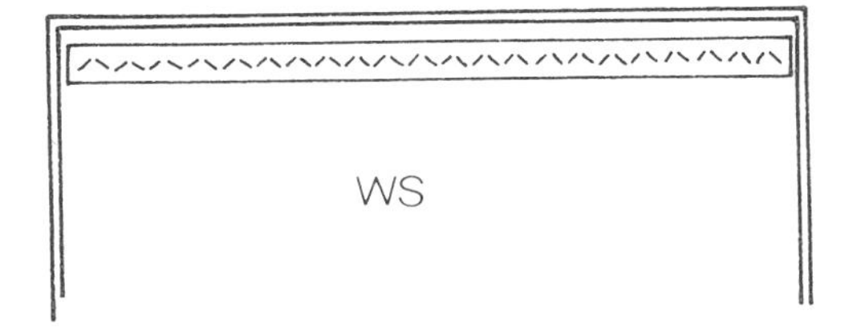

Fig 7.9

Quick seam

Machine the seam as described for the basic seam. Press the stitching flat. Trim both turnings down to 3 mm and work a small zig-zag over the edges. Work in the correct direction, removing pins as you reach them.

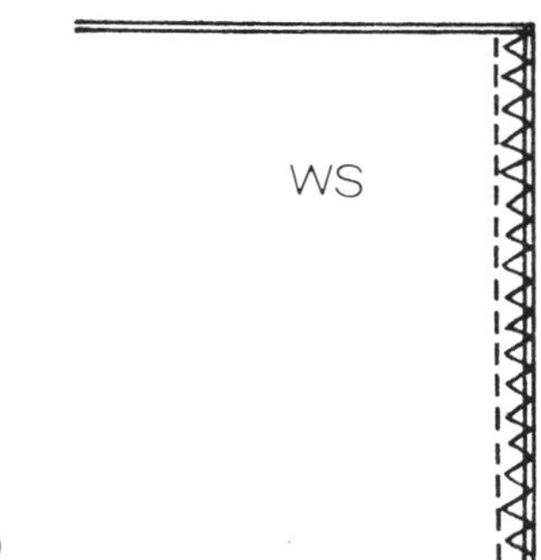

Fig 7.10

Press the seam flat then press it to one side. Press the right side of the garment to finish (fig 7.10).

One-step seam

Set your machine to the blind hem stitch and try it out on fabric to find the most suitable size. Use a small stitch, but a wide zig-zag, and Drima thread to provide 'give' (fig 7.11).

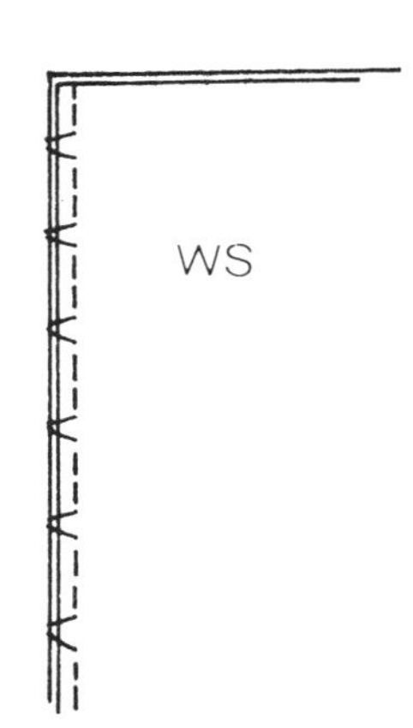

Fig 7.11

Arrange the pieces of fabric in front of you with the raw edges to the left and insert pins across the seam from the right. Trim 12-13 mm (more than 1 cm) off the raw edges. Place the seam under the machine foot and stitch with the needle passing over the raw edges when it zig-zags. Remove the pins as you reach them.

Press the stitching then press the seam to one side.

The overlock stitch on the machine also sews the seam in one movement. Use Drima thread to provide 'give'. Try the stitch on your fabric to find a suitable size. Set it to a wide zig-zag (fig 7.12).

Arrange the pieces of fabric and pin as for the basic seam. Trim both turnings down to 3 mm, cutting off a little more than 1 cm. Place under the machine and work the seam so that the needle clears the raw edges when it moves to the right.

Press the stitching, press the seam to one side.

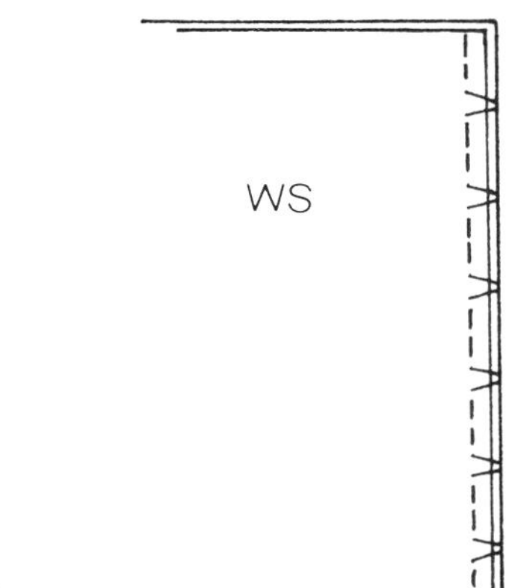

Fig 7.12

> **TIP** If two of these narrow seams have to meet when you work a later seam, reduce the bulk and make it easier to sew by pressing the two matching seams in opposite directions. Then make sure they remain matching by inserting one pin to hold the machine over it (fig 7.13)

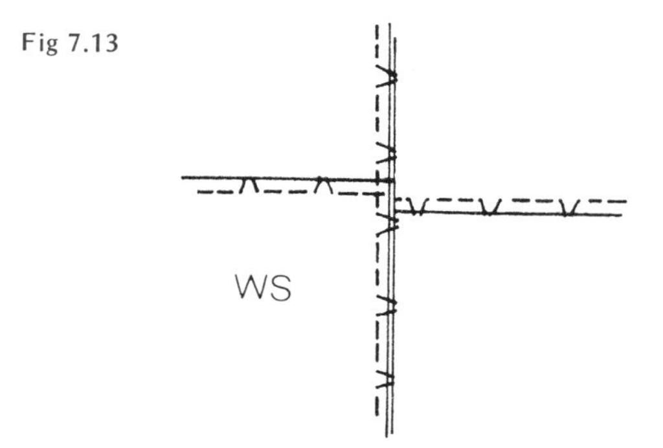

Fig 7.13

Top-stitched seams

These take longer to work because the stitching is visible.

Overlaid seam

Finish both raw edges of the fabric with zig-zag stitch or an alternative.

Decide which piece is to overlay the other — this will be the one with the stitching on. Fold this edge over on the fitting line, i.e. usually 1.5 cm, and press well.

Lay this pressed edge over the other piece of fabric, both with right sides up. Arrange the seam vertically in front of you with the overlaid piece on the left. Insert pins at intervals across the seam. Take

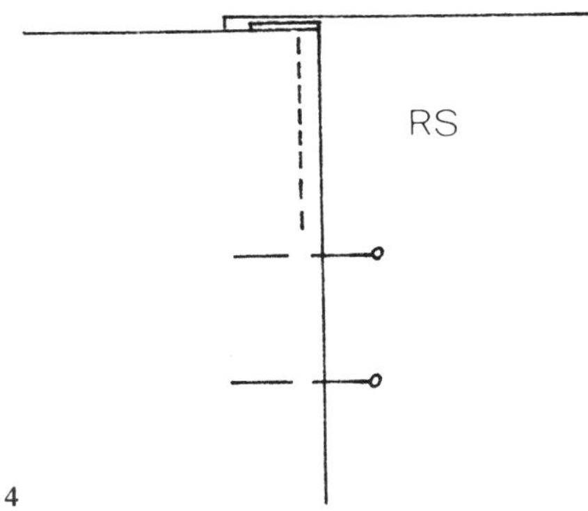

Fig 7.14

it to the machine and stitch with a medium-sized straight stitch, on the fold, very close to the edge. Remove the pins as you reach them (fig 7.14).

If you wish, work another row of stitching beside this, using the foot as a guide for keeping straight. Press the stitching on the right side and wrong side (fig 7.15).

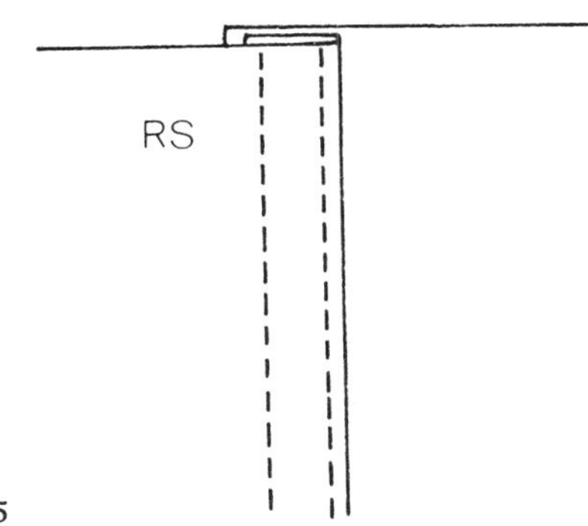

Fig 7.15

Angled seam

If your pattern shows an angled seam, the quickest way to complete it is to work it as for an overlaid seam.

Welt seam

Place the two pieces of fabric with the right sides together, pin and machine as for the basic seam. Press the turnings open to produce a good line then press both firmly to one side. Lift the top turning and trim the one underneath down to 3 mm. With the fabric flat on the sleeve board turn under and press the upper turning. To keep it level and an even width all the way along the seam tuck the raw edge under the narrow turning as far as it will go. Insert a few pins across to hold it. Machine on the fold from end to end removing the pins as you come to them. This row of stitching may be a straight stitch (make it the same size as the previous stitching) a zig-zag or a decorative machine stitch. Press both sides of the seam (fig 7.16).

Fig 7.16

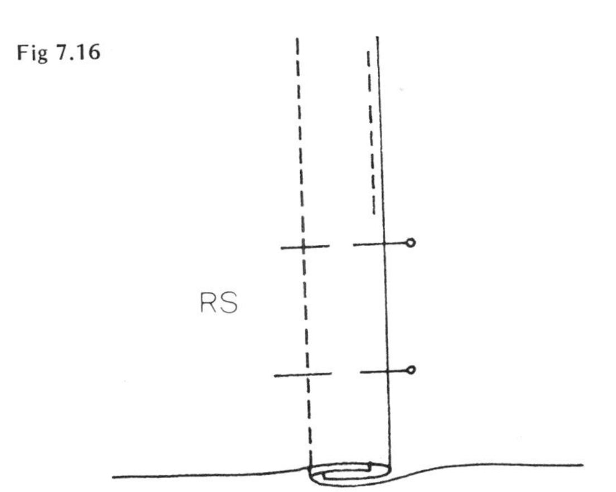

Braid seam

Stitch and press open a basic seam but place the fabric with wrong sides together so that the seam turnings are pressed open on the right side. Trim down both edges to 3 mm. Place braid or bias binding centrally over the join of the seam and insert pins horizontally at intervals. Work a small zig-zag or decorative stitch over both edges, removing the pins as you stitch the first side. Work both rows of stitching in the same direction (fig 7.17).

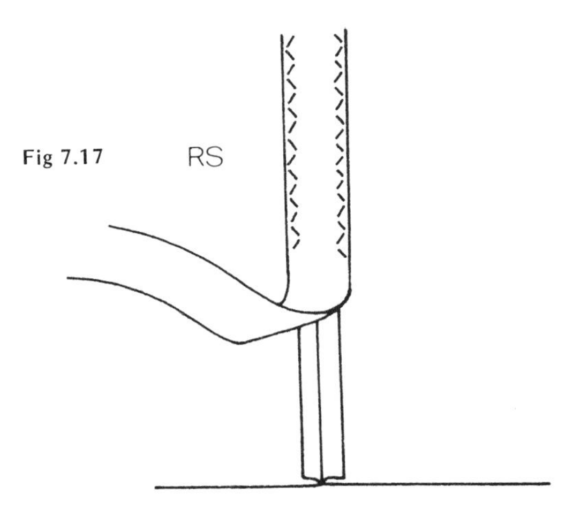

Fig 7.17

Gathered seam

This seam involves gathering one edge until it is the same length as another it has to join.

Mark the points between which you are to gather by putting chalk marks on the edge of the fabric on the right side. Using the largest straight machine stitch work one row of stitching between these points, with the fabric right-side up and the stitching 1-2 mm within the seam allowance. Reverse to start

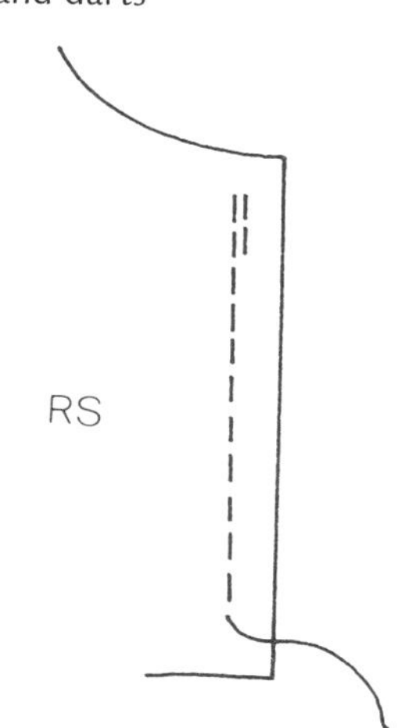

Fig 7.18

in order to anchor the ends of thread. It is only necessary to work one row (fig 7.18).

If the seam is short or you are joining two gathered edges cut a piece of tape or paper the exact length of the edge to be joined — use the pattern as a guide — and pin the ends to the edge with the gathering thread in. Pull up the gathers, holding the under thread, i.e. the one on the wrong side of the fabric, until the edge is the same length as the paper. Insert a pin in the fabric and wind the thread end round the pin. Even out the gathers. Remove the paper and pin the gathered edge to the flat edge with right sides together. Put the first pin in the centre, then add one at each end. Tack on the gathering. Remove the pins — check the other side to make sure you haven't missed any — machine with gathers uppermost 1 mm below the gathering thread (fig 7.19).

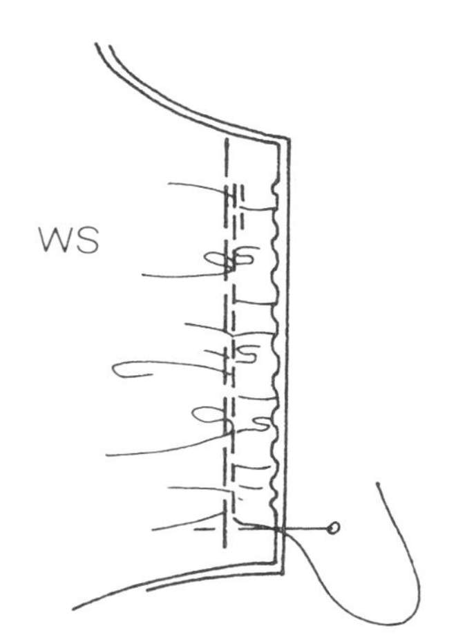

Fig 7.19

Snip the gathering thread at the anchored end and pull it out in one movement.

Press the seam so that both pieces of fabric are right side up. Do not flatten the gathers but be sure to ease the toe of the iron along the seam to flatten the upper fabric.

Work a row of stitching on the right side parallel with the join and not too far from it — a distance of about 3 mm is usually best or the gathered edge shows as a bulky ridge. Set the machine to a straight stitch, small zig-zag or satin stitch. The corded or piped decoration described in the chapter on machine stitching is particularly suitable on medium-weight fabrics. Trim away the surplus fabric on the wrong side (fig 7.20).

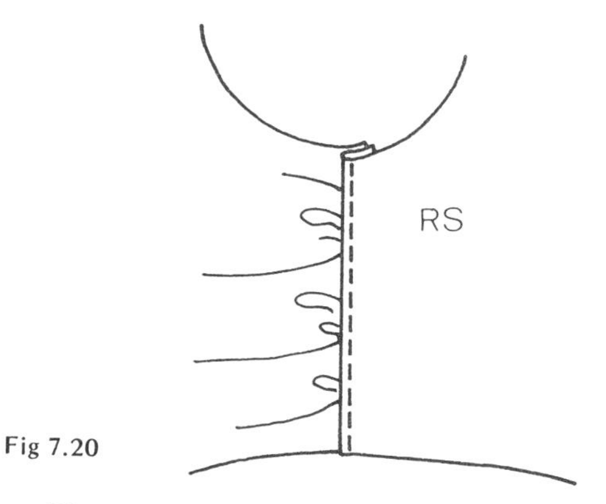

Fig 7.20

The gathered seam may also be made in the same way as an angled seam, that is, by laying one edge over the other and machining on the right side. Work a second row of matching stitching to complete it.

TIP Light-weight fabric can be gathered directly on to another piece of fabric by using the gathering foot. Use for attaching frills, etc., as the gathering cannot be precisely controlled (fig 7.21).

Fig 7.21

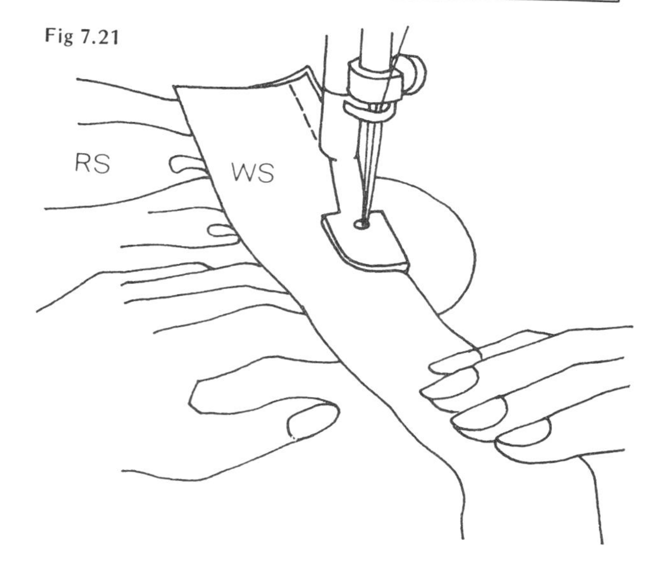

Extra-strong seam

This takes a little longer to do as there are four rows of stitching involved but it is worth it on fabrics such as cord and firm cottons.

Place the two pieces of fabric right-sides together and pin at intervals with the raw edges and the pin heads to the right. Machine, taking the appropriate seam allowance. Remove the pins.

Place the seam wrong-side up on the pressing surface and open the turnings with the toe of the iron. Press both turnings firmly to one side. Turn the fabric right-side up and press again.

Trim both raw edges to a width of 5 mm and zig-zag over both to neaten (fig 7.22).

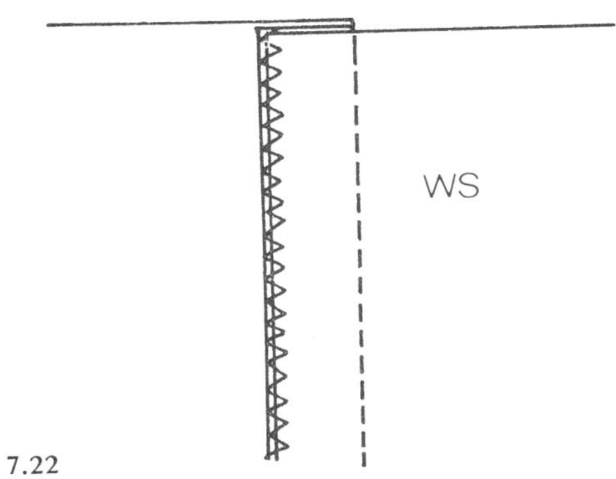

Fig 7.22

With the fabric right-side up, put it under the machine and work two rows of straight stitching, the first very close to the seam join and the second about 3 mm from it, or the width of a toe of the machine foot. If you wish to make the distance between the two parallel rows wider, leave turnings wider than 5 mm over which to zig-zag (fig 7.23).

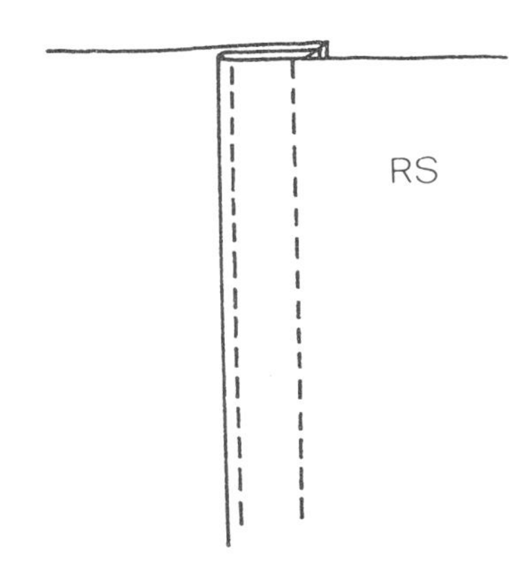

Fig 7.23

DARTS

Look at the design of the garment you are making and see whether you can make the darts into tucks. Darts are time-consuming and difficult to stitch accurately especially at the point. If you make a tuck instead you will be producing the same amount of shaping but with less trouble.

The dart should be marked on the fabric. With the fabric right-side up, fold it on one line of marking and bring it over on to the second line. Insert two pins across the tuck, having the folded edge and the head of the pin to the right. Do not attempt to make the point of the dart meet. With a long dart of perhaps 10 cm shorten it by 4-5 cm. If the dart is shorter then omit only about 2-3 cm (fig 7.24).

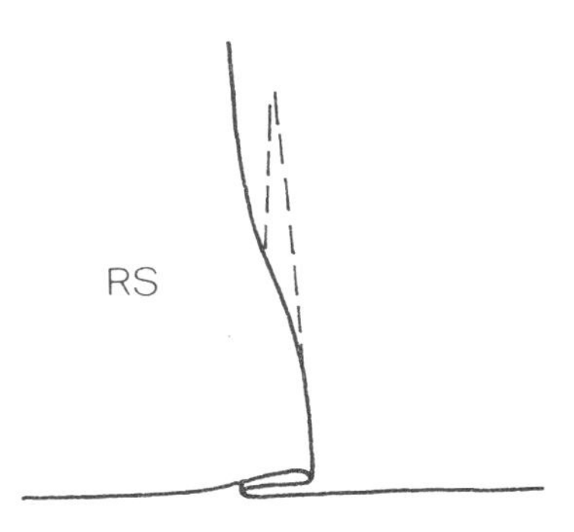

Fig 7.24

Use the toe of the iron and slide it between the pins to flatten the fold slightly. Prepare all darts to make sure pairs of tucks face in opposite directions. Pairs of tucks must be equal in length. Use tailor's chalk or wax chalk and an adjustable marker to chalk off the point at which you want to end the stitching.

Put under the machine and stitch on the edge of the fold, reversing at both ends. Remove the first pin after lowering the foot, and the second pin as you reach it (fig 7.25).

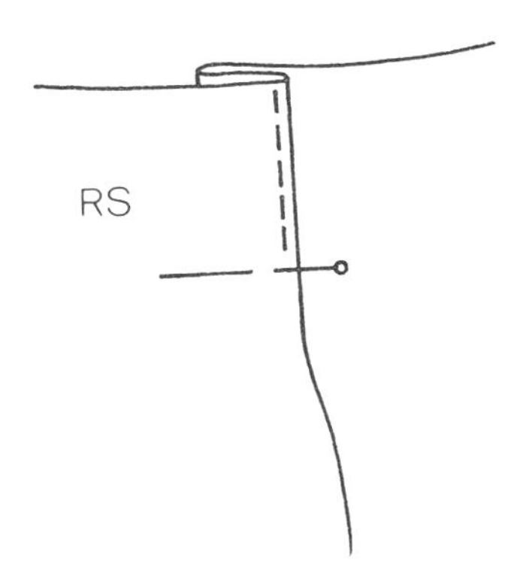

Fig 7.25

Some small darts may be omitted altogether and the surplus fabric eased into the seam. These include darts in the back neck or back shoulder, elbow darts in long sleeves and front darts in skirts and trousers.

In the case of skirts and trousers, ease in a little of the fullness but then trim away the remainder at the side seam in a gradual curve.

With neck, shoulder and elbow darts the surplus must be eased in until the edge fits the place it is joining. Pin each end and then pin at intervals between to distribute it without it forming tucks (fig 7.26).

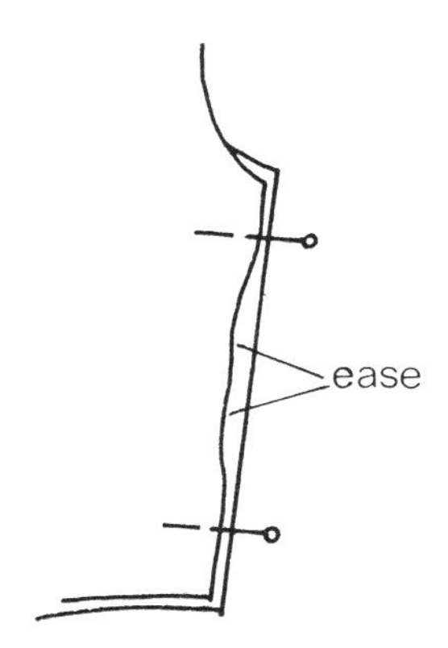

Fig 7.26

If the style and fit of the outfit would be spoiled by using tucks you will have to make darts. Fold the fabric with right sides together and, matching the two lines of dart markings, pin across the dart. Use only three pins. Use the toe of the iron to flatten the fold between the pins. Stitch. Reverse for two stitches. Remove the pins as you come to them (fig 7.27).

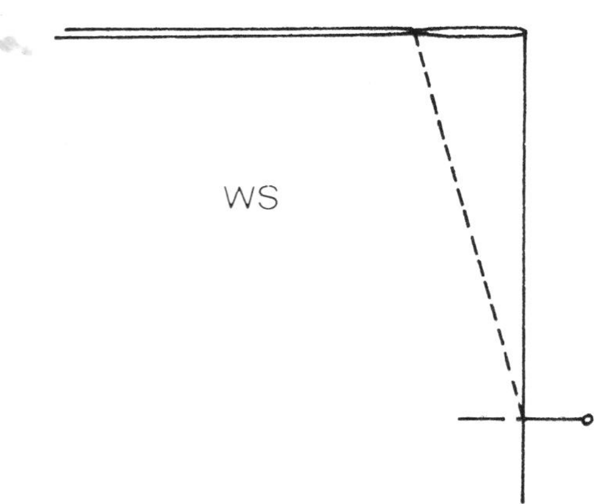

Fig 7.27

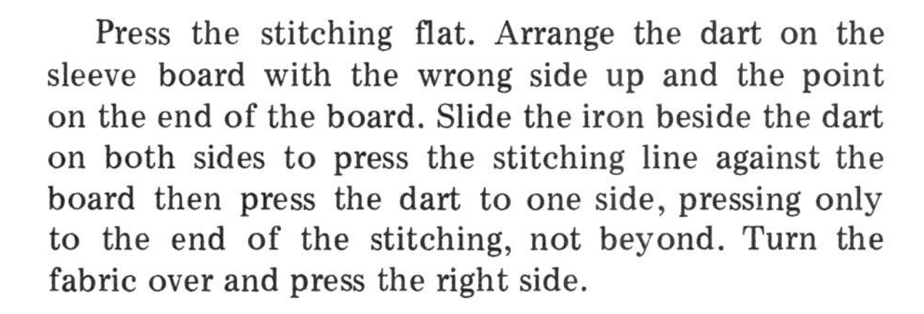

Press the stitching flat. Arrange the dart on the sleeve board with the wrong side up and the point on the end of the board. Slide the iron beside the dart on both sides to press the stitching line against the board then press the dart to one side, pressing only to the end of the stitching, not beyond. Turn the fabric over and press the right side.

TIP If you insert one pin just beyond the point of the dart it helps to keep the fabric flat as you machine.

8 Buttonholes and buttons

BUTTONHOLES

You can see from the chapter on fastenings that there are a number of alternatives to buttonholes, so you will be able to avoid them on quite a number of outfits. However, if they are essential to the design or if there is no suitable and effective substitute choose one of the following types. Buttonholes in a seam are quick to do; machine-made buttonholes are quick but care should be taken; finally, piped buttonholes are time-consuming but they are the easiest of the conventional buttonholes and you cannot go wrong in their construction.

Position and size

Do not buy buttons that are appreciably larger or smaller than those recommended in the pattern, because the size of button has been considered when planning the button extension and width of facing.

The buttonhole slits should begin at a point equal to the diameter of the buttons from the edge of the garment, if they are to be horizontal. This is because when the button is fastened it settles in the end of the buttonhole, taking the strain, and it would extend over the edge of the garment if the buttonhole were too near the edge (fig 8.1).

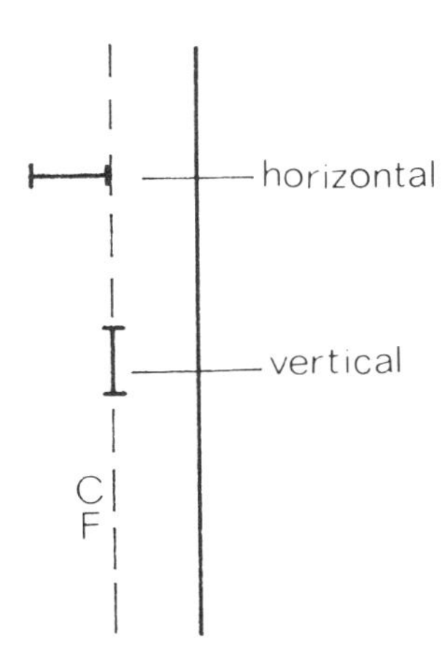

Fig 8.1

If the buttonholes are vertical they are placed on the centre front line and the buttons are attached so that they settle in the top of the buttonhole.

To prevent stretching the buttonholes in use, make the buttonholes slightly bigger than the diameter of the button. Add 3 mm for machine-made and seam buttonholes as there is very little 'give' in buttonholes and any strain would spoil them. Piped buttonholes will 'give' slightly, so allow 2 mm ease.

When using dome buttons or especially thick ones, add extra length to the buttonholes to compensate for the thickness.

Large buttons should be more widely spaced than small ones.

Decide on the position of the top and bottom buttons then space others between.

If a garment fastens up to the neck the top button should be sufficiently below the neck edge so that you do not have to work the buttonhole through the bulk of the neck turnings.

On a blouse that tucks in at the waist, avoid placing a button exactly at the waist.

If the garment is close-fitting, place a button approximately level with the bust points.

On any garment to be worn outside a skirt or trousers the bottom button should be low enough to keep the edges together in wear, but not right at the hem.

Buttonholes in a seam

The decision to make this type of buttonhole has to be made before the garment is cut out. I will describe them at a conventional centre front opening that you would find on a coat, jacket, blouse, shirt or dress; but you can apply the method to a buttonhole or a series of buttonholes in any position where you can reasonably make a seam, such as the top of a pocket. It would not be worth doing this at such points as cuffs and waistbands that are not decorative as there are other fastenings that can be employed. These buttonholes are not suitable for very lightweight fabrics (fig 8.2).

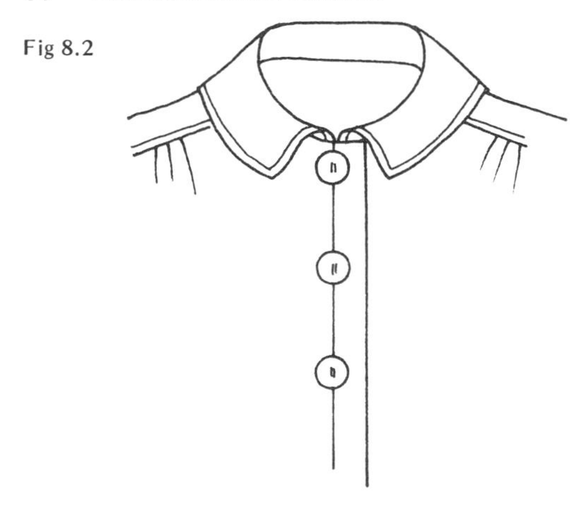

Fig 8.2

Cut the paper pattern on the centre front line. If this is not marked draw it with a pencil and ruler. Place the pattern on single fabric to cut the right side of the garment (or left for a man). Add 3 cm seam allowance at the centre front and cut out. Also cut out the other piece of pattern, adding 3 cm seam allowance. Note that this strip could well be added to the front facing before cutting, to avoid another seam on the edge of the garment (fig 8.3).

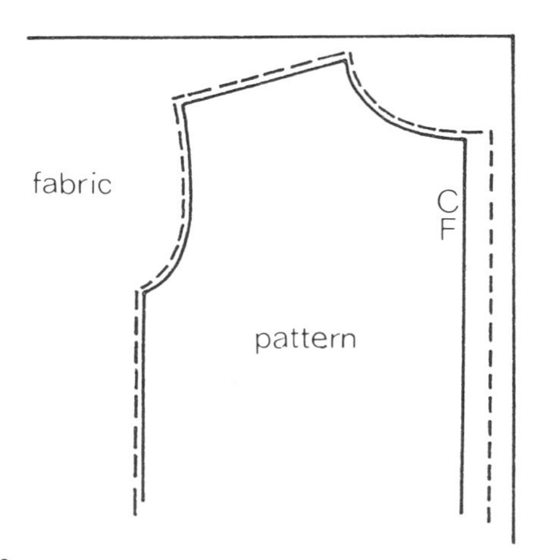

Fig 8.3

The left side of the garment should be cut from single fabric using the original pattern — you may prefer to copy it rather than cut it.

Place the extension or facing to the garment pieces right-sides together and edges meeting. Pin at intervals along the edge. Place the buttons in position, evenly spaced down the centre of the Fold-a-Band. Remember to allow a reasonable space between the neck edge and the first button. Set an adjustable marker to equal the distance between the buttons. Set another marker to the width of the button plus ease, or establish how many perforations in the Fold-a-Band are equal to this distance, and mark with pencil the buttonhole space.

Machine down the centre of the interfacing, stopping and reversing at each buttonhole and starting again at the other side and so on. Remove pins, cut off all thread ends, press the seam open. From the right side top stitch on each side of the seam, (fig 8.4).

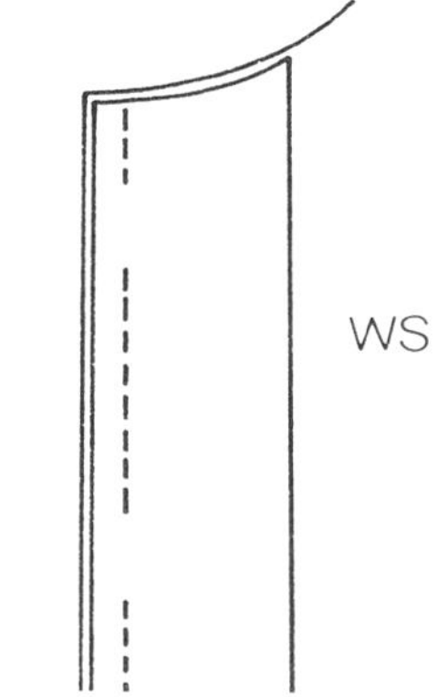

Fig 8.4

Trim down the fabric edge in the facing if it extends beyond the fold line at the edge of the garment (fig 8.5).

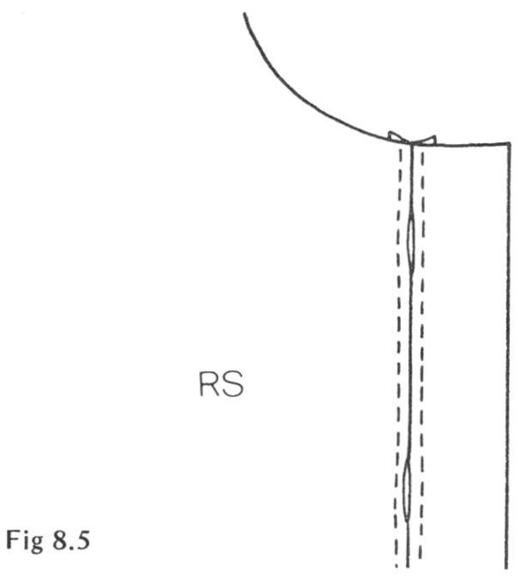

Fig 8.5

Continue with the construction of the garment until the neck is complete and the front facing has been basted in position on the wrong side.

From the right side insert a pin at each end of each buttonhole, through to the facing. Turn the garment over and, using tailor's chalk, mark these pin points with horizontal chalk marks. Remove the pins.

Cut the facing between the pins but stop the cuts 3 mm short of the chalk marks and from there cut outwards until you reach the chalk. Turn in all four

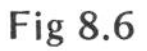
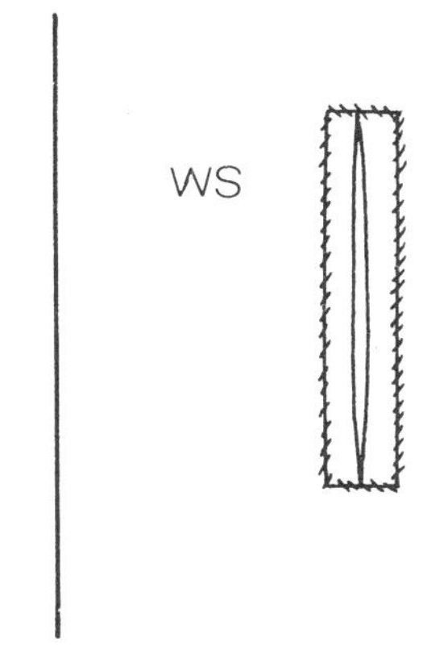

Fig 8.6

sides, two long and two short, and hem into the fabric underneath with small close stitches. Press to finish (fig 8.6).

> **TIP** On fraying fabrics press a strip of Bondaweb on the wrong side of the facing to correspond with the buttonhole position. When the facing is cut fraying will be minimal.

Machine-made buttonholes

This type of buttonhole is worked through all layers, so complete the garment or at least complete all areas requiring buttonholes and work them all at one session.

In addition to interfacing, insert a strip of Wundaweb between the garment and the facing. Press well. This not only reinforces the buttonholes, but more important, it helps to prevent fraying when the buttonholes are cut.

Mark the buttonhole positions with tailor's chalk and a ruler. If they are to be vertical, draw a vertical line and mark off the buttonhole sizes with horizontal dashes. Use two adjustable markers for accuracy, one set to the buttonhole size and one to the size of the space. Alternatively cut pieces of card to measure with.

Horizontal buttonholes are more difficult to mark. Begin by ruling two parallel vertical lines; the distance between them must be exactly the size of the buttonhole. Mark the buttonhole positions with horizontal chalk lines across the parallel lines. The buttonholes should be on the straight grain.

Set your machine to the correct stitch for buttonholes. Attach the buttonhole foot. Thread up the machine, preferably with machine embroidery thread, e.g. Anchor. Have a gimp thread ready if you are working on medium or heavy fabric. The gimp can be double-stranded embroidery thread, a crochet cotton or tailor's gimp (fig 8.7).

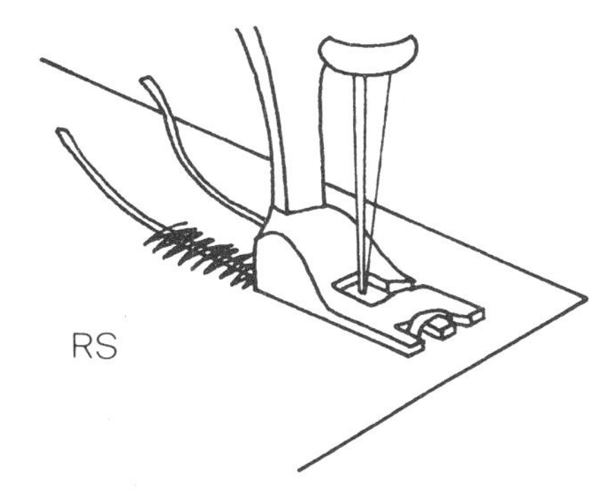

Fig 8.7

Work the buttonholes following the instructions in the machine hand-book; work round twice if using machine embroidery thread.

Snip off all ends of thread. Brush off the chalk and press well on both sides of the garment. Cut the buttonholes, using the points of small scissors or, if they are not sharp enough, use an unpicker but insert a pin at each end of the buttonhole to prevent the unpicker slipping too far.

> **TIP** Prepare a piece of fabric and work a test buttonhole before you start. Cut it and try it for size before making them on the garment.

Piped buttonholes

Suitable for almost any fabric, this is a method of making piped buttonholes using one piece of fabric which makes them slightly quicker to do.

The first stage should be worked as early in construction as possible because it helps to have the fabric flat on the table to attach the pipings.

Attach interfacing to the wrong side of the fabric and mark the buttonhole positions on the right side with tailor's chalk, as described for machine-made buttonholes.

Make the piping by cutting a strip of fabric on the straight grain 3 cm wide. It should be long enough to allow 3 cm of piping for each buttonhole, more if your buttons are more than 2 cm in diameter. If your fabric is very fine, cut the strip 3 cm wide.

Cut a strip of Bondaweb the same width and press it to the wrong side of the strip. Peel off the paper backing and fold the raw edges in to meet each other. Press well with the raw edges together (fig 8.8).

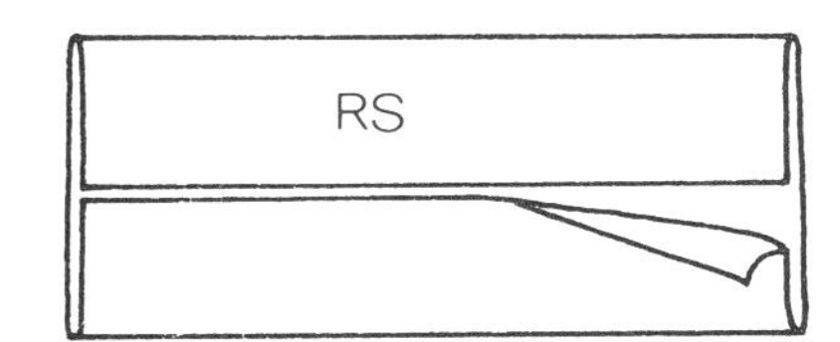

Fig 8.8

Place the piping on the right side of the garment. Leave at least 5 mm extending beyond the chalk line at each end, tack in the middle of the strip. Make sure the cut edges are on the chalk line.

As you have now covered the chalk lines marking the size of buttonhole, re-chalk across the pipings.

Set your machine to a small stitch to make it easier to make all buttonholes exactly the same size. Stitch the piping to the garment by machining in the centre of each side. Stitch exactly to the chalk marks. Begin in the middle of the piece and stitch to the end, turn, stitch to the far end, turn and return to the middle. This manoeuvre provides extra firmness but it also means that you can snip off all thread ends with safety. Remove tackings (fig 8.9).

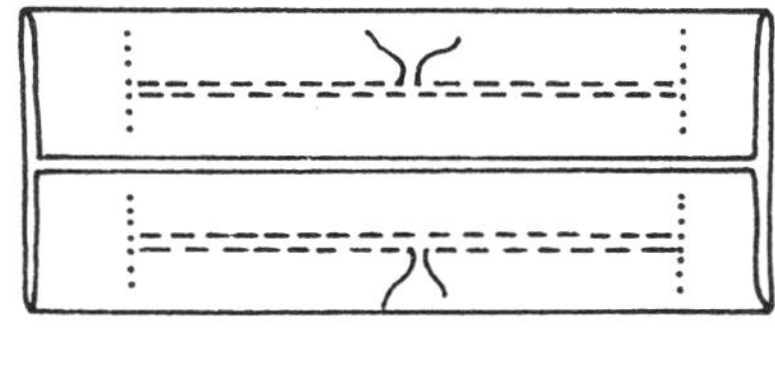

Fig 8.9

Turn the work so that it is wrong-side up and snip between the rows of stitching through the garment but not through the buttonhole piece. Make a small snip and then cut out to all four ends of stitching. On the right side, cut the buttonhole piece along the centre to separate it into two pipings. Push these pipings through to the wrong side and manipulate them with your fingers to flatten the ends of the rectangle now showing. Tack together the two edges of piping. Push the triangle of fabric at each end through to the wrong side and stab stitch back and forth on the fold from the right side to hold it down. Press the buttonhole from both right and wrong sides (figs 8.10 and 8.11).

Fig 8.10

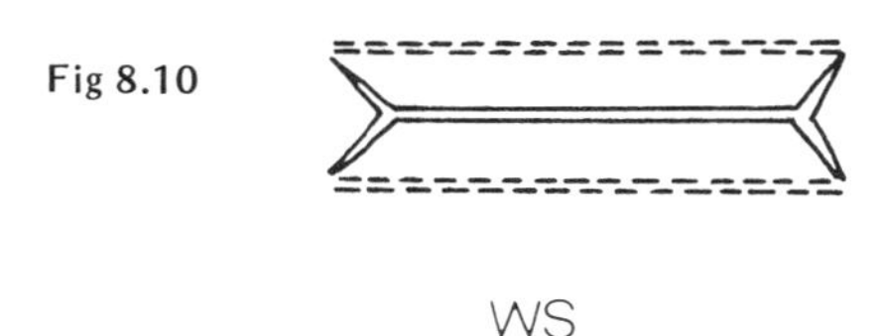

Fig 8.11

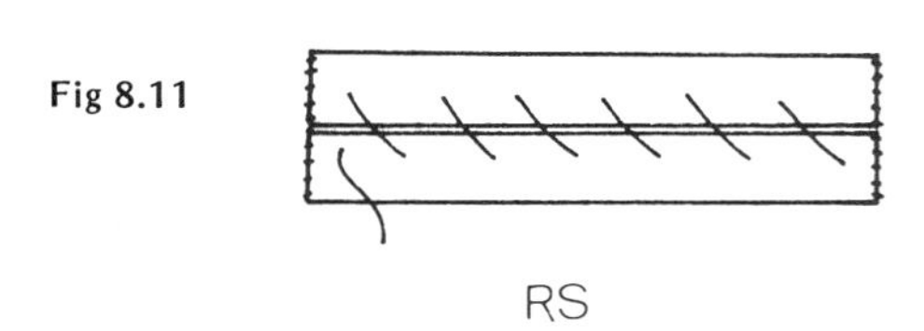

The buttonhole may be machined across the ends and between the piping and the garment. This is not necessary for strength but it helps to hold down springy fabrics. In addition, if there is top stitching elsewhere on the garment then this will match (fig 8.12).

Fig 8.12

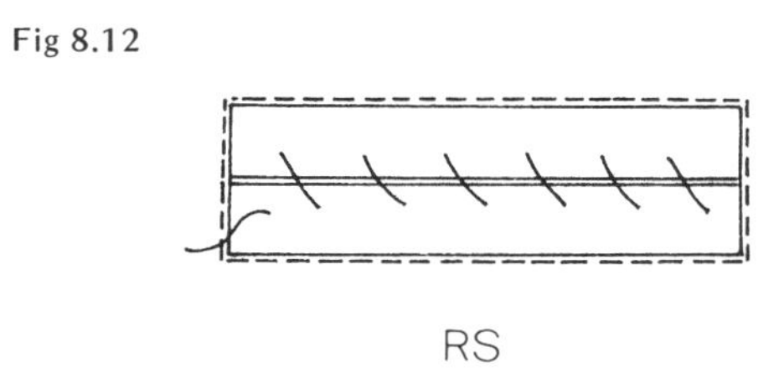

Leave the buttonholes and continue with the construction of the garment. The buttonholes may be finished at any time after the facings are in position. When you are ready to complete them, proceed in the following way.

Before folding the facing back against the garment press a strip of Bondaweb to the wrong side. Cut the strip wide enough and long enough to cover all the buttonholes. Peel off the paper (fig 8.13).

Fig 8.13

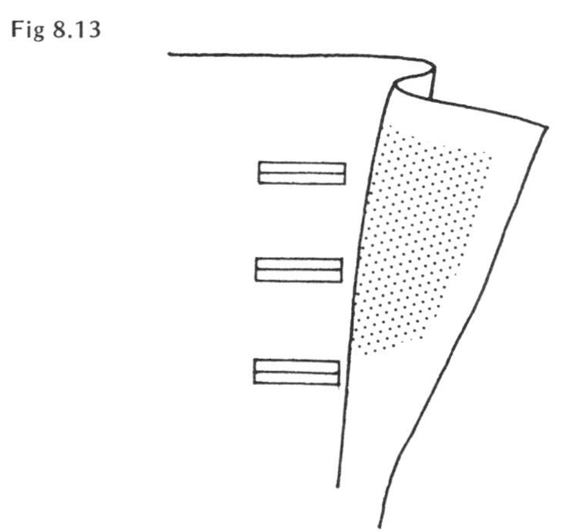

Place the facing in position against the garment and pin or tack round each buttonhole from the right side through the garment and through the facing. Insert a pin through each end of each buttonhole. The points extend through the facing, indicating the exact size of the buttonhole. Snip between the pin-points, remove the pins, turn the edge of the slit under and hem with small stitches to attach the fold of the facing to the back of the buttonhole (fig 8.14).

Press well on both sides to finish.

Fig 8.14

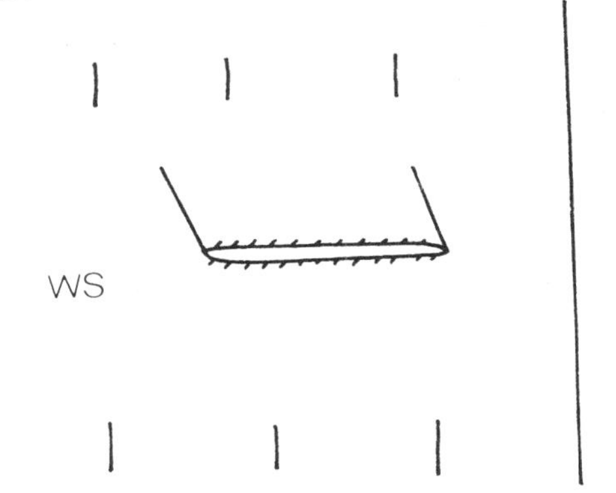

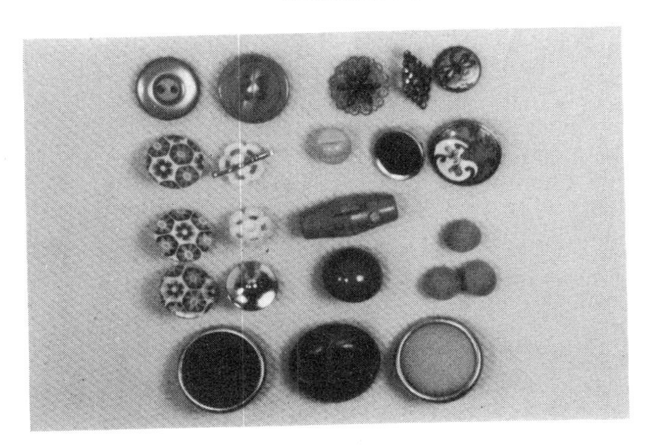

TIPS Count the number of machine stitches used on the first buttonhole and make sure all are the same size.

The facing on the back of the buttonhole may be cut in the same shape as the buttonhole was cut, and the edges turned in to form a rectangle.

If working on check or striped fabric cut the buttonhole piece on the cross to avoid having to match the pattern.

BUTTONS

There is no short cut to sewing on a button. If it is not sewn really well it will quickly come off. However, there are a few tips that make the job much easier.

Needle

Use a larger size needle than the one used for hand-sewing on the remainder of the garment, but make sure it will pass through the fabric without difficulty.

Thread

Use synthetic thread such as Drima. It is strong but fine and will wear well. It may well be the thread you have used for making the garment.

Alternatively, on thick fabrics and outer wear use button thread, such as Anchor, or use Heavy Duty thread. They are thick, strong glazed threads specially made for the purpose.

Reinforcing

Make sure there is a layer of interfacing between the two layers of fabric. On heavy fabric or on clothes which will receive hard wear it is wise to also add a small piece of cotton fabric to stitch through. Raincoats, overcoats and suede and leather coats may have a small backing button sewn on the wrong side attached at the same time as the main button. This will prevent the fabric being torn if the button comes off.

Preparing the garment

Try to ensure that sewing on the buttons is the very last job of all because they get in the way if attached too soon and also pressing is difficult.

Press the entire garment — this is its final press — and hang it to cool.

Arrange it on the table without creasing, establish the button position then draw that part of the garment towards you and sew on the buttons. Try not to crush any part as you sew. Probably the best position is to stand up to do it to avoid the temptation to crumple the garment on your lap. Raise the work by using the sleeve board, lifting only the part of the garment needing a button, on to the board.

Preparing the thread

Cut off a piece of thread about 40 cm long, thread the needle, put in a knot to join the ends. Run your cake of beeswax along the thread several times. To do this, hold the knot and run the wax from knot to needle to avoid an uneven double thread. Without letting go of the knot, put down the wax and twist the thread by rubbing the palm of the outer hand firmly across the thread. This will twist the thread. Wind that twisted section round the thumb holding on to the knot and rub your palms together again. Continue until you reach the needle (fig 8.15).

Unwind the twisted waxed thread from your thumb.

Marking the position

Lap one side of the opening over the other, making

Fig 8.15

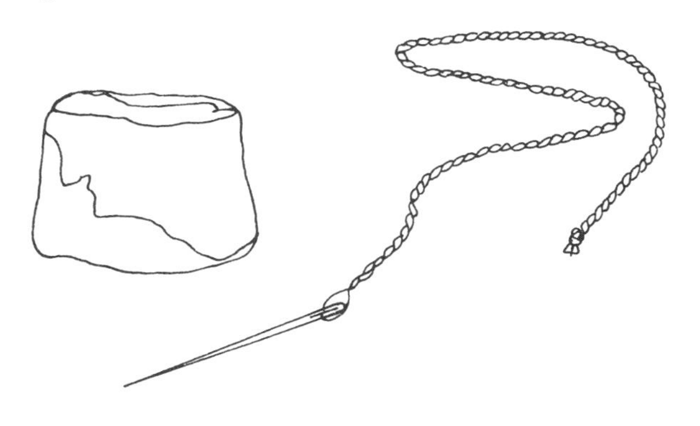

sure any centre front lines, etc., are matched up. If the button is to be attached to a waistband or some other close-fitting area, try on the garment and mark the position of the overlap with a pin.

Insert pins through the garment between the buttonholes to hold. Mark the exact position for attaching the button, using a chalk pancil inserted in the top of a vertical buttonhole, or with a horizontal buttonhole, in the end taking the strain of fastening. Begin by sewing on the bottom button if there are several. Mark only one at a time (fig 8.16).

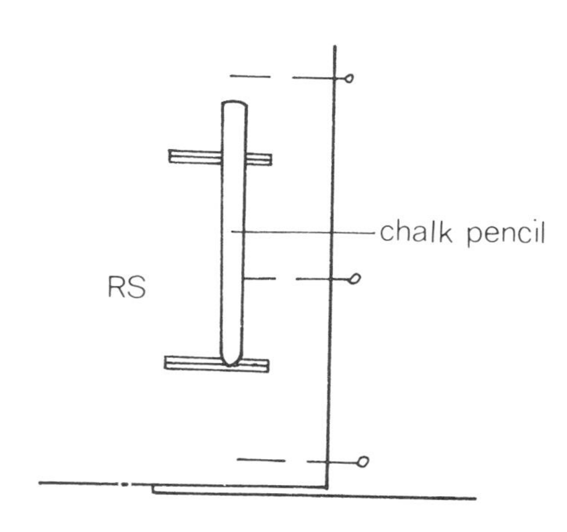

Fig 8.16

Sewing on buttons

Remove the pin anchoring that part of the opening, remove the top layer of garment, insert the prepared needle exactly on the chalk mark. Take two stitches right through all layers, stabbing the needle back and forth and finally bringing it back to the right side of the garment. Cut off the knot in the thread (fig 8.17).

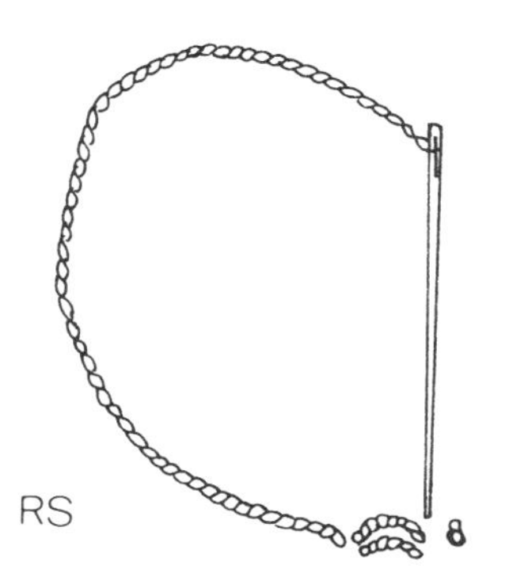

Fig 8.17

Slip the button on to the needle. Insert the needle through the other hole in the button into the garment and out again all in one movement. Pull the thread through and adjust the button — it should not be flat on the fabric but because of the sewing action it stands up on its side, the advantage being that this position ensures extra thread between button and garment. With thick fabrics this extra amount of thread will have to be adjusted and made up to 5 mm long. The shank must be long enough to allow the total thickness of the other layer of garment to lie flat between the button and the garment (fig 8.18).

Fig 8.18

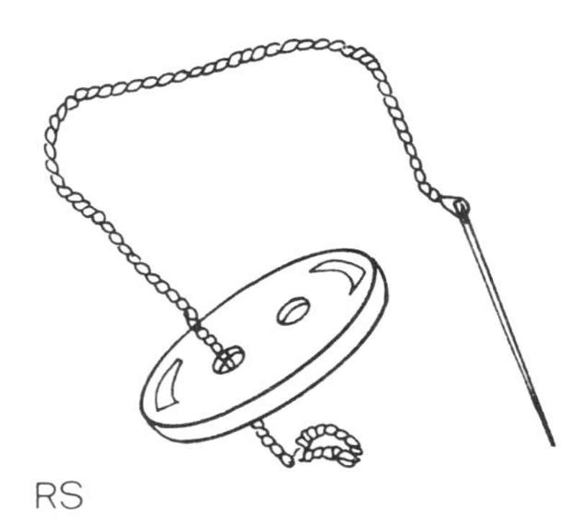

Bring the needle up through the first hole of the button.

Insert it in the second hole, down into the garment and up again below the button. Adjust the thread and button to get the shank threads the same length.

Continue in this way until six stitches have been worked. When sewing on buttons with four holes, make four stitches across one way and then move the needle to the second pair of holes and work three stitches.

You will finish with the needle under the button. From that position take hold of the thread near the button and wind it round the shank to cover it. Wind twice more, nearer to the button and pull hard, then twice more moving back down to the garment (fig 8.19).

Fig 8.19

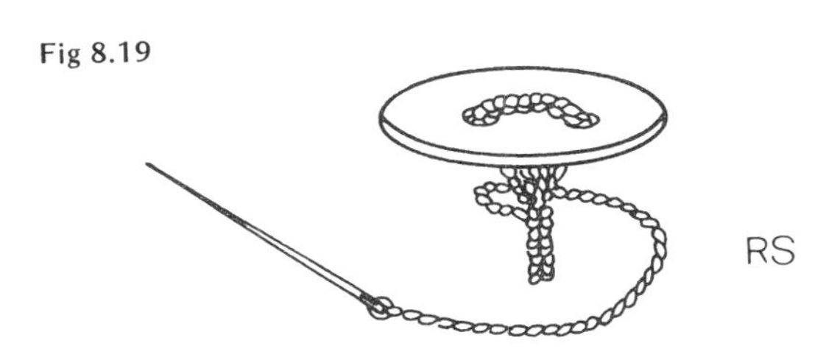

The thread is now near the fabric again. Take two stitches across the base of the shank, through the threads and through the surface of the fabric. Pull the thread tight. Pass the needle to the wrong side or underneath and take two stitches. Cut off the thread close to the surface of the fabric. Fasten the button, mark the position of the next one, unpin and undo the button already attached. Sew on the next button, and so on (fig 8.20).

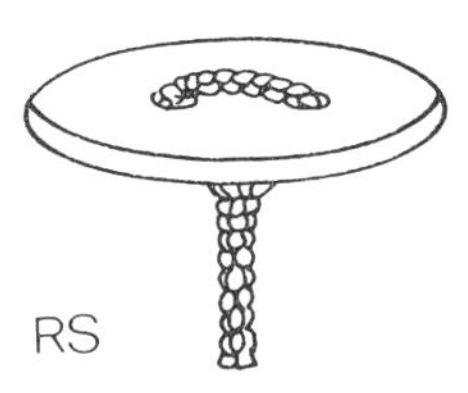

Fig 8.20

When all buttons are sewn on press the area by running the toe of the iron round and underneath each button.

Buttons without through-holes

The buttons may be designed to have the needle and thread passed through a tunnel on the underside. Attach by working six stitches, leaving a shank in the way already described.

Buttons with a shank

These are buttons, often metal or elaborate plastic ones, with a metal loop on the back. The needle should be passed through it six times for a small button, eight for a large one. Do not make a thread shank, sew the button flat to the fabric but tidy up the stitches by winding the thread round between the metal loop and the fabric before fastening off.

Decorative buttons

If the button is decorative, sew it in position using only four stitches before passing the needle across the base to finish off. Do not make a shank; do not wind the thread round the stitches and instead of fastening off on the wrong side, snip the thread after passing the needle across the base of the stitching.

TIPS When preparing the thread, make up one needle of waxed thread before you start for every two buttons to be attached. This will ensure that you use enough stitches and are not tempted to skimp the process.

Each double thread should be about 50 cm long when twisted.

Try to make the stitches fall roughly on top of each other so that they look tidy on the under side of the garment. When complete, before cutting off the thread work loop stitch over these stitches to form a neat bar. If the button has four holes work about three loop stitches across the centre of the threads.

9 Zips and fastenings

ZIPS

Avoid the methods of insertion that take time and extreme care to get right, mainly those where you fight to cover the zip so that it does not show. Confine yourself mainly to the concealed zip, specially made to be invisible and very easy to put in, and when using other zips with visible teeth, make a feature of the zip (fig 9.1).

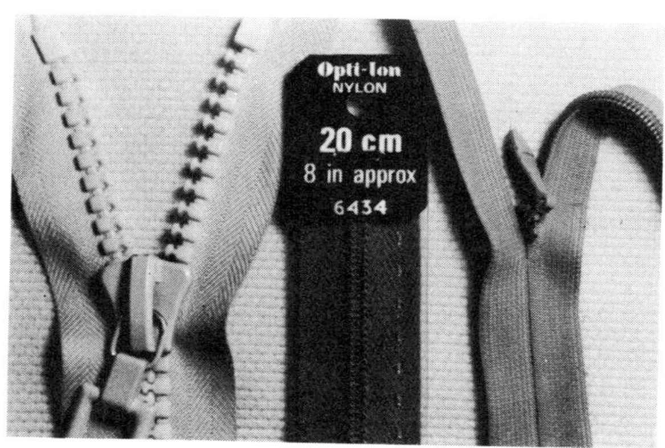

Fig 9.1

Concealed zip

The lightest and most supple zips are made of nylon coil attached to tape. The zips are made in lengths of 20 and 23 cm for skirts and trousers and 56 cm for dresses. The range of colours is not extensive, containing a few pale colours, some medium tones and the usual dark colours, but the colour match is not too important because the zip does not show in wear.

Use at the side or front of skirts and trousers and at the back or front of dresses.

Sew in by hand using backstitch or fit the one-sided zip foot (piping foot) on the machine. It does not require a special foot.

Stitch the garment seam. The gap left should be 1 cm shorter than the length of the zip teeth but you may find it easier to stop the stitching 3 cm below this. Change the machine stitch to the largest size and machine from that point to the top of the zip position (fig 9.2).

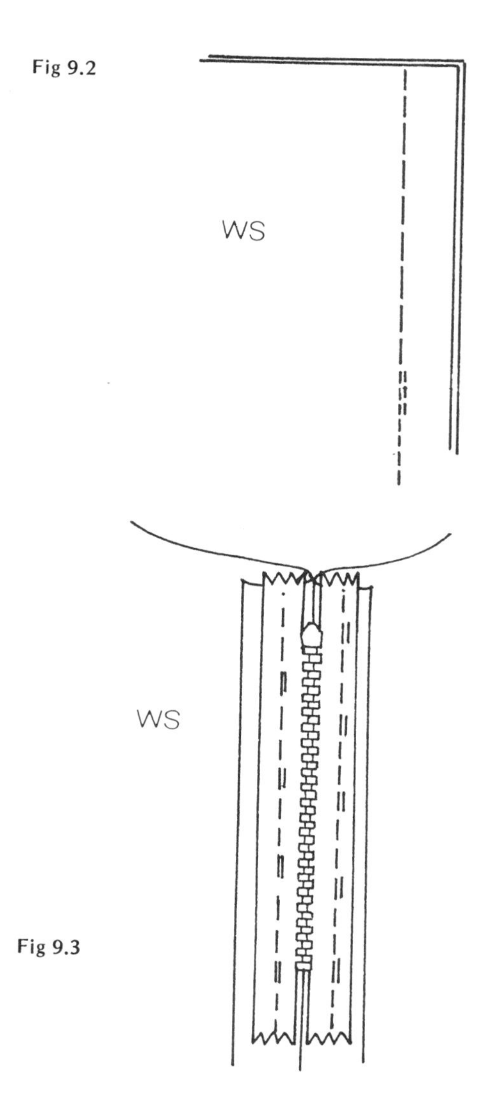

Fig 9.2

Fig 9.3

Press the seam open. Neaten both edges from top to bottom.

With fabric wrong-side up, place the zip right-side down on the seam. Make sure the zip slider is a fraction below the fitting line of the garment. Tack from top to bottom on each side but tack through the zip tape and the seam allowance. Prevent the needle from penetrating the garment beneath by sliding your fingers under the seam allowance. Take a back stitch every third stitch as this zip has a tendency to slide out of place. Make sure the centre of the teeth lies exactly over the seam line (fig 9.3).

Remove the large machining and stitch the zip to the turnings. To do this, roll the teeth over as flat as possible so that the stitching can be placed as close to the teeth as possible. Use a medium-length machine stitch and sew with the zip teeth uppermost. Stitch as far as possible. The slider will be in the way at the bottom so stop machining. Stitch the other side in the same way. Remove the tacking stitches (fig 9.4).

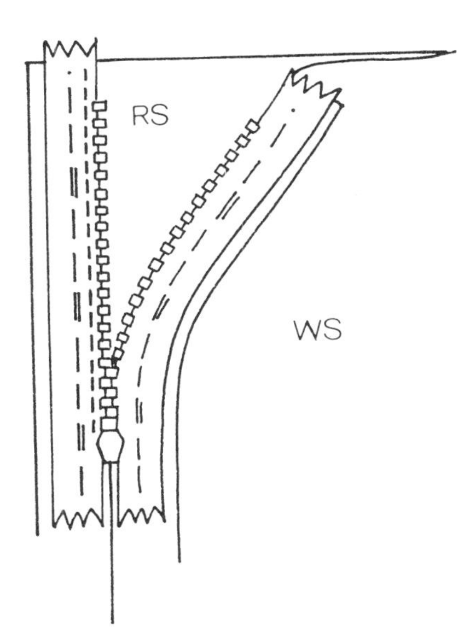

Fig 9.4

Close the zip, running the slider slowly to roll the teeth over gently. Stick a length of Sellotape over the join on the right side, taking it from below the gap in the seam to a point about 5 cm along the zip. Turn the garment wrong-side up, lift the lower end of the zip and slip stitch by hand to close the gap from below the zip stitching to the top of the seam stitching. Pick up a small amount of fabric from each fold of fabric alternately. Do not pull the thread tight. Fasten off. Re-tack the bottom part of the zip tape to the seam allowances and stitch as close as possible to the teeth. If the machine still has the zip foot on you can do this by machine. If not, back stitch by hand. Remove the Sellotape and tacking (fig 9.5).

If you stitch the entire zip by hand and you are doubtful of its strength, machine as well, stitching on the edge of the tape, attaching it to the seam allowance (fig 9.6).

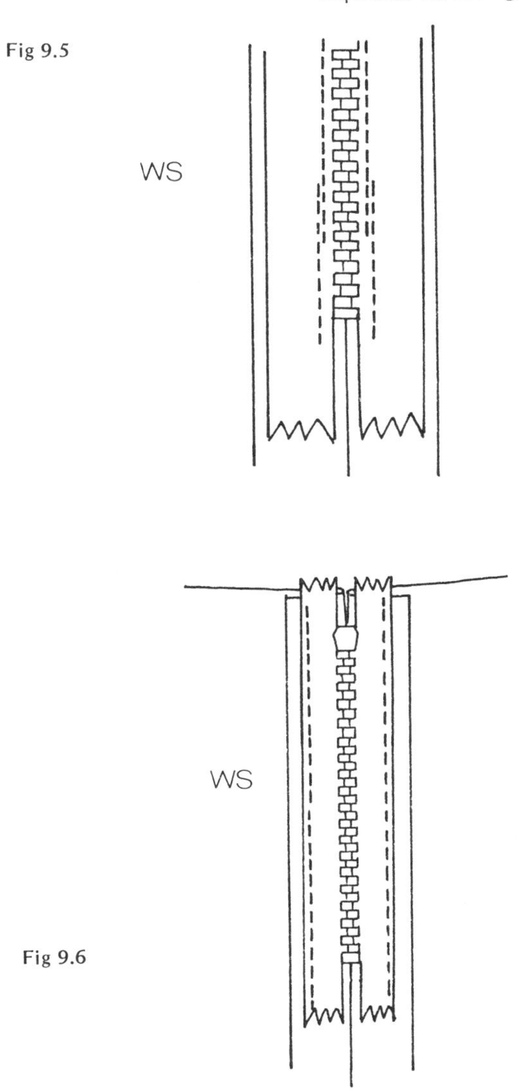

Fig 9.5

Fig 9.6

Visible zips

Use a conventional zip of nylon or metal with coloured teeth. Choose a matching or contrasting zip. There is a wide range of colours in all lengths up to 56 cm.

Zip in a seam

This method is suitable only for the centre front of a garment, or in an asymmetrical front seam. The main difficulty in putting in a zip is that the fabric is so much lighter in weight and different in texture from the zip tape. You can overcome this problem by having ready two pieces of soft iron-on Vilene 2 cm wide and 3 cm longer than the zip.

Stitch the garment seam to the zip base point. Press it open and neaten both edges right to the top of the zip opening. Press a small piece of Bondaweb beside the stitching at the top of the seam stitching (fig 9.7).

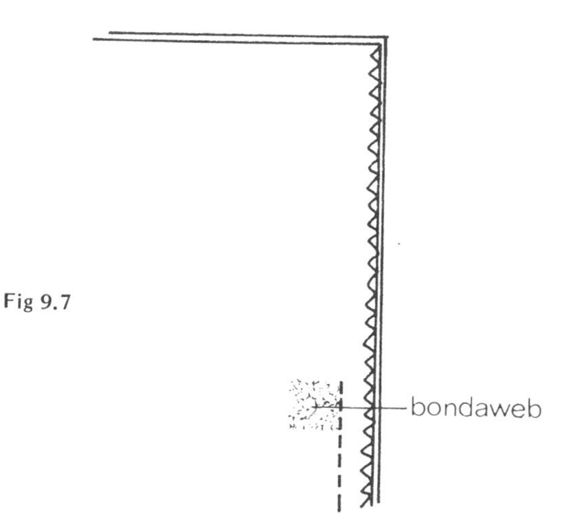

Fig 9.7

At the base, snip at an angle to form a triangle, the base of which is exactly equal to the width of the zip teeth. Fold the triangle to the wrong side and press (fig 9.8).

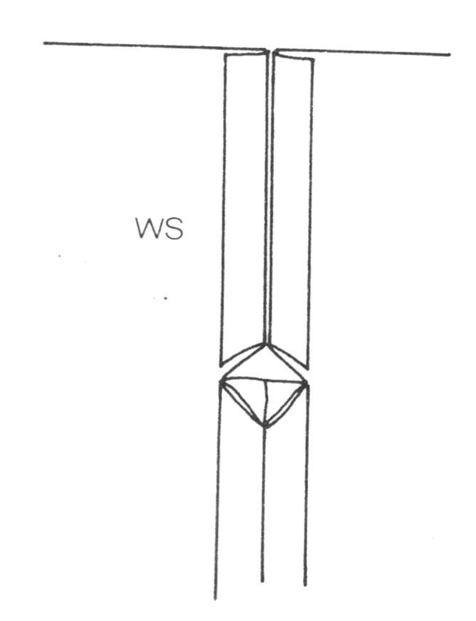

Fig 9.8

Turn in the seam allowance above this and press. Open out the turnings, place the Vilene in position with one edge on the crease. Press. Fold the turnings over and press again (fig 9.9).

Fig 9.9

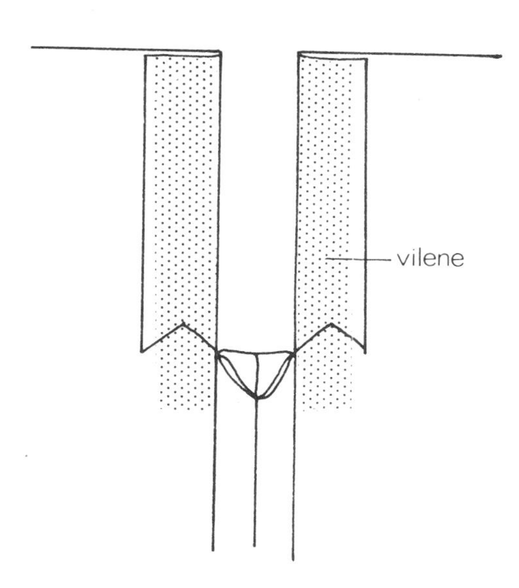

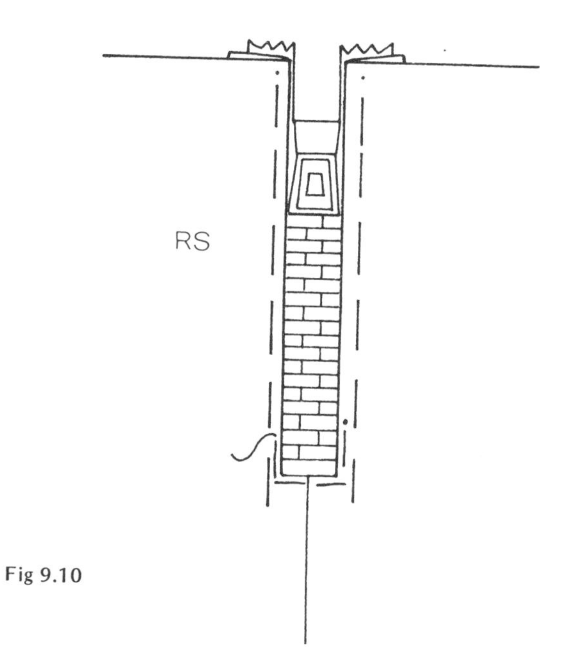

Fig 9.10

Starting at the base, place the zip under the opening and tack round the end stop of the zip. The fold of the fabric should be close against the teeth. Tack along both sides of the zip in this way (fig 9.10).

Stitch, using the zip foot on the machine and a medium-sized stitch. Sew once close to the teeth and again a little distance away — about 3 mm (fig 9.11).

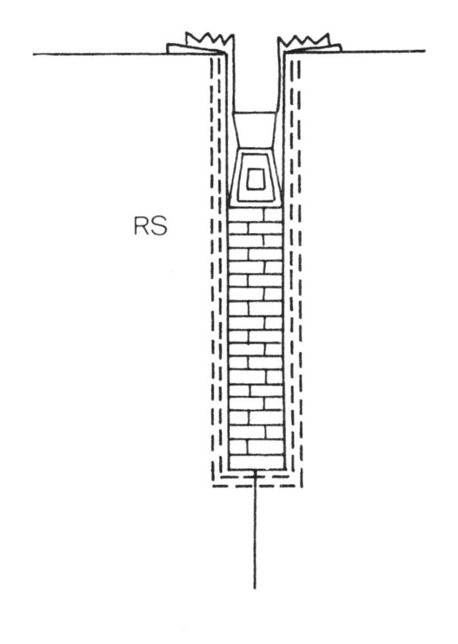

Fig 9.11

Remove tackings. Press up to the teeth but not over them.

Open-ended zip

These are available with nylon and metal teeth and there is in addition the jumbo-size Alpine zip with large plastic teeth. Colours are limited in the latter type but the others are made in a wide range of colours and lengths. Buy the zip and if necessary adjust the length of the garment to fit the zip. The zips are suitable for centre front openings on jackets, blousons, anoraks, track suit tops, etc.

It is easier if the bottom of the garment is completed before the zip is inserted.

It is usual to have a turn-back facing on the garment of about 5 cm, so add this on when cutting out if it is not allowed-for in the pattern. Neaten the facing edge and press a length of Fold-a-Band on the wrong side with the central holes exactly on the centre front line. Alternatively, press a piece of iron-on Vilene to the garment. Your decision will depend upon the edge of the garment. The facing is added for support but also to neaten the neck edge where there may be a collar. If this is so, the facing will be shaped round to the shoulder seam and therefore the Vilene should follow that shaping. The zip will not necessarily extend right up to the neck. Fold the edges back and press (fig 9.12).

Fig 9.12

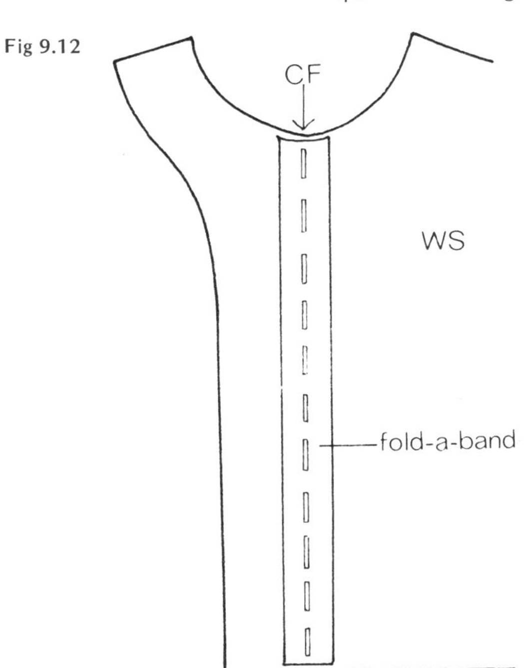

Begin at the bottom and put the zip under the folded fabric edge. The bottom of the zip should be level with the bottom of the garment. Tack, holding the edge of the fabric close to the teeth (fig 9.13).

Fig 9.13

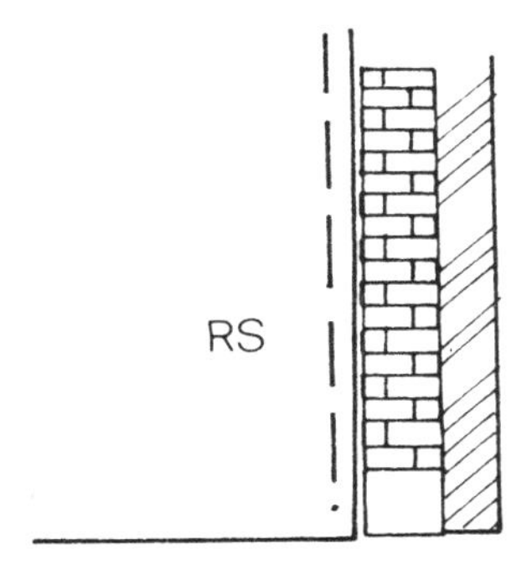

Return to the bottom and tack the other side. The ends of tape may be caught later in a neck finish but if not, trim them off to 1 cm, turn under the ends and hem.

Machine the zip with two rows of medium-sized stitching, the first close to the teeth and the second 3 mm away. Fasten off the stitching strongly, especially at the bottom of the zip where you may find it difficult to sew throught the last little bit of the tape because it is reinforced (fig 9.14).

Fig 9.14

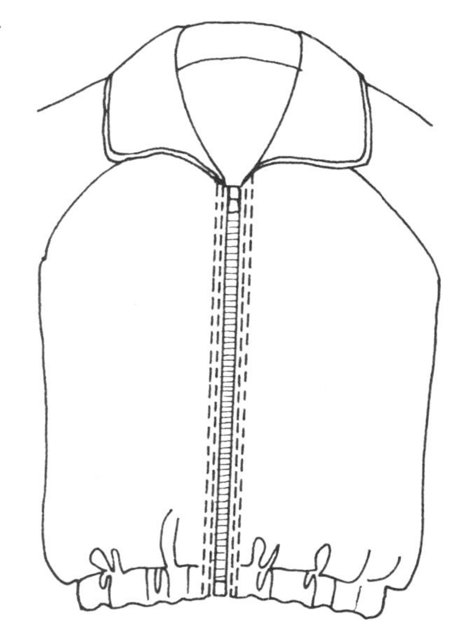

Decorative zip

Use an ordinary or an open-ended zip. This method is suitable for centre front openings. Prepare the edges as for the visible zip but turn the edges to the *right side* of the garment, tack and press and trim them down to 5 mm. Place the zip on top, on the right side of the garment. The zip tape must cover the seam allowances. Tack the zip along each side, turning under the ends of the tape. Stitch in one of the following ways.

— two rows of straight stitching, one on the edge of the tape and another 3 mm inside, in matching thread
— one row of zig-zag stitch along the centre of the tape in matching thread
— a row of machine embroidery stitching worked over the edge of the tape, in matching or contrasting thread (fig 9.15)
— one row of straight or zig-zag stitch in matching thread, covered with contrasting braid which is stitched in place along both edges by hand or machine, or, if narrow, down the centre with one row

TIPS If zip teeth seem tough, run your beeswax along them to lubricate.

Always stitch in the same direction on both sides of the zip.

If the two edges of fabric have to be exactly level, as, for example, when matching stripes or where there is a crossing seam, stitch that part first for about 3 cm, then start again and sew the entire zip.

It is not easy to work a second row of parallel stitching using the zip foot because you have no guide. It helps to put a piece of Sellotape on the fabric with one edge marking the position of the stitching.

Even hems, ordinary zip

If you cannot use any of the methods described above, the next easiest method of insertion is by the even-hem method. Two folds of equal width meet centrally over the teeth. The teeth will inevitably show at some stage, so buy a nylon or metal zip with coloured teeth.

Try to avoid a long centre back zip — replace it with a short one in the back neck and a 30 cm zip in the left side seam.

The even-hem method is also suitable for centre front openings on dresses and trousers and side opening skirts.

If the fabric edges are straight, build up the fabric by inserting a narrow strip of soft iron-on Vilene under the turnings. It helps to allow additional seam allowances — say 2.5 cm — when cutting out (fig 9.16).

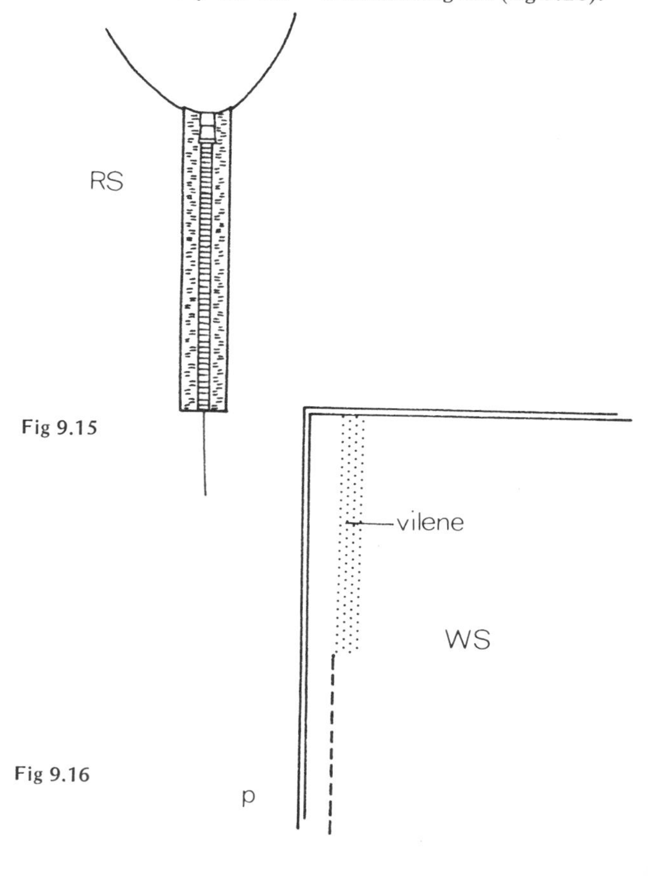

Fig 9.15

Fig 9.16

Stitch the seam to the zip base position. Press open. Neaten the seam right to the top.

Fold back the seam allowances beside the zip and press. Open out again and press the Vilene in position with one edge on the crease (fig 9.17).

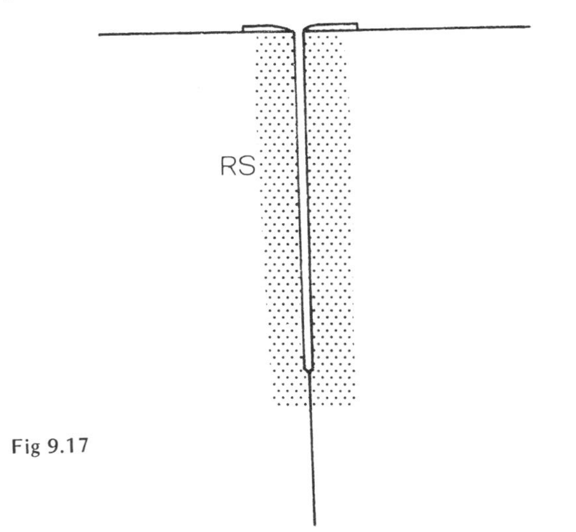

Fig 9.17

Fold turnings back and press again. With garment right-side up place the zip under one edge with the fold half-way over the teeth. Tack beside the teeth (fig 9.18).

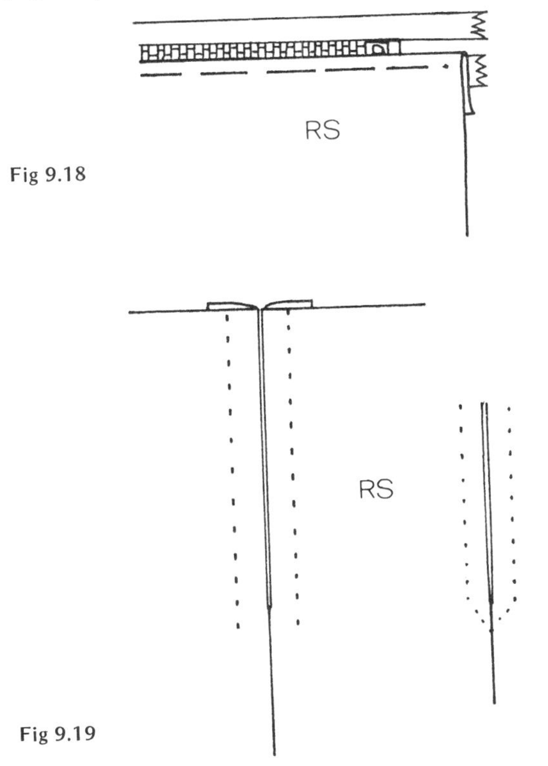

Fig 9.18

Fig 9.19

Tack the second side in the same way.

Hold the two folds together over the zip with a length of Sellotape.

Stitch in the zip with hand prick stitch or using the zip foot on the machine. Do not sew too close to the teeth. Sewing straight across below the bottom of the zip invariably produces a bulge: either work two parallel rows only, or stitch to a V to avoid this (fig 9.19).

Remove tackings and Sellotape. Press the stitching from the right side.

> **TIPS** Always ease rather than stretch fabric on to a zip.
>
> If you widen the seam allowance when cutting out, you can use Fold-a-Band to reinforce the edges.
>
> When putting a zip in a side seam, stitch the seam to the zip base point, insert the zip so that the slider comes at the fitting line at the armhole. After inserting the zip, work a bar tack above the slider and finish the armholes, stitching across just above the top of the zip.
>
> Before inserting an ordinary zip the fabric will lie flatter, especially soft fabric, if a narrow strip of Wundaweb is inserted under the pressed back edges.

FASTENINGS

In order to be effective, i.e. strong and lasting, fastenings must be sewn on well and that is time-consuming. So in order to save time, fastenings that are easy to attach must be chosen.

Velcro

Without a doubt this is the quickest of fastenings to attach, partly because you don't have to spend time locating the exact position, and partly because it is not fiddly to hold while sewing. Available in a variety of colours and three widths, it can be cut to any length or shape.

Use it to fasten waistbands of skirts, trousers and wrap-over skirts, to fasten cuffs and belts.

Use it in circles or squares in place of buttonholes. Sew the buttons on top.

Use it in short lengths in place of a zip in full skirts.

Use a tiny piece to hold collars neatly together at the back of the neck, in place of a hook.

Use it to fix anything detachable or interchangeable.

Use it to fasten straps of dungarees and pinafores, passing the end through a plastic or wooden ring.

Velcro is made of nylon so it is durable and endlessly washable. Because it is so strong, eliminate sharp corners by trimming them off if you are using squares or rectangles. Also Velcro's great virtue is its easy adjustment. As this may leave part of the hook or scratchy side exposed, always use a slightly smaller piece than the softer loop side.

It doesn't really matter which side of the Velcro is positioned where, but it prevents tights being caught when dressing if the soft side faces the body.

When using Velcro in a position where the body is liable to expansion, i.e. waistband, eliminate creaking by leaving ½-1 cm free of stitching at the open end of the band. This allows the end of the Velcro to lift instead of pull (fig 9.20).

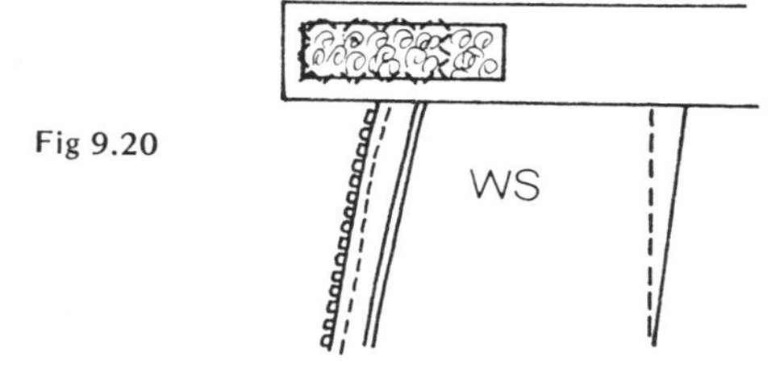

Fig 9.20

In attaching Velcro, machine large pieces if possible, provided the stitching does not show too much, or forms part of a design of stitching such as on a waistband. Set the machine to a small zig-zag stitch and work it over the edge.

If you have difficulty in keeping the Velcro still while stitching, use a small piece of double-sided tape or a spot of Copydex.

When sewing by hand use a small needle that will easily penetrate the Velcro and take small hemming stitches through the edge of it. If you find it difficult the reason is either the needle is too big or your stitches are too big (fig 9.21).

Always use Drima because it is strong.

Fig 9.21

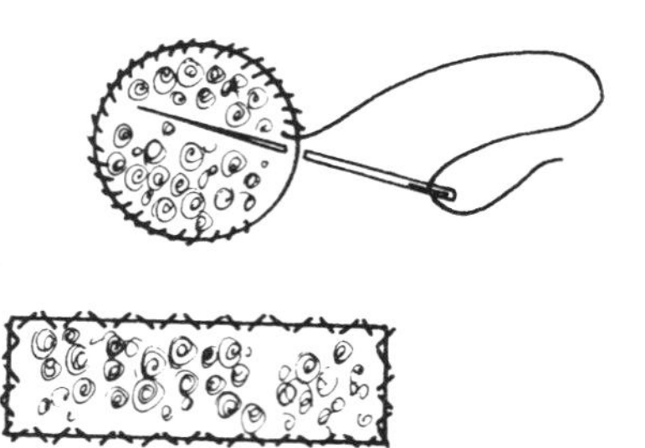

Ties

Ties can be made from fabric, bias binding, cord or flat braid. Use them in place of buttons and buttonholes, frog fastenings and on any edge-to-edge neck opening.

Narrow bias ties can be made in the same way as a tube or rouleau belt or belt loops.

Straight ties can be any width, stitched and turned through or the strip of fabric can be turned in on both sides and then folded again and machined (fig 9.22).

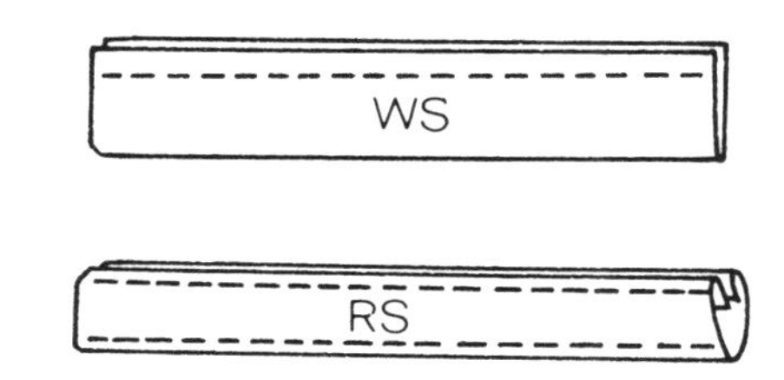

Fig 9.22

Attach by folding under one end and hemming to the wrong side of the garment, or if there is a seam or join available, tuck the end in and stitch on the wrong side. This method may be used where ties are inserted in a bound edge (fig 9.23).

Fig 9.23

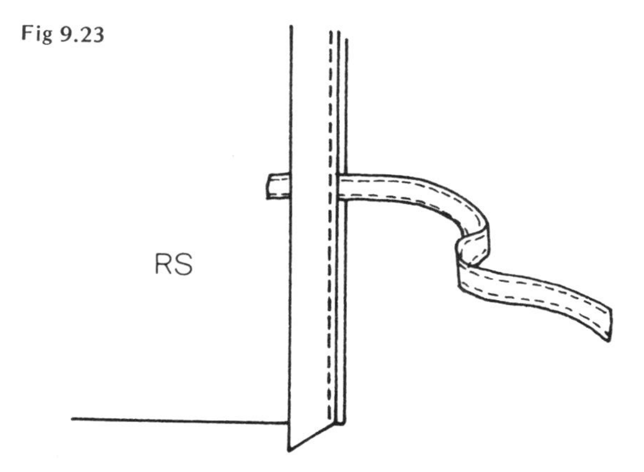

If the ties must be attached on the right side, tie a knot in the end and twirl it round a couple of times decoratively and hem in place (fig 9.24).

The raw ends of tube ties can be tucked in. This ties and cord can be knotted. The ends of flat braid should be mitred; do this by hand or machine.

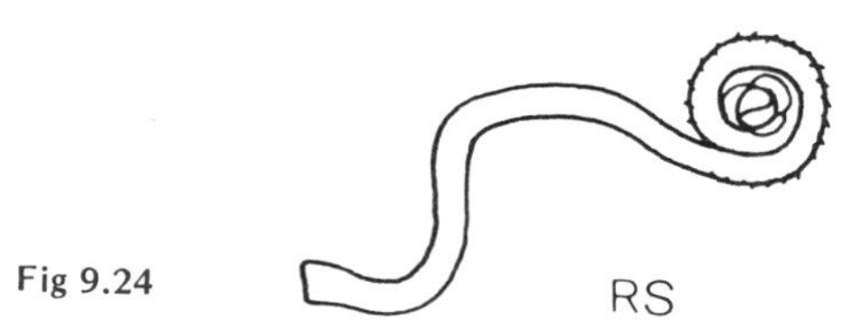

Fig 9.24

Loops

Loops to fit round buttons can be made from cord, straight or bias ties as above, or bias binding, but they should be set into a seam for neatness and they look good only with large buttons or toggles. They may be inserted in a bound edge between the binding and the garment.

If flat braid is used mitre the loop at the fold and press. Insert the loops in a seam or under a braid edge or stitch to the wrong side of the garment, turning under the raw ends of the braid and hemming (fig 9.25).

Fig 9.25

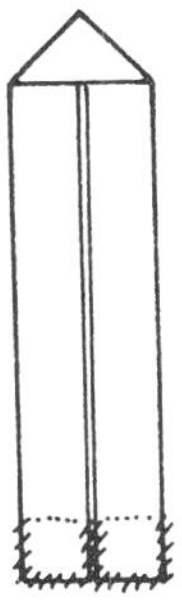

Snaps

There is a variety of metal studs available with decorative tops. Most of these are quickly attached by squeezing on to the fabric and are an excellent method of fastening.

Where several press studs are needed buy those that are fixed to tape. Attach by machining round the edge of the tape with a medium, straight machine stitch.

> **TIP** Use the zip foot so that you can stitch past the press studs easily (fig 9.26).

Trims — the press studs with metal caps that are available which need to be covered with fabric — are not really a short cut because they take a little time to prepare and attach. However, if you wish to avoid buttonholes then they are very useful.

Trouser clips

Use on waistbands of trousers and skirts.

These are big and strong and not too fiddly to attach. The best type is one with a bar with spiky prongs as it doesn't have to be stitched.

If at all possible insert the hook in the end of the waistband. Attach both hook and bar before finishing the band.

It is not easy to establish the position of the bar once the hook is in place, so mark the position with a clearly visible chalk mark, not a pin. Push the prongs of the bar through the waistband from the right side. On the back flatten the prongs.

Fig 9.26

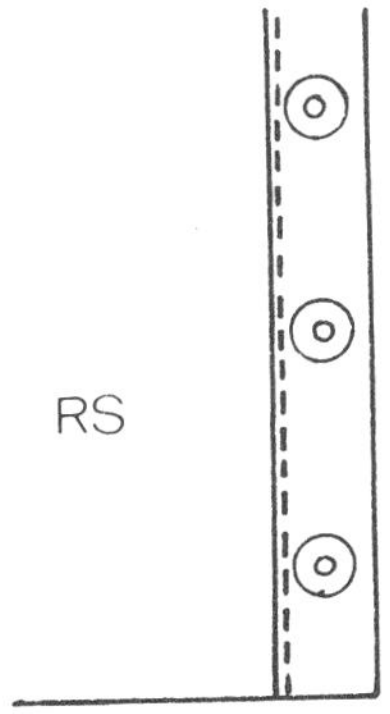

If you have only a single layer of fabric through which to fix the bar, add additional strength by putting a piece of plain cotton fabric on the back. Hold in place with a piece of Wundaweb then insert the bar.

To attach the hook cut a piece of tape or seam binding about 10 cm long. Thread the tape through the loop of the hook in a swing-ticket knot. Place the hook in position at the end of the waistband on the outer part of the band but on the wrong side. Use double-waxed thread and oversew firmly round the holes on each side of the hook. Pull the tape back and lay it flat on the waistband. Hold it down firmly with plenty of hemming stitches. Tuck the waistband backing under the head of the hook and oversew the two folds together between the metal parts of the hook. Finish the waistband (fig 9.27).

Note that you will not be able to machine across the end of the waistband where the hook is.

Fig 9.27

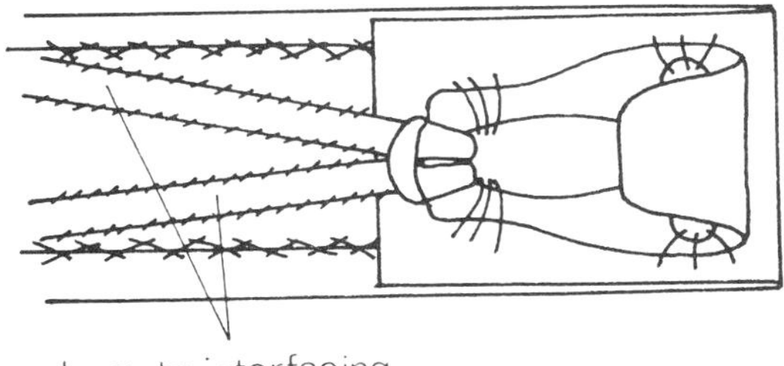

10 Edges and hems

It takes longer to make something unnoticeable than something visible, so most quick methods are ones that are visible when finished. Choose the method of finishing the edge or hem according to the weight and type of the fabric and the effect that you want.

BINDING OR CROSSWAY FINISH

Narrow strips of fabric cut on the cross or bias can be used to finish edges including necklines, armholes, front fastening edges, sleeve hems, jacket and skirt hems, edges of hoods and collars.

Purchased binding is available in a wide variety of plain colours and mainly in three widths. Pretty printed binding is available in narrow widths. The narrow binding is soft, the medium and wide ones are firmer but coarser in texture. Use narrow binding on thick fabrics; it is really too soft for fine fabrics.

Ordinary fabrics, cut into strips, are easier to use as they are firm and they are also more decorative. Keep pieces of all types of fabric including lining materials and nylon jersey; it is useful to be able to find an odd piece of matching or contrasting material, plain or print, to use for crossway strips or facings. With some uses it helps to fold over and press one edge before applying the strip. When using ready-prepared bought binding which has both edges pressed over, it often helps to remove one of these folds by pressing it out.

These strips can also be used for tie belts, rouleau ties, loops for buttons. See those sections for details.

Cutting your own binding

Strip width and direction depends on weave; follow the instructions below.

Woven fabrics

When using woven fabrics the strips are cut at an angle to the selvedge because that provides 'give' that enables you to manipulate the binding round curves. It also provides a contrast in effect to have the weave of the fabric on the bias.

The 'true' bias or true cross can be found at an angle of 45° to the selvedge. The easiest way to find the position is to mark a point on the selvedge and measure from that point an even distance down the selvedge and across the weft or width of the fabric. Draw a chalk line with a ruler, joining these two points, cut on the chalk line and that gives you two true cross edges (fig 10.1).

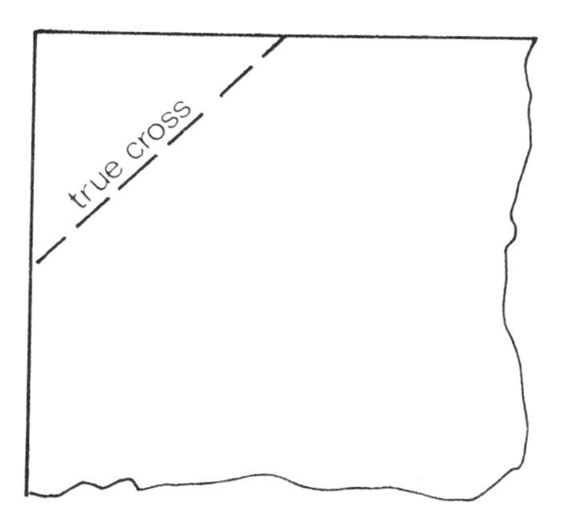

Fig 10.1

The pieces of fabric used will invariably be small scraps from which other pieces have been cut, so the edges will not be straight, but you will be able to follow a straight thread clearly enough to measure on.

Having made the first cut, decide how wide you need the strips. This will depend on the final effect, but allowing two seam allowances of 5 mm each, a strip 2-3 cm wide is about average. It can be trimmed before completion for a very narrow effect. Set an adjustable marker to the width and cut parallel with the bias cut edges of the fabric. Use cutting out shears, make long cuts holding the marker well ahead. If you use small scissors and cut slowly the strip will be uneven. If you try to chalk or pin, the fabric will bubble. If the cut strips are wildly uneven trim them after cutting (fig 10.2).

If the fabric is checked, striped or printed in a line pattern the strips will have to be cut on the true cross but if not, bias strips with a little less 'give'

Fig 10.2

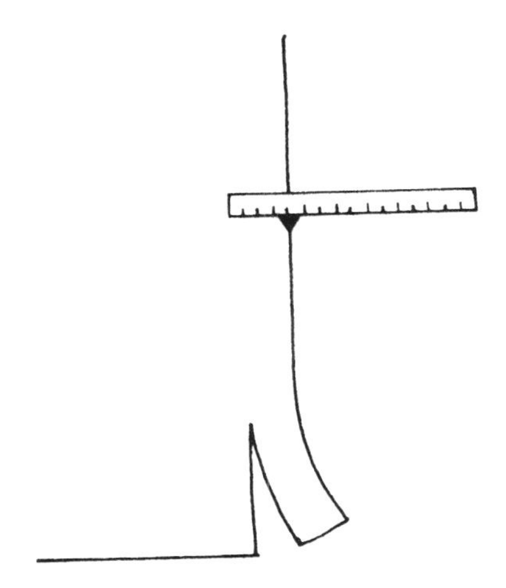

can be cut at an angle less than 45°. The advantage of having less 'give' is that pieces are easier to handle and will be less inclined to bubble when attached to straight edges. Cut in the same way, marking a chalk line for the first cut and then cutting strips from both edges.

Cut more than you need, allowing about 3 cm extra length for each join to be made.

Knitted fabrics

For special effects you may wish to cut bias strips on the cross as described for woven fabrics but the fabric is not easy to handle because there is a tremendous amount of stretch in it that can be almost uncontrollable. The exceptions to this are the firm knits such as nylon jersey, heavy polyester, knits, Raschel knits. On the whole it is the warp knit construction fabrics that will stretch most. Pull the material on the bias and see how much it stretches.

Knit fabrics also give a lot across the width, often to the same degree as on the cross and usually too much for such items as belts and rouleau loops and ties. If the fabric stretches much more than the thread then the stitches will break under the strain of being pulled.

It is usually best to cut binding strips on the warp, parallel with the selvedge on knit fabrics. This provides sufficient 'give' for most purposes. If you are unsure then cut a short piece and try it.

Joining the strips

The strips may have to be joined to make sufficient length. Even if you are using it in several different positions it is more convenient and quicker to prepare one long piece and use it as needed.

Strips of fabric whether straight or bias look best if the joins appear on the garment at an angle.

Lay out the strips wrong-side up with ends meeting. Cut one end at an angle of 45°. Cut the other to fit. Lift up both cut ends and insert a pin across the seam. Cut and pin all other joins (fig 10.3).

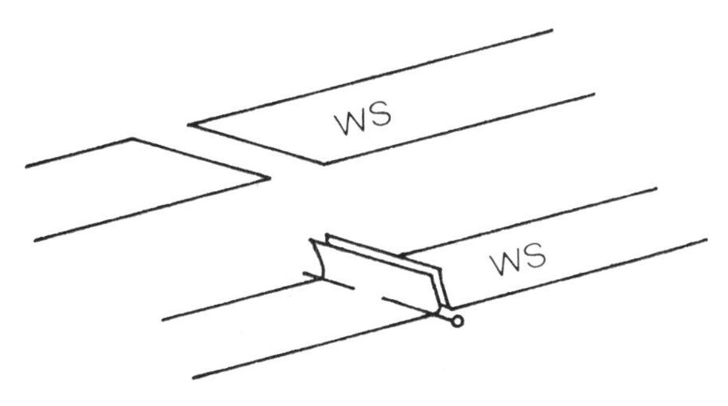

Fig 10.3

Stitch these little seams by hand or machine taking 3-5 mm turnings. Due to the way the ends have been cut, you will have an odd angle of fabric extending at both ends. This can be a useful guide for joining as the stitching must begin and end in that angle so that when opened out the strip has continuous straight edges. You will probably have to pin the first join and test it by opening out the strip before stitching. Stitch all joins.

Press each join carefully. The flattest effect is achieved by using the toe of the iron and opening the seam. Press on the wrong side and then on the right, then trim both raw edges of the join to 3 mm.

However, many fine fabrics, except knits, will wrinkle when pressed in this way. Avoid it by pressing both turnings to one side, first trimming the upper one to 2 mm. Press on the wrong side and the right side (fig 10.4).

With strip right-side up cut off all extending corners of fabric.

Fig 10.4

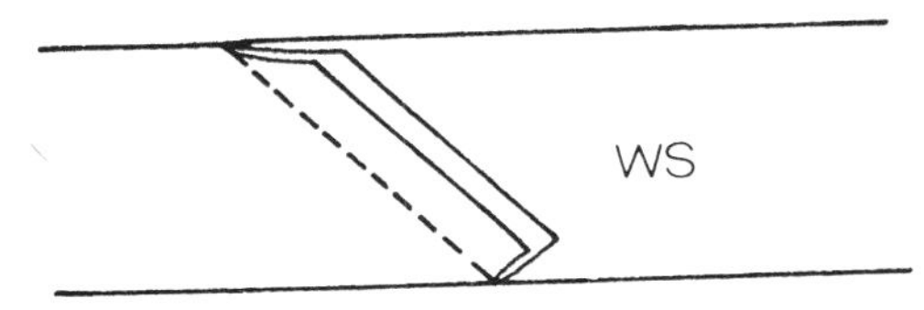

Stretching

Purchased binding has had the excess stretch removed but if you cut your own it should be stretched and pressed to make it easier to handle. Only true cross strips of woven fabric need to be stretched and knit fabric cut on the true cross, others do not 'give' excessively.

Pin one end of the strip to the pressing board, stretch the strip slightly, not to its maximum and pin at the other end of the board. Press with a medium-hot iron and damp muslin. Remove the muslin and leave the strip to cool before moving on to press the next section (fig 10.5).

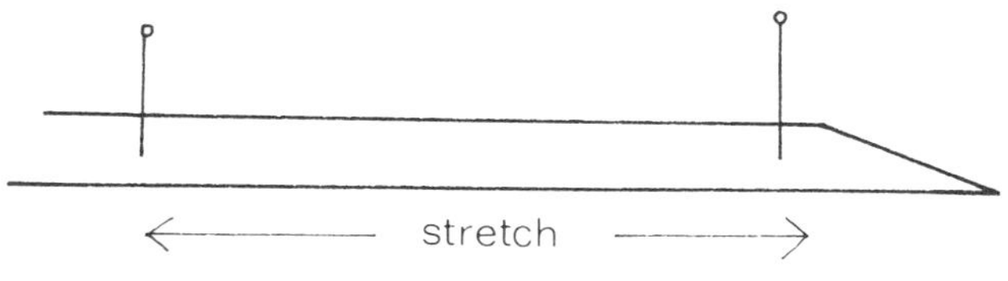

Fig 10.5

FOLDED BIAS FINISH

This edge finish can be of any width from about 1 cm up to 3 cm. It is not suitable for use on an edge that is very shaped. Use matching or contrast fabric.

Where possible, leave one garment seam open, if only at the edge where the bias is to go, rather than attach it to a completed edge. The illustrations below show the bias being attached to a short sleeve but it may also be used wide on a dress hem, or jacket front edges; narrow on a neckline or armhole. If the length is critical, for example on sleeves or a skirt, cut the garment to finished length minus the width of the strip being applied.

Cut pieces twice the finished visible width plus two seam allowances of 5 mm. Fold in half with wrong sides together and press. Place the strip to the right side of the garment with edges arranged so that you can stitch, taking a 5 mm turning on the bias strip but the usual seam allowance on the garment. Insert a few pins across the strip. Machine in place with strip uppermost (fig 10.6). Trim all three raw edges to 3-4 mm and neaten by working zig-zag stitch over them. Press so that the strip extends beyond the garment edge but the turnings lie back into the garment.

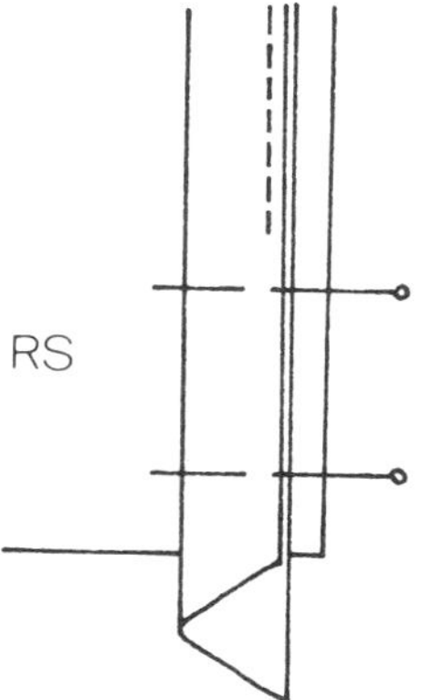

Fig 10.6

Fold the garment, sleeve, etc., right sides together, line up the joins just made and insert a pin to hold in place. Stitch the seam, starting on the join and machining to the hemline. Turn the garment over and complete the seam. Press. Stitching in two stages in this way ensures that the strip is exactly level at the seam (fig 10.7).

Fig 10.7

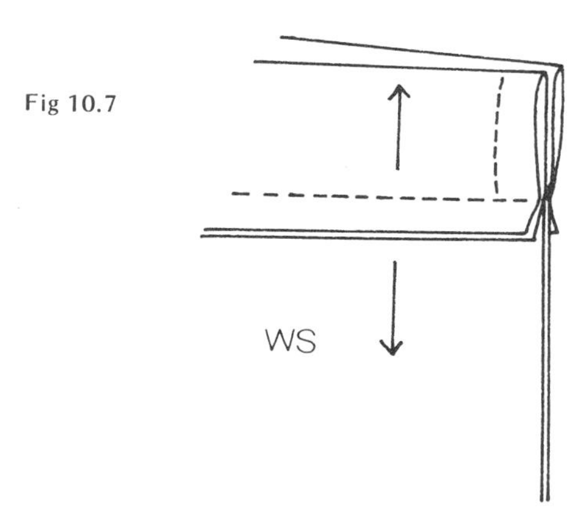

FLAT BIAS FINISH

The bias strip is folded to the right side to be finished and can be almost any width although if there are curves to manipulate keep it to no more than 2 cm. Use to finish any edge including necklines, armholes, edges of jackets, boleros. It is particularly effective when applied to quilted fabric as it provides a contrast in texture. Use matching or contrasting fabric. This finish is only successful with woven binding. The binding can be the final process as the join is not difficult to make. This method does not add to the length.

Cut bias pieces the finished width plus two seam allowances of 5 mm. Join and then press under 5 mm all along one edge.

Begin placing the binding in position at a point where a join will not be visible, for example at the back of the neck, side seam or centre back. If there is a seam the join should fall where the seam comes. Leave an end about 2 cm long for joining.

Place the strip right-side down to wrong side of garment edge. Take 5 mm turning on the bias but the normal seam allowance or whatever is necessary on the garment. If you are skilled at controlling your machine the binding can be stitched on without tacking. Be sure to take an even seam allowance all along, perhaps using the machine foot as a guide. You will find that you tend to slightly pull the bias strip while machining and this produces a good finish. Do not pin or the binding will wrinkle. This process is particularly easy when using a light binding on a

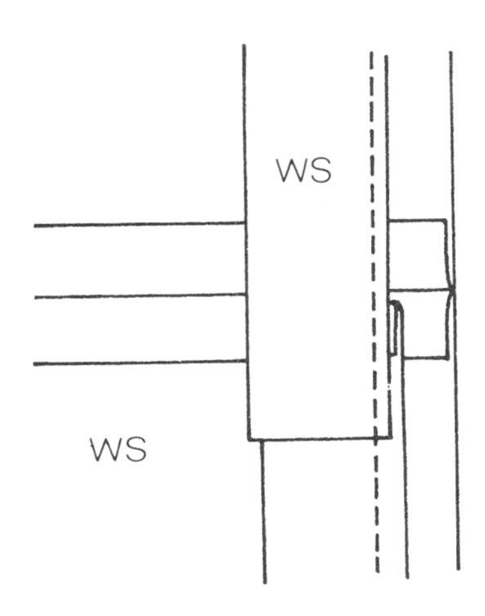

Fig 10.8

thicker or firmer fabric such as quilting.

On reaching the end, fold over the end of the binding underneath and continue stitching the strip over the fold. The folded edge should be exactly level with the garment seam. Fasten off the stitching. (fig 10.8).

A flatter but more time-consuming join can be made as follows. Begin and end the machining 4 cm away from the ends of binding. Using the iron, press over both ends of binding at an angle so that the folds meet. Lift up these ends and place the pressed creases together. Stitch the join by hand or machine. Trim the raw edges to 3 mm and press. Complete the machining to attach the strip to the garment.

To finish, place the garment wrong-side up on the pressing board. Use the toe of the iron and run it between the garment and the binding, pushing against the join to turn the binding over so that it extends beyond the garment. Trim the garment edge down to 3 mm.

With garment wrong-side towards you roll the binding completely to the right side, roll the edge and tack so that the join is just visible. Press.

Turn to the right side and tack the binding flat to the garment. If you haven't time to tack, pin across the binding at intervals.

Work a straight zig-zag or embroidery stitch along this edge and also along the garment edge if you wish. Press. If the main fabric is printed, match the stitching with one of the colours (fig 10.9).

This finish may also be applied to the right side of the garment and finished on the wrong side. Work the final machine stitching from the right side to make sure it is even.

NARROW BOUND FINISH

This can be applied to any straight or shaped edge such as necklines, sleeve hems, jacket edges. Keep the finish narrow or it may pucker.

Fig 10.9

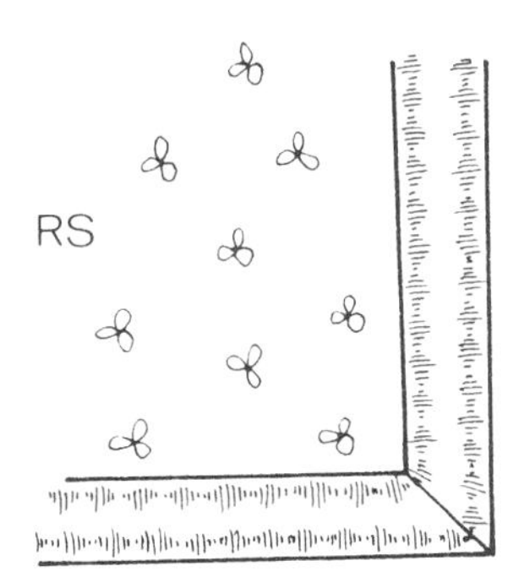

The garment is lengthened by the finished width of the binding, so if the length is critical apply it taking a longer seam allowance on the garment. It may be applied before or after seams have been stitched.

Use the narrow purchased binding, plain or printed, or cut strips twice the finished width plus two 5 mm seam allowances. Join and press over one edge with the iron.

Joins should be placed out of sight at the side or back of the garment. Place the binding right-side down to the wrong side of the garment. Take 5 mm seam allowance on the binding but the usual amount (or 5 mm more) on the garment. Machine in place leaving at least 2 cm if a join has to be made. You will slightly stretch the binding as you stitch but this produces a good result.

Make a join by one of the two methods described under *Flat bias finish*.

To finish, use the toe of the iron and run it between the garment and the binding, pushing against the join to press the binding over so that it extends beyond the garment edge (fig 10.10).

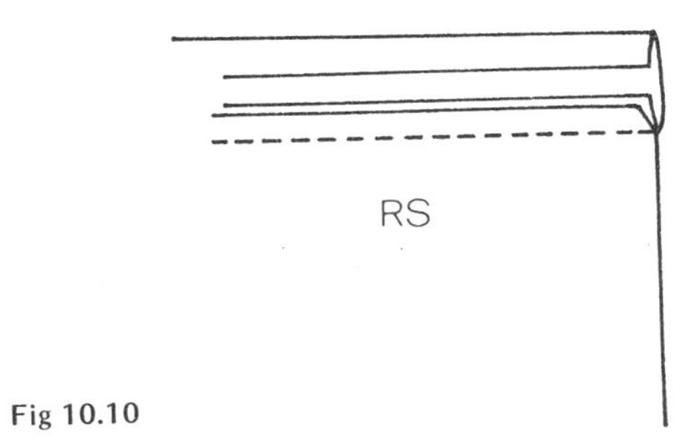

Fig 10.10

Trim the garment edge to 4 mm, or 3 mm if the fabric is thick.

With right side garment towards you, roll the binding over to the right side and tack with the folded edge, just covering the machining beneath.

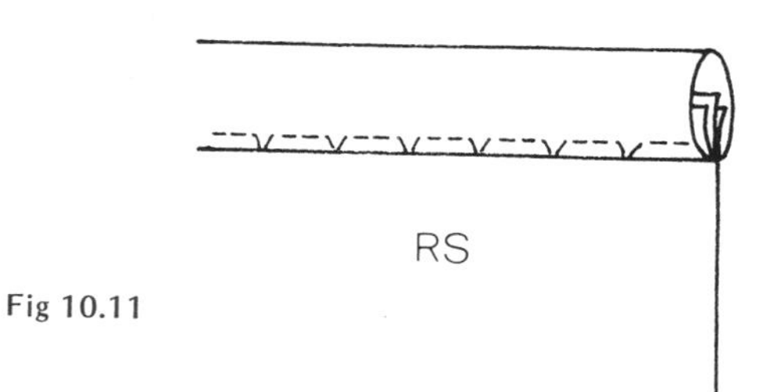

Fig 10.11

It is not wise to stitch this without tacking.

Press. Work a straight, zig-zag or machine embroidery stitch along the edge of the binding using a matching or contrasting thread.

This finish may be applied to the right side and finished on the wrong side of the garment, in which case finish by hand hemming into the machining or, if machining, work the stitching from the right side for an even result (fig 10.11).

NARROW HEMS

Fluted hem

This is very successful on jersey and knits and also on bias edges of fine fabrics such as chiffon. Use the fluted hem on dresses and skirts, sleeves, scarves, collars, frills.

Cut the garment edge to the required length plus 3-5 mm.

Set the machine to satin stitch of medium width, about 2 to 2½. Place the garment edge under the foot, right-side up, turning under 3-5 mm or as little as possible, depending on the thickness of the fabric. Work two or three machine stitches over the fold to start then satin stitch along the edge. The machine needle must clear the folded edge on the right with every stitch. Stretch the fabric by pulling it at the front as it approaches the needle, and also at the back behind the foot. This opens out the satin stitch to a zig-zag. Pull the fabric as much as possible for the best results (fig 10.12).

After machining the hem, trim off the surplus raw edge of fabric. Use small scissors and cut carefully. The fabric may flute up a little more after removing this edge. Do not press the hem.

Contrasting thread may be used.

Fig 10.12
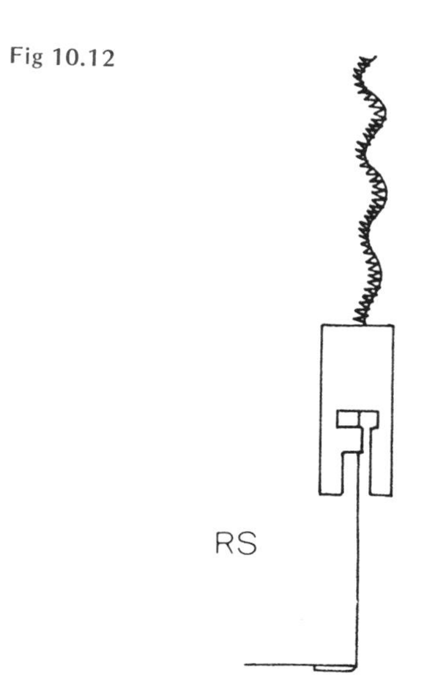

Machined-twice hem

This is suitable for any fine woven or jersey fabric and can be used on any garment edge. It produces good results on flared skirts as the two rows of stitching stabilise and add weight.

Trim the garment to the correct length plus 5-6 mm.

Set the machine to a medium-length straight stitch. Work the first row of machining 2 mm inside the raw edge. Feed the fabric into the machine evenly to avoid stretching.

To work the second row place the hem under the machine foot wrong-side up, fold the raw edge over twice forming a very narrow hem. The first row of machining is hidden but it provides a firm edge to grasp, making it easy to roll the hem. Work the second row of machining on the fold (fig 10.13).

Fig 10.13
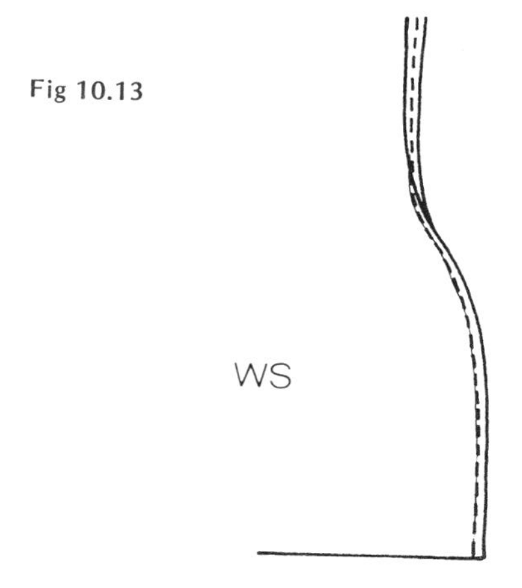

Rolled hem

Use the hemming foot on your machine for this. It is suitable for any fine woven or jersey fabric but work a trial hem on spare fabric just to make sure it is a suitable finish and to practise holding the fabric correctly. Use on any garment edge. It is particularly

useful as a time-saver on long edges of frills, over dresses, wedding trains and veils, etc.

Trim the garment to the correct length plus 5 mm. When working on woven fabrics cut the fabric just before hemming, because fraying yarns make the hem untidy and it is difficult to trim them off.

Set the machine to a small- to medium-length straight stitch.

Insert the garment hem wrong-side up and feed the edge into the curl of metal on the foot. Lower the foot and start machining. Hold the fabric edge vertically and hold it taut as it enters the roll. Watch the needle to make sure it is catching the hem down continuously (fig 10.14).

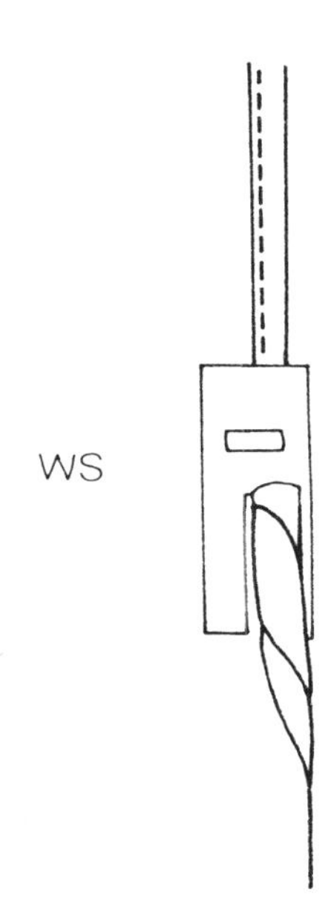

Fig 10.14

Shell hem

This is similar to the rolled hem above and suitable for all light and jersey fabrics. Trim the garment to the correct length plus 5 mm.

Use the shell-hem foot on the machine and a zig-zag stitch, setting about 2½-3 depending on the weight of the fabric. Try the hem out on a spare piece of fabric and adjust the length and width of stitch in order to produce a satisfactory effect.

Insert the garment hem wrong-side up and feed the edge into the curl of the foot. Lower the foot and machine, holding the fabric edge taut and vertical as you feed it in (fig 10.15).

This hem is particularly successful on springy fabrics as the width of the zig-zag holds the edge down well.

Fig 10.15

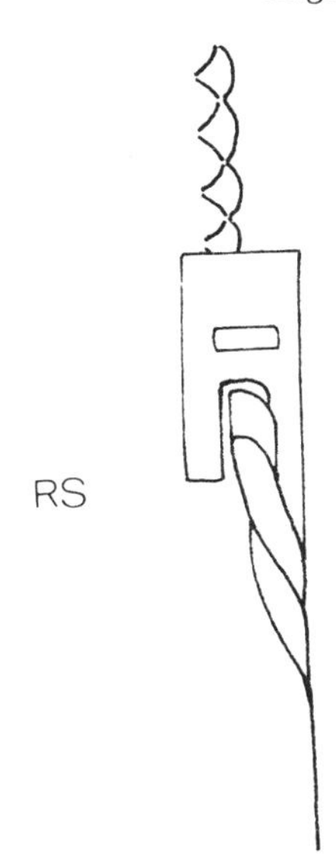

Ribbon finish

This is an attractive finish on light-weight straight hems. Use on nightwear, lingerie, linings, and also where you are short of fabric for a conventional hem. Use narrow ribbon to match exactly or to contrast.

Trim the garment to the correct length minus two-thirds the width of the ribbon. Set the machine to a small zig-zag stitch.

Place the ribbon right-side up to wrong-side hem, with the edge of the ribbon level with the raw edge of the fabric. Work zig-zag stitch over the edge (fig 10.16).

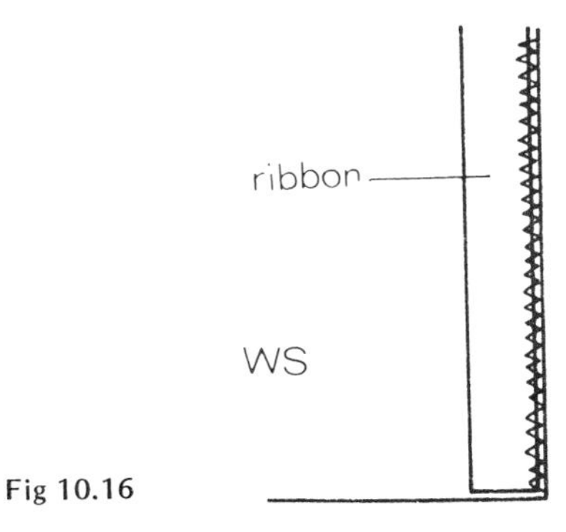

Fig 10.16

Using the iron fold this narrow stitched edge over to the right side of the garment so that the ribbon extends beyond the hem edge. The right side of the ribbon now corresponds with the right side of the fabric (fig 10.17).

Fig 10.17

Set the machine to a slightly larger stitch, or better still to an embroidery stitch that will cover the zig-zag underneath, and work the stitch over the edge of the ribbon.

Braid and petersham ribbon can also be used successfully in this way and it can be of any width. Wide ribbon is not successful as it is light in weight and tends to wrinkle.

CONVENTIONAL HEM

This takes longer to do and requires more care but can be used on all except light transparent fabrics. It is the usual method for skirts, dresses and trousers.

If the hemline is straight or only slightly shaped the hem depth can be 5 cm deep. If the skirt is shaped, reduce the depth to 2 or 3 cm in order to avoid the problem of excess fullness in the hem. With circular or very shaped hems the fabric is probably very light in weight so one of the narrow hems described previously will be more suitable.

When using Wundaweb in the hem the depth should be the width of the adhesive plus 5 mm, i.e. 3.5 cm. It is important to keep to this depth which allows sufficient fabric to cover the Wundaweb.

Decide on the length of the garment and mark the fold line with chalk dashes on the right side. Trim the seam allowance of side seams and other seam to 5 mm where the seam falls within the hem, but leave seams at full width in the actual fold of the hem. If too much is trimmed the hem becomes limp and the shape of the hem may be lost.

Fold the garment on the chalk line and tack 3 mm from the folded edge. The stitches should not be too small but they should be even in size at about 3 cm. This row of tacking cannot be omitted (fig 10.18).

Arrange the hem wrong-side up on the pressing surface and press the fold. Make sure you do not allow the iron to rest on the raw edge of the hem. Control it by using the iron sideways to press the fold.

Fig 10.18

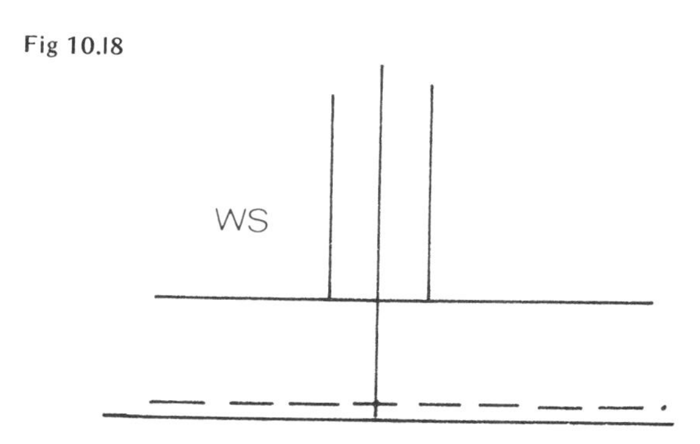

Trim the surplus fabric away so that the hem is a suitable depth. Neaten the raw edge by working a medium-sized zig-zag stitch over the raw edge. It is as well not to omit this even if the fabric does not fray, because the stitching stabilises the edge.

The hem section must now be attached to the garment.

If using Wundaweb, arrange the hem on the pressing surface with wrong side of garment uppermost. Settle a short section of the hem, making sure it is unwrinkled. Slide the Wundaweb between the hem and the garment. Push one edge right down to the tacking, lay the hem edge back in position to completely cover the Wundaweb and press. Use a damp cloth and hot iron and press sharply several times, using the iron sideways and pressing over the hem fold but not on the neatened edge, otherwise an impression of it will show through.

The adhesive web must be completely melted to be effective, so press sharply three or four times in one position and gently lift the hem edge to make sure it has stuck before moving on. Because of the pressure needed, Wundaweb is not suitable for pile fabrics. It is advisable to test it first on others with a surface interest, e.g. crêpe, bouclé and also when using fine transparent fabrics.

When inserting Wundaweb in a curved hem, cut the Wundaweb at intervals and overlap it to make it fit the curve.

Narrower hems can be made, cutting the Wundaweb down the middle but it is only sufficient on a lightweight fabric on a hem that does not need to weight the garment, for example, a frill.

To stitch the hem down, first tack a little below the neatening to hold the hem to the garment.

Thread a small needle with a short piece of matching thread and knot the end. Hold the hem with the lower fold towards you, lift the neatened edge and roll it back towards you and, starting the thread in the fabric of the hem, work catch stitch. Work from right to left picking up one thread from the garment, moving forward 5 mm and taking a couple

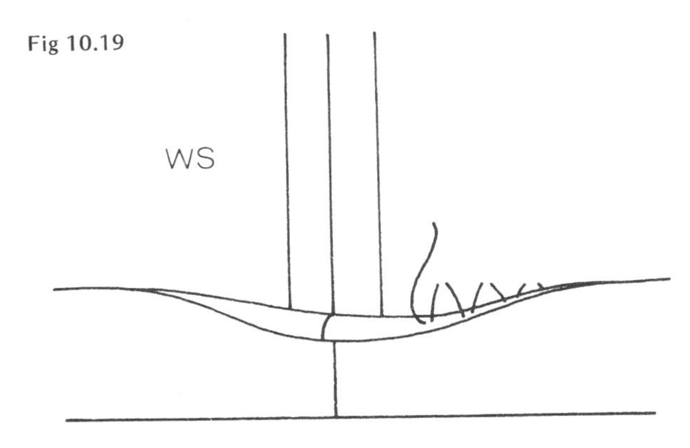

Fig 10.19

of threads from the hem fabric, move forward, pick one thread from the garment and so on. This is a slow job and it should not be hurried. If the thread is pulled through the garment too quickly it dislodges the weave and can make the hem show (fig 10.19).

Do not pull the thread tight but leave each diagonal of thread fairly loose. Do not try to close the hem fabric tight up against the garment. When sewing on jersey fabric leave an extra loop of thread 1 cm long every 4 cm. This allows for the fabric to stretch in wear but not pull the thread so tight that the hem shows.

Begin and end all lengths of thread in the hem edge, not in the garment.

Remove all tacking and press the hem. Arrange it on the pressing surface wrong-side up and press the hem fold. Use the iron sideways on the fold to ensure that you do not press the stitched edge. Pressing will cause a ridge to show on the right side.

Turn the hem right-side up and press very lightly over the hem and the garment. The hem is quite likely to be the final process so this may be the final pressing of the entire garment.

On medium to heavy fabrics it may be necessary to press more heavily for good results. To do this, arrange the hem wrong-side up and press the fold as described, but then place a piece of spare fabric, folded, up against the hem edge but on the single layer of garment. This fabric will cushion the pressure of the iron and a hem mark will be less likely on the garment. Now press with gentle, not sharp, pressure over the whole hem area.

> **TIP** Allow a hem to cool and dry before hanging the garment — the weight of the hem fold pulling on the stitches while the fabric is warm and damp may cause stretching but will certainly create a line on the right side.

FRINGE EDGE

Use bought fringing and place it on the of the garment edge with the right-side down. Machine in position with a medium-length straight stitch. Stitch close to the edge of the fringe. Press the fabric back away from the fringe. Set the machine to a small zig-zag stitch or a decorative stitch and work it on the right side close to the edge. Trim away the surplus fabric on the underneath (figs 10.20 and 10.21).

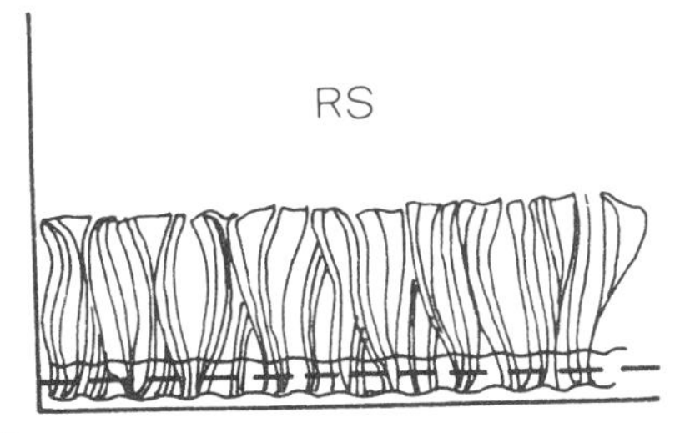

Fig 10.20

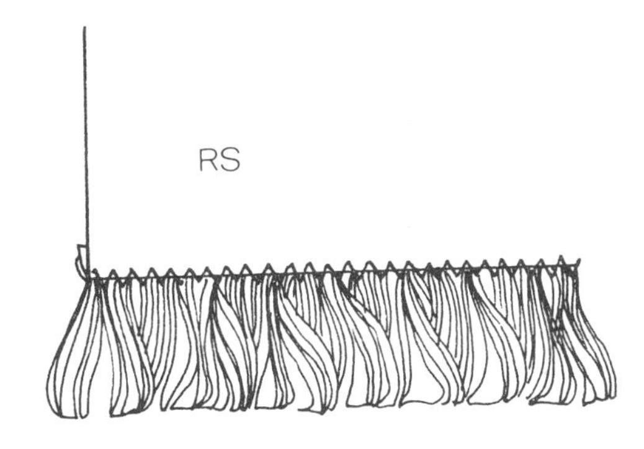

Fig 10.21

CASING EDGE

A casing may be added to an edge to have elastic, cord, etc., threaded through. A casing may be preferable to a hem where there is insufficient fabric to turn up, where the fabric is bulky or where the edge is too shaped to turn a good hem.

Use lining fabric, nylon jersey, fine cotton fabric or the fabric of the garment. Cut bias strips wide enough to contain the elastic or cord plus 1 cm. Join the strips if necessary. Press under one end of the casing.

Place casing strip right-side down on to the right side of the garment taking the correct seam allowance on the garment but only 5 mm on the casing. Machine with a straight stitch. At the end turn over the casing and stitch across it (fig 10.22).

Fig 10.22

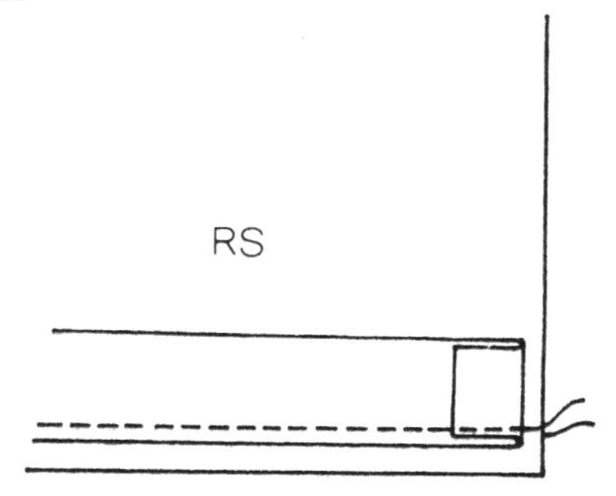

Slide the toe of the iron between the casing and the garment, pushing the casing over until it is right-side up and flat. Turn fabric wrong-side up and roll the casing over; press.

Machine near the edge using a straight, zig-zag or decorative stitch. Turn under the remaining raw edge of the casing and press. Insert pins across the casing to stop it from moving and machine on the fold using the same stitch as on the other edge. Remove the pins as you approach them (fig 10.23).

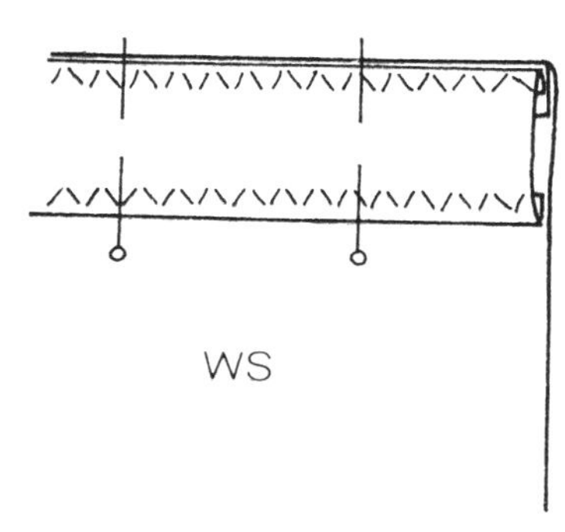

Fig 10.23

11 Facings

Facings are used to neaten shaped edges such as necklines and armholes, to provide a double layer of fabric where buttons and buttonholes are to be used, and also to make certain areas, such as revers, double sided.

Interfacing is often inserted between the facing and the garment so there is the added advantage that the facing covers the interfacing on the inside.

CUTTING THE FACING

The edge to be faced may be shaped, in which case the facing is cut with one edge corresponding in shape. In the case of necklines and armholes the pattern provided will usually be in two pieces. Save time by pinning the pieces together and cutting the facings in one piece as follows.

Necklines

Place the neckline facings together at the shoulder, overlapping the paper if seam allowances are allowed. Pin. Place the new pattern on to the fabric, folded double with the centre back edge on the fold. Cut out (fig 11.1).

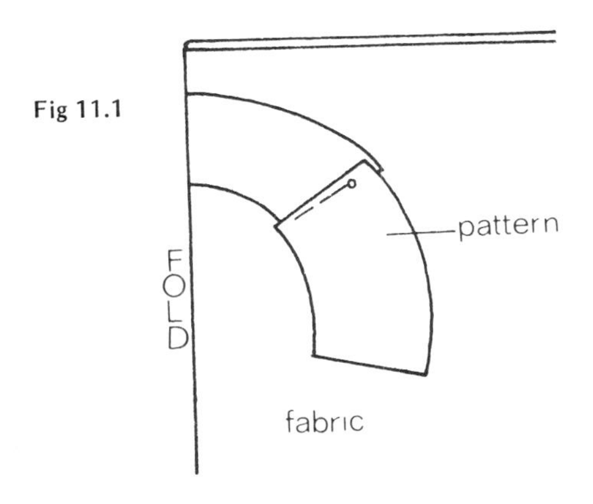

Fig 11.1

If the neckline is to be turned back at the front to form a rever it may look better if the centre front edge of the facing piece is placed on the straight grain to ensure that the grain or pattern matches the centre front of the garment. If you decide to do this, cut out allowing a seam allowance at the centre back and make a seam (fig 11.2).

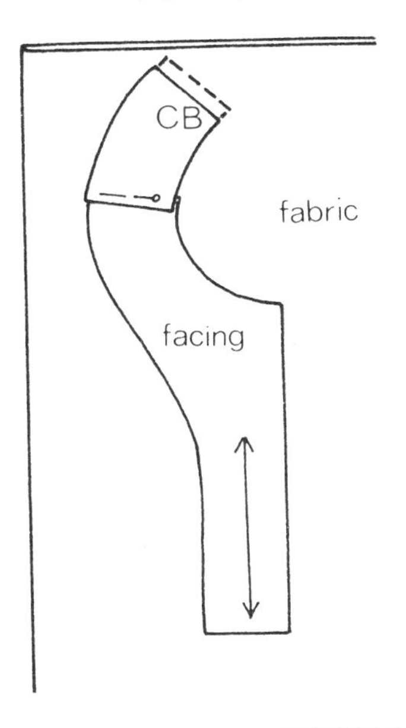

Fig 11.2

TIPS If you fold the fabric wrong-side out you can cut out and stitch the facing join accurately before removing the pattern. Do not neaten the raw edges of the join but do press them open and trim them to 5 mm.

Although cutting the facings by these methods means that the fabric grain does not correspond with the garment grain at every point, this will not affect the handling or wear of the garment. After all, if the fabric is soft or liable to 'give' you will be interfacing it anyway to hold it in place.

Buttoned edge

If the edge to be faced is straight you can save time by cutting it so that it is part of the garment and is simply folded back into position. If the edge is slightly shaped it is usually possible to straighten it without spoiling the design. To do this pin the pattern to paper or light Vilene and draw a straight line, using a felt pen and ruler, joining the two extreme corners of the pattern. This new line will be the fold-over line. Trim off any surplus paper beyond this line.

If the pattern edge is already straight, begin by cutting off the seam allowance if it is there, then pin to paper. Fold back the seam allowance, if there is one, on the facing pattern and pin it to the paper with its long edge against the edge of the piece already in position. Pin.

If the edge is shaped, still fold the paper to a straight edge, drawing a line first if you need it.

Cut out round the outside of this new shape to produce the pattern with fold-back facing. Leave the paper pieces in position to provide the markings, fold line, centre front that you will be transferring to the fabric (fig 11.3).

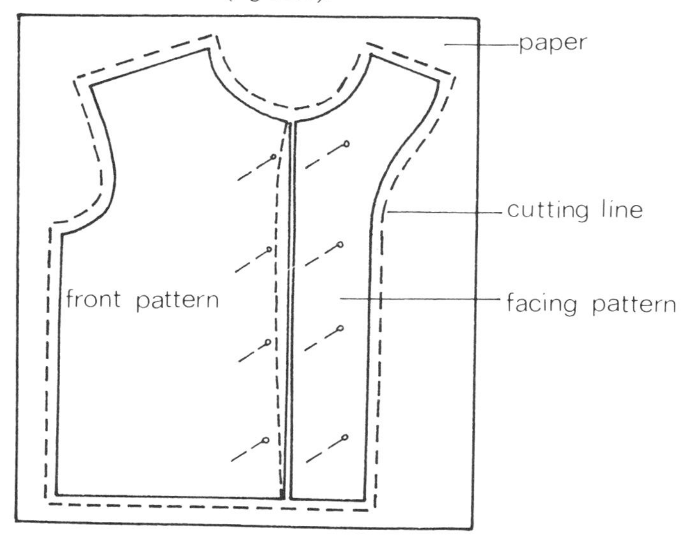

Fig 11.3

Armholes

If the garment is sleeveless place the two armhole-facing pattern pieces together at the shoulder, overlapping the paper if seam allowances have been provided. Fold the fabric and pin down this new one-piece facing. Arrange it so that the straight grain runs along the part that will face the armhole across the shoulder. Cut out (fig 11.4).

Fig 11.4

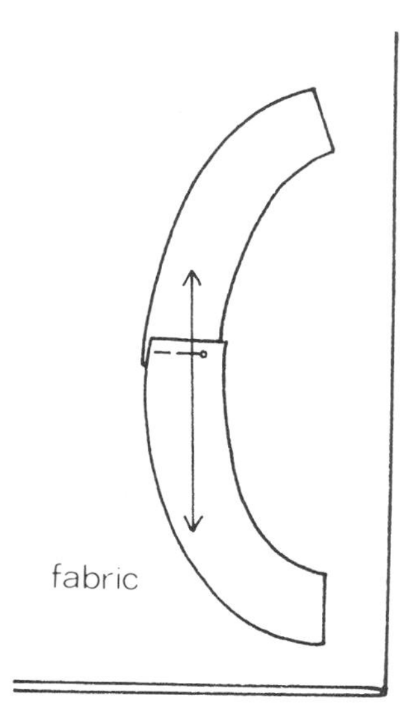

Neck and armholes all-in-one

If the pattern provides separate neck and armhole pieces save time by using instead one facing to cover both areas.

Begin by pinning the neck-facing pattern on top of the dress pattern. Do this with the front and the back, matching the edges. Pin this assembly to paper or light Vilene. Outline the edge with felt pen following the neckline and any part of the centre front or centre back edge that is covered by the original facing. Outline the entire shoulder edge, the armhole edge and 10-12 cm of the side seam (fig 11.5).

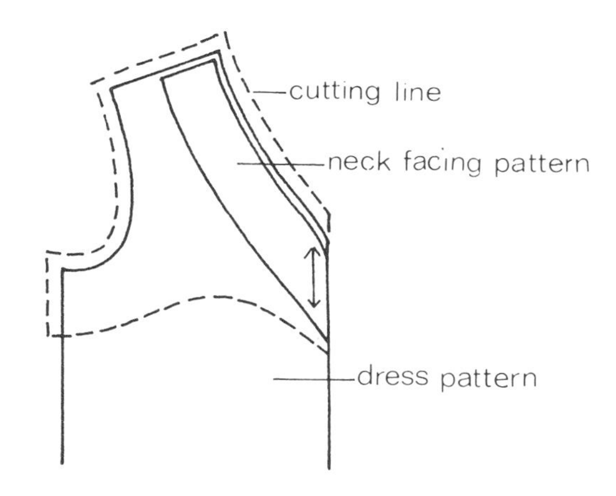

Fig 11.5

Remove the original pattern and draw a gently curving line across the new pattern from the side seam to join the base of the line you have drawn at the centre front. Mark the straight grain position parallel with the centre front edge and the centre back edge.

Place the pattern pieces on folded fabric with the centre front and centre back to the fold unless there is to be an opening in the garment. Cut out.

TIPS Improve a plain round neckline by adding a lace collar. These can be bought in packs in a variety of designs. Place collar in position on right side of garment and tack. Place the facing right-side down on top and stitch round the neckline.

Decorate a plain fabric by cutting the facings in print and attaching them to the wrong side of the garment, folding them to the right side to stitch down.

You can often improve an edge and make it easier to handle by cutting the facing wider than the pattern, but do not cut facings narrower than 10 cm plus a seam allowance, and 5 mm for neatening the outer edge.

Interfacing

Support faced necklines and buttoned openings with interfacing and also those that fold back or are liable to be worn undone, for example zipped at centre front. Do not interface armholes, although a shoulder may be interfaced, see *Interfacing*, chapter 12. Also see that chapter for information on choice of interfacing and methods of attaching.

After cutting out the facings remove the pattern, cut 1 cm from the outer edge of the pattern and pin the remainder to folded interfacing. Cut out. This ensures that the facing will cover the interfacing.

Attach the interfacing pieces to the wrong side of the garment. Stitch garment seams and press. If you are turning the facings to the right side of the garment for decoration attach the interfacing to the right side but stitch the seams in the usual way (fig 11.6).

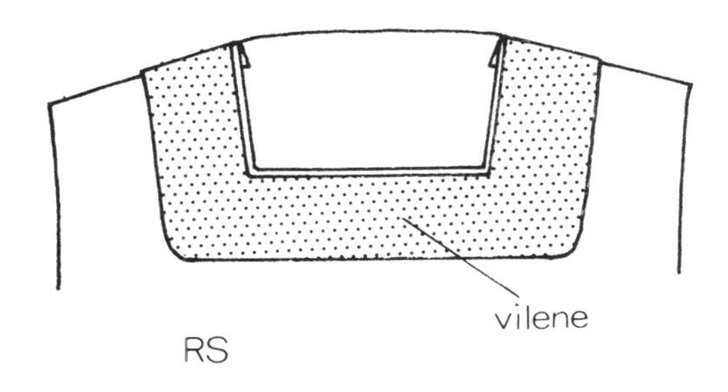

Fig 11.6

Do not interface an area that is to be gathered. If necessary trim down the facing pattern by more than 5 mm to make it sufficiently narrow to pass beside gathers. If the front neckline is entirely gathered, interface the back neck only.

PREPARING THE FACING

Make the joins. Place the fabric right-sides together and insert one pin some distance from the edge. Machine, remove pin, press open. Trim the raw edges down to 3 mm. Press again.

Neaten the entire outer edge, that is, any cut edge of facing that will not be joined to the garment. Either zig-zag over the edge or if the fabric is fine, place it under the machine right-side up and turning under the raw edge by the smallest possible amount, edge stitch with a straight or small zig-zag stitch. Press the stitching (fig 11.7).

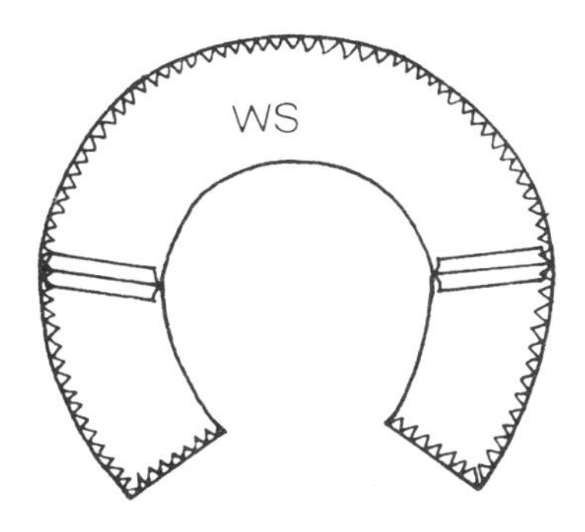

Fig 11.7

TIPS On a soft or stretchy fabric, prevent fluting by working a row of straight stitching first 3 mm inside the raw edge. You then have a firm line on which to turn the edge to stitch again.

Mark the centre front and back of a neckline on the garment and the facing. There may be a seam at that point, in which case that will suffice but if not, fold both evenly, and quickly crease the fabric with the iron for a distance of about 2 cm down from the neck edge.

ATTACHING THE FACING

Arrange the neck edge on the table right-side up. Place the facing right-side down on top with centre backs matching. Insert one pin near the raw edges at right angles to the edge.

Put one hand under the garment and lift the neckline off the table, bring the ends of the facing round to the centre front (or it may be the back) and pin to the garment (fig 11.8).

Fig 11.8

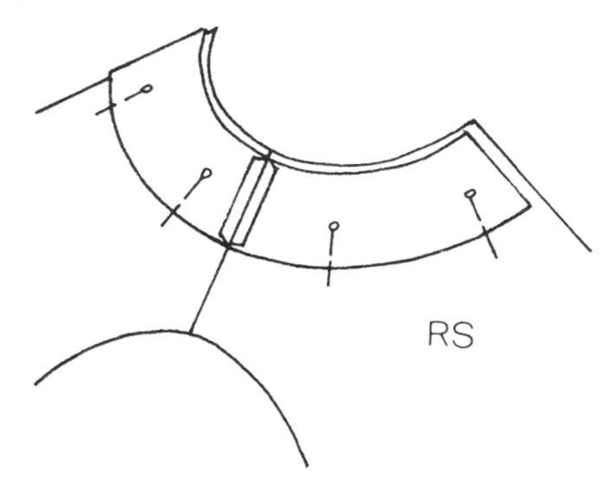

Holding the neckline in this position and keeping the raw edges together, insert pins at an angle, well away from the raw edge.

Put the neckline under the machine, and stitch for 2 cm across the centre back, 5 mm in from the edge. Remove the pin just as you lower the foot. Move round to the front and work a short row of stitches at the centre front. This anchors the facing at the vital points (fig 11.9).

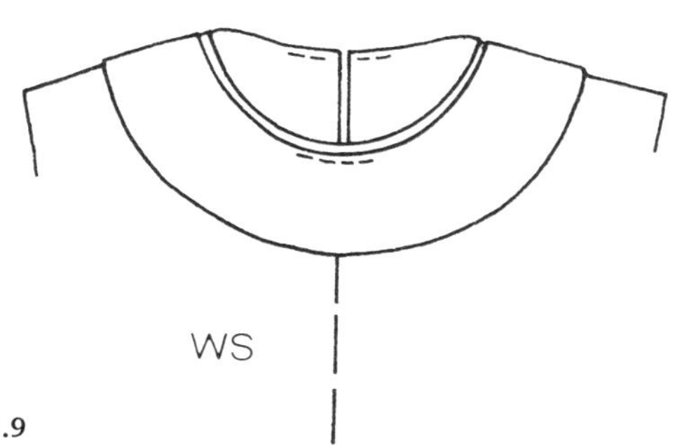

Fig 11.9

Turn the work over so that you have the garment uppermost and stitch by machine right round the neck on the marked seam line or taking 1.5 cm seam allowance.

Remove all pins. Press the stitching flat and then push the toe of the iron under the facing but on top of the garment, and run it round the neck as far as you can. Push the iron forward slightly to turn the facing over so that it is right-side up (fig 11.10).

If you had to turn any corners you will not be able to insert the iron but press up to it on both sides.

Using small scissors, make snips through the raw edges and also the interfacing every 5 mm round all curves. Snip to within a thread of the stitching (fig 11.11).

Fig 11.10

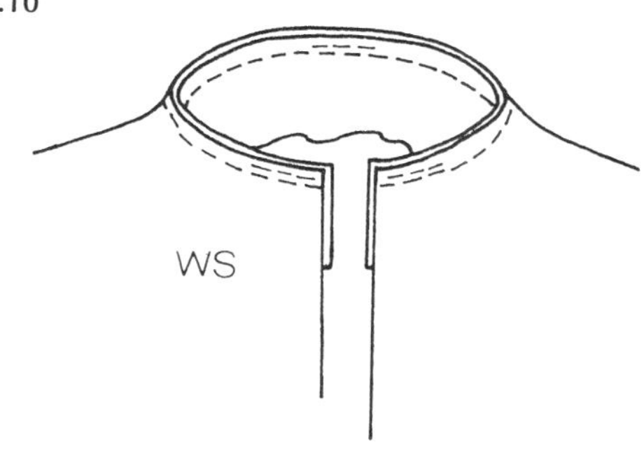

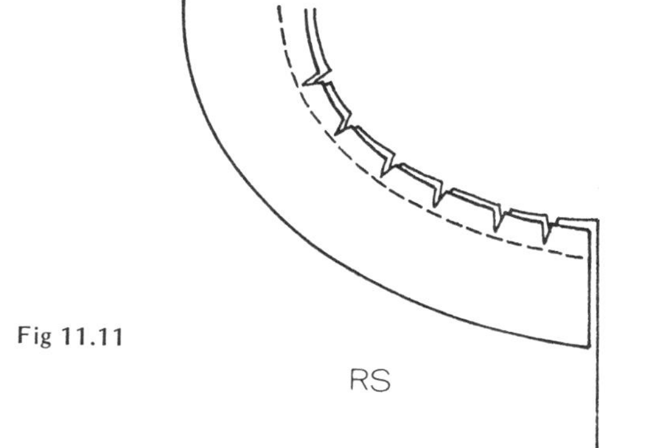

Fig 11.11

> **TIP** Angle the snips and you are unlikely to cut through the machine stitching — cutting straight up to a line is dangerous and difficult to control, but if the blades are angled they tend to rest beside the stitching.

Using medium-sized scissors, trim the snipped turnings down to 3 mm and then cut the facing edge down a little further if the fabric is anything but very light weight. At corners cut the surplus away completely, cutting across the corner and then snipping back even further.

FINISHING THE FACING

Hold the garment with the right side towards you, roll the facing over out of sight, hold the edge and roll so that the join is quite exposed, and tack 3 mm from the edge. Press the edge. Turn the garment over so that the facing is uppermost, slip short pieces of Wundaweb between the facing and the garment at intervals of about 5 cm and press well with a hot iron and a damp cloth (fig 11.12).

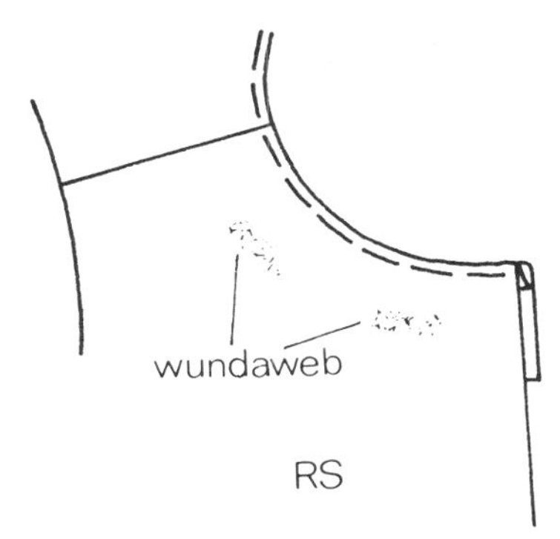

Fig 11.12

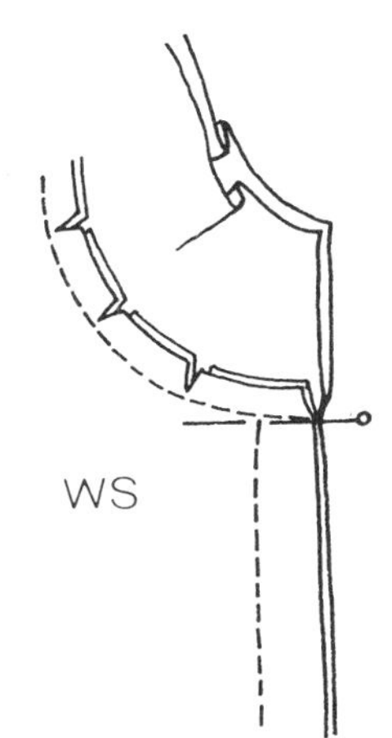

Fig 11.13

TIPS When stitching corners, stop and work one machine stitch across the corner. This makes it easier to turn out than a sharp right angle.

Put a small folded piece of Wundaweb on the end of your left thumb when turning corners through. Push your thumb into the corner, roll the facing over and pull the garment right side out. When pressed, the Wundaweb will melt, prevent fraying and slightly stiffen the corner.

When inserting the Wundaweb to hold the finished facing in position, put the first pieces at the centre front and centre back, press to avoid buckling and then place two or three more pieces between these.

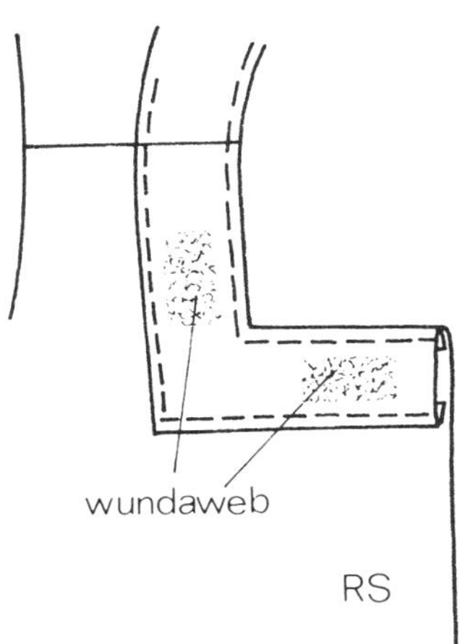

Fig 11.14

Armhole facing

Neaten the facing edge but do not join the ends. Stitch and press garment shoulder seams only. Attach the armhole facing and snip and trim the turnings. Fold the garment right-sides together, matching the side seams and insert one pin across this seam exactly on the facing and armhole join. Stitch the seam from armhole to hem. Remove the pin, turn the garment over and complete the stitching across the facing. Press open the seam. Trim the turnings within the facing to 3 mm and neaten the seam (fig 11.13).

TIP If you find it difficult to establish the angle at which to machine across the facing in order to ensure that it lies flat when turned down inside the garment, press open and neaten the remainder of the seam, roll the armhole facing to the wrong side and tack and press the edge, at the same time pressing the two ends of facing. The folds of facing should meet. Finish by slip stitching by hand.

Decorative facing

Do not neaten the outer edge of the facing. Attach to the wrong side, trim, snip, roll tack and press the edge. Set your adjustable marker to the width at which you wish to finish the facing, hold it in your left hand and turn under the raw edge of the facing level with the marker. Tack the edge as you fold. Press the edge. While at the ironing surface, slip pieces of Wundaweb under the facing and press (fig 11.14).

Finish by working a machine stitch, straight, zig-zag or embroidery.

TIP If the facing has a shaped or decorative outer edge, do not cut it to shape when cutting out. Cut a straight outer edge but mark with tailor tacks or carbon paper the shaped outer edge. After attaching the facing, turn in and tack on this marked line, snipping away the surplus fabric as you go.

Combined neck and armhole facing

Place the back and front facings with right sides together and join the shoulder and under-arm seams. Press open and trim the edges down to 3 mm. Arrange the facing round the neck of the garment, pinning and stitching as described previously and trimming and tacking the edge too. The facing is now completely on the wrong side of the garment (fig 11.15).

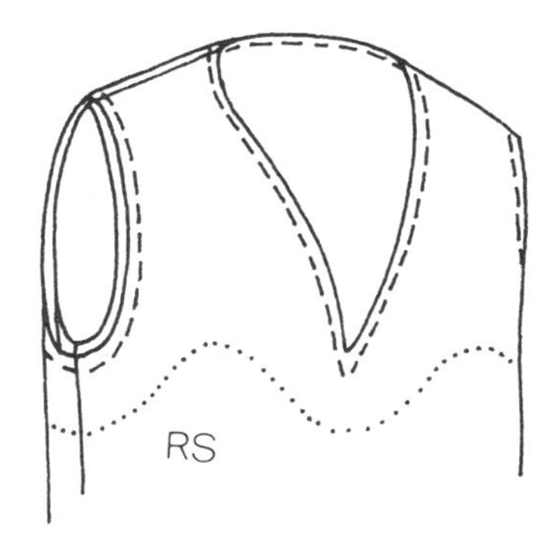

Fig 11.15

With the right side of the garment outwards, turn in the armhole edge and tack close to the fold. The edge will spring up again, so snip it almost to the fold. Trim the raw edge down to 5 mm and press the folded edge.

Still with the right side outwards spread the facing out underneath until it is in the correct position, armhole edges matching. Insert pins, at an angle, round the armhole, well within the edge. Turn the garment wrong side out, insert pieces of Wundaweb between the facing and the garment. Start by putting one piece at the shoulder area and another at the under-arm then space two more on each side between these two. The Wundaweb should not be too close to the armhole edge (fig 11.16).

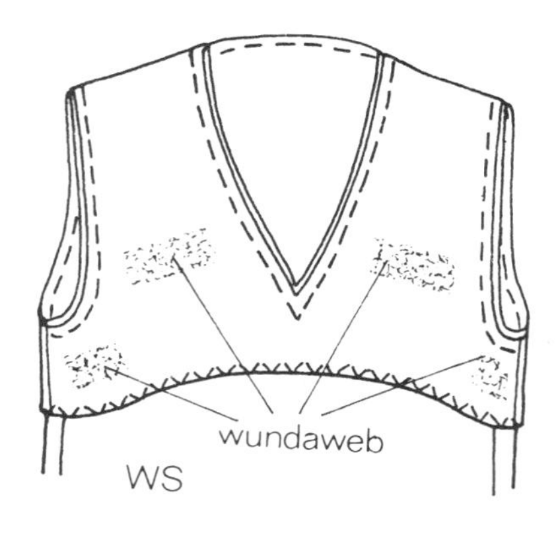

Fig 11.16

Trim the facing edge until it extends beyond the garment edge by only 3 mm. Snip this edge every 1 cm.

With the facing side towards you, turn in this raw edge and tack it to the garment with the edge 1 mm back from the armhole. Press.

Finish by slip-stitching round the armhole, or by machining. Use edge stitching, a zig-zag stitch or a decorative stitch (fig 11.17).

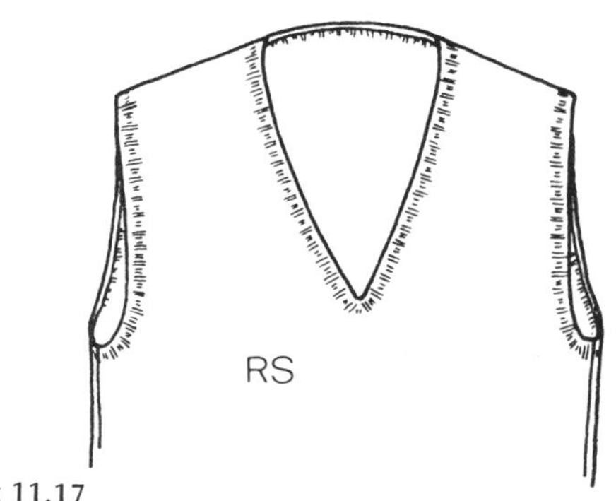

Fig 11.17

12 Interfacing

WHAT, WHY AND WHERE?

The answer to why is that interfacing adds crispness and form to those parts of the garment where it is applied. This not only strengthens those areas but also ensures that the garment continues to look good while worn.

What to use for interfacing depends on the fabric and style of the garment. Some places may need heavy reinforcement, e.g. waistbands and shirt collars, while some may only require the lightness of adhesive web to provide extra body.

Where to interface? The following list is a general guide but of course you wouldn't always interface all these areas. You must select the interfacing for the area according to the particular fabric and style. Any part that will be handled in wear must be interfaced, plus any style features.

1 All collars	Stand collars — firm Roll collars — soft or medium
2 Cuffs	Wide cuffs — firm Narrow bands — medium
3 Dress yokes	Soft
4 Skirt or trouser yokes	Soft
5 Waistbands	Very firm or medium
6 Belts	Very firm, medium or soft
7 Neckbands	Soft or medium
8 Strap neckline openings	Soft or medium
9 Patch and seam pockets	Soft
10 Pocket welts and flaps	Medium or firm
11 Necklines and shoulders — no collars	Soft
12 Piped buttonholes	Soft
13 Fastening areas	Soft or medium
14 Weak points — slits, etc.	Soft
15 Hems	Soft
16 Pleats	Soft

TYPES OF INTERFACING

There are soft, medium and firm interfacings that can be sewn in and a similar choice of the type that is ironed in place. These are sold by the metre about 82 cm wide or in pre-packs containing one piece. Both types have to be cut to shape.

There are packs of a pre-cut strip, one is soft and iron-on, the other an adhesive web. There is also an adhesive web with paper backing (torn away after pressing in place) in packets containing a sheet which you cut to shape. There is a wide variety of belt stiffenings and petershams of varying widths, some in pre-packs, some sold by the metre. These are referred to in detail in the section on waist finishes.

All the iron-on and adhesive interfacings are quick to use because sewing is eliminated, but be sure you are using ones that are suitable for your fabric. Try out a small piece on a scrap of fabric if in doubt.

Vilene is the most widely available interfacing in the biggest range. There is something suitable for every fabric and every process. The chart on the following page is the entire range at present and I have indicated which will produce the results listed as desirable in the chart on this page.

HOW TO INTERFACE

Attach the interfacing to the garment piece itself on the wrong side of the fabric. Never interface a facing: it makes it stand away from the garment; it becomes too important compared with the garment; it does nothing to support the garment; it does not reinforce the piece of fabric taking the strain of wear because facings take no strain. Attaching interfacing to the facing is a technique employed in making ready-to-wear clothes because it is quicker and requires little accuracy, but it is not a technique that we should copy. Many people complain that neck and armhole facings, and front facings of a ready-made blouse, dress, etc., pop out, and this is solely because they are interfaced.

The principle is the same for collars and cuffs: it is the piece which is part of the garment that is interfaced, i.e. the outer cuff (or the whole cuff), the

Types of interfacing

Vilene	*Area*	*Which fabrics*	*Result*
Softline	Collars, cuffs, yokes, tie belts, neckbands, patch and seam pockets, neck and shoulder fastening areas	Medium and light, including velveteen, wools, silk, cotton	Soft
Transparent	Collars, cuffs, openings	Fine, including silks, voile, georgette	Soft
Superdrape	Collars, cuffs, pocket flaps, openings, shoulders, yokes	Medium, including all jersey and soft fabrics with 'give'	Slightly crisp but fine
Soft iron-on	Collars, cuffs	Firm, including cotton woven synthetic	Medium
Firm iron-on	Belts, waistbands, pocket flaps	Firm	Very crisp
Fold-a-Band	Pleats, hems, turn-back cuffs, openings, straps, cuffs, bands, waistbands, belts, welts	All except very fine and pile fabrics	Medium
Wundaweb	Hems, openings, fraying areas, buttonholes	All except very fine or transparent and pile fabrics	Slightly crisp but fine
Bondaweb	Buttonhole pipings, openings, appliqué, fraying areas	All except pile fabrics	Soft
Light sew-in	Collars, cuffs, openings, yokes	All fine and medium	Soft
Soft sew-in	Stand collars, bands, cuffs, pocket flaps	Medium and heavy	Medium but firm
Medium sew-in	Stand collars, bands, cuffs, pocket flaps, openings	Fine and medium	Crisp but fine
Heavy sew-in	Belts, waistbands	Any	Very firm

under collar, the piece attached to the neckline that is outermost when the collar is standing up and not folded into a style. The exceptions are when using Fold-a-Band and Wundaweb. They are strips and are therefore attached equally to garment and facing.

Interfacing is a very important step in construction and one not to be skimped. The quickest way to do it is to use iron-on methods.

If the result is unsatisfactory it means you have used the wrong weight of interfacing; the most common fault is using one that is too stiff for the fabric. Choose the one that is most like your fabric then it will be easy to handle. Problems nearly always occur if you have an area that is far stiffer than the remainder of the garment. The secret of successful interfacing is that it should be impossible to detect it by looking at the outside of the finished garment.

Iron-on interfacing

Attach before beginning to construct the garment.

Fold a sheet of dressmaker's carbon paper with the right side out and slip it between the layers of a folded piece of Vilene (fold it with shiny or adhesive side outside).

If the interfacing shape is to correspond with a pattern shape such as cuff, collar, pocket, yoke or front edge, place the pattern on the Vilene, using the fold if the pattern requires it.

Using a tracing wheel mark round the outer edges of the pattern. Where you are cutting interfacing for a buttoned opening, mark the neck and part of the shoulder, run the wheel down the centre front line but mark the cutting edge 1-2 cm beyond this. At the outer edge mark a cutting line on the Vilene 2 cm narrower than the garment facing. This ensures that the Vilene extends beyond the centre front line and folds back making a better edge to the garment, and it ensures that the interfacing will be covered by the facing on the inside.

Remove the paper pattern and cut the Vilene. On outside edges cut 2-3 mm within the dotted line. This ensures that the Vilene is smaller than the fabric piece and so the adhesive will not stick to the ironing surface.

Place all fabric to be interfaced with wrong side up, place Vilene pieces with the adhesive side down and insert a pin towards one side of the piece. Carry to the pressing board, press up to the pin, remove the pin, press the other half in position (fig 12.1).

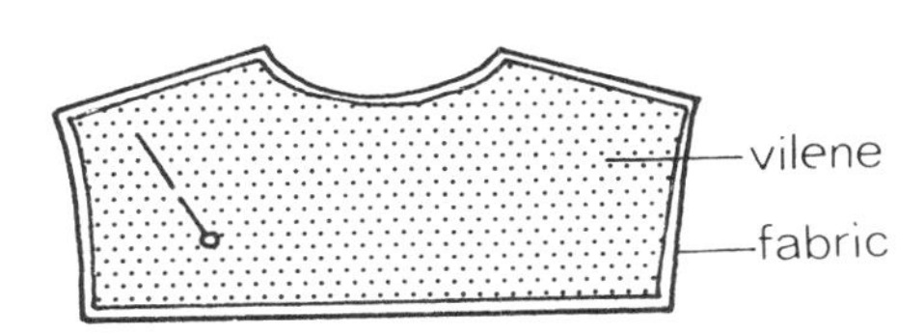

Fig 12.1

Hold the iron in position for a couple of seconds before moving it. Press all parts several times with a steady plonking movement. Do not slide the iron. Use a damp cloth when attaching Softline. Allow the pieces to cool.

Strip interfacing

Mainly used during construction or to complete a process.

When using Wundaweb press a fold, or tack and press, cut a piece of Wundaweb slightly longer than needed and place it carefully between the layers of fabric.

Make sure the edge goes right to the tacking or into the folded edge; if it has to reach into a corner tuck it well in, folding the surplus Wundaweb over. When using several strips, cut to length, cutting lengthways too if necessary, put all pieces in position and smooth out the top fabric. When putting Wundaweb into a small unbroken hem such as trousers or sleeves, insert the whole length of Wundaweb and pull the fabric of the hem, tugging it to make it lie flat. This prevents the fabric from wrinkling (fig 12.2).

Fig 12.2

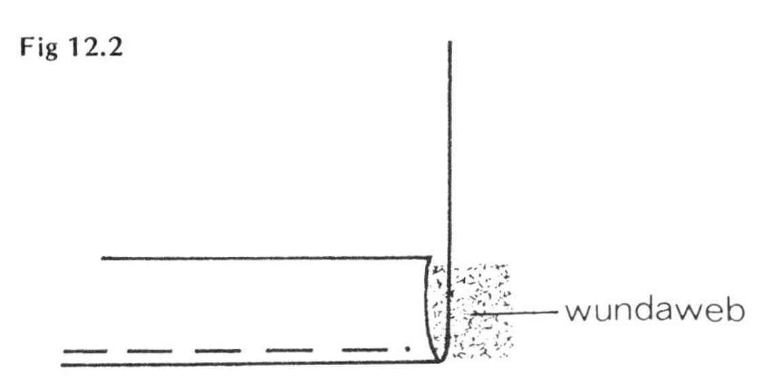

Use a damp cloth and a hot iron, press with steady plonking movements and press three or four times on each area. Make sure the adhesive web has thoroughly melted. It helps when pressing a large area to go along it a second time after allowing a few moments to cool; it is then easier to detect the unstuck areas.

Do not attempt to hurry, or you will have to do it again. When you think you have pressed sufficiently, turn the garment right-side up and press again, but lightly.

To use Fold-a-Band, press a crease in the fabric if there is to be a fold, e.g. pleat, slit, turn-back cuff, pocket top.

When using it at the start of a process, e.g. cuff or waistband, it is easiest to cut it to size and place it on the wrong side of a piece of fabric, matching the perforations to the straight grain, press in position and then cut out the fabric using the edge of the Fold-a-Band as a guide but adding seam allowances (fig 12.3).

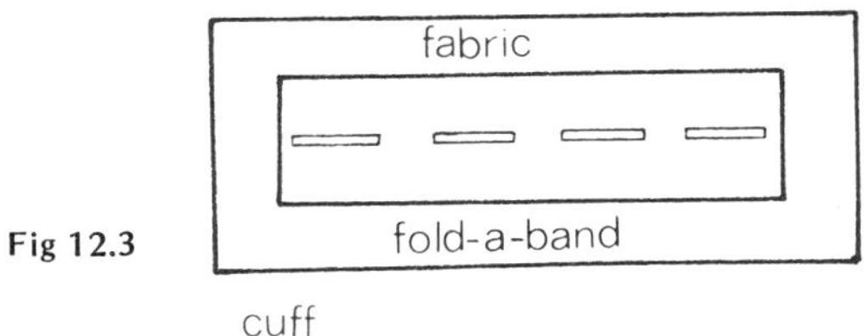

Fig 12.3

If using it to make an opening such as centre front or neck slit make sure there is a straight line marked on the wrong side of the fabric as a guide. Use tailor's chalk and a ruler or carbon paper.

Place the Fold-a-Band with the adhesive side down to the wrong side of the fabric, aligning the oblong perforations with the crease or marked line. Use a medium-hot iron. Press one side of the interfacing in position, then the second side.

If the full width is not needed press the first side in position then trim down the second side before pressing that too.

To use Bondaweb cut to size and shape and press in position on the wrong side of the fabric. Use a medium-hot iron and damp cloth. Press well with a firm plonking movement until the paper appears mottled. Remove the cloth and allow the fabric to cool: leave it for at least 10 minutes. Lift one corner of the paper and peel it off. Continue sewing, complete buttonholes, opening, etc., then when the Bondaweb has been covered with fabric, press again and it will stick.

Sew-in interfacing

Cut in the same way as for iron-on pieces but it is not necessary to reduce the size of the pieces.

Arrange all fabric pieces to be interfaced with wrong side up. Place interfacing on top and attach to fabric with basting. Start with a knot, make the stitches about 3 cm long. There is no need to fasten off the thread ends (fig 12.4).

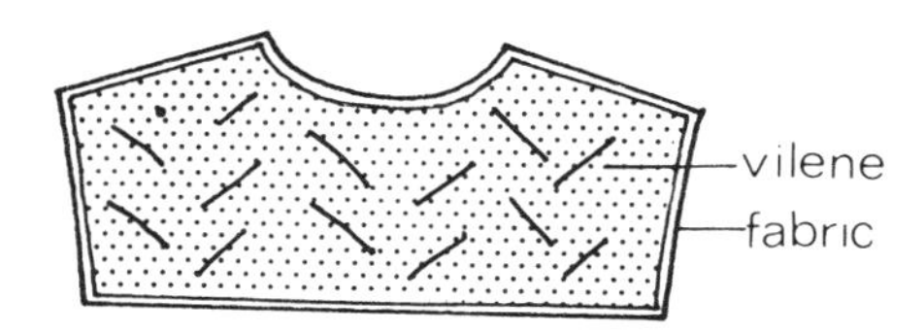

Fig 12.4

Work on the garment and on completion remove the basting stitches.

If the interfacing is very heavy, as on waistbands, it should be cut to size excluding turnings, and the edge attached to the seam allowance of the fabric using herringbone stitch or a machine stitch, or even a strip of Wundaweb.

TIPS Where there is a dart, interface the area, stitch the dart then cut away the interfacing close to the stitching before pressing the dart. If the fabric is bulky, split the entire dart including the fabric, trim away the interfacing and press the dart open (fig 12.5).

Where interfacing extends to a gathered area, shape the interfacing to avoid the gathering, reducing its width to as little as 2-3 cm if necessary (fig 12.6).

If a complete area is to be tucked, e.g. yoke, interface first with the lightest weight iron-on interfacing.

Fig 12.5

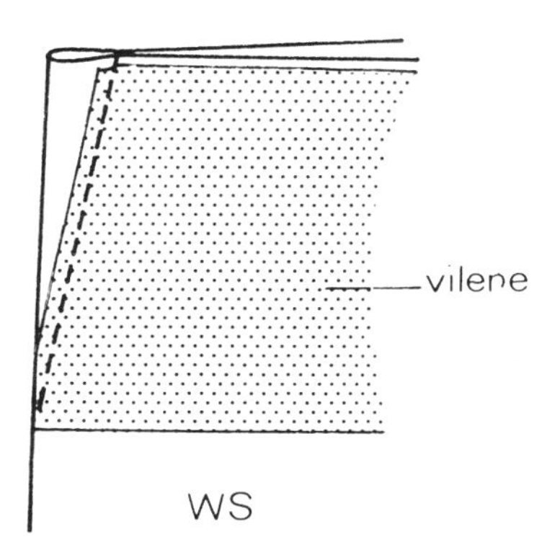

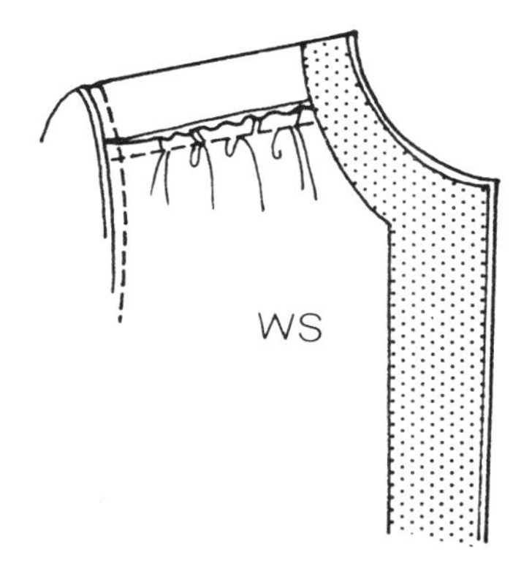

Fig 12.6

GENERAL RULES

When interfacing large areas or those to be folded, e.g. roll or fold collars, openings, yokes, patch pockets, use soft or light interfacing.

When interfacing small, flat unfolded sections, e.g. stand collars, cuffs, bands, pocket flaps, straps, belts, waistbands, use firmer interfacing if a stiffer result if wanted.

In edges such as pleats, hems, slit openings and for reinforcing weak points, use adhesive such as Wundaweb or Bondaweb, and for an accurate straight line or fold use Fold-a-Band.

When stitching matching corners or curves mark the pairs of stitching lines with pencil dots for accuracy.

13 Appliqué

Attach the motif as early as possible in construction while the fabric is still flat. If its position has to be carefully decided then partly make up the garment and add the appliqué before side seams are completed.

Decide on the design. Keep the outline as simple as possible with very few additional rows of stitching that will require careful finishing of threads at the end. Most outlines can be simplified, even initials. Trace the motif shown here, or draw your own design on soft sew-in Vilene and cut out. Pin this to the garment and adjust it until it looks right. Unpin the Vilene but mark its position on the garment with a chalk cross (figs 13.1 and 13.2).

Decide on the fabric for the motif. It does not have to contain the same fibres but it should be washable and of a colour that will not run. The piece can easily be washed before use to test this and to pre-shrink it. Remember that contrasting textures are particularly attractive, for example satin on towelling, and so are contrasting prints and colours.

Decide on the thread colour. This can match either of the fabrics or you can introduce a new colour. Use Anchor Machine Embroidery No. 30 or 50, or, for a heavier result, use normal sewing thread such as Drima.

Set the machine to satin stitch. Stitch length: ¾.

Fig 13.1

Fig 13.2

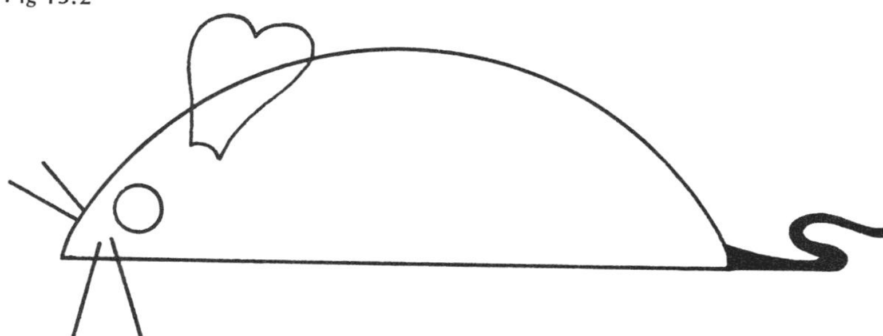

Zig-zag: 1½. Attach the satin stitch foot.

Pin the Vilene template to the fabric and mark round it with a dotted pencil line. Trim away some of the surplus fabric but leave at least 2 cm extending beyond the pencil line. Place the fabric on the right side of the garment. Slip a piece of Wundaweb between the two and press until it adheres.

Put paper underneath and work satin stitch round the design following the line. Try to start and finish at a point convenient for fastening off or for moving on to the next part of the design. If the design has two sections that will partly overlap, work on the underneath one first but avoid a ridge by satin stitching only round that part that will not be covered by the upper part (fig 13.3).

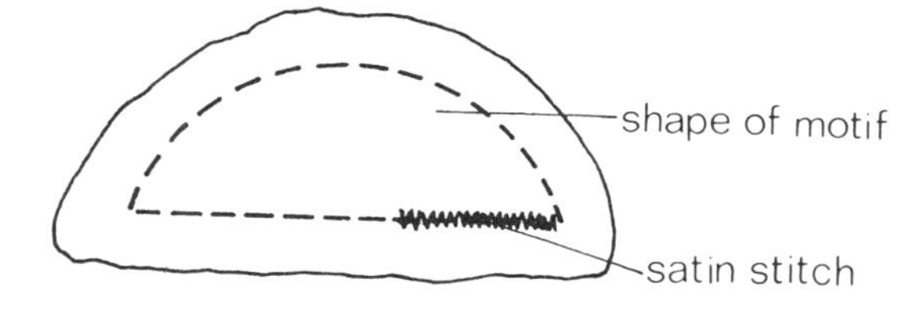

Fig 13.3

Remove the garment from the machine. Tear off the paper. Trim the thread ends and carefully trim away the excess fabric close to the satin stitch. Adjust the stitch to work a zig-zag width of 2, still keeping to a stitch length of ¾. Work round the motif again, stitching exactly over the first row. The slightly wider stitch will cover the first stitching. Remember to put a fresh piece of paper underneath (fig 13.4).

Fig 13.4

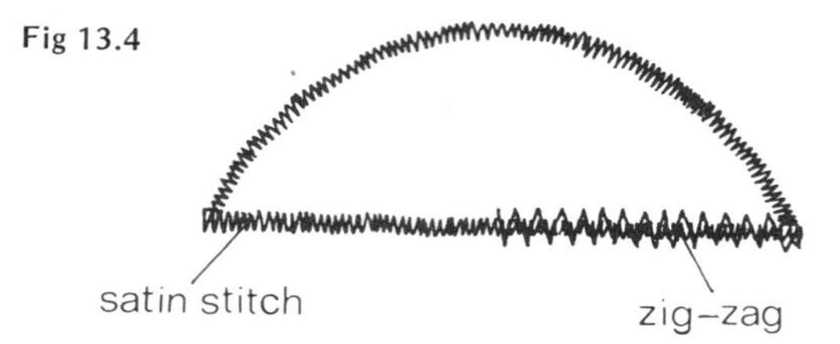

TIP Slip a thin piece of polyester wadding, ½ cm smaller all round than the design, underneath the fabric. Use two pieces of Wundaweb to keep it in position. The resulting appliqué will be slightly padded.

14 Equipment

BASIC TOOLS

You have probably already got at least some of these basic items of equipment, but if you are buying new ones, note the special points to help you choose.

Pins The long ones with coloured plastic heads are easy to pick up and clearly visible.

Tape measure The types marked off in 10 cm sections of different colours are quick to read.

Needles Have packets of Betweens in assorted sizes.

Tailor's chalk Wax squares are less likely to break. Keep edges sharpened.

Adjustable marker (A short metal rule with movable red arrow.) An invaluable tool, much quicker to use than a tape.

Chalk pencil (A white pencil with a brush on the end.) Useful for marking points on fabric.

Pin-holder The magnetic tube holder is spill-proof. It has a piece of Velcro attached and can be used on the wrist or fixed to a surface.

Beeswax One cake will last for years. Essential for waxing thread when sewing on buttons, useful for smoothing out double thread that snarls.

Bodkin (Now made in plastic.) Invaluable for speeding up the removal of tacking threads.

Rouleau turner (Long metal needle with a large eye at one end and a knot at the other.) The only way to turn thin tubing successfully but also useful for turning belts and ties.

Elastic threader (A short, flat metal needle with a large eye.) The most efficient way of threading elastic because it passes easily through casing and will bend to go round curves.

Hem marker The most accurate way of marking a level hemline on a skirt if you have someone on hand at the right moment to use it. The best ones have a heavy metal base and firm upright. The container holding the powdered chalk is moved to the level of what will be the bottom of the skirt. The marks should be made every 10 cm or so, with you moving gently round on one spot. You do not turn up the fabric for marking.

Thread snips (Small scissor-like blades for snapping threads, not fabric.) Very useful by your machine.

Tracing wheel (A spiked wheel with a handle.) The type with a long handle is more comfortable to use than the miniature one. When pushed along dressmaker's carbon paper it transfers pattern markings to fabric.

Use the paper in narrow strips folded double with the carbon side out, slip this between two layers of fabric — right side out — and run the wheel over the paper pattern. The most useful colour paper is orange as it is visible on most fabrics yet does not show through to the right

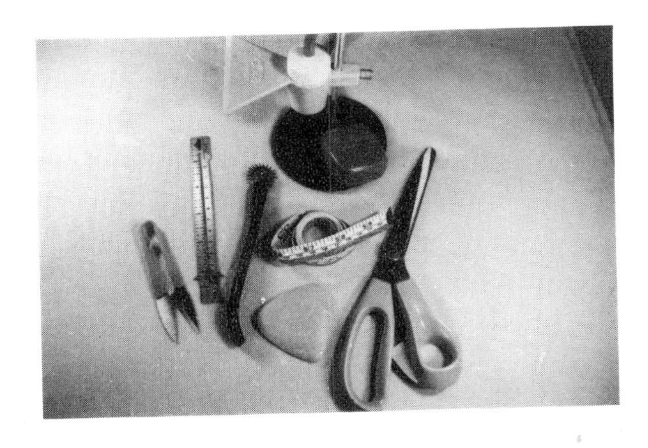

side as dark colours tend to do.

Never mark the right side of the fabric with carbon paper as it often proves impossible to get out.

Small and medium scissors It is always quicker to use the correct tool and it is easier to pick up and use the right size scissors for the job than struggle slowly with the wrong ones.

Cutting out shears Expensive but worth the saving in time and frustration to invest in a really big pair. They are faster and more accurate and much more comfortable to hold.

Thimble A thimble is vital. Trying to sew without one is slow and painful. Use one correctly and hand sewing becomes quick, even and pleasurable. The only type that is completely comfortable and goes unnoticed in wear, so you can keep it on all the time you are sewing, is a tailor's thimble.

OTHER ESSENTIALS

Apart from equipment that you keep ready for use, each time you make something you will buy fabric, thread and other items such as zips. But sewing is easier and much quicker if you have access to some other items that you can choose from and use if appropriate. It helps to build up stocks of these things.

Wundaweb Not only for hems: small pieces hold down facings, etc.

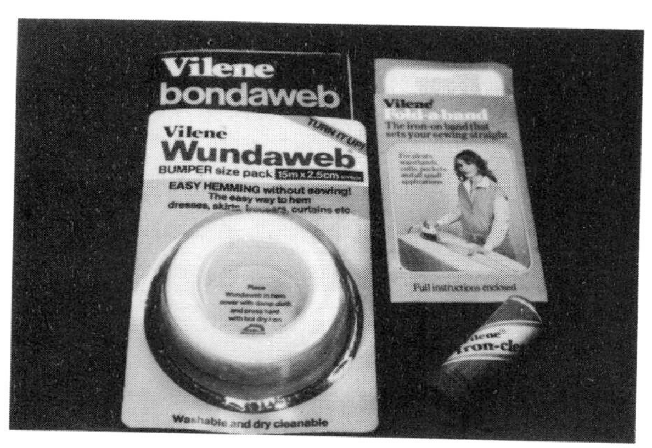

Bondaweb For quick application of motifs, etc., also in small areas to prevent fraying.

Velcro Cut to size and shape for fastenings in any position on any garment.

Elastic petersham Comfortable, useful as a waist stay. An aid to quick fitting.

Trouser clips Large clips for waistbands. Quicker to sew on than two small hooks.

Fold-a-Band Iron-on tape cut to an accurate width with centre marking. Saves hours of measuring in cuffs, bands, straps, belts.

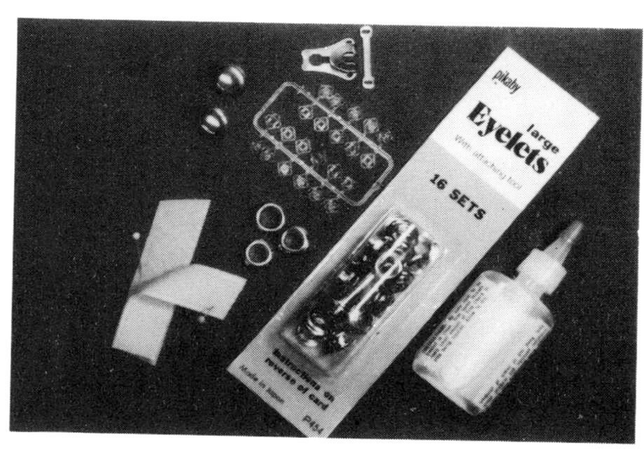

Trims Metal button moulds you cover with fabric. Special press studs are sewn under them.

Studs Metal-capped studs, decorative and quick to apply. Useful in all positions.

Shirring elastic Keep both black and white. Two or three rows of shirring are as effective as one piece of narrow elastic, but more decorative.

Iron-on binding In limited colours, but useful for decorative repairs.

Eyelets The quickest fastening — eyelets and a piece of cord.

Ribbons and narrow petersham ribbon Useful for skirt loops, as a stay in jersey seams and for decoration.

Plastic press studs Transparent, so they are practically invisible, but because they are square they are easy to hold while sewing on.

Fray-Check Keep handy to drop one spot on badly fraying fabrics while handling a process.

PART TWO
The designs

Introduction

The designs in this book have been carefully worked out so that they are quick to make, and as far as possible they avoid the time-consuming processes and activities such as buttonholes, collars and fitting. They have been arranged in order of simplicity — most people will find the early designs take less time to make than those towards the end.

THE PATTERNS

The pattern shapes have been simplified as much as possible without loss of style so that in some cases you can draw the outline with tailor's chalk directly on to the fabric. The measurements are indicated and there are instructions on altering the size if necessary. Although simple in shape, most of the designs are variable. They can all be shortened or lengthened, pockets can be added or omitted, ready-made decoration such as braid or piping can be added if you wish. Many people stick rigidly to a pattern, thinking it will be ruined if they don't. A few variations are suggested with each design. Try them. Try a few ideas of your own as well.

The advantage of diagram-patterns is that you can see all the pattern pieces and their relative shapes at once. It is a good way of learning construction and seeing the way pieces fit together, without having to rely on numbered points — it is obvious when looking at these small-scale diagrams which is the neckline, shoulder, armhole, side seam, etc.

A disadvantage of some diagram-patterns is that they take time to copy. Often they appear so mathematically confusing that the dressmaker doesn't know how or where to start and may well be exhausted before starting to actually sew.

To help to overcome this problem I have described how to draw each pattern, suggesting where to begin, describing the shape of a curve and so on. Also, where a pattern shape is symmetrical I suggest folding a piece of paper and then drawing half the pattern. When cut it becomes the entire piece. This is not only much more accurate, it is very quick.

The grid

It is possible to rule 5 cm squares on a large sheet of plain paper to make a grid, but it is extremely tedious and may not be entirely accurate. It is obviously much better to buy squared pattern paper or, the alternative is to use a cutting board. It has various markings, including 5 cm squares.

For drawing the actual patterns, pin pieces of Light Sew-In Vilene on top of the grid. You can easily see the lines and it keeps the squared paper unmarked. The Vilene makes a good durable pattern. You could, of course, use sheets of tissue or other plain paper as an alternative.

Copying the pattern

The following hints make the job much easier:

Cut the Vilene or paper to size before starting to draw the pattern. It helps when locating points measured in from the edge; the pieces are easier to handle; and you will feel more confident to be working within the confines of a specific area which you know is to be filled.

Use fine felt-tipped pens on Vilene but do not draw continuous lines — they fade and also wrinkle the Vilene. Use a dotted or dashed line even when drawing with a ruler.

Do not try to draw solid lines at curves — that is easy only for draughtsmen. Draw a dotted or dashed line in a sweeping curve.

Never worry about a slight wobble in any line, it is easily corrected when you cut out the pattern piece.

Never add extra 'just in case'. Look at the measurements given and check before you start. The easiest way to check a length measurement is to measure an existing garment. To adjust the patterns in this book, draw in the line as it is given and then draw another line representing the adjustment. If you are enlarging a pattern and the piece of Vilene or paper is not big enough make a note at the pattern edge to add when you are cutting out the fabric.

Use a ruler for straight lines. Even curves are easier to draw if there is a straight line there as a guide. If you haven't a long ruler use a piece of wood — a piece of dowel or thin batten.

Always draw the arrow representing the straight grain.

Always mark 'place to fold' where appropriate.

Always put 'cut two' etc., to remind you when cutting out.

Always write the size on each piece and after use fold up all the pattern pieces together, put a pin through them to hold, and on the outside draw a sketch of the garment — easier to identify than a description.

Caftan

A loose, ankle-length caftan to wear as a robe, holiday cover-up or casual evening dress. It has a slit neck, bound and tied, and two rows of vertical stitching to form side seams.

If the border fabric suggested is used there is only the hem to do in addition to the neck.

Very quick to make — one piece of fabric and takes as little as an hour.

Size: Fits any size up to 150 cm hip

Length: 120 cm from base of front neck slit to hem

Fabric: 3 m. 115 cm border print fabric. If narrow fabric is used buy 6 m of 90 cm fabric and join at the centre front and centre back making a piece of fabric 180 cm wide. After stitching the side seams, trim so that sleeve is correct length. 1 m binding or crossway fabric.

Haberdashery: 1 reel Drima
Wundaweb

The pattern: There is no need to make a pattern for this caftan; cut out in fabric.

Cutting out: Fold the fabric right-side out with the folded end and selvedges level. Insert a couple of pins at the centre of the fold and draw a chalk line at right angles to it 25 cm long. Make a small snip at the fold and cut the top layer of fabric only. The first 8 cm of the cut represents the back neck, the remainder is the front neck (fig 1).

From the slit, measure 37 cm out towards the selvedges on each side. Draw a vertical chalk line from there to the raw edges of the fabric. Mark off a point 30 cm from the fold down each line. At the hem measure up 40 cm on each line and mark a point.

Making up: Insert a few pins diagonally across the chalk lines. Stitch on the chalk fastening off the thread at the start and finish of each row. The space between the stitching and the fold forms the armhole. Bind the neck slit, making the join at the 8 cm point so that it does not show. To add ties cut the remainder of the binding in two, stitch, neaten one end of each piece and either insert the raw ends under the neck binding before stitching, or fold under and hem to the wrong side after completing the binding (fig 2).

Turn up the hem at the back and front of the caftan, securing with Wundaweb.

Variations: Trim away the four corners at the hem and turn a narrow machined hem on the back and the front.

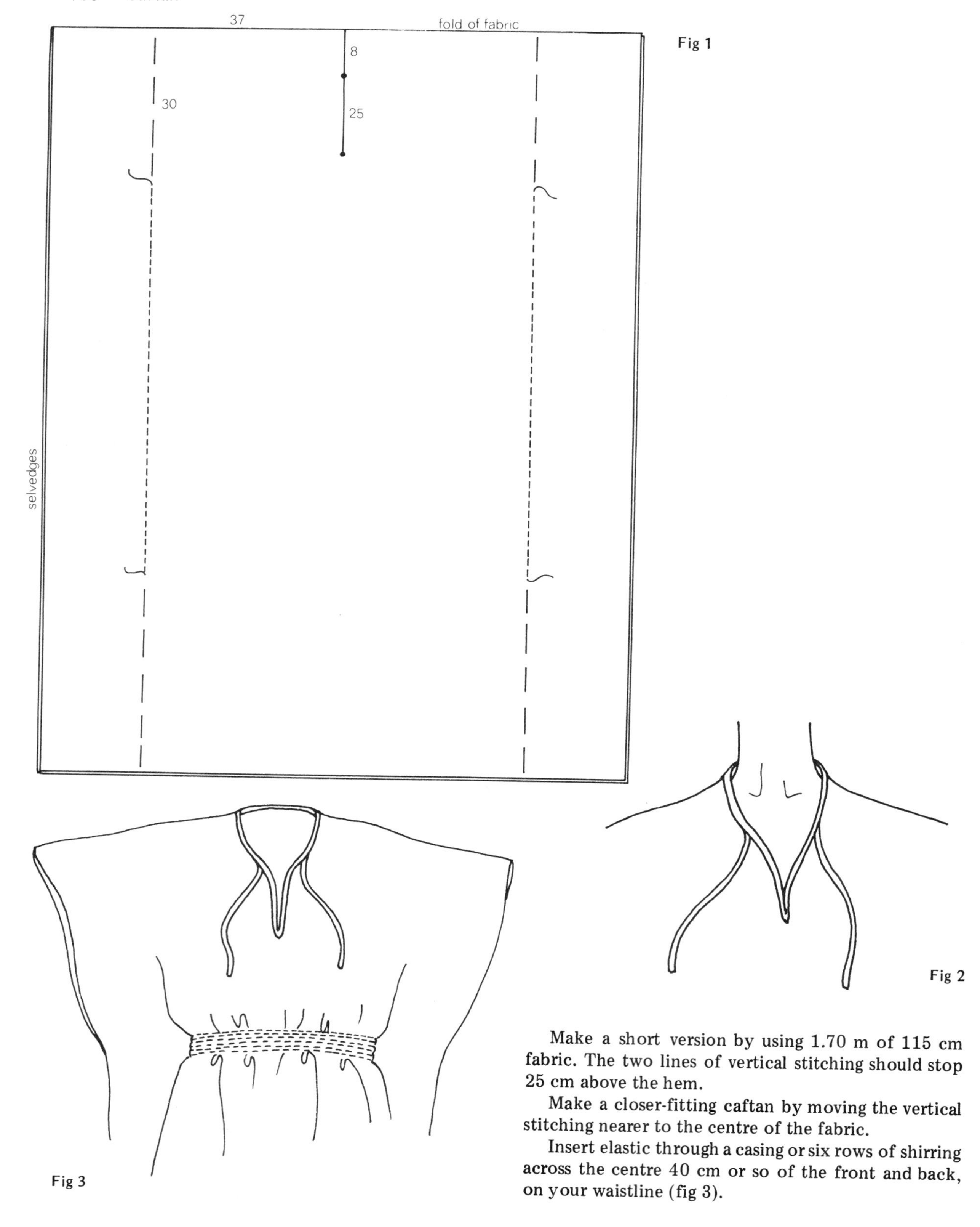

Fig 1

Fig 2

Fig 3

Make a short version by using 1.70 m of 115 cm fabric. The two lines of vertical stitching should stop 25 cm above the hem.

Make a closer-fitting caftan by moving the vertical stitching nearer to the centre of the fabric.

Insert elastic through a casing or six rows of shirring across the centre 40 cm or so of the front and back, on your waistline (fig 3).

Wrap

A simple jersey cover-up in plain or print, knotted at the front or side. Make it in towelling and it can be worn after swimming and for changing. Men can use it too. Buy an extra 60 cm of fabric and you can make a matching bikini.

The wrap can be made in only the time it takes to machine the edges — as little as half an hour.

Size: Up to 102 cm hips
Length: 107 cm
Fabric: 1.10 m jersey, knit, velour, stretch towelling
Haberdashery: 1 reel Drima
Wundaweb

The pattern: The wrap consists of one piece of fabric so there is no need to cut a pattern.

Cutting out: Fold the fabric down the centre with

Fig 1

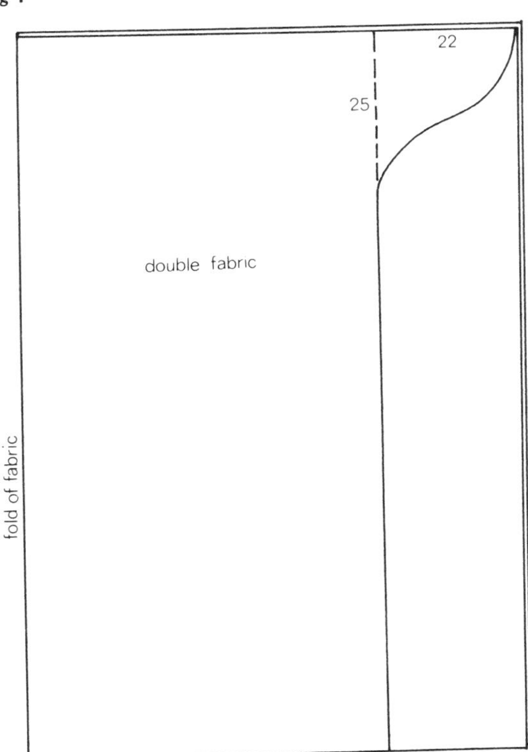

right sides out. Make sure the two cut ends are trimmed level. Measure in 22 cm and down 25 cm from the corner. Draw a curve using tailor's chalk, making it convex for half its length and concave below that. A plastic curve may be of help.

From the base of the curve draw a chalk line to the bottom of the fabric, parallel with the selvedges (fig 1).

Cut the double fabric on the chalk line.

Making up: Turn narrow machined hems on both the vertical edges.

Turn narrow machined hems at the top and bottom of the wrap.

Variations: Make double from two layers of contrasting fabric.

Make shorter for a briefer cover-up.

Tie bikini

Bra top and pants made in double fabric and adjusted to size and fastened with cord or rouleau. Can be worn under the Caftan (p. 105) or the Wrap (p. 107).

Quick to make if using purchased cord, otherwise it takes a little longer.

Size: 12-14. Adjust to smaller or one size larger by subtracting or adding small amounts. Adjust the pants at the centre of each pattern piece. Adjust the top along the straight edge that forms the side. If in doubt about adjusting the pattern measure an existing bikini or cut out as shown and fit before stitching.

Seam allowances: 1.5 cm
2 cm at sides of pants

Fabric: 60 cm of jersey, knit, velour, stretch towelling

Haberdashery: 1 reel Drima
4 m cord
3 m narrow elastic

The pattern: Make a pattern by following the diagrams. Half the pants, back and front is shown for ease of drawing. If you fold the paper first, copy the pattern and cut it out, then when opened out you have a full-size pattern. For the front use paper 30 cm deep and 20 cm wide when folded. For the back it should be 30 cm deep and 23 cm wide when folded.

The crutch seam is slightly curved, the waist edge and sides are straight. The leg curve on the front is concave but on the back is almost straight. The latter is easy to draw if you put in a straight line first (fig 1).

The bra cup has a curved edge under the bust, a sloping edge at the side and the edge with greater slope runs from centre front between busts up to the point where ties are attached. It will help if you cut the paper to size first, 22 x 27 cm. Make two copies of the bra section.

Cutting out: Fold fabric on straight grain with wrong side out. Place front and back pants' pattern one below the other, matching the straight grain arrow to the line of knitting on the fabric. Place both bra pattern pieces in position one above the other, with straight grain correctly positioned.

Pin and cut out.

Making up pants: Place back and front together and join the short crutch seam. Make the lining pieces to

Fig 1

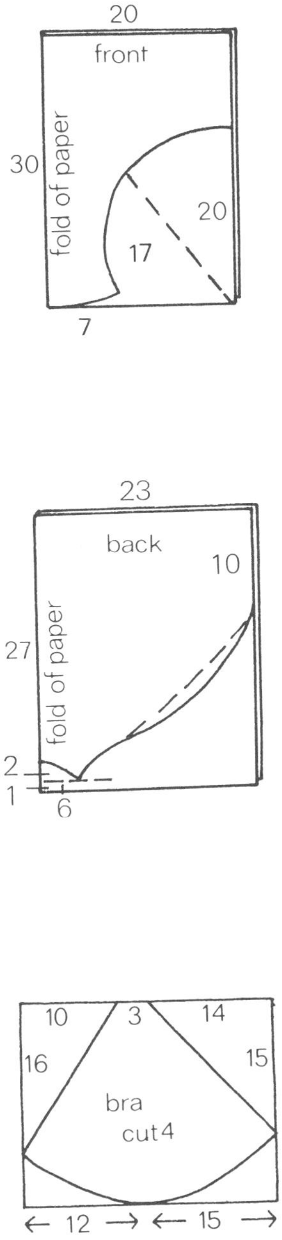

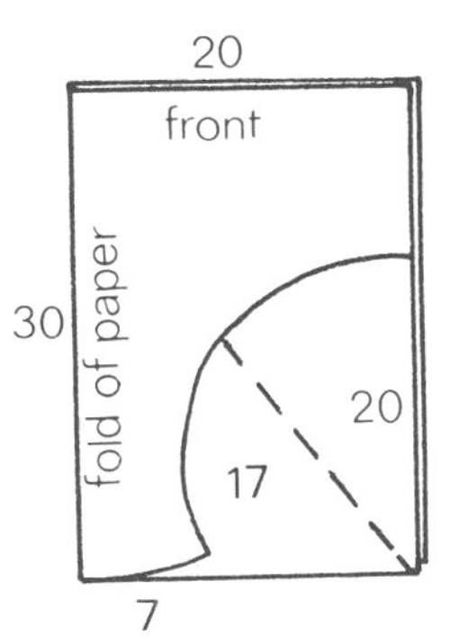

23
back
10
27
fold of paper
2
1
6

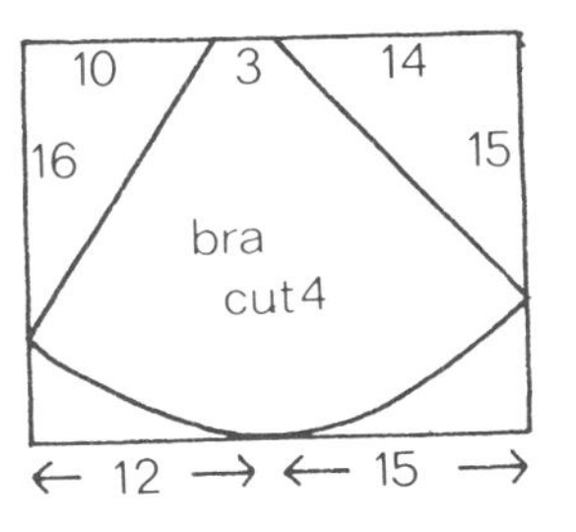

match and place both right sides together. Machine the curves of the legs, trim and turn pants right-side out. Tack along raw edges through both layers to hold. Turn a double hem along the tops of the pants 3 mm wider than the elastic and machine. Machine round both leg curves the same distance from the edge as on the top edge (fig 2).

Fig 2

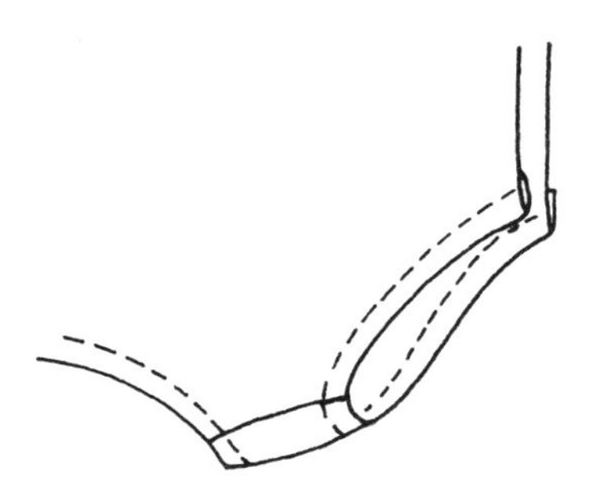

Cut two pieces of elastic 52 cm long and insert one in each leg casing.

Cut two pieces 37 cm long and insert in the upper edges. Adjust length if necessary.

Secure all ends in the casings with double machining. Turn a double hem 2 cm wide on each of the four sides of the pants and machine. Slot 60 cm cord through each tie (fig 3).

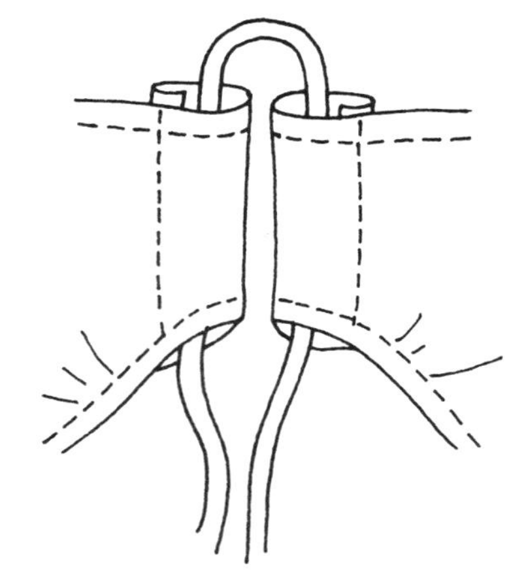

Fig 3

Making up bra: Insert the end of a 60 cm piece of cord at the top corner of one pair of fabric pieces.

Place fabric pieces together in pairs, right sides together. Stitch all round. Take 5 mm seam allowance on the curved edge leaving a 5 cm gap in one straight edge. Trim edges, turn right side out. Slip stitch the gap (fig 4).

Fig 4

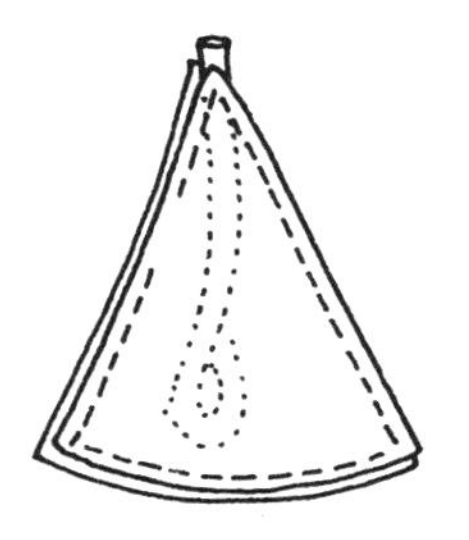

Machine along the two straight edges of the triangles just far enough inside the edge to allow the elastic to pass through (the same distance as on the pants). Thread elastic, pulling up the fabric until it is slightly gathered (check this by trying it on) and secure the ends with machining (fig 5).

Fig 5

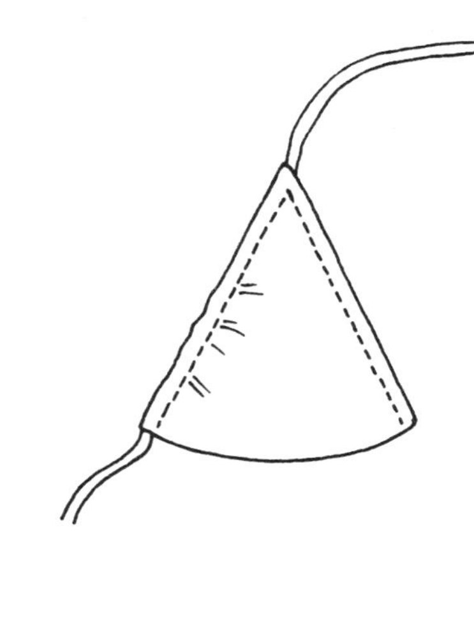

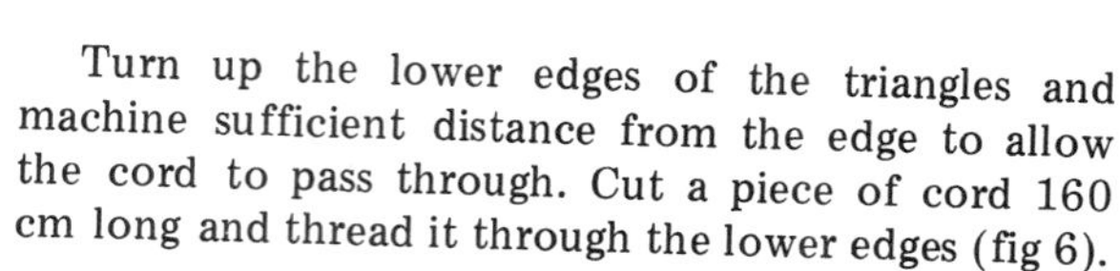

Turn up the lower edges of the triangles and machine sufficient distance from the edge to allow the cord to pass through. Cut a piece of cord 160 cm long and thread it through the lower edges (fig 6).

Fig 6

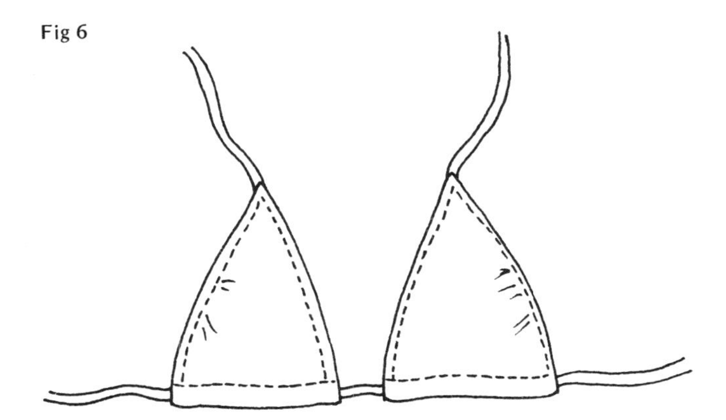

Variations: Make the bikini lining in contrasting fabric. Both the colour and also the texture can be varied.

For more support put the bra triangles on to reversed curved petersham. Make the two bra pieces and insert elastic. Insert a gathering thread along the curved edge of each triangle and pull up a little (try on and adjust). Attach curved petersham to fabric. Attach it to the bra sections with centre front corners meeting. Try on and adjust length of petersham allowing at least 7 cm for an overlapping fastening or 2 cm if a metal clasp is to be used. Complete the petersham band as for a waistband. Attach fastener.

TIP Knot the ends of the cord or attach small wool bobbles to prevent them from pulling out.

Single-seam skirt

Full, long skirt made from one piece of fabric. Easy to make and the perfect choice for border fabrics, stylised prints, awkward geometrics and diagonal designs. Although there are no side seams, there are pockets. The waist is finished with wide elastic in a casing. Could be made in a couple of hours.

Can be worn with the Tie Bikini (p. 109) any version of the Sweater (p. 128) or with the Robe cardigan or waistcoat version (p. 123).

Size: Up to 100-105 cm hip, waist adjustable

Length: 100 cm waist to ankle, can be adjusted to fit or according to the border on the fabric.

Seam allowance: 1.5 cm
5 cm at hem or according to print

Fabric: 2.10 m of 115 cm fabric (the usual width for border design) or
1.80 m of 140 cm fabric or
1.80 m of 150 cm fabric

Haberdashery: 2 reels Drima
Small piece of iron-on Vilene, e.g. Softline for pockets. 35 cm wide x 30 cm deep.
Waist length of wide elastic or elastic petersham
Wundaweb

The pattern: The skirt is a very simple shape that can be cut out in fabric without a pattern.

Cutting out: Straighten the fabric edges and fold the piece in half across the width with the wrong side out. Measure up from the double selvedge 110 cm or whatever length is correct for you. You may have to vary this amount depending on the border and on the width of the unprinted edge at the selvedge. Trim off surplus fabric at the opposite selvedge if necessary. Measure along this the waist edge and find the half-way point. Mark off 4 cm on either side of this point. Measure 45 cm down and rule straight chalk lines from the points at the top edge to this point. From the base of this dart shape, measure straight down for a further 25 cm. Mark this point on the wrong side of the fabric on the upper and under layer. Mark the dart shape on the wrong

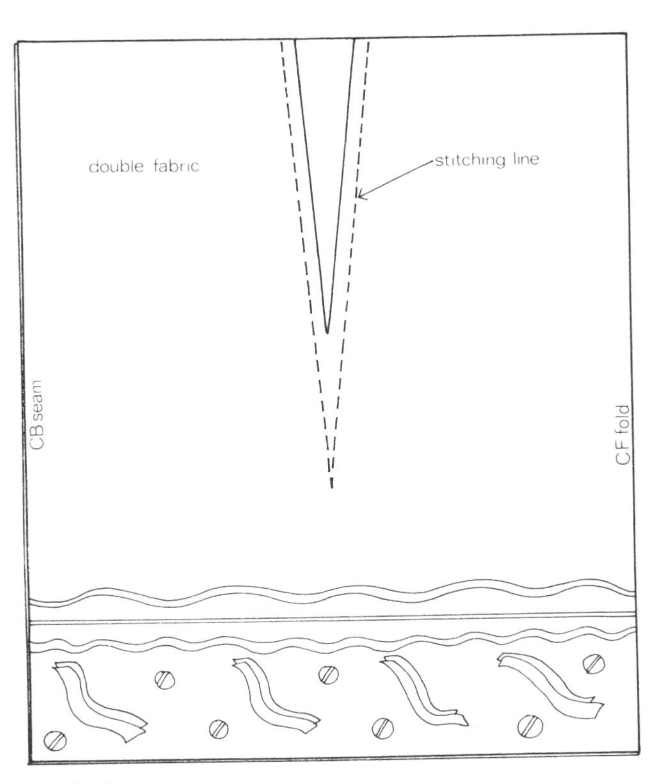

Fig 1

side of both layers. Cut out the dart on the lines (fig 1).

Fold the Vilene right-side out. Draw the shape of the pocket shown with pencil or felt pen. A plastic curve may help with the shape. The straight edge is 23 cm long then the bag curves down for a depth of 5 cm before curving upwards. On the straight edge mark a point 8 cm down as a guide for joining later. Cut out. Then cut four pieces in fabric (fig 2).

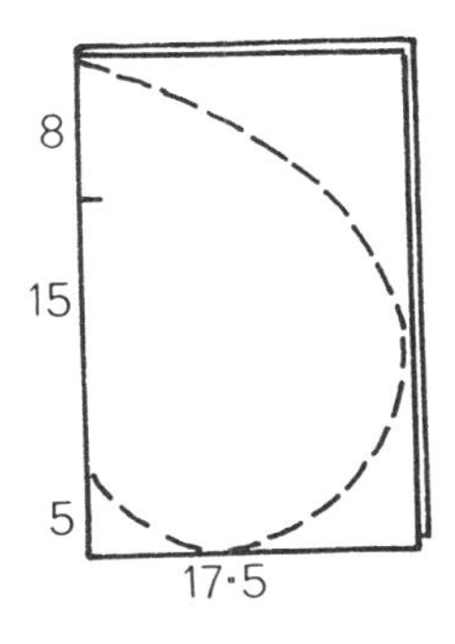

Fig 2

Making up: Join and finish the centre back seam. Turn up the hem and complete with Wundaweb.

Press the Vilene pocket shapes to the wrong side of one pair of fabric pockets.

Place each one to the edge of the cut out dart, right sides together, on the edge nearest the seam and with the top of the pocket 10 cm below the top of the skirt. Stitch, taking 5 mm turnings. Press joins open.

Attach the other two pocket pieces to the front edges of the dart 10 cm below the waist.

Fold fabric right-sides together and pin the dart to form a tapering seam.

Stitch from the waist to the point marked on the pocket edge. Close the pocket opening with stitching. Stitch from the base of the pocket to the point marked on the fabric below the cut dart. Neaten edges, press the dart open and flat. Complete the pocket. Neaten the top edge of the skirt and fold it over to form a casing 4 mm wider than the elastic. At the centre back seam, unpick the machine stitches for a little way to allow the casing to lie flat and to provide an opening for the elastic. Work a bar tack to prevent the stitching from coming undone further.

Press the casing and stitch, working two rows of machining.

Thread elastic or elastic petersham through the casing. Adjust to size and join.

Fitting: If you have a hollow back trim the waist edge to a curve between the side darts before making the casing.

Variations: Make the skirt mid-calf length.

Use plain fabric and make your own border with braid and embroidery or appliqué. Do this before marking or cutting the fabric.

Omit the pockets for speed.

Add patch pockets — taking the pattern from the Hooded Snuggler (p. 134).

Add a waistband in place of elastic. Decide on the width of the waistband and shorten the skirt by twice this amount. You may well be able to cut the band from wasted border design. Stitch the back seam but insert a 20 cm zip in the top of the seam. Complete the side darts and pockets then gather the waist edge on to the prepared waistband.

Slip-on dress

Soft, easy bias dress in drapy fabric with drawn-up neck and waistline. Make long pieces of rouleau to thread through the neck and tie round the waist.

Quick to make, only two seams, the fluted hem and the neckline.

Size: To fit up to 97 cm bust

Fig 1

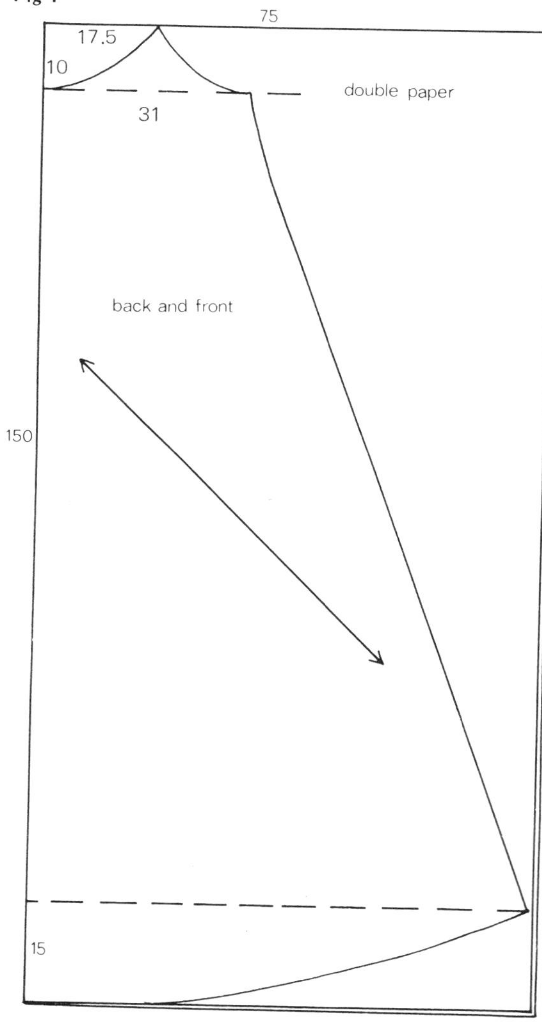

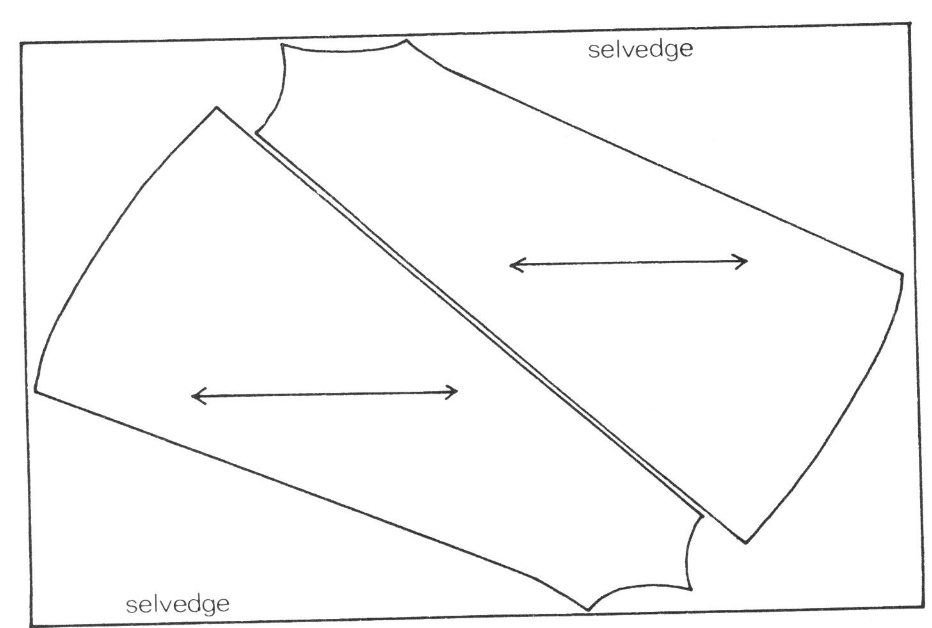

Fig 2

Length: Back neck to hem 145 cm (allowing 7 cm for blousing at waist).

Reduce the fullness in the dress by taking 3-4 cm off the pattern at the centre front and centre back.

Seam allowance: 1.5 cm
2 cm at hem

Fabric: Use light-weight jersey,
3.90 m of 140 cm fabric or
3.70 m of 150 cm fabric

The dress could also be made successfully in other fine soft fabrics such as voile, chiffon, georgette, crêpe but they may not be as wide. Buy extra fabric and cut out, allowing for a join near the hem.

You will need 4.40 m of 115 cm fabric

Haberdashery: 3 reels Drima
Small beads for the ends of the rouleau

The pattern: The back and front are alike, so make one piece of pattern. The pattern takes a piece of paper 75 cm wide and 150 cm long. Join sheets together. It will be easier to cut out the fabric if you have two pattern pieces, so use two sheets of paper.

Copy the pattern shape shown starting 10 cm down from the fold. The under-arm point is 31 cm from the fold and from there the side seam is a straight line to a point 15 cm above the bottom of the paper. Curve the hem down to the fold and curve the top of the dress from the centre fold up to the top of the paper 17.5 cm in from the fold. From there curve down to the under-arm. A plastic curve may help (fig 1).

Mark the straight grain position at an angle of 45° across the pattern.

Cut out the folded paper and open out.

Cutting out: Fold the fabric right-side out, across the width. Make sure the selvedges and ends are together. Place the pattern piece with the straight grain arrow parallel with the selvedge, anchor it and chalk round. Remove the pattern and position again following the diagram. Pin down and cut out (fig 2).

Cut out the first piece marked with chalk.

When using narrow fabric draw a line on the pattern marking where the selvedge cuts across. After cutting both pieces lay the pattern on the spare fabric and cut out the remaining triangle of pattern. Match the grain correctly and remember to allow a seam allowance along the straight edge to be seamed. After cutting out join these pieces to the main skirt (fig 3).

Cut crossway strips from the surplus pieces of fabric. Cut 2 m for the neck, 2 m for the belt and sufficient to face the top edge of the dress.

Making up: Stitch the side seams. Using the crossway strip face or bind the armholes. Face the front and back neckline of the dress, finishing the ends of the crossway strip to leave a slot for threading the ties.

Make the rouleau ties and thread through the necklines.

Put the dress on and adjust the ties.

Mark the waistline with a fitting petersham, blousing the top for a depth of up to 7 cm. Mark the hemline at the desired length.

Trim the hem surplus and flute the edge. Use crossway strips of fabric to attach a casing to the inside of the waistline. Insert elastic in the casing.

Make the rouleau tie belt. Attach beads to the

rouleau ends.

Variations: Work rows of shirring to mark the waist and omit the belt.

Wear a narrow purchased belt.

Make a wider tie belt.

Shorten the pattern to mid-calf length cutting off about 35 cm and make it as a disco dress, a slip or a nightdress.

Use ribbon instead of rouleau in the neck and attach lace to the hem.

Fig 3

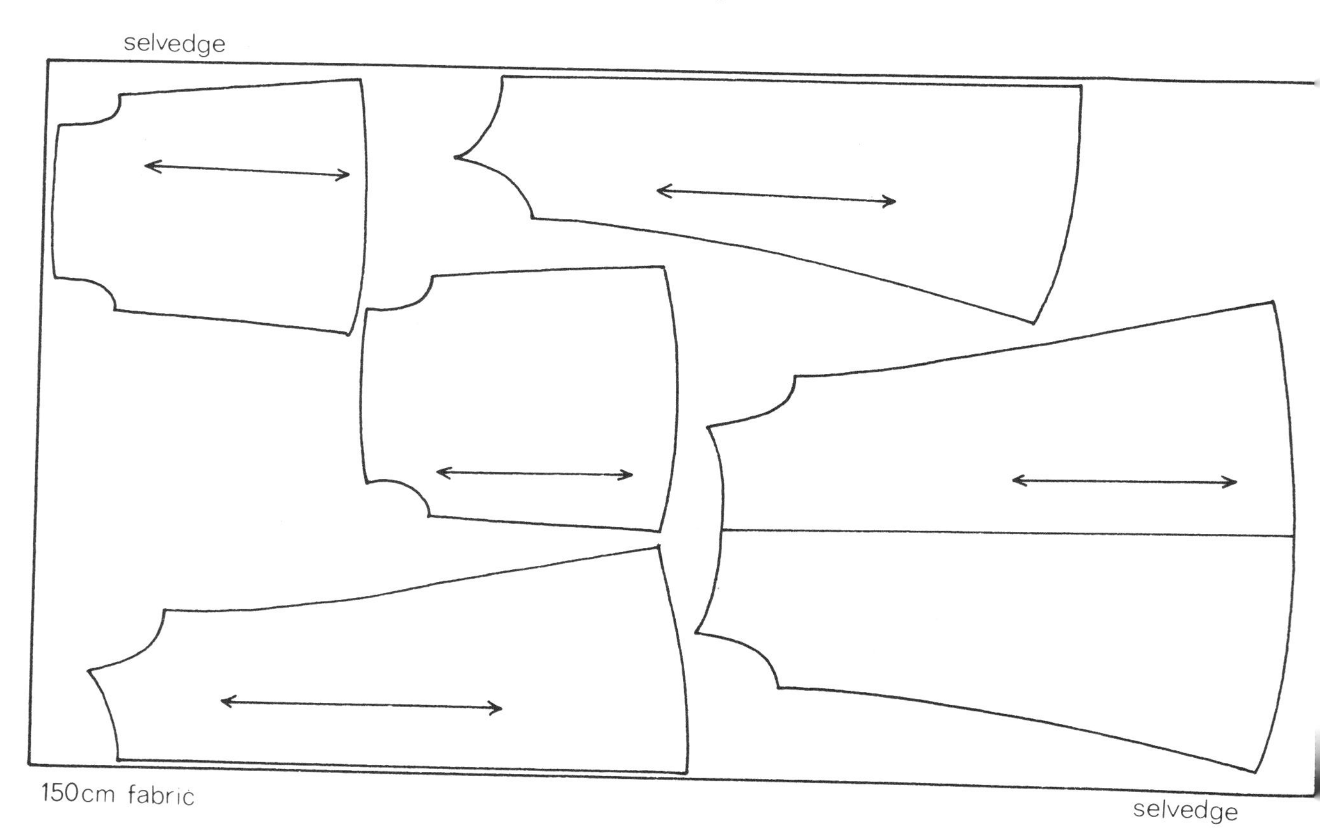

Wrap skirt

Wrap skirt with waistband and stitched edges, it is fastened with Velcro to make it adjustable.

Size: To fit 97 cm hip

Length: 76 cm

Adjust the size by adding or subtracting a little at the centre back and sides of the pattern.

Seam allowance: 1.5 cm
5 cm on hem
7 cm allowed for fold-back facing on front of skirt

Fabric: Any light or medium fabric including wool and synthetics in woven or jersey construction, cotton, polyester and cotton, cord, denim.

1.80 m of 140 or 150 cm fabric

Haberdashery: 3 reels Drima
Petersham or interfacing for waistband
16 cm Velcro 3 cm wide
85 cm Fold-a-Band
Wundaweb

The pattern: You will need a piece of squared paper 85 cm long and 40 cm wide for the back. The edge on the left is the centre back and will be placed to the fold of the fabric. At the hem, the width of the skirt is 1 cm less than the size of the paper and the hem curves up to a point 2.5 cm above the bottom edge of the paper.

Rule a line across the paper 70 cm above the hemline at the centre back. Measure 26 cm along this line and rule from there down to the outer point of the hem (fig 1).

Measure 6 cm in along the horizontal line and mark a point directly above it but at the edge of the paper. Draw a slight curve from there to join the side line to complete the side seam.

Draw the waistline by first measuring 10 cm in from the side seam and 2.5 cm down and draw a curve. Rule a dart as shown, making it 1.5 cm wide, and coming to a point on the line below.

Complete the waist by drawing a curve from the dart to the centre back edge.

To make the front pattern use a piece of paper 85 cm long and 90 cm wide. Fold the paper under at a point 25 cm in from the right-hand edge. Write

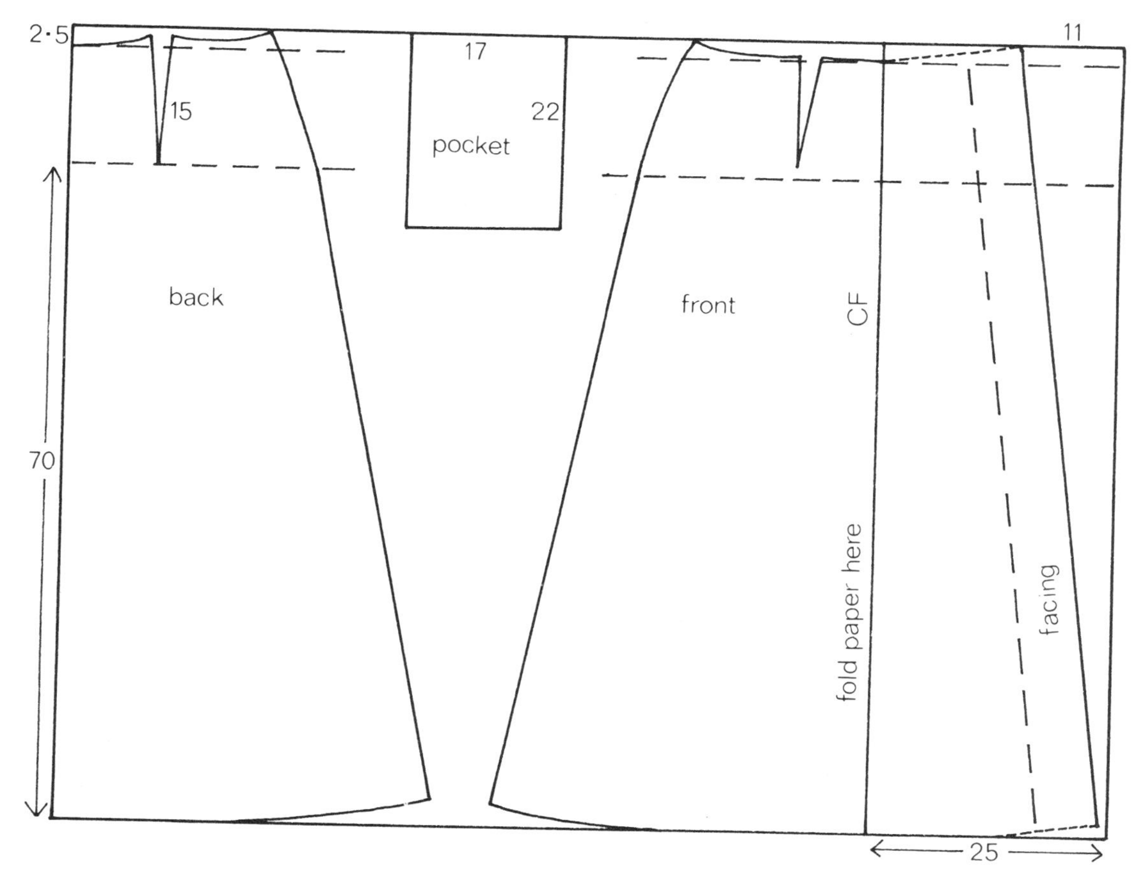

Fig 1

on the fold 'centre front' and put grain arrows on it.

At the bottom edge of the paper draw the hem in the same way as for the back.

Mark a line across the paper 70 cm above the hem and rule a straight side seam as for the back.

Measure in 5 cm on this line and curve in the remainder of the side seam up to the top edge of the paper.

Start the waistline curve by drawing a line dropping by 1 cm by the time it reaches the dart position 10 cm in. Make the dart 1 cm wide but it should stop short of the line below by 2 cm. Complete the waist curve by dropping the line to a point 2 cm below the top of the paper by the time it reaches the fold.

Cut out the pattern with the paper still folded. Open it out and shape the skirt wrap-over by ruling a straight line from the hem edge up to a point 11 cm in from the right-hand edge of the paper. Trim off the paper.

Cutting out: Place the pattern on the fabric folded as shown. Match the straight grain on the front. Pin and cut out (fig 2).

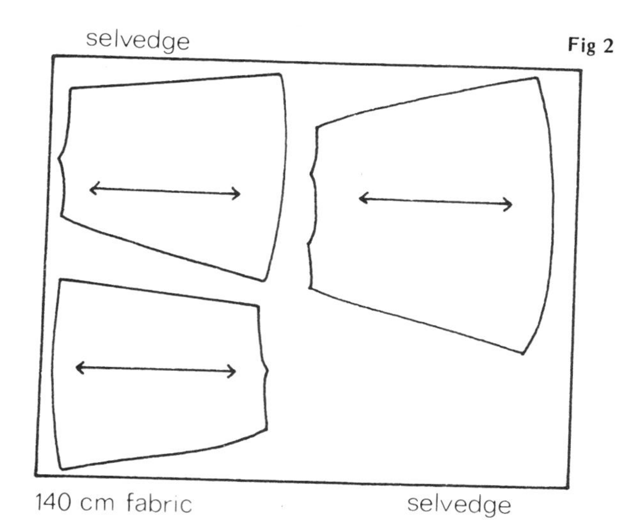

Fig 2

Mark the darts, the centre back, centre front and also mark the fold line of the front facing 7 cm inside the edge of the fabric.

Making up: Press Fold-a-Band to the wrong side of each skirt front, locating the perforations over the facing fold line. Neaten the raw edges of the facing extension (fig 3).

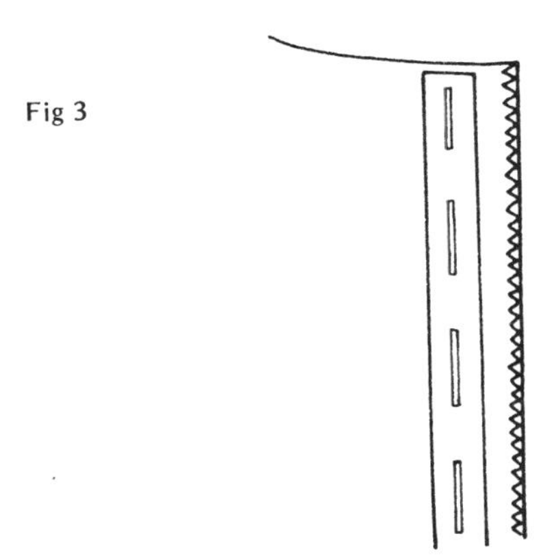

Fig 3

Place back skirt right-side up and front skirts on top right-side down, matching the side seams. Tack. Tack in the front and back darts. Try the skirt on, matching the centre front lines. Adjust if necessary. Attach pockets if desired — see *Variations.*

Complete the darts and side seams. Fold back the front facings and tack. Press. Make a straight or curved waistband and attach. Try on the skirt and mark the position of the wrap-over on the band. Mark the hemline.

Open out the front facing and turn up the hem. Fold facing back into position and hold back by inserting a length of Wundaweb between the skirt and the facing (fig 4).

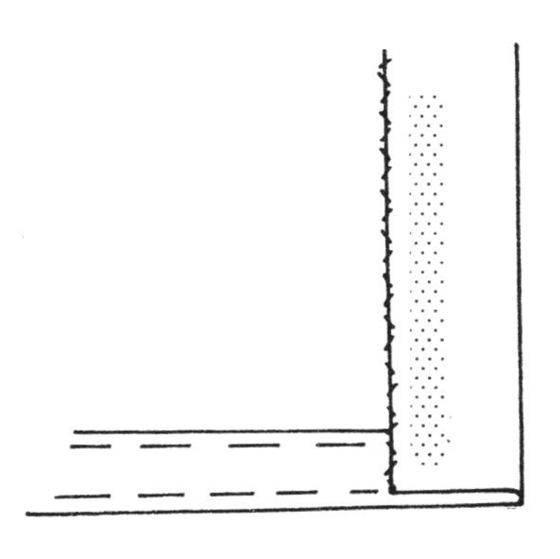

Fig 4

Work decorative stitching down front edge and round the hem. Attach the Velcro to the waistband.

Variations: Before attaching waistband trim the seam allowance of the front edges and trim the hem off the bottom, enclose the raw edges in braid. Attach waistband.

Sew two large buttons to the outside of the waistband (fig 5).

Fig 5

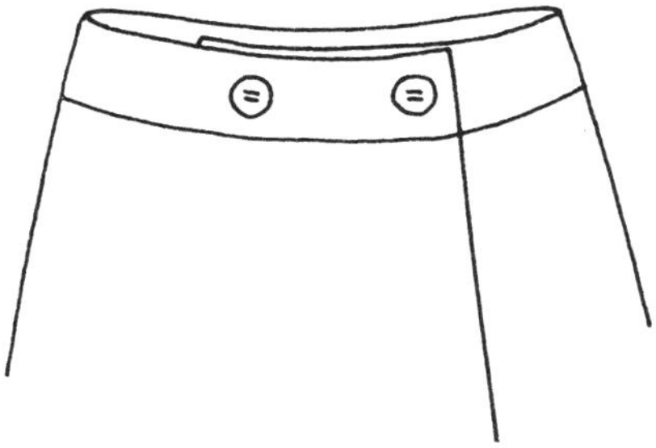

Add a patch pocket. Attach it after stitching the darts and side seams. Place the top of it so that the right corner just covers the point of the dart.

Insert seam pockets. Use the pattern given for the Single-Seam Skirt (p. 112) and attach them to the side seams 10 cm below the waist edge, before stitching the side seams.

Vary the length of the skirt — cut it only 50 cm long, trim it with ric-rac braid or embroidery. Alternatively attach long ends of braid or contrasting fabric to the waistband and to the skirt and tie (this is in addition to the Velcro). Wear it for sports and holidays. Team it with the sleeveless version of the Sweater (p. 128), the whole outfit in cotton jersey, towelling, velour, track suit fabric, etc.

Lengthen the pattern to ankle length and make the skirt in soft cotton, light-weight jersey or panne velvet.

Tunic

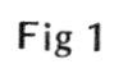
Fig 1

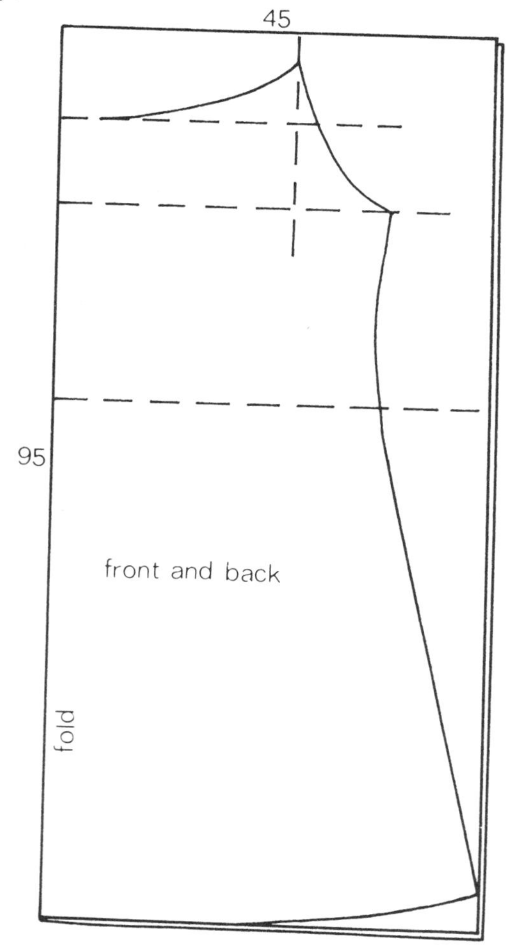

Loose tunic with elastic or drawstring neck. Lift with a hipline sash and wear it with the Trousers (p. 131). Very quick to make with raglan sleeves, elastic in the wrists and machined hem.

Size: 10-14

Length: 92 cm

Adjust by adding or subtracting a small amount at the centre edge of the pattern.

Seam allowance: 1.5 cm
2 cm at hem, neck and sleeve hems

Fabric: 2.60 m of 115 cm jersey fabric, or 2.40 m if it is 150 cm or more wide

Haberdashery: 2 reels Drima (3 if fluting the hem)
1.50 m narrow elastic for neck
50 cm narrow elastic for sleeves
Shirring elastic for waist

Fig 2

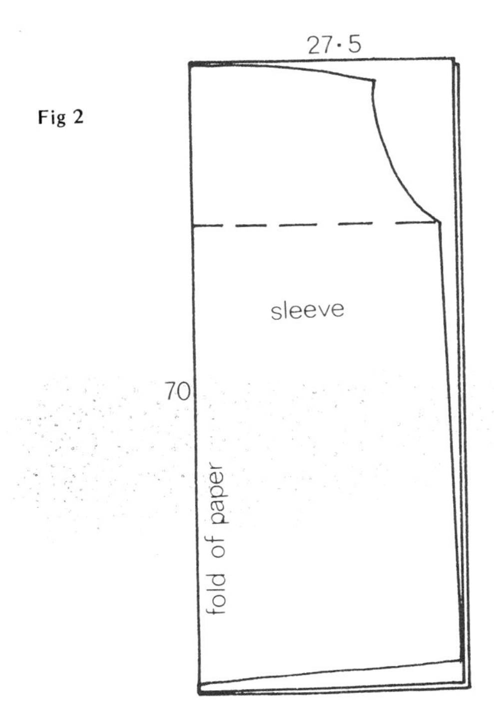

The pattern: The front and back are the same so cut one pattern piece. The diagram shows half the sleeve so draw it on a folded piece of paper.

For the main pattern piece use a piece of paper 45 cm wide and 95 cm long. Begin at the bottom left and mark the hemline, curving it up to a point 5 cm above the bottom of the paper.

Measure 55 cm up the left-hand edge of the paper and rule a line across. Mark a point 34 cm along and draw the side seam from there to the hem. Curve the line in slightly for 5 cm then gently out for 10 cm before ruling the remainder with a ruler (fig 1).

Rule a horizontal line across the paper 21 cm over the first, another 9 cm above that and a vertical one 24 cm in from the left-hand edge.

Curve the armhole and neckline as shown and complete the side seam.

To make the sleeve pattern fold a piece of paper 55 cm wide and 70 cm long (fig 2).

At the bottom of the folded edge measure up 4 cm and from there curve the hemline to a point 5 cm above the bottom of the paper by the time it reaches the edge of the paper.

Rule a sleeve seam 48 cm long from this point but slope it in 1 cm.

At the top of the paper rule a horizontal line 19 cm long 2 cm down. Curve the top of the sleeve as shown and from there curve the armhole.

Cutting out: Cut out the front and back and two sleeves with the straight grain of the fabric running down the centre of each (fig 3).

If making a sash from matching fabric cut it from the surplus piece.

Making up: Stitch tunic side seams and sleeve seams.

Turn up a 2 cm hem at the bottom of the sleeves and stitch to form a casing.

Set sleeves into armholes, matching sleeve seam to tunic side seam.

Turn in a 2 cm hem round the neck and tops of sleeves and stitch to form a casing. Insert elastic

Fig 3

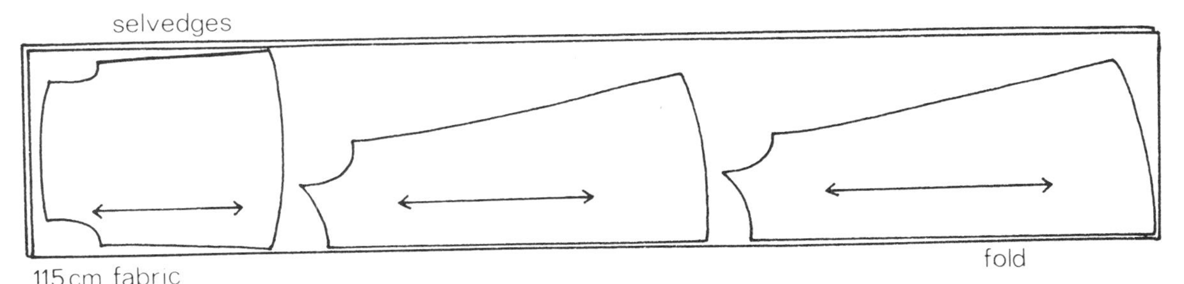

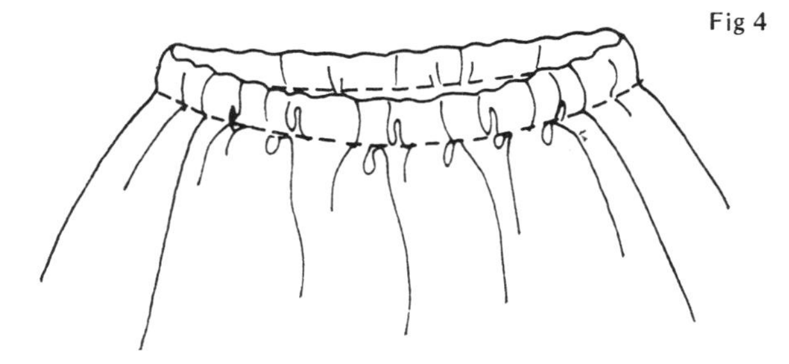

Fig 4

and pin. Try on dress and adjust elastic. Mark the waistline, blousing the tunic as much as desired (fig 4).

Join the elastic. Work several rows of shirring round the waistline and insert elastic in the sleeves. Machine the hem. Make the sash.

Variations: Insert ribbon in the neckline instead of elastic.

Shorten the sleeves to elbow length or shorter.

Leave short sleeves loose without elastic.

Lengthen the pattern to dress length.

Fabric: 3.20 m of 115 cm fabric or 2.70 m of 150 cm fabric.

Robe

Wrap-over robe with bands and wide sleeves, and fold-back cuffs. A comfortable all-purpose garment.
Size: 14-16
Length: Back neck to hem 145 cm
Adjust width by adding or subtracting small amounts at the centre back and side seams of the pattern.
Seam allowance: 1.5 cm
5 cm on hem
Fabric: Use velour, stretch towelling, plush or other jersey fabric of 150 cm width
Haberdashery: 2 reels Drima
Fold-a-Band for cuffs
The pattern: You will need pieces of paper 155 cm long for the back and front patterns, join sheets to obtain this length.

For the back pattern use a piece of paper 35 cm wide. Begin at the bottom and mark the hemline, curving it up to a point 1 cm above the edge of the paper (fig 1).

Draw a line across the paper 110 cm above the hem and measure across it 30 cm. Draw the side seam from the hem to this point and then curve it out by 1 cm to a point 10 cm above.

At the top of the paper measure down 6 cm and draw a horizontal line. Mark the end of the shoulder seam 29 cm along it. Draw the armhole as shown. Draw the neckline 9 cm wide starting 4 cm below the top of the paper and curving up 2 cm. Complete the shoulder seam.

To draw the front pattern take a piece of paper 155 cm long and 50 cm wide. Fold under the edge on the right turning 15 cm underneath. The folded edge of paper is the centre front. Mark it as such and put grain arrows on it.

At the bottom of the paper measure across from the right 32 cm and draw a curved hemline. Mark horizontal guide lines on the paper 110, 10 and 30 cm above this. Draw the lower part of the side seam sloping it in to a point 29 cm from the centre front. Curve it more as shown for the last 10 cm. Above this, curve the seam out again for 1 cm to the line above.

Measure along the top guide line 29 cm and from

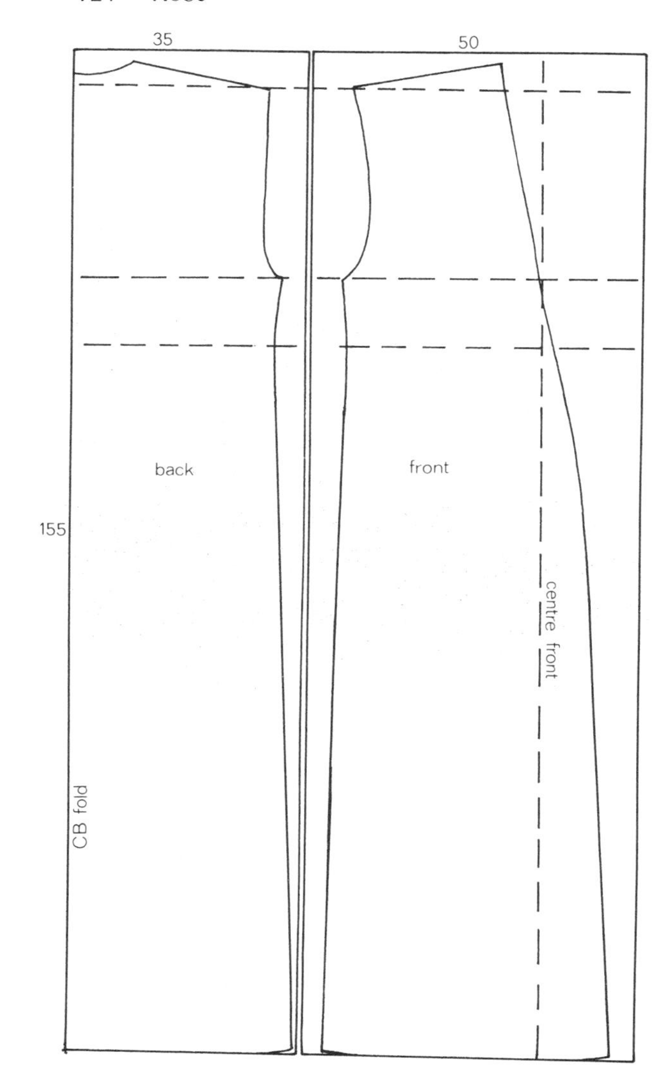

Fig 1

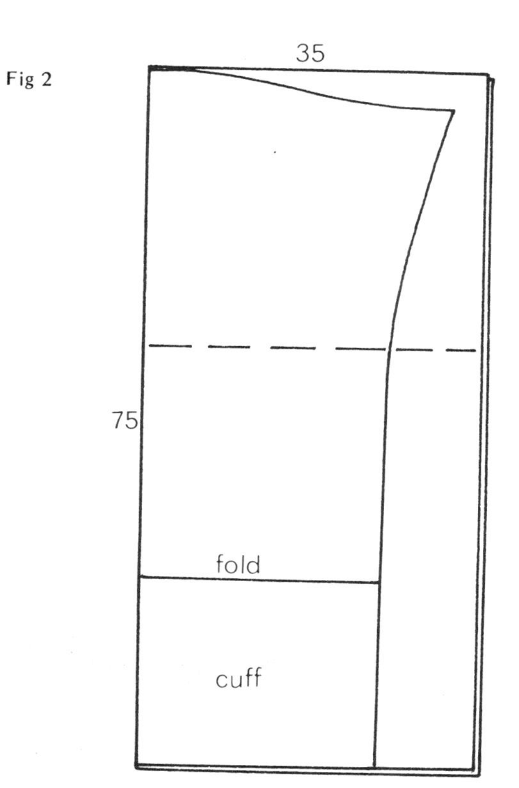

Fig 2

there draw the armhole in a curve as shown.

Measure along the top edge of the paper 6 cm and start the shoulder seam line 1.5 cm below this.

The neckline runs in a slightly concave curve from that point down to the next guide line, joining the guide line exactly on the fold of the paper.

Open out the paper and continue curving the front edge but now slightly convex for 30 cm before completing it, using a ruler. This line should meet the bottom of the paper 4 cm in from the edge.

To make the sleeve pattern fold a piece of paper 70 cm wide and 75 cm long. Measure from the fold 25 cm along the bottom edge. From there draw a line up to a point 45 cm above the hem. Draw the sleeve head as shown sloping it down to a point 3.5 cm below the top of the paper and 3 cm in from the edge. From there complete the sleeve seam as shown. Cut out and open the paper for the complete sleeve pattern (fig 2).

Draw a line across the pattern 20 cm above the hem to mark the fold line for the cuff.

Cutting out: Place the back to a fold. Cut the front and sleeve with the straight grain running lengthwise (fig 3).

Cut two bands for the edges 164 cm long and 12 cm wide.

For the belt cut a piece of fabric, or pieces to join, 12 cm wide and 160 cm long.

Making up: Join the shoulder seams, reinforcing them to prevent stretching.

Press Fold-a-Band to the wrong side of each sleeve, locating the perforations over the cuff fold line (fig 4).

Insert the sleeves into the armholes. Join the sleeve and side seam in one continuous seam.

Turn up the sleeve hem on the Fold-a-Band and stitch the edge of the cuff to the sleeve. Turn back the cuffs and hold in position with three bar tacks worked between the cuff and the sleeve (fig 5).

Turn up and complete the hem.

Join the two bands, fold the strip in half with wrong sides together and attach to the edges of the robe as a double fabric edge. At the hem of the robe

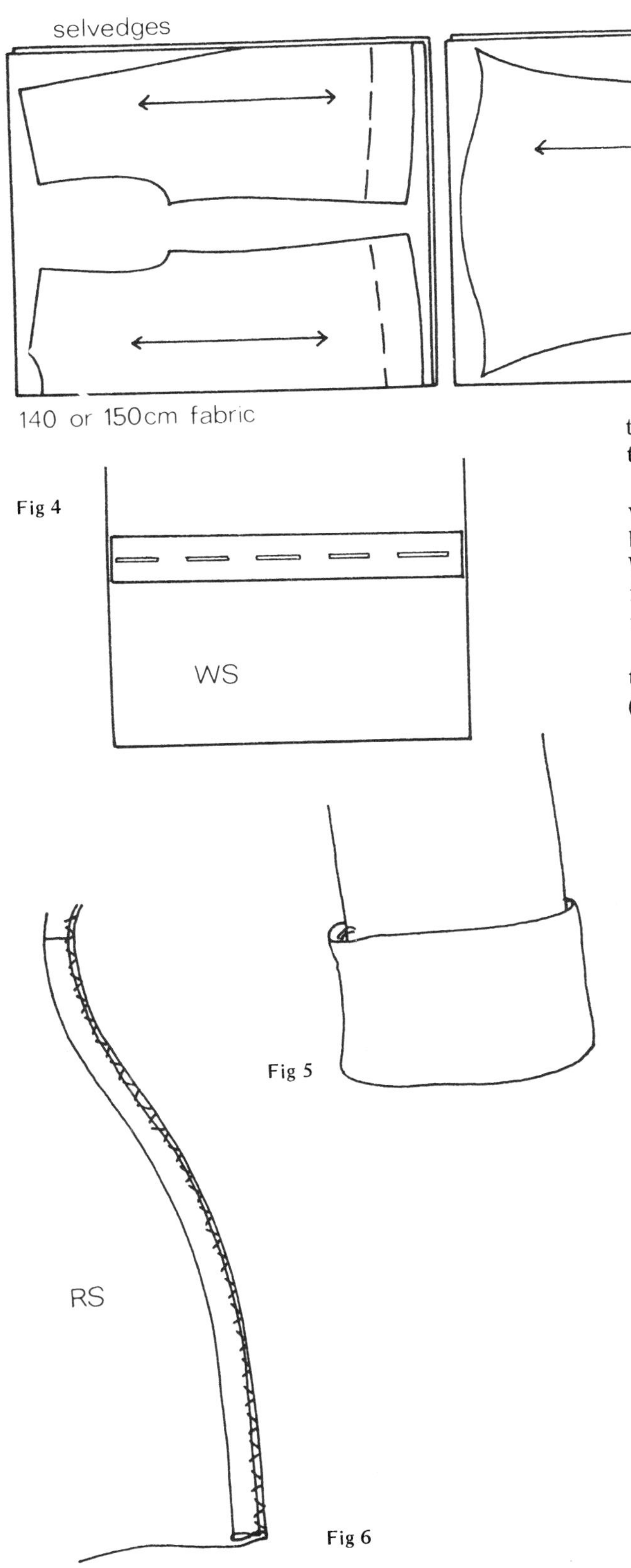

Fig 3

Fig 4

Fig 5

Fig 6

turn in the end level with the hem before folding the band (fig 6).

Make two fabric belt loops and attach at the waist. Also make a fabric hanger and attach to the back of the neck.

Variations: Add pockets. Use the patch pocket given for the Wrap Skirt (p. 117) or add seam pockets using the pattern from the Single-Seam Skirt (p. 112).

Sew a small piece of Velcro at the waist where the robe wraps over to stop it from falling open (fig 7).

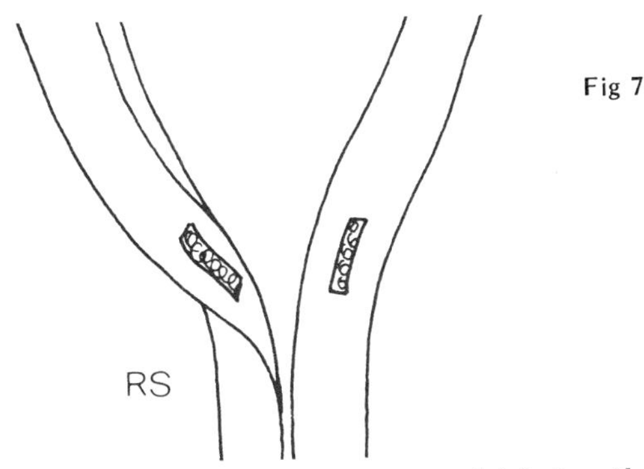

Fig 7

Shorten the pattern by 75 cm to thigh length, and team it with trousers. Make bands and belts in contrasting fabric. The jacket could be made in a wide variety of fabrics including crêpe, polyester and cottom, satin, panne velvet.

Fabric: 3 m of 90 cm fabric
2 m of 140 or 150 cm fabric plus extra if contrast is used

Use jersey, wool or synthetic coating, brushed fabrics to make a cardigan.

Fabric: 2 m of 140 or 150 cm fabric

Omit the sleeves and bands, re-shape the front edge so that is does not extend beyond the centre front and make a warm waistcoat from fur fabric, brushed coating, blanket cloth, etc., finish the edges with the braid and add braid ties.

Fabric: 1 m of 140 or 150 cm fabric

Bias skirt and shawl

A pretty skirt cut on the cross with a quickly made matching shawl. The skirt has pockets and is gathered into a waistband.

There is a concealed zip in the centre back seam.

Size: To fit 71 cm waist

Length: 76 cm

To reduce or increase the size adjust the pattern at the centre front and centre back.

Seam allowance: 1.5 cm
2 cm hem

Fabric: Use any plain or checked medium-weight fabric. If woven fabric is used the shawl edges can be fringed, if jersey fabric is used attach bought fringe (5.70 m).

2.40 of 140 cm wide fabric or
2.20 of 150 cm wide fabric

Haberdashery: 2 reels Drima
Petersham or stiffening for waistband
Velcro or hooks, trouser clips to fasten
20 cm concealed zip

Fig 1

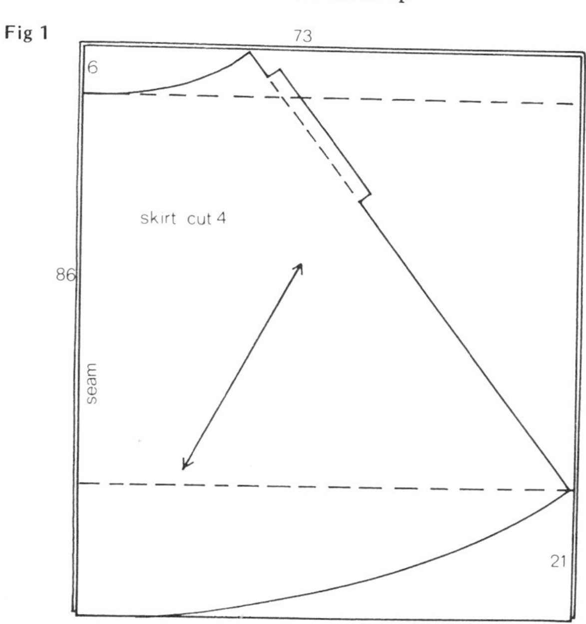

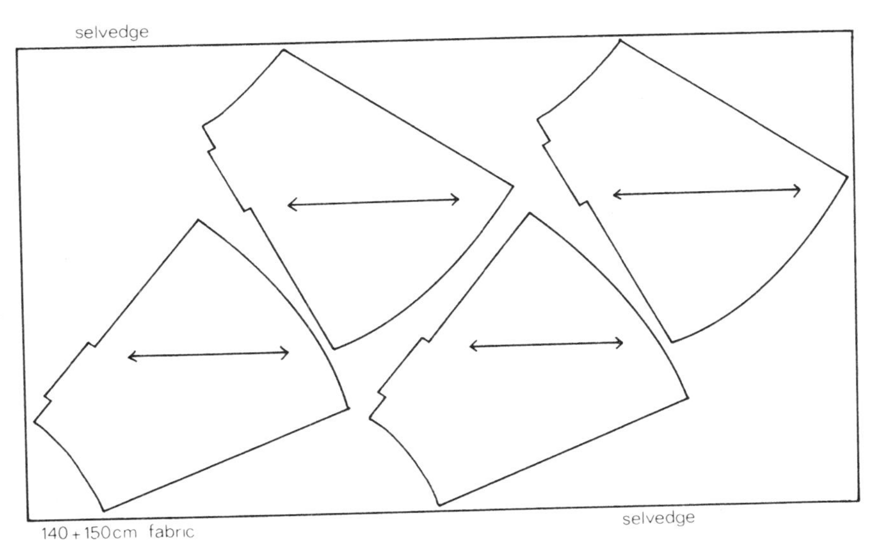

Fig 2

Iron-on Vilene (Softline), 30 cm x 40 cm for the pockets

The pattern: You will need one piece of paper 73 cm wide by 86 cm deep. The front and back skirt pattern pieces are the same but as only half the pattern is shown it helps when you come to cutting out if you make two copies of the pattern — use two pieces of paper (fig 1).

Begin at the bottom left and draw in the hemline. Draw an even curve to a point 21 cm above the bottom of the paper.

Draw a horizontal guide line across the paper 6 cm below the top edge and mark a point 25 cm along. Curve in the waistline as shown. From the side waist point rule a straight line to the hem. Add 1.5 cm to the side seam where the pockets will be attached so that the join will not be obvious if checked fabric is used. Begin the extension 5 cm below the waist and make it 28 cm in length.

Fold the Vilene in half and draw the pocket shape from the Single-Seam Skirt (p. 112) on it with pencil or felt pen. Mark a point 8 cm below the top to indicate the opening. Cut out.

Cutting out: Place the pattern pieces on single fabric and pin with the straight grain positioned as shown. Cut out.

Cut four pocket pieces using the Vilene as a guide (fig 2).

Cut a square of fabric 140 cm x 140 cm for the shawl.

Making up: Mark the centre back and centre front. Stitch and press centre back and centre front seams. Insert the zip in the back seam. Press the Vilene to the wrong side of two of the pocket pieces. Attach these to the extensions on the back skirt. Press. Attach the other two pocket pieces to the front extensions.

Join the side seams, closing up the pocket opening with stitching. Complete the seams and the pockets.

Insert a gathering thread in the skirt waist or make small unpressed pleats.

Cut and interface a waistband and attach it, gathering the skirt to fit. Attach fastenings to the waistband.

Try on the skirt and mark the hemline. Turn up and complete the hem.

Pull fibres from all edges of the shawl to make a fringe of a suitable depth. Work zig-zag stitch round the edge of the fabric to prevent further fibres coming away (fig 3).

If using jersey fabric turn a narrow hem all round and machine it. Attach the fringe by hand or machine.

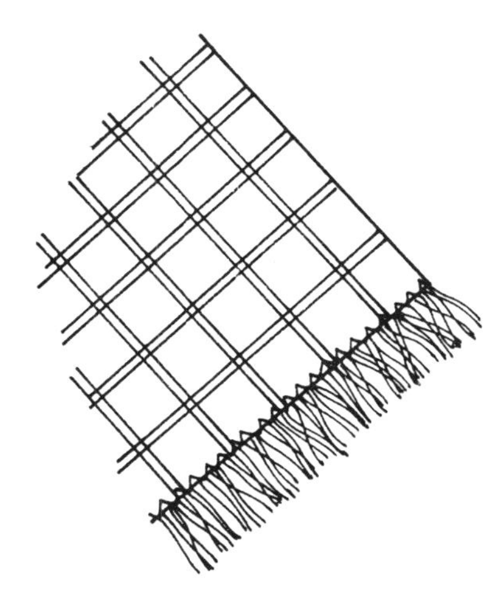

Fig 3

Sweater

Fig 1
70
11
5
10·5
16·5
back
front
fold
fold
10
sleeve
51
fold of fabric
16
25
22
wrist
20
fold fabric here
waist
fold fabric here
20
40
28
neckband
fold
CF
extend for
deeper band

Fig 2

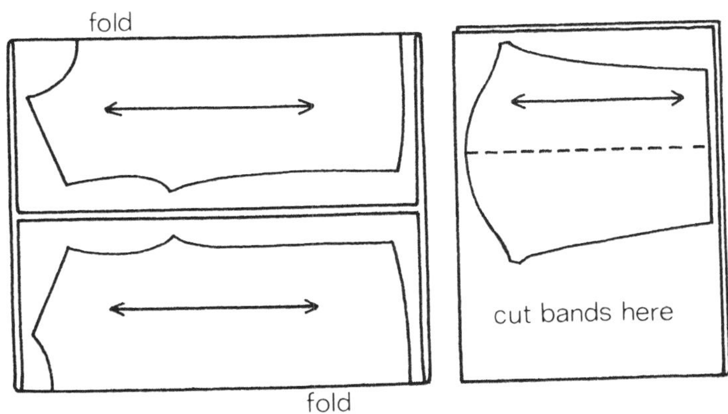

A loose blouson jersey top with extended shoulder and bands of fabric or ribbing at neck, cuffs and hem. It can be made in a couple of hours.

Size: 14-16

Length: 67 cm

For a smaller size take small amounts from centre back, centre front and side seams of pattern. Re-draw the side seams and armholes within the line shown following the original shape.

Seam allowance: The usual 1.5 cm has been allowed on all edges, but if you are using one of the narrow seams suitable for jersey this can be reduced to 4 mm before cutting out in fabric.

Fabric: Use medium to thick knits and jersey including velour, track suit fabric, stretch towelling, panne velvet, plush, fancy knit fabrics, fur fabric. Use self fabric or ribbed knit fabric or hand knitting for the bands.

1.40 m of either 140 cm or 150 cm fabric, or 1.20 m if contrast ribbing is used.

Haberdashery: 2 reels Drima
45 cm narrow ribbon, tape or seam binding for shoulder seams.

The pattern: You will need a piece of paper 70 cm wide and 80 cm deep to draw the front and back sweater pattern. Only half the sleeve pattern is shown. Either fold the fabric, chalk the pattern as shown directly on to the fabric and cut out (cut two sleeves in this way), or fold a piece of paper 50 cm wide and 51 cm deep and draw the sleeve pattern (fig 1).

The bands for neck, wrists and hem can be cut directly in fabric.

Draw the hemline for the back and front 3 cm above the edge of the paper, curving it up slightly to a point 30 cm in. From there draw a vertical line to the top of the paper. Draw the side seams sloping in slightly and then curving out and beyond the marker line 43 cm above the bottom of the paper.

Draw a marker line 13 cm below the top of the paper. Draw in the back neckline 10 cm down curving to 11 cm in and rule a 22 cm shoulder seam from there onto the marker line below.

The front neckline starts 16.5 cm down and curves up to 10.5 cm in. Rule the shoulder seam but note that it joins the armhole curve 1.5 cm above the marker line.

To draw half the sleeve mark the hemline 16 cm long 4 cm above the bottom of the paper. Rule a marker line 10 cm below the top and rule the sleeve seam. Above that point draw a slightly angled line 2 cm long before curving the sleeve head as shown. The curve is slightly concave for 10 cm but convex for the top of the arm.

Cutting out: Fold the fabric sides to middle and cut the back and front to a fold. Re-fold the remainder of the fabric in order to cut the sleeves and bands (fig 2).

Cut pieces of ribbing or fabric to sizes shown to fold double for attaching.

Making up: Stitch shoulder seams, using a slight zig-zag stitch or one of the narrow or stretch seams. Insert tape to prevent stretching.

Insert sleeves, placing centre of sleeve head to shoulder seam with right sides together; ease sleeve to fit armhole and stitch the seam.

Stitch side seam and sleeve seam in one operation.

Join all bands, fold them wrong sides together and attach. The full sleeve will have to be gathered to the ribbing or fabric. The neck and hem bands

Fig 3

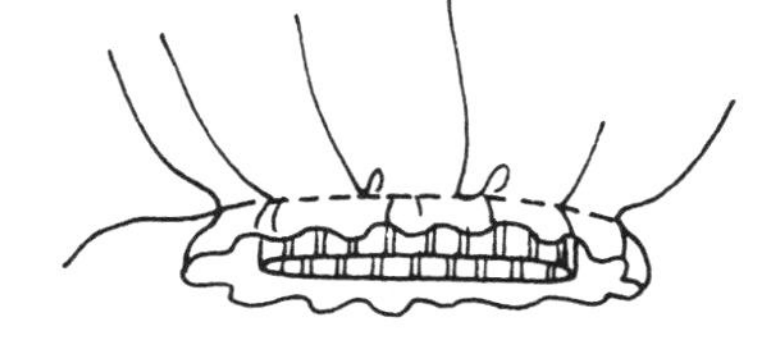

need stretching slightly to fit (fig 3).

Variations: Cut a V neck and attach a double band of fabric.

Cut a piece of ribbing or fabric 50 cm deep for the round neck and attach it as a cowl.

Omit the sleeves, cut a V neck, bind the neck and armholes with self fabric; shorten the pattern by 15 cm and insert a drawstring through a casing at the waist. Made in light-weight jersey, it is a perfect top to go with the Single-Seam Skirt (p.112), the Wrap Skirt (p.117) or the Bias Skirt (p.126).

Trousers

Easy trousers with straight leg, elastic or drawstring in waist. Wear with any of the tops shown in the book.
Size: 16
Length at side seam: 107 cm
Width of leg at hem: 54 cm
For smaller sizes reduce the pattern at side seams by the following amounts:

For size 10 — 32 mm
For size 12 — 22 mm
For size 14 — 12 mm

Also re-shape the crutch seam as shown for each size.

Fig 1

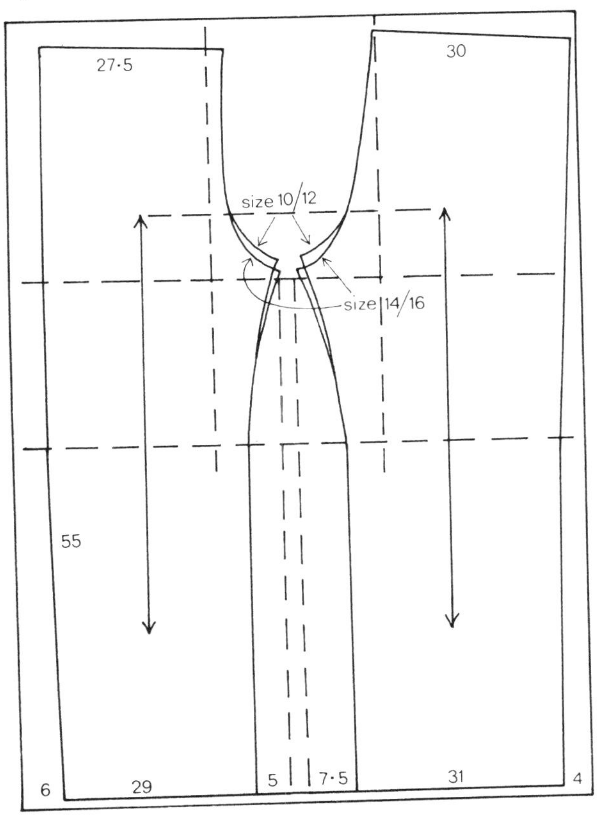

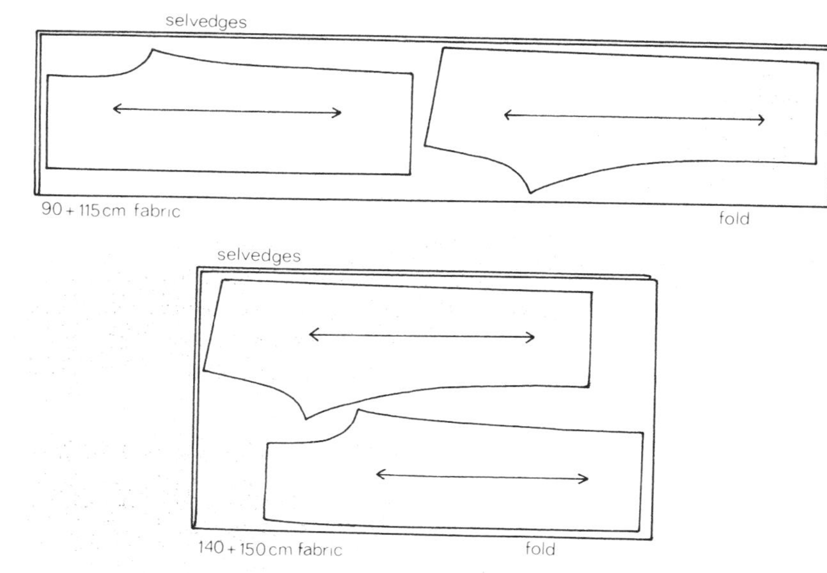

Fig 2

To adjust the leg length alter at the hem.
Seam allowance: 1.5 cm
3 cm at waist
4 cm at hem

Fabric: Use any light-weight woven or jersey fabric, including cotton, satin, viscose, ciré, synthetic jersey, panne velvet, velour, stretch towelling, velveteen.
2.40 m of 90 cm fabric or
2.40 m of 115 cm fabric or
1.50 m of 140 cm fabric or
1.30 m of 150 cm fabric

Haberdashery: 2 reels Drima
80 cm elastic 20 mm wide

The pattern: You will have to join pieces of paper to make a piece 120 cm long and 85 cm wide.

Draw the hemline of back and front legs 2 cm above the bottom edge. Mark off the leg widths as shown. Draw perpendicular guide lines for the inside leg and 82 cm long. Draw the inside leg and outside leg seams straight up to 55 cm from the bottom of the paper then shape as shown (fig 1).

To draw the crutch seam, rule perpendicular guide lines at 30 cm and 55 cm measuring from the left-hand edge of the paper.

The front seam drops straight almost to the guide line below before curving out to meet the inside leg seam. The back crutch starts higher and slopes out by 5 cm before curving to the inside leg. Follow whichever curve is appropriate to the size you are making.

Cutting out: Follow the diagram for cutting out (fig 2).

Making up: Arrange the front legs on a table with right sides up and place the back legs on top right-sides down. Match up the outside leg edges and join. Match the inside leg edges and join (fig 3).

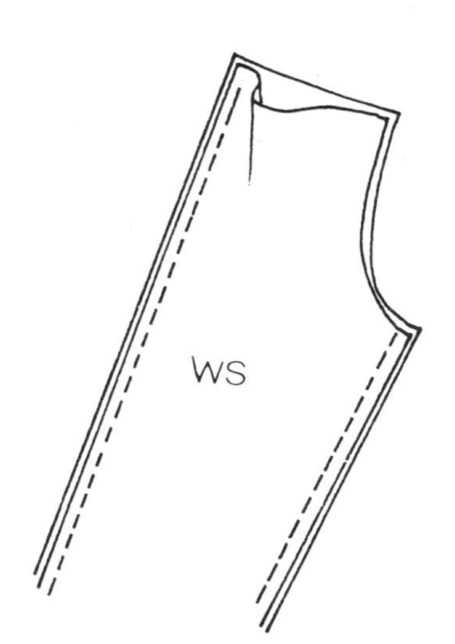

Fig 3

Fig 4

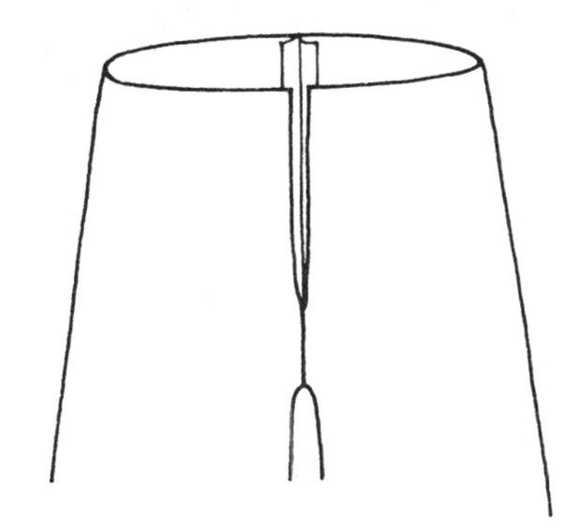

With legs right-side out, pin in side leg seams together (fig 4).

Turn over 3 cm at the waist and machine to form a casing. Cut elastic to size and insert. Join securely.

Turn up hems and adjust length. Make a deep hem or a Wundaweb hem.

Variations: Use cord or rouleau instead of elastic.

Make the hems into stitched casings and insert cord ties or elastic.

Pleat the waist into a waistband: reduce the height at the waist by 1.5 cm, insert a 20 cm zip in the front seam, and add a waistband. The band can be fastened conventionally or it can have long ties.

Hooded snuggler

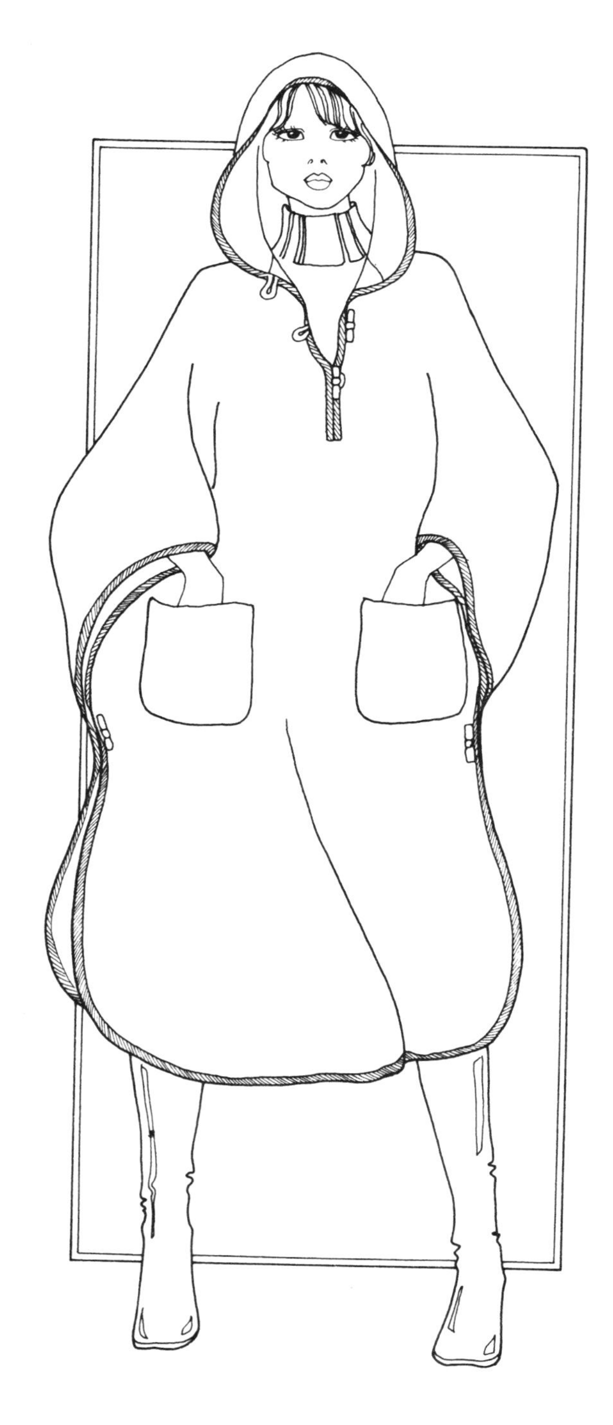

Neither a cape nor a poncho but a warm, loose casual thing to snuggle into. One piece of fabric — no shoulder seams — a hood, pockets and braid round the edges.

Size: All sizes

Length: 112 cm

Seam allowance: 1.5 cm. No allowance at outer edge as braid is to be attached.

Fabric: Any thick, spongy fabric, including coating, blanket cloth, mohair, reversible cloth. Unsuitable for one-way fabrics.

2.70 m of 140 or 150 cm fabric

Haberdashery: 2 reels Drima
5.50 m braid 4 cm wide
7 toggle buttons

The pattern: This is a simple shape that can easily be drawn on the fabric. Fold the fabric and find the half-way point along the fold. Mark the shoulder line then draw the neckline. Cut it out and cut down the centre front fold for 29 cm for the neck opening (fig 1).

At the far side mark the points for attaching the buttons at the sides. They are 10 cm in from the edge of the fabric and 32 cm down from the shoulder at the front and 40 cm at the back.

The edge of the snuggler is parallel with this line and then curves round to 30 cm from the fold. From there draw a straight hemline.

The pocket position is 15 cm below the neck slit and 10 cm from the centre front.

For the hood pattern you will need a piece of paper 31 cm wide and 45 cm deep. Use the patch pocket pattern from the Wrap Skirt (p. 117) but cut it larger by 2 cm all round (fig 2).

Cutting out: Cut the main part in fabric. Cut two hood sections. Cut two pockets.

Making up: Attach braid to outer edge.

Make and attach the pockets.

Stitch the centre back seam of the hood as a welt seam.

Join hood to neckline with a welt seam.

Bind the face edge of the hood and the slit neckline (fig 3).

Make braid loops and attach to the right side of

Fig 1

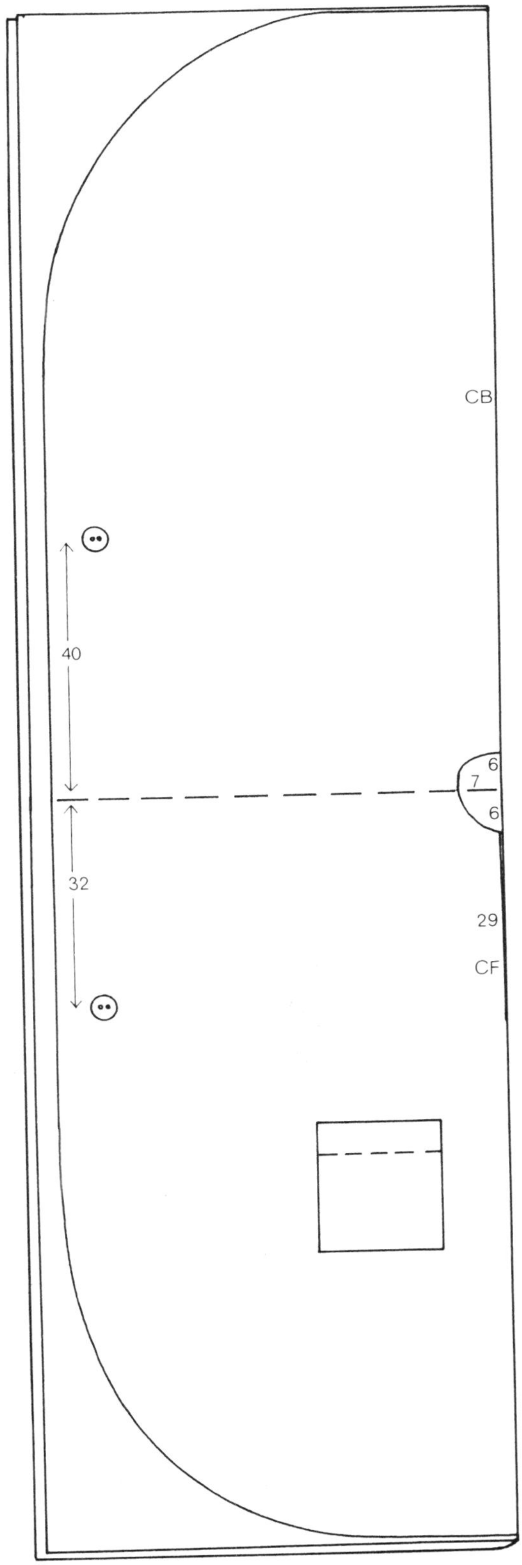

the opening. Sew buttons to correspond with the loops. Sew pairs of buttons to hold the sides closed.
Variations: Make ties from the braid instead of loops and buttons.

Turn machined hems instead of using braid. Shorten the pattern by 30 cm for a short version.

Fig 2

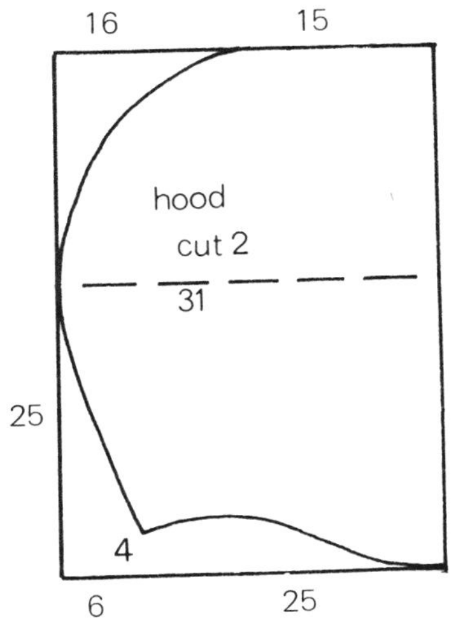

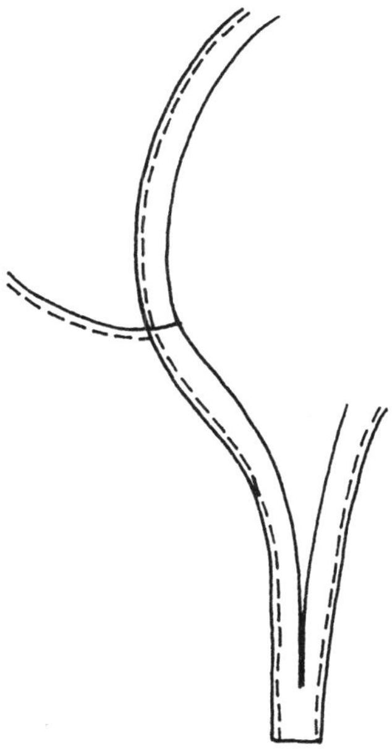

Fig 3

Zip jacket

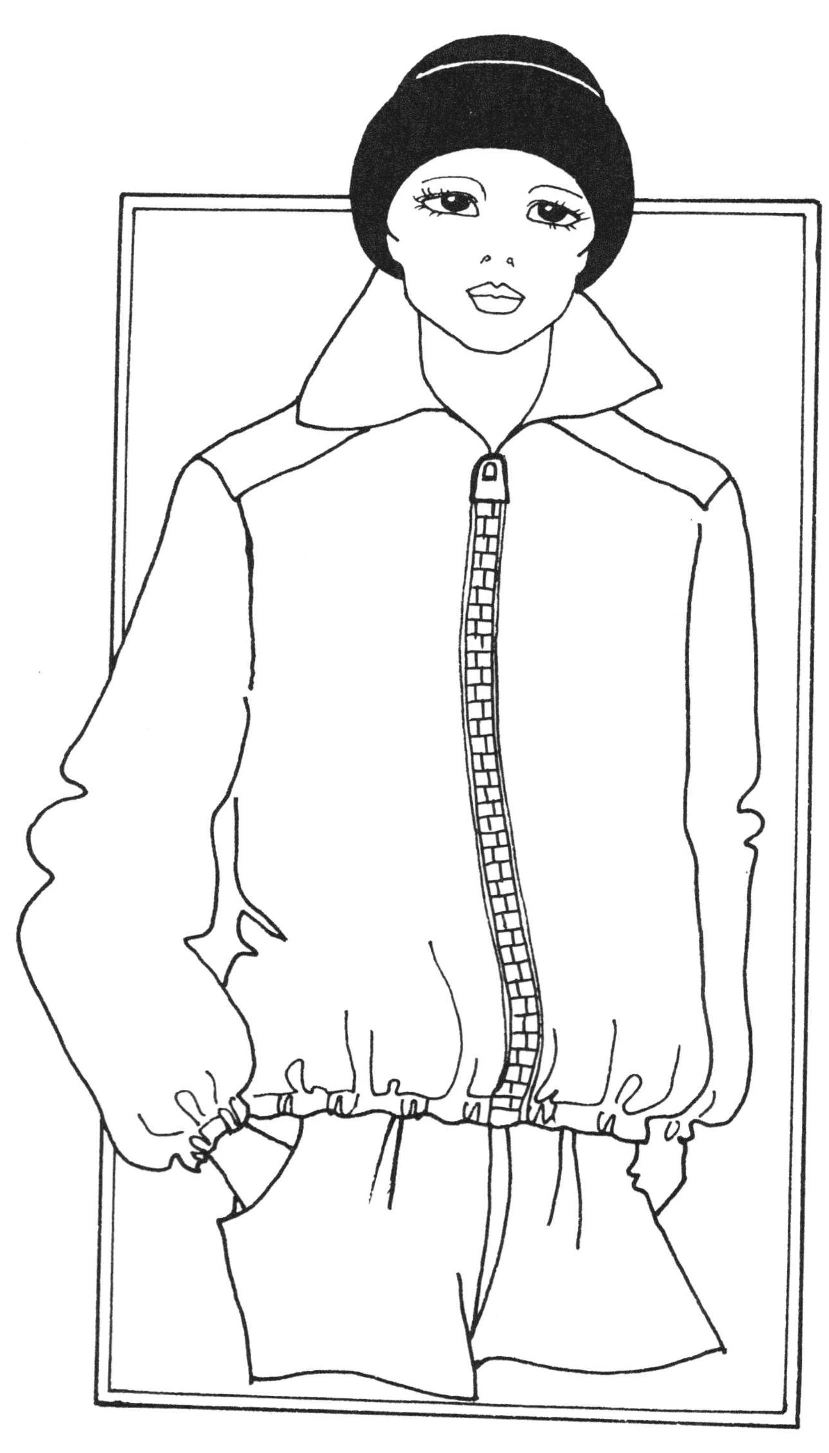

A hip-length blouson with chunky zip and collar. This includes more processes than any other design but the extended shoulder and elastic wrists and hem make it easy to get a good result.

Can be worn with the Trousers (p. 131), in which case put elastic or cord through the hems.

Size: 12-14

For a smaller size take equal amounts from centre front and centre back.

Length: Back neck to hem 64 cm

Seam allowance: 1.5 cm
3 cm on hems

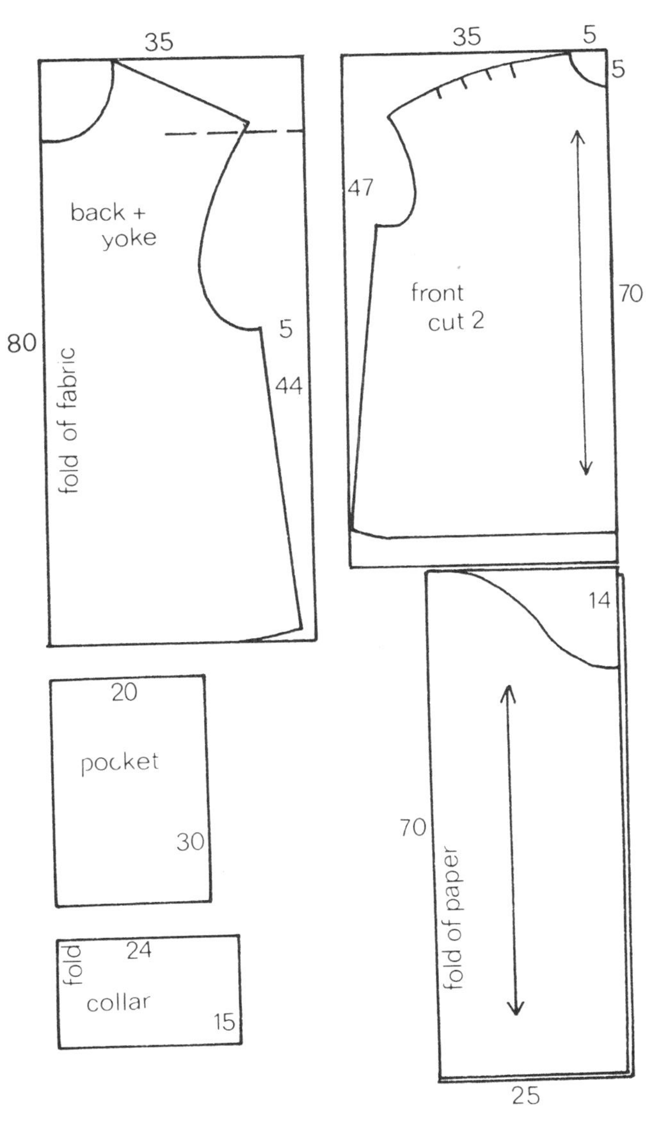

Fig 1

Fabric: Velour, jersey velvet, panne velvet, velveteen, needlecord, corduroy, nylon cirê, proofed poplin, stretch towelling, candlewick, cotton jersey.

1.40 m of 150 cm fabric

Haberdashery: 2 reels Drima
Small piece iron-on Vilene 48 x 15 cm for collar e.g. Softline
1.50 m elastic 1 cm wide
60 cm open-ended nylon zip or big Alpine zip

The pattern: For the back you need a piece of squared paper 35 cm wide and 80 cm deep. Draw in the hemline, curving it up slightly to finish at a point 2 cm before the edge of the paper. Measure 44 cm up the edge of the paper to find the armhole level. Draw in the side seam sloping in 5 cm (fig 1).

Draw the neckline 11 cm down and 10 cm in at the top corner. Rule the shoulder yoke seam 19 cm long, sloping down to 10 cm below the top of the paper. Curve the armhole as shown. The top 15 cm slope gently but under the arm it dips sharply from the side seam before starting to rise.

For the front use a piece of paper 35 cm wide and 70 cm deep. Rule in the hemline as shown, 4 cm above the bottom of the paper but curve it up slightly. The under-arm level is 47 cm up from the bottom of the paper. Rule the side seam, sloping it in 4 cm.

The neckline is a curve 5 cm deep by 5 cm wide. The outer point of the shoulder yoke seam is 9 cm down and 7 cm in from the edge of the paper. Curve the seam from there to the neck point.

Mark two tucks 3 cm wide and 2 cm apart in the middle of that seam.

For the sleeve fold a piece of paper 70 cm deep and 50 cm wide to draw half the sleeve. Draw the sleeve head to a point 14 cm down, curving the top 10 cm gently, the next 5 cm at a slant and the last 10 cm should be slightly concave. Cut out the sleeve head shape, open out the pattern for the complete sleeve.

Cutting out: Fold the fabric and place the back to the fold with the front beside it on the selvedge. Pin the sleeve below the front and cut out.

Cut the collar from the remainder still with the fabric double. The collar is 15 cm deep and 24 cm long. The fold of the fabric becomes the centre back of the collar.

Pockets may be cut from the remainder. They should be 30 cm deep and 20 cm wide.

Making up: Pin the tucks, folding the fabric out towards the armhole. Join the front and back shoulders with an overlaid seam or handle as a welt seam (fig 2).

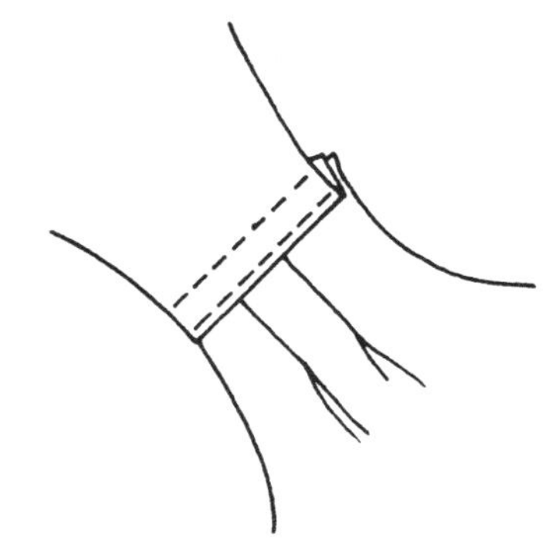

Fig 2

Insert the sleeves, easing the sleeve into the armhole.

Stitch the sleeve and side seam in one movement (fig 3).

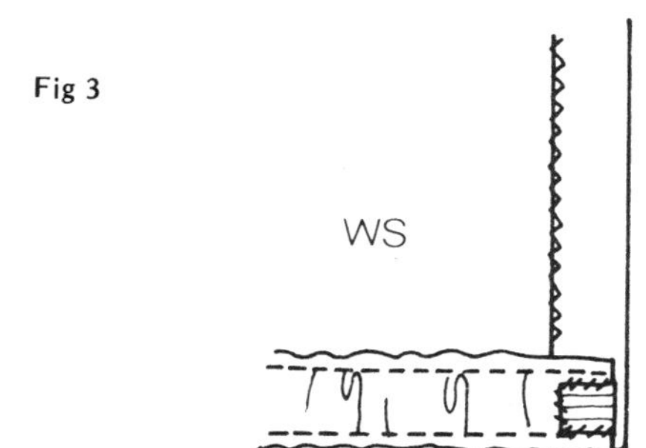

Fig 3

Turn up the sleeve hems. Turn up the hems of the jacket. Insert elastic.

Insert the zip. Attach the collar to the neckline, following the single layer method for shirt collars. *Variations:* Attach the patch pockets after cutting out but before working any processes.

Place the pockets 6 cm above the hemline and 3 cm from the centre front edge (fig 4).

Use cord to drawstring the hem.

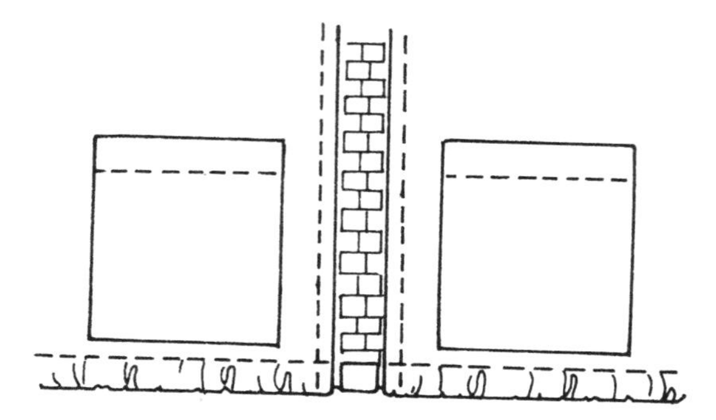

Fig 4

Hat and scarf

Pull-on hat and long scarf. A classic set quick to make but to be worn with practically anything.

Size: All sizes

Fabric: Only suitable for stretchy knitted fabrics
80 cm of 140 or 150 cm fabric
50 cm fringe or knitting yarn to make fringe

Haberdashery: 1 reel Drima

The pattern: Both scarf and hat are simple rectangles that can be cut from fabric to the sizes shown in the diagram (fig 1).

Cutting out: Cut all pieces across the width of the fabric.

Making up: Fold hat section in half and join the seam. Fold tube wrong-sides together and gather up the crown edges separately, drawing them together and tucking in the raw ends of fabric. Fold edge back to form brim. Narrow elastic such as shirring elastic could be inserted in the fabric at the fold to tighten the hat (fig 2).

Fig 1

55
42·5
42·5
hat
scarf
scarf
70
fold
80

Fig 2

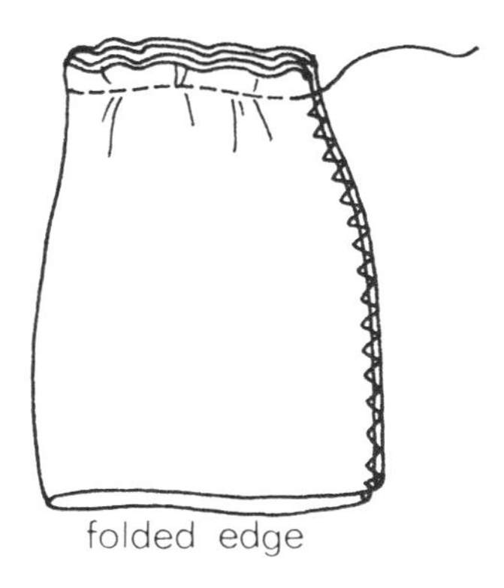

Join the scarf pieces end to end. Fold in half lengthwise and stitch to form a tube (fig 3).

Turn right side out. Attach fringe to ends.

Variation: Cut scarf longer and tie ends in a knot.

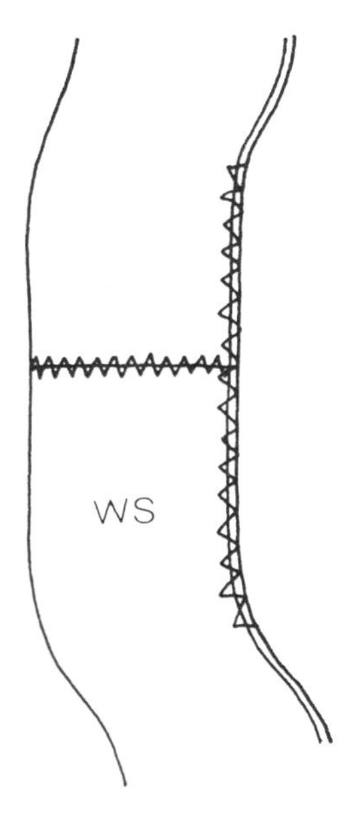

Fig 3

Bag

Simple tote bag style. Use as a handbag or general carrying bag.

Fabric: Use any strong, stiff fabric such as canvas, hessian, heavy PVC, ticking, deck chair canvas, calico, or a softer fabric and back it before making with firm iron-on Vilene.

1.10 m of fabric 45 cm wide or
55 cm of 90 cm fabric

Haberdashery: 1 reel Drima
3.80 m webbing 2.5 cm wide
Stiff card and thin foam sheet

The pattern: Cut the bag from double fabric to the size shown. Mark off 10 cm at the bottom corners as shown and also mark the position of the webbing (fig 1).

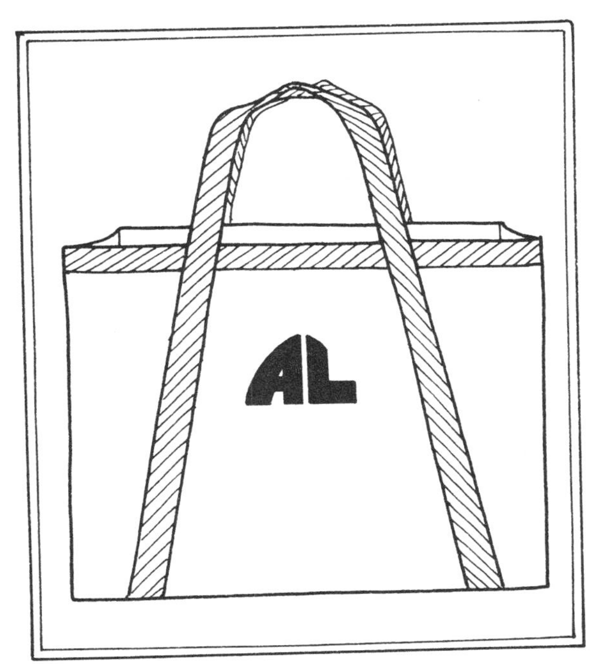

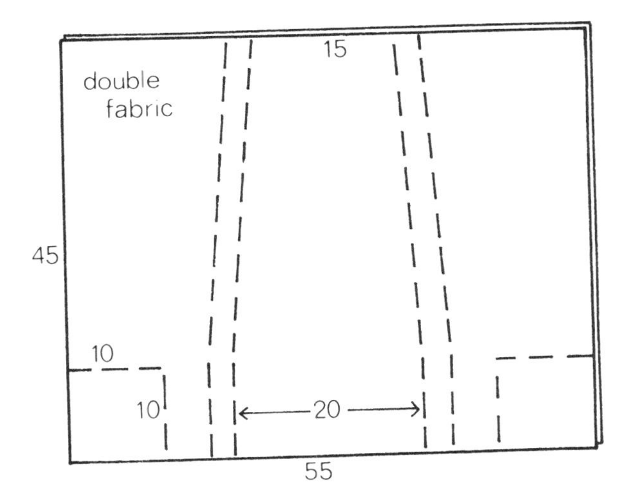

Fig 1

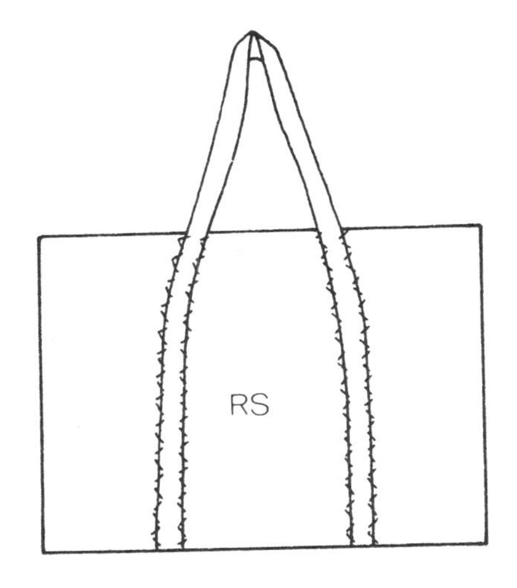

Fig 2

Making up: Attach the webbing handles (fig 2).

Stitch the four corners by folding the fabric right-sides together, matching the marks and stitching as a dart.

Make a seam across the base of the bag and up each side in one operation (fig 3).

Fig 3

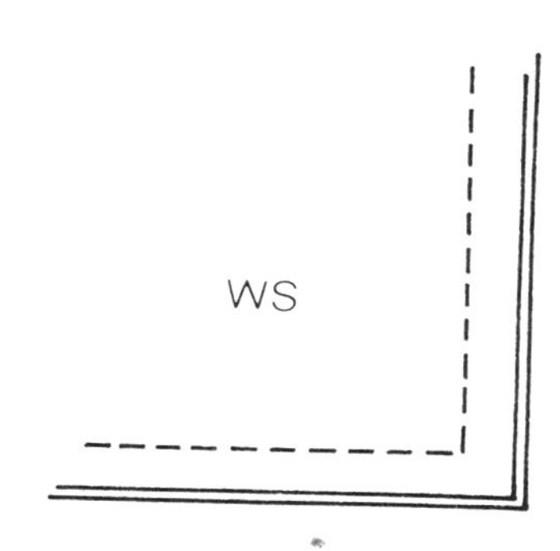

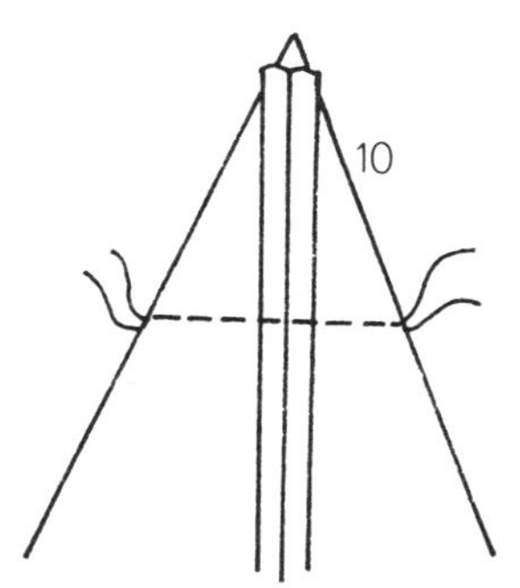

Fig 4

Fold across base seam and stitch as a dart 10 cm from the point (fig 4).

Cut a piece of strong card 35 cm long and 20 cm wide. Slip it into the base of the bag and trim it to fit easily. Glue a piece of foam sheeting to one side and cover the whole with an odd piece of fabric or with sheet plastic.

Index

TASCHEN's FAVOURITE
SPAS

Angelika Taschen

TASCHEN's FAVOURITE
SPAS

TASCHEN

Europe

12–181

Africa & the Middle East

182–217

Asia

North America

Latin America

FR, Six Senses Spa 122
FR, Spa Vinothérapie Caudalie 130
IE, Espa 28
US, Japanese Spa 352
US, Aman Spa 364
US, Mii Amo Destination Spa 360
US, Osmosis Day Spa Sanctuary 370
FR, Spa Vinothérapie Caudalie 148
PT, Aquapura Spa 176
ES, Spa Vinothérapie Caudalie 170
324 Mayflower Inn & Spa, US
330 Mandarin Oriental Spa, US
338 Shibui Spa, US
MX, Verana Day Spa 376
CR, El Silencio Lodge & Spa 388
344 The Standard Spa, US
BR, Le Spa Natura 394

58 Gräflicher Park Hotel & Spa, DE
34 Grand Spa Resort A-Rosa, DE
40 Heiligendamm Spa, DE
46 Brune Balance Med & Spa, DE
54 Adlon Day Spa, DE
12 Pädaste Spa, EE
22 Espa, RU
64 Aiyasha Spa, DE
68 Grand Spa Resort A-Rosa, AT
74 Balance Center & Spa, AT
82 Susanne Kaufmann Spa, AT
90 Aurelio Spa, AT
156 Kami Spa, IT
182 Six Senses Spa, JO
196 Anantara Spa, AE
190 Six Senses Spa, QA
98 Dolder Grand Spa, CH
106 Delight Spa & Beauty, CH
110 Therme Vals, CH
116 Kronenhof Spa, CH
MV, Como Shambhala Retreat 276
200 Maia Spa, SC
210 Le Spa de Constance, SC
138 Buddha-Bar Spa, FR
160 Six Senses Spa, ES
164 Spaciomm, ES
JP, Ginzan Hot Spring Fujiya Inn 318
218 Aman Spa, IN
228 Ananda Spa, IN
236 Aman Spa, BT
308 Aman Spa, CN
302 The Oriental Spa, CN
294 Zen Spa Red River, VN
286 The Nam Hai Resort & Spa, VN
246 Como Shambhala Urban Escape, TH
254 Six Senses Spa, TH
262 Six Senses Spa, TH
268 Espa, TH

Deep relaxation for body and soul

The spa takes its name from the small town of Spa in the Ardennes, whose hot springs made it one of the most popular health resorts among European royalty in the 18th and 19th centuries. Since then, however, it has spread far beyond the borders of Belgium and come to mean a great deal more than just therapeutic baths for aristocrats. Today, the spa is known the world over as a place in which to take time out from one's daily routine, to indulge the senses, pamper the skin and feel healthier, more beautiful and more relaxed. The treatments offered span the globe, too, and show how far back the traditions of healing techniques date: India's Ayurveda and traditional Chinese medicine are among humankind's oldest teachings, Roman baths and Greek laconia remind us of the bathing rituals of antiquity, while steam baths such as the Oriental hammam, the Russian banya and the Mexican temazcal have enjoyed widespread use and popularity for centuries. Some spas harness the power of the same plants that the Native Americans used, giving traditional treatments a modern twist, others offer scrubs, oils and creams made with herbs and fruits from their own gardens, while others still provide skin care in the form of Italian fango mud or French grape extracts.

For authentic treatments, it's not even necessary to travel to the country of origin: traditional Japanese onsens can also be found in North America, lomi lomi massages are practised as professionally in Rome as in Hawaii and Finnish saunas can be experienced in Hong Kong or in any major European city.

Just as important as the therapy itself is the spa's atmosphere. The beachfront location of a straw-roofed pavilion or the view out over a city skyline ensures an unforgettable spa experience. An interior design with fine wood, stone and silk finishes can make as positive an impression as a highly skilled therapist. And the aromatic teas, freshly squeezed juices and light but delicious spa cuisine offer inspiring ideas that can then be tried out at home.

When it comes to picking the best or most suitable spa, you might be forgiven for feeling envious of those royals, whose options were limited to just a handful of health resorts. Today, the range of wellness destinations is so vast that choosing between them can be quite a challenge. This book by Angelika Taschen aims to make that choice a little easier. It presents 55 selected spas from around the world – spas that are as remarkable for their stunning locations and unique interiors as they are for their first-class treatments and therapists.

Tiefenentspannung für Körper und Seele

Das Spa verdankt seinen Namen dem Städtchen Spa – einem in den Ardennen gelegenen und im 18. und 19. Jahrhundert dank seiner heißen Mineralquellen sehr beliebten Kurort von Europas Kaisern und Königen. Auf Belgien, heilende Bäder und eine adlige Klientel ist ein Spa heute jedoch nicht mehr beschränkt. Überall auf der Welt bezeichnet das Spa einen Ort, an dem man eine Auszeit vom Alltag nehmen kann, seine Sinne verwöhnt, sich pflegen und schön machen lässt, Erholung findet und der Gesundheit Gutes tut. Aus aller Welt stammen die möglichen Anwendungen, von denen viele zugleich Zeugen für die lange Historie der Heiltechniken sind: Indische Ayurveda und traditionelle chinesische Medizin gelten als zwei der ältesten Lehren der Menschheit, das römische Bad sowie das griechische Laconium erinnern an Pflegerituale der Antike, der orientalische Hamam, die russische Banja oder das mexikanische Temazcal sind Beispiele für Schwitzbäder, die bereits eine jahrhundertealte Tradition haben. Es gibt Spas, die auf die Wirkkraft indianischer Pflanzen setzen und traditionelle Behandlungen modern interpretieren, andere stellen ihre Peelings, Öle und Cremes aus im eigenen Garten kultivierten Kräutern und Früchten her, und wieder andere pflegen ihre Gäste mit italienischem Fango oder Extrakten aus französischen Weintrauben.

Für eine authentische Spa-Behandlung kann man in ihr Ursprungsland reisen, muss aber nicht: Traditionelle japanische Onsen gibt es auch in Nordamerika, Lomi-Lomi-Massagen werden in Rom so professionell wie auf Hawaii durchgeführt, und eine finnische Sauna findet man in Hongkong ebenso wie in jeder europäischen Metropole.

So wichtig wie die Therapie selbst ist im Spa das Ambiente – die Lage eines strohgedeckten Pavillons direkt am Strand oder der Blick aus einem Spa auf die Skyline einer Metropole können einen Spa-Besuch perfekt machen. Das Design eines Spas mit edlen Hölzern, Naturstein und Seidenstoffen behält man in ebenso guter Erinnerung wie einen ausgezeichneten Therapeuten. Und aromatische Tees, frisch gepresste Säfte sowie eine köstliche, leichte Spa Cuisine inspirieren die eigene Küche und Kochkunst.

Geht es um die Wahl des besten, des passendsten Spas, beneidet man für einen Augenblick die Kaiser und Könige, die sich nur zwischen einer Handvoll Heilbäder entscheiden mussten. Heute ist das Wellness-Angebot fast unüberschaubar und die Wahl eine echte Herausforderung. Angelika Taschen macht es den Lesern dieses Buches ein bisschen leichter und stellt ihnen 55 Spas in aller Welt vor, die sich durch eine herrliche Lage und ihr einzigartiges Design in gleicher Weise auszeichnen wie durch erstklassige Anwendungen und hervorragende Therapeuten.

Relaxation profonde physique et mentale

Au départ, Spa est le nom d'une petite ville des Ardennes possédant des sources thermales chaudes et devenue, au 18ᵉ et au 19ᵉ siècle, l'une des villes d'eaux préférées des empereurs et des rois en Europe. Devenu nom commun, il a dépassé les frontières de la Belgique, ne se limite plus à l'hydrothérapie et n'est plus l'apanage des grands. Partout, un spa est un endroit dans lequel on peut oublier le quotidien, redécouvrir ses cinq sens, se faire chouchouter et embellir, se reposer et s'occuper de sa santé. Les soins proposés – nombre d'entre eux témoignent aussi de la longue histoire des méthodes thérapeutiques – sont originaires du monde entier : l'Ayurveda indien et la médecine traditionnelle chinoise sont deux des plus anciennes sagesses, les thermes romains et le laconium grec évoquent les rituels de soins antiques, le hammam oriental, le banja russe ou le temazcal mexicain sont des bains de sudation connus depuis des siècles et très appréciés. Certains spas misent sur les vertus curatives des plantes indiennes et offrent une interprétation moderne de traitements traditionnels, d'autres fabriquent leurs produits de gommage, leurs huiles et leurs crèmes avec les fleurs et les fruits cultivés dans leur jardin, d'autres encore soignent leurs hôtes avec de la boue volcanique provenant d'Italie ou des extraits de raisins français.

Celui qui désire un traitement spa authentique peut évidemment se rendre dans le pays où celui-ci est né, mais rien ne l'y oblige : on trouve aussi des onsen traditionnels japonais en Amérique du Nord ; le massage Lomi-Lomi est pratiqué avec autant de professionnalisme à Rome qu'à Hawaii, et on trouve un sauna finlandais à Hongkong aussi facilement que dans chaque métropole européenne.

L'atmosphère qui règne dans le spa est aussi importante que les soins prodigués – le pavillon au toit de paille sur la plage ou la vue sur les toits de la capitale qu'offre un spa peuvent rendre le séjour parfait. On garde en mémoire avec autant de plaisir le design d'un spa, ses bois nobles, sa pierre naturelle et ses étoffes de soie que les conseils d'un excellent thérapeute. Quant aux infusions aromatiques, aux jus de fruits et de légumes fraîchement pressés ainsi qu'à la cuisine spa légère et savoureuse, ils inspireront notre art culinaire et nos habitudes alimentaires.

Lorsqu'il s'agit de sélectionner le meilleur spa, le plus adapté à nos besoins, on envie un moment les monarques qui n'avaient guère l'embarras du choix. Aujourd'hui, l'offre de centres de remise en forme est presque inextricable, et choisir un véritable défi. Angelika Taschen facilite la tâche aux lecteurs de cet ouvrage. Les 55 spas du monde entier qu'elle présente ici se distinguent par leur emplacement magnifique et un design unique ainsi que par des soins haut de gamme et des thérapeutes très compétents.

Pädaste Spa

at Pädaste Manor

This manor house, the origins of which date back to the 14th century, was once the family seat of German-Baltic aristocrats. Today, it's home to a delightful spa hotel in which guests can enjoy a sweat in a traditional wood-fired sauna, cool off in the Siberian cold tub and relax with natural Estonian herb and mud treatments.

Einst war dieses Herrenhaus, dessen Ursprünge bis ins 14. Jahrhundert zurückreichen, der Sitz einer deutsch-baltischen Adelsfamilie. Heute beherbergt es ein entzückendes Hotel mit Spa, wo man in der traditionell holzbefeuerten Sauna schwitzt, sich im sibirischen Zuber abkühlt und bei Anwendungen mit estnischen Kräutern und Schlamm ganz natürlich entspannt.

Ce manoir dont l'origine remonte au 14e siècle a été autrefois la résidence d'un baron balte. Il abrite aujourd'hui un hôtel ravissant doté d'un spa où l'on peut transpirer dans le sauna chauffé traditionnellement au bois, se refroidir dans le baquet sibérien et se relaxer tout naturellement pendant les applications d'huiles essentielles d'herbes d'Estonie et de boue.

Pädaste Spa
at Pädaste Manor
Muhu Island 94716
Estonia
Tel. +372 454 88 00
Fax +372 454 88 11
info@padaste.ee
www.padaste.ee
Open from early March
to late October

LOCATION
Situated on Pädaste Bay, Muhu Island, off the west coast of Estonia. The journey from Tallinn by car and ferry takes 2 h.

ROOMS
11 rooms and 12 suites in 2 separate buildings; 1 farmhouse (sleeps 2–6).

FOOD
The hotel restaurant "Alexander" offers Nordic Islands' cuisine made with vegetables and herbs from its own garden. In summer, lunches are served on the "Sea House Terrace".

SPA FACILITIES
2,600 sq ft with 3 treatment rooms, Muhu sauna, Siberian cold tub, seawater hot tub and herbal steam bath.

SIGNATURE TREATMENTS
The invigorating clover-rich Muhu hay bath and anti-rheumatic Muhu mud wrap.

BOOK TO PACK
"The Czar's Madman" by Jaan Kross.

LAGE
An der Pädaste-Bucht der Insel Muhu vor der Westküste Estlands gelegen. Der Transfer per Auto und Fähre ab Tallinn dauert 2 h.

ZIMMER
11 Zimmer und 12 Suiten in 2 Gebäuden, 1 Bauernhaus (2–6 Gäste).

KÜCHE
Gemüse und Kräuter für die nordischen Menüs im »Alexander« stammen aus dem eigenen Garten. Im Sommer genießt man den Lunch auf der »Sea House Terrace«.

SPAAUSSTATTUNG
240 qm mit 3 Behandlungsräumen, Muhu-Sauna, sibirischem Zuber, Meerwasser-Zuber, Kräuter-Dampfbad.

SIGNATURE TREATMENTS
Das belebende, kleereiche Muhu-Heubad und der Muhu-Schlammwickel mit antirheumatischer Wirkung.

BUCHTIPP
»Der Verrückte des Zaren« von Jaan Kross.

SITUATION
Dans la baie de Pädaste de l'île Muhu, au large de la côte ouest de l'Estonie. Le transfert en voiture et en bac à partir de Tallinn dure 2 h.

CHAMBRES
11 chambres et 12 suites dans 2 bâtiments, 1 ferme (2–6 pensionnaires).

RESTAURATION
Les légumes et les fines herbes qui composent les menus nordiques du restaurant « Alexander » proviennent du jardin. L'été, le dîner est servi sur la « Sea House Terrace ».

SERVICES DU SPA
240 mètres carrés avec 3 cabines de soins, sauna Muhu, baquet sibérien, baquet d'eau de mer, bain de vapeur aux huiles essentielles.

SOINS SIGNATURE
Bain de foin vitalisant Muhu au trèfle et enveloppement de boue Muhu aux vertus antirhumatismales.

LIVRE À EMPORTER
« Le Fou du tzar » de Jaan Kross.

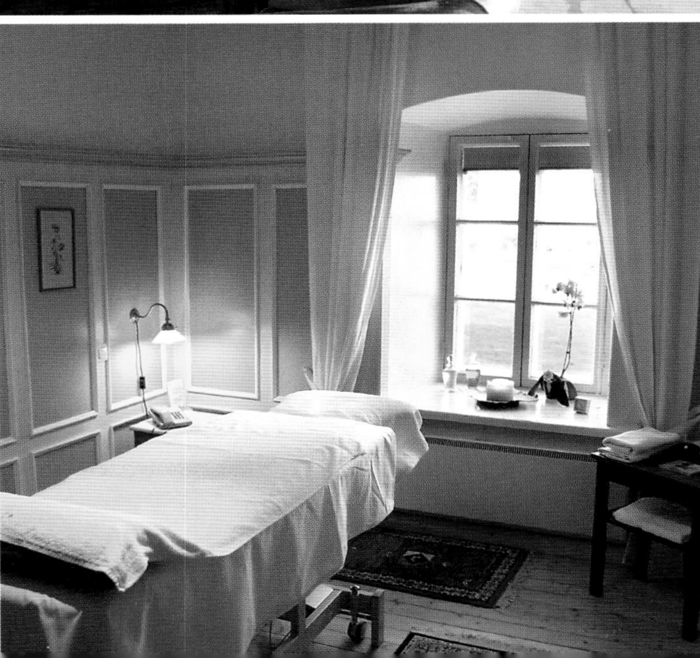

Espa

at The Ritz-Carlton Moscow

This luxurious spa is a real feast for the eyes, with subtle shades of marble, polished wenge wood and Swarovski crystals that bathe the black and gold-clad pool in sparkling light. It's a treat for the skin too, thanks to natural Espa products and sumptuous treatments that combine the latest scientific advances with European therapies and Eastern healing traditions such as Ayurveda.

In diesem luxuriösen Spa verwöhnen farbiger Marmor, poliertes Wenge-Holz sowie Swarovski-Kristallle, die den schwarz-gold ausgekleideten Pool in funkelndes Licht setzen, das Auge. Die Haut pflegen natürliche Espa-Produkte sowie traumhafte Anwendungen, die neuste wissenschaftliche Erkenntnisse mit europäischen Therapien und fernöstlichen Heiltraditionen wie Ayurveda verbinden.

Dans ce spa luxueux, le marbre aux couleurs tendres, le wengé poli et les cristaux de Swarovski autour du bassin aux carreaux noir et or enchantent le regard. La peau est choyée par les produits naturels Espa et par des soins mariant les découvertes scientifiques modernes aux thérapies européennes et aux traditions curatives d'Orient comme l'Ayurveda.

Espa
at The Ritz-Carlton Moscow
Tverskaya Street 3
Moscow 125009
Russia
Tel. +7 495 225 88 88
Fax +7 495 225 84 00
rc.mowrz.leads@ritzcarlton.com
www.ritzcarlton.com

LOCATION
On the edge of Red Square with views of the Kremlin; 45 min from the airports Domodedovo and Sheremetyevo.

ROOMS
278 rooms and 66 suites.

FOOD
The spa has its own café. The hotel's "O2 Lounge" serves sushi, while "Ginkgo" offers pan-Asian cuisine.

SPA FACILITIES
21,528 sq ft with 14 treatment rooms; mixed area with indoor pool, hot pool, steam bath, sauna, lifestyle showers and ice fountain; women's area with steam bath, sauna, lifestyle showers and ice fountain; fitness centre and hair salon.

SIGNATURE TREATMENT
The "Energy Balancing Ritual", a body massage with hot volcanic stones and Espa oils.

BOOK TO PACK
"War and Peace" by Leo Tolstoy.

LAGE
Am Rand des Roten Platzes mit Blick auf den Kreml gelegen; 45 min von den Flughäfen Domodedowo und Scheremetjewo entfernt.

ZIMMER
278 Zimmer und 66 Suiten.

KÜCHE
Zum Spa gehört ein Café. Im Hotel serviert die »O2 Lounge« Sushi, das »Ginkgo« pan-asiatische Menüs.

SPAAUSSTATTUNG
2.000 qm mit 14 Behandlungsräumen; Bereich für Damen und Herren mit Innenpool, Heißpool, Dampfbad, Sauna, Lifestyleduschen, Eisbrunnen; Damenbereich mit Dampfbad, Sauna, Lifestyleduschen, Eisbrunnen; Fitnesscenter, Friseursalon.

SIGNATURE TREATMENT
Das »Energy Balancing Ritual«, eine Körpermassage mit heißen Vulkansteinen und Espa-Ölen.

BUCHTIPP
»Krieg und Frieden« von Leo Tolstoi.

SITUATION
Au bord de la place Rouge avec vue sur le Kremlin ; à 45 min des aéroports de Domodedovo et Cheremetievo.

CHAMBRES
278 chambres et 66 suites.

RESTAURATION
Le spa abrite un café. À l'hôtel, le « O2 Lounge » propose des sushis, le « Ginkgo » une cuisine pan-asiatique.

SERVICES DU SPA
2000 mètres carrés avec 14 cabines de soins ; espace mixte avec piscine intérieure, bassin d'eau chaude, bain de vapeur, sauna, douches lifestyle, fontaine de glace ; espace dames avec bain de vapeur, sauna, douches lifestyle, fontaine de glace ; centre de remise en forme, salon de coiffure

SOIN SIGNATURE
L'« Energy Balancing Ritual », un massage du corps aux pierres volcaniques chaudes et aux huiles Espa.

LIVRE À EMPORTER
« Guerre et Paix » de Léon Tolstoï.

Espa

at The Ritz-Carlton Powerscourt

Built in 2007, this Palladian hotel sits amidst the green hills, ancient woodlands and shimmering lakes of County Wicklow. The hotel's spa, whose interiors combine wood, slate and glass, takes its cue from the beautiful surroundings – and offers stunning views of the nearby Sugar Loaf Mountain as well as treatments featuring natural products by Espa.

Seit 2007 thront dieses von Palladio inspirierte Hotel inmitten der von grünen Hügeln, uralten Wäldern und glitzernden Seen geprägten Landschaft von County Wicklow. Die Schönheit der Umgebung greift das Spa mit Interieur-Elementen aus Holz, Schiefer sowie Glas auf – zudem bietet es wunderschöne Ausblicke auf den Sugar Loaf Mountain und Behandlungen mit natürlichen Produkten von Espa.

Depuis 2007, cet hôtel de style palladien trône au milieu des collines vertes, des forêts séculaires et des lacs scintillants du comté de Wicklow. Aménagé avec des éléments de bois, d'ardoise et de verre, le spa reflète la beauté du paysage environnant. On profite ici d'une vue splendide sur la Sugar Loaf Mountain et de soins Espa, à base de produits naturels.

The Ritz-Carlton Powerscourt
Powerscourt Estate
Enniskerry
County Wicklow
Ireland
Tel. +353 1 274 88 88
Fax +353 1 274 99 99
dubrt.leads@ritzcarlton.com
www.ritzcarlton.com

Espa
Tel. +353 1 274 97 10

LOCATION
Situated on an approx. 1,000-acre estate to the south of Dublin, 25 min from the city centre and 40 min from the airport.

ROOMS
76 rooms and 124 suites.

FOOD
The spa's café serves salads and wraps.

SPA FACILITIES
30,000 sq ft with 20 treatment rooms, 2 spa suites, men's and women's thermal suites, each with separate steam bath, sauna, ice fountain, vitality pool, lifestyle showers and tepidarium; 20-m indoor pool, hammam, hot pool, sauna and fitness centre.

SIGNATURE TREATMENTS
"Garden of Inspiration" rituals such as the holistic body treatment with oil-and-salt scrub, massage and face mask.

BOOK TO PACK
"Waiting for Godot" by Samuel Beckett.

LAGE
Auf einem 404 ha großen Grundstück südlich von Dublin gelegen – das Zentrum ist 25 min entfernt, der Flughafen 40 min.

ZIMMER
76 Zimmer und 124 Suiten.

KÜCHE
Das Spa-Café serviert Salate und Wraps.

SPAAUSSTATTUNG
2.788 qm mit 20 Behandlungsräumen, 2 Spa-Suiten, Thermal-Suiten für Damen und Herren jeweils mit Dampfbad, Sauna, Eisbrunnen, Vitality-Pool, Lifestyleduschen und Tepidarium; 20-m-Innenpool, Hamam, Heißpool, Saunen, Fitnesscenter.

SIGNATURE TREATMENTS
Die »Garden of Inspiration«-Rituale: ganzheitliche Körperbehandlung mit Salz-Öl-Peeling, Massage und Maske.

BUCHTIPP
»Warten auf Godot« von Samuel Beckett.

SITUATION
Dans une propriété de 404 ha au sud de Dublin – le centre est à 25 min, l'aéroport à 40 min.

CHAMBRES
76 chambres et 124 suites.

RESTAURATION
Le café du spa propose salades et wraps.

SERVICES DU SPA
2788 mètres carrés avec 20 cabines de soins, 2 suites spa, suites thermales pour dames et messieurs avec bain de vapeur, sauna, fontaine de glace, piscine Vitalité, douches lifestyle et tepidarium ; piscine intérieure de 20 m, hammam, bassin d'eau chaude, saunas, centre de remise en forme.

SOINS SIGNATURE
Les rituels « Garden of Inspiration » : soins holistiques du corps avec gommage à base d'huile et de sel, massage et masque.

LIVRE À EMPORTER
« En attendant Godot » de Samuel Beckett.

Grand Spa Resort

at A-Rosa Sylt

The nearby North Sea plays a starring role at this chic and modern spa resort set amidst the windswept sand dunes of List. Built by Helmut Riemann Architekten, it boasts an almost 1,000-foot-long pipeline that feeds fresh seawater into the heated pools, plus treatment rooms in which guests can enjoy sea views and authentic thalassotherapy.

In diesem Spa Resort, das vom Architekturbüro Helmut Riemann als modernes, mondänes Kurhaus in die Sanddünen von List gesetzt wurde, spielt die Nordsee die Hauptrolle: Durch eine 300 Meter lange Pipeline wird frisches Meerwasser in die Pools geleitet und dort beheizt, und in den Behandlungsräumen genießt man bei Meerblick Thalassotherapien.

La mer joue le rôle principal dans ce Spa Resort, que le cabinet d'architectes Helmut Riemann a placé comme une « Kurhaus » moderne et mondaine au milieu des dunes sauvages de List : un pipeline de 300 m de long apporte l'eau de mer dans les bassins chauffés et, dans les cabines de soins, on fait une cure de thalassothérapie originale en regardant la mer.

Grand Spa Resort
at A-Rosa Sylt
Listlandstraße 11
25992 List
Germany
Tel. +49 4651 96 75 00
Fax +49 4651 96 75 07 99
sylt@a-rosa.de
www.a-rosa.de

LOCATION
On the north-eastern coast of Sylt, just a stone's throw from the sandy beach; 9 miles from the island's airport and about half a mile from the ferry terminal at List.

ROOMS
147 rooms and 30 suites.

FOOD
The spa bistro serves fresh juices and healthy meals, and there are 3 hotel restaurants.

SPA FACILITIES
37,700 sq ft with 18 treatment rooms, spa suite, indoor and outdoor pools, laconium, caldarium, Finnish saunas, saunarium, Kneipp pool, hammam with rasul, fitness area, yoga room and hair salon.

SIGNATURE TREATMENT
"La Vie Aquatique", a thalassotherapy treatment with sand scrub, water-lily bath, body massage and mud pack.

BOOK TO PACK
"The Rider on the White Horse" by Theodor Storm.

LAGE
An Sylts Nordostküste nur wenige Schritte vom Sandstrand entfernt gelegen. Zum Flughafen Westerland fährt man 15 km, zum Hafen List 1 km.

ZIMMER
147 Zimmer und 30 Suiten.

KÜCHE
Das Spa-Bistro serviert frische Säfte und gesunde Gerichte; zudem bietet das Hotel 3 Restaurants.

SPAAUSSTATTUNG
3.500 qm mit 18 Behandlungsräumen, Spa-Suite, Innen- und Außenpool, Laconium, Caldarium, finnischen Saunen, Biosauna, Kneippbecken, Hamam mit Rasul, Fitnessbereich, Yogaraum, Friseursalon.

SIGNATURE TREATMENT
»La Vie Aquatique«, eine Thalassotherapie mit Peeling, Wasserlilienbad, Körpermassage und Schlickpackung.

BUCHTIPP
»Ebbe und Flut« von Irina Korschunow.

SITUATION
Sur la côte nord-est de Sylt, tout près de la plage de sable. L'aéroport de Westerland est à 15 km, le port de List à 1 km.

CHAMBRES
147 chambres et 30 suites.

RESTAURATION
Le bistro du spa sert jus de fruits et plats diététiques ; l'hôtel abrite 3 restaurants.

SERVICES DU SPA
3500 mètres carrés avec 18 cabines de soins, suite spa, piscine intérieure et extérieure, laconium, caldarium, saunas finlandais, sauna bio, bassin Kneipp, hammam avec soins au rassoul, espace de remise en forme, salle de yoga, salon de coiffure.

SOIN SIGNATURE
« La Vie Aquatique », une thalassothérapie avec gommage, bain aux nénuphars massage du corps et enveloppements de boue.

LIVRE À EMPORTER
« Le Goût des pépins de pomme » de Katharina Hagena.

Heiligendamm Spa

at the Grand Hotel Heiligendamm

Behind its pristine white seafront façades, the Grand Hotel Heiligendamm now boasts elegant interiors in the blue, green and sand shades of the Baltic coast (a redesign by Anne Maria Jagdfeld), as well as a 32,000-square-foot luxury spa housed in the hotel's Severin Palais. A homage to Heiligendamm's long history as a spa resort, it offers traditional wellness treatments from Europe and the East.

In der »Weißen Stadt am Meer«, deren Interieurs Anne Maria Jagdfeld elegant in den Blau-, Grün- und Sandtönen der Ostseeküste designt hat, beherbergt das Severin Palais, ein 3.000 Quadratmeter großes Luxus-Spa. Als Hommage an die glanzvolle Bädertradition von Heiligendamm entworfen, bietet es klassische Wellnessanwendungen aus Europa und dem Orient.

Dans la « ville blanche en bord de mer » dont Anne Maria Jagdfeld a élégamment décoré les intérieurs dans les teintes bleu, vert et sable du littoral de la Baltique, le Severin Palais abrite un spa luxueux de 3000 mètres carrés. En hommage à la brillante tradition balnéaire de Heiligendamm, il propose des soins de bien-être classiques, originaires d'Europe et d'Orient.

Heiligendamm Spa
at the Grand Hotel Heiligendamm
Prof.-Dr.-Vogel-Straße 6
18209 Bad Doberan-Heiligendamm
Germany
Tel. +49 38203 74 00
Fax +49 38203 740 74 74
info@grandhotel-heiligendamm.de
www.grandhotel-heiligendamm.de

LOCATION
112 miles north-east of Hamburg airport, 149 miles north of Berlin-Tegel airport.

ROOMS
136 rooms and 79 suites in 5 buildings.

FOOD
The "Spa Lounge & Bar" serves the Heiligendamm Spa Cuisine.

SPA FACILITIES
32,000 sq ft with 15 treatment rooms, yoga suite, 18-m indoor pool, whirlpool, Finnish sauna, steam bath, caldarium, ice room, Kneipp pool, women's sauna area, hammam, fitness area and medical wellness area offering traditional Chinese medicine.

SIGNATURE TREATMENT
The "Ila Experience", a full body massage and facial with products based on Ayurvedic principles.

BOOK TO PACK
"Buddenbrooks" by Thomas Mann.

LAGE
180 km nordöstlich des Flughafens Hamburg gelegen und 240 km nördlich vom Flughafen Berlin-Tegel.

ZIMMER
136 Zimmer und 79 Suiten in 5 Gebäuden.

KÜCHE
Die »Spa Lounge & Bar« serviert die Heiligendamm Spa Cuisine.

SPAAUSSTATTUNG
3.000 qm mit 15 Behandlungsräumen, Yogasuite, 18-m-Innenpool, Whirlpool, finnische Sauna, Dampfbad, Caldarium, Eisraum, Kneippbecken, Saunabereich für Damen, Hamam, Fitnessbereich, Medical-Wellness-Bereich mit traditioneller chinesischer Medizin.

SIGNATURE TREATMENT
Die »Ila Experience«: ein Facial und eine Ganzkörpermassage mit auf Ayurveda-Prinzipien basierenden Produkten.

BUCHTIPP
»Buddenbrooks« von Thomas Mann.

SITUATION
À 180 km au nord-est de l'aéroport de Hambourg et à 240 km au nord de l'aéroport de Berlin-Tegel.

CHAMBRES
136 chambres et 79 suites dans 5 bâtiments.

RESTAURATION
Le « Spa Lounge & Bar » propose la Heiligendamm Spa Cuisine.

SERVICES DU SPA
3000 mètres carrés avec 15 cabines de soins, suite yoga, piscine intérieure de 18 m, bain à remous, sauna finlandais, bain de vapeur, caldarium, salle froide, bassin Kneipp, espace sauna pour dames, hammam, espace de remise en forme, espace Medical Wellness avec médecine traditionnelle chinoise.

SOIN SIGNATURE
L'« Ila Experience » : soin du visage et massage du corps avec des produits basés sur les principes de l'Ayurveda.

LIVRE À EMPORTER
« Les Buddenbrook » de Thomas Mann.

Brune Balance Med & Spa

at Gut Klostermühle Alt Madlitz

This lakeside estate on Madlitzer See takes its name from a watermill that was built by monks in the 14th century and later became part of a country manor. The current manor house was transformed by Walter and Renate Brune into a hotel with its own spa and centre for integrated medicine. The European and Oriental therapies were developed in conjunction with Berlin's Charité teaching hospital.

Seinen Namen verdankt dieses Anwesen am Madlitzer See einer im 14. Jahrhundert von Mönchen erbauten Wassermühle, die später Teil eines Gutshofes wurde. Diesen verwandelten Walter und Renate Brune in ein Landhotel mit Spa sowie einem Zentrum für integrative Medizin – die ganzheitlichen Therapien aus Europa und Fernost wurden mit der Charité Berlin entwickelt.

Située au bord du lac de Madlitz, la propriété doit son nom à un moulin à eau construit par les chartreux au 14e siècle et intégré plus tard à une ferme. Walter et Renate Brune l'ont transformée en un hôtel doté d'un spa et d'un centre de médecine intégrative qui élabore avec l'Hôpital universitaire de Charité à Berlin des thérapies holistiques originaires d'Europe et d'Orient.

Gut Klostermühle Alt Madlitz
Mühlenstraße 11
15518 Madlitz-Wilmersdorf
Germany
Tel. +49 33607 592 90
Fax +49 33607 592 91 50
info@gutklostermuehle.com
www.gut-klostermuehle.com

Brune Balance Med & Spa
Tel. +49 33607 592 91 20
Fax +49 33607 592 91 21
info@brunebalancemed.com

LOCATION
In Brandenburg, near the German-Polish border, 47 miles east of Berlin.

ROOMS
80 rooms and suites in 5 buildings, 3 apartments and 2 cottages.

FOOD
The "Finckenlounge" serves healthy-eating and detox cuisine featuring organic ingredients, the "Klostermühle" international cuisine and the "Kloster-scheune" regional cuisine.

SPA FACILITIES
27,000-sq-ft medical centre and spa with 16 treatment rooms, indoor and outdoor pool, 2 saunas, salt-water steam bath, salt-water grotto and fitness area.

SIGNATURE TREATMENTS
Individually planned balance programme combining conventional medicine with alternative therapies.

BOOK TO PACK
"Under the Pear Tree" by Theodor Fontane.

LAGE
Im Märkischen Seenland gelegen, 75 km östlich von Berlin.

ZIMMER
80 Zimmer und Suiten in 5 Gebäuden, 3 Ferienwohnungen, 2 Ferienhäuser.

KÜCHE
Die »Finckenlounge« serviert Vital- und Detox-Menüs aus Bioprodukten, die »Klostermühle« internationale Küche und die »Klosterscheune« regionale Küche.

SPAAUSSTATTUNG
Medizinisches Zentrum sowie Spa auf 2.500 qm mit 16 Behandlungsräumen, Innen- und Außenpool, 2 Saunen, Sole-Dampfbad, Solegrotte, Fitnessbereich.

SIGNATURE TREATMENTS
Individuelle Balanceprogramme, die Schulmedizin und Naturheilkunde verbinden.

BUCHTIPP
»Wanderungen durch die Mark Brandenburg« von Theodor Fontane.

SITUATION
Au Brandebourg, dans un paysage riche en lacs, à 75 km à l'est de Berlin.

CHAMBRES
80 chambres et suites dans 5 bâtiments, 3 appartements, 2 cottages.

RESTAURATION
Le « Finckenlounge » propose une cuisine légère et tonifiante à base de produits bio pour éliminer les toxines. Également sur place le « Klostermühle » sert une cuisine internationale et la « Klosterscheune » une cuisine régionale.

SERVICES DU SPA
Centre médical et spa sur 2500 mètres carrés avec 16 cabines de soins, piscine intérieure et extérieure, 2 saunas, bain de vapeur d'eau salée, grotte à eau salée, espace de remise en forme.

SOINS SIGNATURE
Programmes Balance individuels qui combinent les traitements de la médecine conventionnelle et de la naturopathie.

LIVRE À EMPORTER
« Effi Briest » de Theodor Fontane.

HOTEL ADLON
HOTEL ADLON
HOTEL ADLON

Adlon Day Spa

at Hotel Adlon

Created by interior designer Anne Maria Jagdfeld, the fabulous Adlon Day Spa offers treatments and beauty menus based on traditional rituals and high-tech cosmetic research. The luxurious spa suites are each equipped with a bath or jacuzzi plus a shower with integral steam bath and a sauna.

Im außergewöhnlichen Adlon Day Spa, das von der Interior-Designerin Anne Maria Jagdfeld gestaltet wurde, werden Behandlungen und Beauty-Programme angeboten, die auf traditionellen Schönheitsritualen und auf kosmetischer High-Tech-Forschung basieren. Die luxuriösen Spa-Suiten sind mit einer Badewanne oder einem Jacuzzi, Dusche mit integriertem Dampfbad und einer Sauna ausgestattet.

Les soins et les programmes Beauté que propose l'inhabituel Adlon Day Spa, décoré par la designer Anne Maria Jagdfeld, sont basés sur les rituels d'esthétique traditionnels et la recherche cosmétique de pointe. Les suites spa luxueuses sont dotées d'une baignoire ou d'un jacuzzi, d'une cabine de douche avec bain de vapeur et d'un sauna.

Hotel Adlon
Unter den Linden 77
10117 Berlin
Germany
Tel. +49 30 226 10
Fax +49 30 22 61 22 22
hotel.adlon@kempinski.com

Adlon Day Spa
Behrenstraße 72
10117 Berlin
Germany
Tel. +49 30 301 11 72 00
info@adlon-day-spa.de
www.adlon-day-spa.de
Open Tuesday to Saturday from 9am to 10pm, Sunday and Monday from 9am to 8pm

LOCATION
The spa is situated at the rear of Hotel Adlon, about 7 miles from Tegel airport.

ROOMS
304 rooms and 78 suites.

FOOD
In addition to light, aromatic spa dishes, guests can enjoy fruity cocktails from the "Shōchū Bar".

SPA FACILITIES
9,687 sq ft with 13 treatment rooms, 3 spa suites, indoor pool, Watsu pool, sauna, steam bath and hair salon, plus yoga and personal-training areas.

SIGNATURE TREATMENTS
Treatments using Ila products and based on Ayurvedic healing techniques.

BOOK TO PACK
"Berlin Alexanderplatz" by Alfred Döblin.

LAGE
Das Spa liegt auf der Rückseite des Adlon, 12 km vom Flughafen Tegel entfernt.

ZIMMER
304 Zimmer und 78 Suiten.

KÜCHE
Die leichte und aromatische Spa-Küche wird durch frische Fruchtcocktails aus der »Shōchū Bar« ergänzt.

SPAAUSSTATTUNG
900 qm mit 13 Behandlungsräumen, 3 Spa-Suiten, Innenpool, Watsu-Pool, Sauna, Dampfbad, Friseursalon und Bereiche für Yoga und Personal Training.

SIGNATURE TREATMENTS
Die Anwendungen mit Ila-Produkten, basierend auf ayurvedischen Heilmethoden.

BUCHTIPP
»Berlin Alexanderplatz« von Alfred Döblin.

SITUATION
Le spa est situé à l'arrière de l'Adlon, à 12 km de l'aéroport de Tegel.

CHAMBRES
304 chambres et 78 suites.

RESTAURATION
La cuisine du spa, légère et aromatique, est complétée par les cocktails aux fruits du « Shōchū Bar ».

SERVICES DU SPA
900 mètres carrés avec 13 cabines de soins, 3 suites spa, piscine intérieure, bassin Watsu, sauna, bain de vapeur, salon de coiffure et espaces réservés au yoga et à l'entraînement personnalisé.

SOINS SIGNATURE
Traitements exclusifs avec des produits Ila basés sur des traditions ayurvédiques.

LIVRE À EMPORTER
« Berlin Alexanderplatz » d'Alfred Döblin.

Gräflicher Park Hotel & Spa

Bad Driburg is known for its naturally carbonated healing waters. Their therapeutic effect was described by poet Friedrich Hölderlin back in 1796. Laid out in the style of an English landscape garden, the 150-acre Gräflicher Park is home to three such springs – and to the Counts of Oeynhausen-Sierstorpff, who have lived here for seven generations and whose stylish hotel and garden spa offer truly personal service.

Schon Friedrich Hölderlin schwärmte 1796 von der wohltuenden Wirkung des Bad Driburger kohlensäurehaltigen Heilwassers. Gleich drei Quellen sprudeln im 60 Hektar großen englischen Landschaftspark der Grafen von Oeynhausen-Sierstorpff, die hier seit sieben Generationen zu Hause sind und ihre Gäste im stilvollen Hotel sowie im Garten-Spa ausgesprochen persönlich betreuen.

En 1796, Friedrich Hölderlin s'émerveillait déjà de l'effet bienfaisant des eaux aux vertus curatives de Bad Driburg. Trois sources jaillissent dans le parc anglais paysagé de 60 hectares, propriété du comte d'Oeynhausen-Sierstorpff depuis sept générations. Sa famille veille très personnellement sur les hôtes de l'élégant hôtel et du spa aménagé dans les jardins.

Gräflicher Park Hotel & Spa
Brunnenallee 1
33014 Bad Driburg
Germany
Tel. +49 5253 952 30
Fax +49 5253 952 32 05
info@graeflicher-park.de
www.graeflicher-park.de

LOCATION
19 miles east of Paderborn; 93 miles south-west of Hanover airport.

ROOMS
135 rooms and suites.

FOOD
"Caspar's Restaurant" serves seasonal regional cuisine; the rustic grill restaurant "Pferdestall" features a show kitchen and is housed in a stable block dating back to 1860.

SPA FACILITIES
16,100 sq ft with bathhouse, 3 spa suites, 3 saunas, 2 steam baths, indoor and outdoor pool, whirlpool, hot tub, wet tables, medical spa (F. X. Mayr method) and fitness room.

SIGNATURE TREATMENTS
The traditional moor-mud and carbonated mineral water baths.

BOOK TO PACK
"Selected Poems and Fragments" by Friedrich Hölderlin.

LAGE
30 km östlich von Paderborn gelegen; 150 km südwestlich vom Flughafen Hannover entfernt.

ZIMMER
135 Zimmer und Suiten.

KÜCHE
»Caspar's Restaurant« serviert saisonale regionale Menüs. Der 1860 erbaute »Pferdestall« ist ein uriges Grillrestaurant mit Schauküche.

SPAAUSSTATTUNG
1.500 qm mit Badehaus, 3 Spa-Suiten, 3 Saunen, 2 Dampfbädern, Innen- und Außenpool, Whirlpool, Heißbecken, Wet Tables, Medical Spa (F. X.-Mayr-Methode), Fitnessraum.

SIGNATURE TREATMENTS
Die traditionellen Moorbäder und Kohlensäure-Mineralbäder.

BUCHTIPP
»Sämtliche Gedichte« von Friedrich Hölderlin.

SITUATION
À 30 km à l'est de Paderborn ; à 150 km au sud-ouest de l'aéroport de Hanovre.

CHAMBRES
135 chambres et suites.

RESTAURATION
Le « Caspar's Restaurant » offre des menus avec des produits de saison. La cuisine du « Pferdestall », rôtisserie rustique datant de 1860, est visible par le client.

SERVICES DU SPA
1500 mètres carrés avec maison de bains, 3 suites spa, 3 saunas, 2 bains de vapeur, piscine extérieure et intérieure, bain à remous, bassin d'eau chaude, tables de massage pour soins humides, Medical Spa (méthode F. X. Mayr), espace de remise en forme.

SOINS SIGNATURE
Bains de tourbe et bains d'eau minérale carbogazeuse traditionnels.

LIVRE À EMPORTER
« Poèmes : 1806–1843 » de Friedrich Hölderlin.

Aiyasha Spa

In 2008, doctors Stefan Duve, Wolfgang Niederdorfer and Hans-Peter Schoppelrey opened a day spa to go with their skin and laser practice next to Munich's opera house. Fine wood, natural stone, real gold, Balinese candles and exotic fresh flowers ensure the interior alone is superbly relaxing – and the Far Eastern treatments and detox programmes work wonders.

Dieses Day Spa haben die Ärzte Stefan Duve, Wolfgang Niederdorfer und Hans-Peter Schoppelrey 2008 als Ergänzung zu ihrer Haut- und Laserpraxis an der Münchner Oper eröffnet. Bereits das Interieur mit Edelhölzern, Naturstein, echtem Gold, balinesischen Kerzen und frischen exotischen Blüten ist Entspannung pur – und die asiatischen Anwendungen sowie individuellen Detox-Programme wirken Wunder.

Les médecins Stefan Duve, Wolfgang Niederdorfer et Hans-Peter Schoppelrey ont ouvert ce spa de jour en 2008 pour compléter leur cabinet de dermatologie et de soins laser près de l'opéra de Munich. Bois nobles, pierre naturelle, or, bougies balinaises et fleurs exotiques contribuent déjà à la détente – quant aux soins asiatiques et aux programmes détox individuels, ils font des miracles.

Aiyasha Spa
Perusastraße 5
80333 Munich
Germany
Tel. +49 89 21 02 45 50
www.aiyasha-spa.de
Open daily from 9am to 9pm

LOCATION
In Munich's city centre, 23 miles south of the airport.

ROOMS
The spa doesn't have rooms of its own but can recommend accommodation in the local area.

FOOD
No restaurant; Aiyasha tea is served before and after treatments.

SPA FACILITIES
9,149 sq ft with 5 treatment rooms, each with private changing room and shower, Thai massage suite, yoga room, steam bath and shop.

SIGNATURE TREATMENT
"Aiyasha Signature Green Tea Detox Massage" with lymph drainage and detoxifying massage oil made from green tea.

BOOK TO PACK
"Success" by Lion Feuchtwanger.

LAGE
Im Zentrum Münchens gelegen, 37 km südlich des Flughafens Franz Josef Strauß.

ZIMMER
Das Spa bietet keine Zimmer, empfiehlt aber gerne nahe Unterkünfte.

KÜCHE
Kein Restaurant, vor und nach den Behandlungen wird Aiyasha-Tee serviert.

SPAAUSSTATTUNG
850 qm mit 5 Behandlungsräumen jeweils mit privater Umkleide und Dusche, Suite für Thai-Massagen, Yogaraum, Dampfbad, Shop.

SIGNATURE TREATMENT
»Aiyasha Signature Green Tea Detox Massage« mit entschlackendem Massageöl aus grünem Tee sowie einer Lymphdrainage.

BUCHTIPP
»Erfolg« von Lion Feuchtwanger.

SITUATION
Au centre de Munich, à 37 km au sud de l'aéroport Franz-Josef-Strauß.

CHAMBRES
Pas de chambres, le spa fournit volontiers des adresses d'hébergements proches.

RESTAURATION
Pas de restaurant, une infusion Aiyasha est servie avant et après les soins.

SERVICES DU SPA
850 mètres carrés avec 5 cabines de soins équipées de vestiaires privés et d'une douche, suite pour massages thaï, espace de yoga, bain de vapeur, boutique.

SOIN SIGNATURE
L'« Aiyasha Signature Green Tea Detox Massage » avec une huile de massage détoxifiante à base de thé vert ainsi qu'un drainage lymphatique.

LIVRE À EMPORTER
« Les Arpenteurs du monde » de Daniel Kehlmann.

Grand Spa Resort

at A-Rosa Kitzbühel

From the outside, this stone-built resort, which opened in 2005, resembles a traditional Tyrolean castle, complete with turrets, oriels and a shingle roof made from larch wood. Inside, however, it combines traditional elements with modern design, and features a spa that takes guests on a round-the-world trip, courtesy of treatments from Hawaii, Brazil, Thailand and Bali.

Von außen wirkt dieses 2005 eröffnete Resort aus Naturstein mit seinen Erkern, Türmchen und einem Schindeldach aus Lärchenholz wie ein typisches Tiroler Schloss. Innen jedoch verbindet es traditionelles mit modernem Design – und inspiriert seine Gäste im Spa sogar zu einer Reise rund um die Welt: Hier pflegen Anwendungen aus Hawaii, Brasilien, Thailand und Bali.

Avec ses murs en pierre de taille, ses oriels, ses tourelles et son toit en bardeaux de mélèze, la résidence hôtelière ouverte en 2005 ressemble à un château tyrolien. À l'intérieur cependant, la tradition et le design moderne font bon ménage et le spa propose un voyage autour du monde avec des soins originaires d'Hawaii, du Brésil, de Thaïlande et de Bali.

Grand Spa Resort
at A-Rosa Kitzbühel
Ried Kaps 7
6370 Kitzbühel
Austria
Tel. +43 5356 65 66 09 92
Fax +43 5356 65 66 08 19
kitzbuehel@a-rosa.de
www.a-rosa.de

LOCATION
Nestled in the Kitzbühel Alps, 50 miles south-west of Salzburg.

ROOMS
104 rooms and 46 suites.

FOOD
The restaurant "Streif" serves particularly light and healthy cuisine and even offers diners the option of consulting a nutritionist.

SPA FACILITIES
32,300 sq ft with 16 treatment rooms, spa suite, 7 saunas, hammam, rasul, ice grotto, indoor and outdoor pool, plus yoga and fitness area.

SIGNATURE TREATMENT
The "A-Rosa Way of Life" concept for all-round health.

BOOK TO PACK
"On Her Majesty's Secret Service" by Ian Fleming.

LAGE
In den Kitzbüheler Alpen gelegen, 80 km südwestlich von Salzburg.

ZIMMER
104 Zimmer und 46 Suiten.

KÜCHE
Besonders leicht und gesund kocht das Restaurant »Streif«, in dem man sich auch von Ökotrophologen beraten lassen kann.

SPAAUSSTATTUNG
3.000 qm mit 16 Behandlungsräumen, Spa-Suite, 7 Saunen, Hamam, Rasul, Eisgrotte, Innen- und Außenpool, Bereich für Yoga und Fitness.

SIGNATURE TREATMENT
Das Konzept »A-Rosa Way of Life« für eine ganzheitliche Gesundheitsvorsorge.

BUCHTIPP
»Das Nötigste über das Glück« von Bernhard Aichner.

SITUATION
Dans les Alpes de Kitzbühel, à 80 km au sud-ouest de Salzbourg.

CHAMBRES
104 chambres et 46 suites.

RESTAURATION
Le restaurant « Streif » propose une cuisine particulièrement saine et légère. On peut aussi demander conseil à des nutritionnistes.

SERVICES DU SPA
3000 mètres carrés avec 16 cabines de soins, suite spa, 7 saunas, hammam, soin au rassoul, grotte de glace, piscine intérieure et extérieure, espace de yoga et de remise en forme.

SOIN SIGNATURE
Le concept « A-Rosa Way of Life » pour des soins de prévention holistique.

LIVRE À EMPORTER
« Au service secret de Sa Majesté » de Ian Fleming.

Balance Center & Spa

at the Mavida Balance Hotel

Designed by Ilona Hagleitner, Mavida is all about promoting inner balance. The timelessly elegant spa is finished in natural wood, slate and Crema Marfil tiles, offers Oriental therapies such as shiatsu and Thai yoga, as well as astrological readings and exclusive Mavida Crystal Spa products that harness the power of natural oils, mountain crystals and precious stones.

Hier dreht sich alles um innere Balance: Im zeitlos elegant mit Naturhölzern, Schiefer und Crema-Marfil-Fliesen designten Spa bietet Ilona Hagleitner asiatische Konzepte wie Shiatsu und Thai-Yoga an. Sie ergänzt diese mit Astrologie sowie einer exklusiven Mavida-Crystal-Spa-Pflegeserie, die auf die Kraft von natürlichen Ölen, Bergkristallen und Edelsteinen setzt.

Ici tout favorise l'harmonie intérieure : dans ce spa aux lignes classiques et élégantes en bois, schiste et dalles de Crema Marfil, Ilona Hagleitner propose des concepts asiatiques comme le Shiatsu et le yoga thaïlandais auxquels s'ajoutent l'astrologie et une ligne de soins Mavida Crystal Spa, misant sur les vertus des huiles naturelles, des cristaux de roche et des pierres précieuses.

Balance Center & Spa
at the Mavida Balance Hotel
Kirchenweg 11
5700 Zell am See
Austria
Tel. +43 6542 54 10
Fax +43 6542 567 60
info@mavida.at
www.mavida.at

LOCATION
Situated in the Salzburger Land region, 56 miles south of Salzburg.

ROOMS
43 rooms and 4 suites.

FOOD
The Austro-Mediterranean hotel restaurant offers healthy and low-calorie options as well as other light dishes.

SPA FACILITIES
15,100 sq ft with 9 treatment rooms, shiatsu room, spa suite, indoor and outdoor pool, floatation pool, Blue Box with relaxation loungers, 2 saunas, Kneipp pool, tepidarium, ice fountain and fitness centre with personal trainer.

SIGNATURE TREATMENT
The "Balance Massage" with warm oil and herbal essences.

BOOK TO PACK
"Decisive Moments in History" by Stefan Zweig.

LAGE
Im Salzburger Land gelegen; 90 km südlich von Salzburg.

ZIMMER
43 Zimmer und 4 Suiten.

KÜCHE
Das österreichisch-mediterrane Restaurant serviert auch Vitalmenüs, Diät- und Schonkostgerichte.

SPAAUSSTATTUNG
1.400 qm mit 9 Behandlungsräumen, Shiatsu-Raum, Spa-Suite, Innen- und Außenpool, Floatation-Pool, Blue Box mit Entspannungsliegen, 2 Saunen, Kneippbecken, Tepidarium, Eisbrunnen, Fitnesscenter mit Personal Training.

SIGNATURE TREATMENT
Die »Balance Massage« mit warmem Öl und Kräuteressenzen.

BUCHTIPP
»Sternstunden der Menschheit« von Stefan Zweig.

SITUATION
Dans l'État de Salzbourg ; à 90 km au sud de Salzbourg.

CHAMBRES
43 chambres et 4 suites.

RESTAURATION
Le restaurant propose une cuisine autrichienne aux influences méditerranéennes, mais aussi des menus légers et diététiques pour ceux qui suivent un régime.

SERVICES DU SPA
1400 mètres carrés avec 9 cabines de soins, espace Shiatsu, suite spa, piscine intérieure et extérieure, bassin de flottaison, Blue Box avec couchettes de relaxation, 2 saunas, bassin Kneipp, tepidarium, fontaine de glace, centre de remise en forme avec entraînement personnalisé.

SOIN SIGNATURE
Le « Balance Massage » à l'huile tiède et aux huiles essentielles de plantes.

LIVRE À EMPORTER
« Les Très Riches Heures de l'humanité » de Stefan Zweig.

MAVIDA
MAVIDA

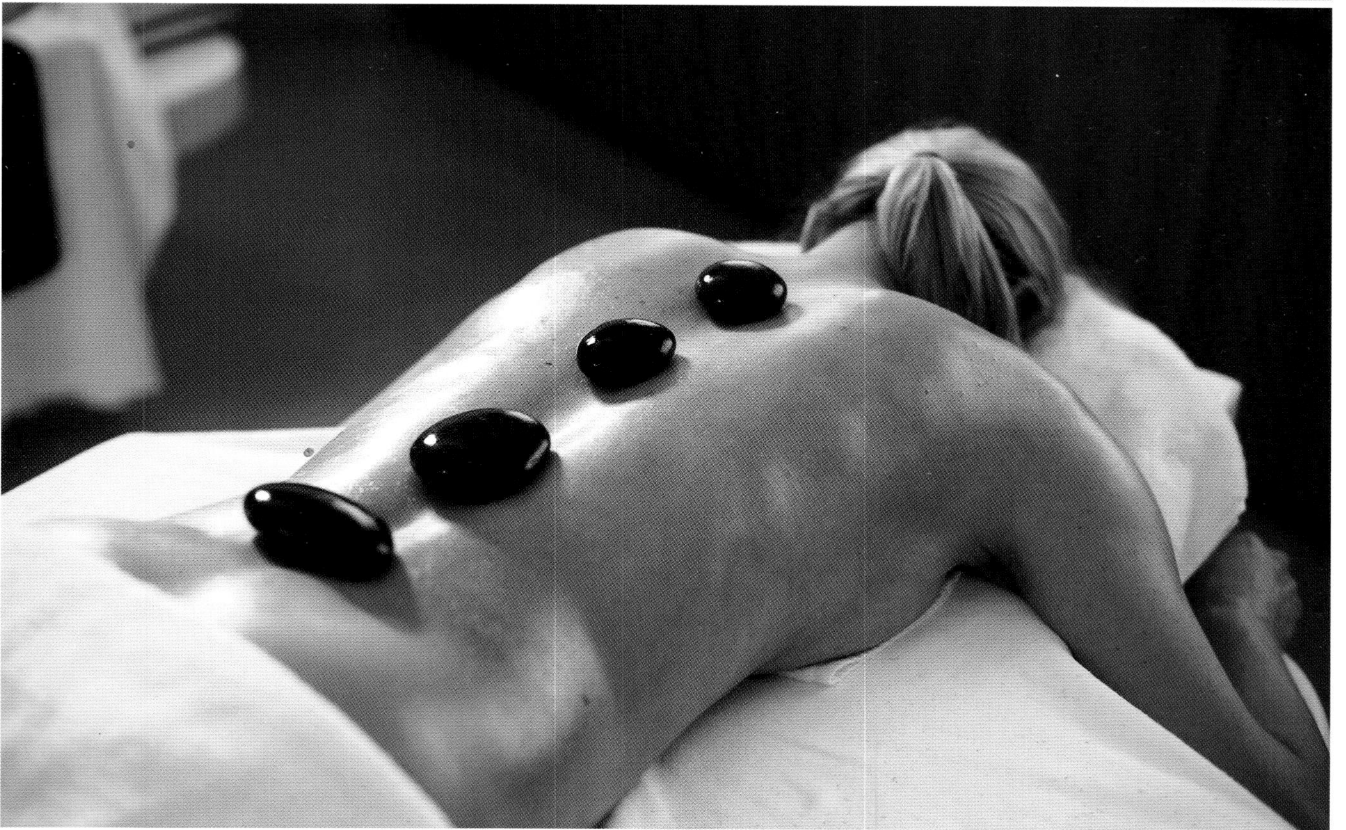

Susanne Kaufmann Spa

at Hotel Post

There are two very good reasons for a wellness break at the Kaufmanns' Hotel Post, which the family has run since 1850: Susanne Kaufmann's first-class treatments using products with local plant-based ingredients, and the purist design of the spa, which was extended in 2009, by Susanne's brother Oskar Leo Kaufmann.

Für einen Wellnessurlaub im Hotel Post, das die Familie Kaufmann seit 1850 führt, gibt es gleich zwei gute Gründe: die ausgezeichneten Anwendungen, für die Susanne Kaufmann Pflegeprodukte mit pflanzlichen Wirkstoffen aus dem Bregenzer Wald verwendet, und die puristische Architektur des 2009 erweiterten Spas, der von Susannes Bruder Oskar Leo Kaufmann entworfen wurde.

Il y a deux bonnes raisons de passer des vacances de remise en forme à l'Hotel Post, que dirige la famille Kaufmann depuis 1850 : les soins remarquables pour lesquels Susanne Kaufmann utilise des substances végétales de la forêt de Brégence et l'architecture minimaliste du spa agrandi en 2009 et conçu par Oskar Leo Kaufmann, le frère de Susanne.

Susanne Kaufmann Spa
at Hotel Post
Brugg 35
6870 Bezau
Austria
Tel. +43 5514 220 70
Fax +43 5514 22 07 22
office@hotelpostbezau.com
www.hotelpostbezau.com

LOCATION
Bezau lies 22 miles south-east of Bregenz.

ROOMS
58 rooms and 4 suites.

FOOD
The main hotel restaurant offers healthy full-board options for lunch and dinner, while "Irma", named after Susanne Kaufmann's grandmother, offers authentic regional cuisine.

SPA FACILITIES
15 treatment rooms, 3 saunas, steam bath, solarium, indoor pool, whirlpool, salt-water pool, traditional Chinese medicine centre, fitness room.

SIGNATURE TREATMENT
The "Bregenz Mountain-Herb Ritual", a herbal whey bath and an Alpine herb oil massage.

BOOK TO PACK
"Brother of Sleep" by Robert Schneider.

LAGE
Bezau liegt 35 km südöstlich von Bregenz.

ZIMMER
58 Zimmer und 4 Suiten.

KÜCHE
Das Hauptrestaurant bietet eine »Vitalpension« mit leichtem Mittag- und Abendessen an. Regionale Menüs serviert das »Irma«, benannt nach Susanne Kaufmanns Großmutter.

SPAAUSSTATTUNG
15 Behandlungsräume, 3 Saunen, Dampfbad, Solarium, Innenpool, Whirlpool, Solebecken, Zentrum für traditionelle chinesische Medizin, Fitnessraum.

SIGNATURE TREATMENT
Das »Bregenzer Bergkräuterritual« mit einem Kräuter-Molkebad und einer Alpenkräuteröl-Massage.

BUCHTIPP
»Schlafes Bruder« von Robert Schneider.

SITUATION
Bezau est à 35 km au sud-est de Brégence.

CHAMBRES
58 chambres et 4 suites.

RESTAURATION
Le restaurant principal propose une « Vitalpension » avec déjeuner et dîner légers. L' « Irma », qui porte le prénom de la grand-mère de Susanne Kaufmann, sert des spécialités régionales.

SERVICES DU SPA
15 cabines de soins, 3 saunas, bain de vapeur, solarium, piscine intérieure, bain à remous, piscine d'eau salée, centre de médecine chinoise traditionnelle, espace de remise en forme.

SOIN SIGNATURE
Le « rituel brégençois aux herbes de montagne » avec bain aux extraits de plantes et au petit-lait et massage aux huiles essentielles de plantes alpestres.

LIVRE À EMPORTER
« Frère Sommeil » de Robert Schneider.

HOTEL
POST
HERMADA
HERMADA

SUSANNE KAUFMANN
Körperöl
100 ml e

Aurelio Spa

at Aurelio Lech

This boutique hotel allows guests to enjoy a stylish combination of spa break and skiing holiday, thanks to its location next to the Schlegelkopf piste. The fabulous wellness centre, whose purist look was created by Mlinaric, Henry & Zervudachi, offers treatments featuring local Alpine herbs as well as exotic ingredients such as caviar and Ligne St. Barth products from the Caribbean.

In diesem Boutiquehotel lassen sich Ski- und Spaferien stilvoll verbinden: Das Aurelio Lech liegt direkt an der Schlegelkopfpiste und besitzt einen wunderbaren Wellnessbereich. Dieser wurde von Mlinaric, Henry & Zervudachi puristisch designt und bietet sowohl Anwendungen mit heimischen Alpenkräutern als auch mit exotischen Produkten wie Kaviar und der karibischen Ligne St. Barth.

Dans ce boutique-hôtel, les vacances de ski et le séjour spa peuvent être combinés avec élégance. Situé devant la piste du Schlegelkopf, l'Aurelio Lech possède un merveilleux espace wellness dont le design puriste est signé Mlinaric, Henry & Zervudachi. Les soins sont à base de plantes alpestres, de caviar ou de fruits et fleurs des Caraïbes dans la ligne St. Barth.

Aurelio Lech
Tannberg 130
6764 Lech am Arlberg
Austria
Tel. +43 5583 22 14
Fax +43 5583 34 56
reservation@aureliolech.com
www.aureliolech.com
Open from early December to mid-April and from mid-July to early September

Aurelio Spa
Tel. +43 5583 221 45 50
spa@aureliolech.com

LOCATION
Lech is situated in Vorarlberg, 58 miles east of Bregenz and 77 miles west of Innsbruck.

ROOMS
14 rooms and 5 suites.

FOOD
The spa has its own health bar offering fresh fruit, teas and snacks.

SPA FACILITIES
10,800 sq ft with 6 treatment rooms, 2 indoor pools (23 and 18 m), sound pool, whirlpool, 2 saunas, aroma steam bath, lifestyle showers, fitness room and hair salon.

SIGNATURE TREATMENT
The "Diamond Peel Microdermabrasion", a scrub using a diamond-tipped head.

BOOK TO PACK
"The Terrors of Ice and Darkness" by Christoph Ransmayr.

LAGE
Lech liegt in Vorarlberg, 94 km östlich von Bregenz und 124 km westlich von Innsbruck.

ZIMMER
14 Zimmer und 5 Suiten.

KÜCHE
Zum Spa gehört eine Vitalbar, die frische Früchte, Tees und Snacks anbietet.

SPAAUSSTATTUNG
1.000 qm mit 6 Behandlungsräumen, 2 Innenpools (23 und 18 m), Klangbecken, Whirlpool, 2 Saunen, Aroma-Dampfbad, Erlebnisduschen, Fitnessraum, Friseursalon.

SIGNATURE TREATMENT
Die »Diamond Peel Microdermabrasion«, ein Peeling mit Diamantaufsätzen.

BUCHTIPP
»Der fliegende Berg« von Christoph Ransmayr.

SITUATION
Dans le Vorarlberg, à 94 km à l'est de Brégence et à 124 km à l'ouest d'Innsbruck.

CHAMBRES
14 chambres et 5 suites.

RESTAURATION
Le spa abrite un « Vitalbar » qui propose des fruits frais, des thés et infusions ainsi que des repas légers.

SERVICES DU SPA
1000 mètres carrés avec 6 cabines de soins, 2 piscines couvertes (23 et 18 m), bassin avec musique subaquatique, bain à remous, 2 saunas, bain de vapeur aromatique, douches lifestyle, espace de remise en forme, salon de coiffure.

SOIN SIGNATURE
La « Diamond Peel Microdermabrasion », un gommage au diamant.

LIVRE À EMPORTER
« La Montagne volante » de Christoph Ransmayr.

FINN SAUNA
AURELIO

Dolder Grand Spa

at The Dolder Grand

The grande dame among Zurich's hotels was recently given a four-year facelift by Sir Norman Foster. Completed in 2008, the refurbished interior includes a glamorous and refined spa conceived by Sylvia Sepielli. Many of its treatments take their inspiration from Japan – the five "Sunaburo" hot-stone baths were even developed exclusively for The Dolder Grand.

Sir Norman Foster hat der Grand Lady der Züricher Hotellerie von 2004 bis 2008 eine Schönheitskur verordnet. Das Spa gestaltete er dabei nach einem Konzept von Sylvia Sepielli so edel wie glamourös. Viele Anwendungen sind japanisch inspiriert – die fünf »Sunaburo« Ruhewannen mit warmen Kieselsteinen wurden sogar exklusiv für das Dolder entwickelt.

De 2004 à 2008, Sir Norman Foster a refait une beauté à la grande dame de l'hôtellerie zurichoise, aménageant le spa luxe et glamour conçu par Sylvia Sepielli. Nombre de soins sont d'inspiration japonaise – les cinq bassins de repos « Sunaburo » entourés de pierres chaudes ont même été réalisés exclusivement pour le Dolder.

The Dolder Grand
Kurhausstraße 65
8032 Zurich
Switzerland
Tel. +41 44 456 60 00
Fax +41 44 456 60 01
info@thedoldergrand.com
www.thedoldergrand.com

Dolder Grand Spa
Resort & Spa
Tel. +41 44 456 64 00
spa@thedoldergrand.com

LOCATION
Situated high above Zurich, 6 min to the east of the city centre and 20 min from the airport.

ROOMS
114 rooms and 59 suites.

FOOD
The spa's café serves healthy snacks and refreshing drinks.

SPA FACILITIES
43,000 sq ft with men's and women's spas, aqua zone (indoor pool, indoor and outdoor whirlpools, saunarium and steam bath), 19 treatment rooms, 2 spa suites, medical wellness area, mind-body studio (yoga), movement studio (Pilates), hair salon and fitness room.

SIGNATURE TREATMENT
"Organic Signature Massage by Kerstin Florian", which includes a foot bath, dry brushing and full-body massage.

BOOK TO PACK
"I'm not Stiller" by Max Frisch.

LAGE
Erhöht über Zürich gelegen, 6 min östlich des Zentrums, 20 min vom Flughafen entfernt.

ZIMMER
114 Zimmer und 59 Suiten.

KÜCHE
Das Spa-Café serviert gesunde Snacks und frische Vitaldrinks.

SPAAUSSTATTUNG
4.000 qm mit Damen- und Herren-Spas, Aqua-Zone (Innenpool, Innen- und Außen-Whirlpools, Sanarium, Dampfbad), 19 Behandlungsräumen, 2 Spa-Suiten, Medical-Wellness-Bereich, Mind-Body-Studio (Yoga), Movement-Studio (Pilates), Friseursalon, Fitnessraum.

SIGNATURE TREATMENT
»Organic Signature Massage by Kerstin Florian« mit Fußbad, Trockenbürsten- und Ganzkörpermassage.

BUCHTIPP
»Stiller« von Max Frisch.

SITUATION
Au-dessus de Zurich, à 6 min à l'est du centre, à 20 min de l'aéroport.

CHAMBRES
114 chambres et 59 suites.

RESTAURATION
Le café du spa propose des snacks sains et légers et des boissons vitaminées fraîches.

SERVICES DU SPA
4000 mètres carrés avec un spa pour dames et un spa pour messieurs, aquazone (piscine couverte, bain à remous intérieur et extérieur, sanarium, bain de vapeur), 19 cabines de soins, 2 suites spa, espace Medical Wellness, Mind-Body Studio (yoga), Movement Studio (Pilates), salon de coiffure, salle de remise en forme.

SOIN SIGNATURE
« Organic Signature Massage by Kerstin Florian » avec bains de pieds, friction tonique à la brosse et massage complet.

LIVRE À EMPORTER
« Stiller » de Max Frisch.

Delight Spa & Beauty

at Waldhaus Flims

The four buildings of the Waldhaus were completed from 1875 to 1904, and guests can still choose between grand hotel, chalet, summer house and Art Nouveau pavilion when booking their stylish room. To mark its 100th anniversary in 2004, the resort opened the Delight Spa, which boasts cinematic mountain views and offers treatments featuring Alpine herbs and the spa's own aromatic oils.

Von 1875 bis 1904 wurden die vier Gebäude des Waldhauses erbaut. So hat man heute die Wahl zwischen stilvollen Zimmern im Grandhotel, Chalet, Sommerhaus oder Jugendstilpavillon. Zum 100. Geburtstag 2004 eröffnete das Delight-Spa, das kinotaugliche Blicke auf die Berge bietet und mit Alpenkräutern sowie Aromaölen aus eigener Herstellung verwöhnt.

Les quatre bâtiments de la Waldhaus ont été construits de 1875 à 1904 et, jusqu'à ce jour, on peut séjourner au Grand Hotel, au Grand Chalet, à la Villa Silvana ou au pavillon Belle Époque. Le Delight Spa, ouvert en 2004, à l'occasion du centenaire, offre une vue sublime sur les montagnes ; ses hôtes sont choyés à l'aide de produits à base de plantes alpestres et d'huiles essentielles fabriquées sur place.

Waldhaus Flims
Via dil Parc
7018 Flims
Switzerland
Tel. +41 81 928 48 48
Fax +41 81 928 48 58
info@waldhaus-flims.ch
www.waldhaus-flims.ch

Delight Spa & Beauty
Tel. +41 81 928 48 68
Fax +41 81 928 48 69
spa@waldhaus-flims.ch

LOCATION
Flims is situated in Graubünden,
87 miles south-east of Zurich.

ROOMS
124 rooms and 26 suites in 4 buildings.

FOOD
7 restaurants. The "Grand Restaurant Rotonde" serves light cuisine prepared with fresh market ingredients.

SPA FACILITIES
27,000 sq ft with 9 treatment rooms, 2 wellness suites, medical beauty centre, indoor pool, outdoor vitality pool, natural swimming pond, Finnish sauna, earth sauna, aroma and steam baths, hammam and fitness area.

SIGNATURE TREATMENT
The deeply relaxing "Delight" special massage using essential oils.

BOOK TO PACK
"Thus Spoke Zarathustra" by Friedrich Nietzsche, which the author worked on while staying in Graubünden.

LAGE
Flims liegt in Graubünden, 140 km südöstlich von Zürich.

ZIMMER
124 Zimmer und 26 Suiten in 4 Häusern.

KÜCHE
7 Restaurants. Leichte marktfrische Küche serviert das »Grand Restaurant Rotonde«.

SPAAUSSTATTUNG
2.500 qm mit 9 Behandlungsräumen, 2 Wellnesssuiten, Medical Beauty Center, Innenpool, Außen-Erlebnisbad, Bio-Schwimmteich, finnischer Sauna, Erdsauna, Aroma- und Dampfbädern, Hamam, Fitnessbereich.

SIGNATURE TREATMENT
Die tiefenentspannende »Delight«-Spezialmassage mit ätherischen Ölen.

BUCHTIPP
»Also sprach Zarathustra« von Friedrich Nietzsche, an dem der Autor in Graubünden arbeitete.

SITUATION
Dans le canton des Grisons, à 140 km au sud-est de Zurich.

CHAMBRES
124 chambres et 26 suites dans 4 bâtiments.

RESTAURATION
7 restaurants. Le « Grand Restaurant Rotonde » sert une cuisine du marché et légère.

SERVICES DU SPA
2500 mètres carrés avec 9 cabines de soins, 2 suites bien-être, Medical Beauty Center, piscine intérieure, piscine ludique extérieure, étang de natation naturel, sauna finnois, sauna enterré, bains de vapeur et bains aromatiques, hammam, espace de remise en forme.

SOIN SIGNATURE
Le massage profond des tissus aux huiles essentielles « Delight ».

LIVRE À EMPORTER
« Ainsi parlait Zarathoustra » de Friedrich Nietzsche qui l'a conçu durant son séjour dans le canton des Grisons.

Therme Vals

Designed by architect Peter Zumthor and opened in 1996, Therme Vals was built into the mountainside using 60,000 slabs of local quartzite. Finished using a range of techniques and arranged in layers with the utmost precision, these blocks of stone lend a fascinating and almost surreal backdrop to the baths, whose Vals spring water has a natural temperature of 86 degrees Fahrenheit.

Aus 60.000 Platten Valser Quarzit hat Peter Zumthor diese 1996 eröffnete Therme in den Berg gebaut. Die mit unterschiedlichen Techniken bearbeiteten Steine wurden mit äußerster Präzision aufeinandergeschichtet. Sie schaffen eine faszinierende, fast surreale Kulisse für die Bäder mit Valser Mineralwasser, das mit einer Temperatur von 30 Grad Celsius seiner Quelle entspringt.

Peter Zumthor a construit dans la montagne avec des pierres plates de quartzite de Vals des thermes ouverts au public en 1996. Les 60 000 plaques travaillées selon diverses techniques et empilées avec une extrême précision créent un décor fascinant, presque surréaliste, pour la source d'eau minérale de Vals qui jaillit à une température de 30 degrés Celsius.

Hotel Therme Vals
7132 Vals
Switzerland
Tel. +41 81 926 80 80
Fax +41 81 926 80 00
hotel@therme-vals.ch
www.therme-vals.ch
Open from mid-June to early April

Therme Vals
Tel. +41 81 926 89 61
therme@therme-vals.ch
Open from early June to early April

LOCATION
Vals is situated 4,108 ft above sea level in the Alps of Graubünden, 30 miles south-west of Chur.

ROOMS
140 rooms in 4 different 1960s buildings, 60 of which have been redesigned by Peter Zumthor.

FOOD
2 restaurants that use organic meat and locally grown products. Wide range of vegetarian dishes.

SPA FACILITIES
Indoor and outdoor pool, fire pool (107 degrees Fahrenheit), ice pool (57 degrees Fahrenheit), petal bath, sound pool, spring grotto, drinking stone, steam stone, hair salon.

SIGNATURE TREATMENT
The deeply relaxing stone massage with full-body scrub.

BOOK TO PACK
"Thinking Architecture" by Peter Zumthor.

LAGE
Vals liegt 1.252 m hoch im Bündner Oberland, 50 km südwestlich von Chur.

ZIMMER
140 Zimmer in 4 Bauten aus den 1960ern. 60 Räume hat Peter Zumthor neu gestaltet.

KÜCHE
2 Restaurants, die Produkte aus einheimischen Gärten und biologischer Tierhaltung verwenden. Große vegetarische Auswahl.

SPAAUSSTATTUNG
Innen- und Außenpool, Feuerbad (42 Grad Celsius), Eisbad (14 Grad Celsius), Blütenbad, Klangbad, Quellgrotte, Trinkstein, Dampfstein, Friseursalon.

SIGNATURE TREATMENT
Die tiefenentspannende Steinmassage inklusive Ganzkörperpeeling.

BUCHTIPP
»Architektur denken« von Peter Zumthor.

SITUATION
Vals se trouve à 1252 m d'altitude dans l'Oberland grisonnais, à 50 km au sud-ouest de Coire.

CHAMBRES
140 chambres dans 4 bâtiments des années 1960. 60 pièces ont été réaménagées par Peter Zumthor.

RESTAURATION
2 restaurants qui utilisent des produits des jardins de la région et de l'élevage biologique. Grand choix de plats végétariens.

SERVICES DU SPA
Piscine intérieure et extérieure, bain de feu (42 degrés Celsius), bain de glace (14 degrés Celsius), bain de fleurs, bain sonore, bain en pierre, fontaine à eau de source, salon de coiffure.

SOIN SIGNATURE
Massage aux pierres procurant une détente profonde, gommage corporel inclus.

LIVRE À EMPORTER
« Penser l'architecture » de Peter Zumthor.

Kronenhof Spa

at the Grand Hotel Kronenhof

This grand hotel with ceiling frescos, ornamental stuccowork, crystal chandeliers and crackling open fires was built between 1848 and 1898 on the site of a simple guest house. In the last major renovation, the listed building gained a spa that looks out on forests and glaciers, offering treatments with mountain treasures such as wild herbs, honey and marmot oil.

Aus einem schlichten Gasthaus wurde zwischen 1848 und 1898 dieses majestätische Grand Hotel mit Deckenmalereien und Stuckornamenten, Kristalllüstern und knisternden Kaminen. Seit der letzten Rundumrenovierung besitzt das denkmalgeschützte Haus auch ein Spa, das auf Wälder sowie Gletscher blickt und mit Bergschätzen wie Wildkräutern, Honig oder Murmelöl verwöhnt.

Entre 1848 et 1898, une simple auberge s'est métamorphosée en Grand Hotel doté de plafonds peints et d'ornements stuqués, de lustres de cristal et de cheminées crépitantes. Depuis la dernière grande rénovation, la maison classée monument historique possède un spa ouvert sur les forêts et les glaciers. Le visiteur profite des trésors alpestres que sont les plantes sauvages, le miel et l'huile de marmotte.

Grand Hotel Kronenhof
7504 Pontresina – St. Moritz
Switzerland
Tel. +41 81 830 30 30
Fax +41 81 830 30 31
info@kronenhof.com
www.kronenhof.com
Open from mid-June to mid-October and early December to mid-April

Kronenhof Spa
Tel. +41 81 830 30 76
spa@kronenhof.com

LOCATION
In Pontresina, 5,900 ft above sea level, 4 miles east of St. Moritz.

ROOMS
65 rooms and 47 suites.

FOOD
The "Grand Restaurant" offers healthy options, while light lunches can be enjoyed in the "Pavillon".

SPA FACILITIES
21,500 sq ft with 13 treatment rooms, spa suite, 20-m indoor pool, vitality pool, kids' pool, Finnish sauna, women's saunarium, steam bath, relaxing floatation grotto, salt-water grotto, Kneipp pool, fitness area and hair salon.

SIGNATURE TREATMENTS
The "Kronenhof Aroma Massage" with natural oils and the "Kronenhof Mountain Massage" with hot stones.

BOOK TO PACK
"Narcissus and Goldmund" by Hermann Hesse.

LAGE
1.800 m hoch in Pontresina gelegen, 6 km östlich von St. Moritz.

ZIMMER
65 Zimmer und 47 Suiten.

KÜCHE
Im »Grand Restaurant« werden auch Vitalmenüs serviert; leichte Lunches genießt man im »Pavillon«.

SPAAUSSTATTUNG
2.000 qm mit 13 Behandlungsräumen, Spa-Suite, 20-m-Innenpool, Erlebnisbad, Kinderpool, finnischer Sauna, Biosauna für Damen, Dampfbad, Relax-Floatation-Grotte, Solegrotte, Kneippbecken, Fitnessbereich, Friseursalon.

SIGNATURE TREATMENTS
Die »Kronenhof Aroma-Massage« mit Naturölen und die »Kronenhof Berg-Massage« mit heißen Steinen.

BUCHTIPP
»Narziß und Goldmund« von Hermann Hesse.

SITUATION
À 1800 m d'altitude dans la commune de Pontresina, à 6 km à l'est de Saint-Moritz.

CHAMBRES
65 chambres et 47 suites.

RESTAURATION
Le « Grand Restaurant » sert un Menu Vital ; légers déjeuners au « Pavillon ».

SERVICES DU SPA
2000 mètres carrés avec 13 cabines de soins, suite spa, piscine intérieure de 20 m, bassin ludique, bassin pour enfants, sauna finlandais, sauna bio pour dames, bain de vapeur, grotte de flottaison relax, grotte à l'eau salée, bassin Kneipp, espace de remise en forme, salon de coiffure.

SOINS SIGNATURE
Le « Kronenhof Massage Aromatique » aux huiles essentielles et le « Kronenhof Massage Alpin » aux pierres chaudes.

LIVRE À EMPORTER
« Narcisse et Goldmund » de Hermann Hesse.

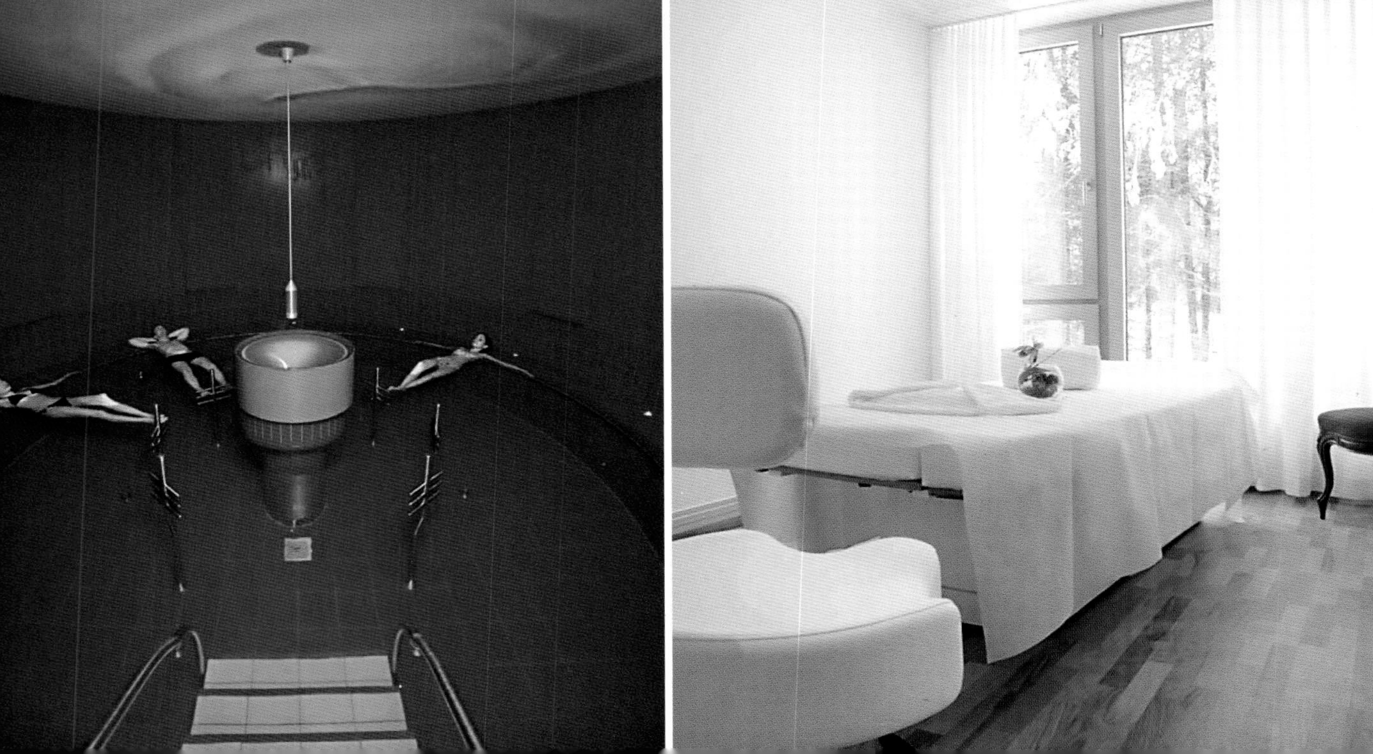

Six Senses Spa

at The Westin Paris

In late 2009, Six Senses opened its first French spa – at The Westin Paris. A hanging garden by Patrick Blanc and architect Pierre David's cocoon-like light-oak treatment rooms with subtly shimmering paper room dividers make it an oasis of calm, but the city remains a constant yet discreet presence thanks to real-time images of the Paris skyline projected onto one of the walls.

Ende 2009 eröffnete Six Senses im Hotel The Westin Paris sein erstes Spa in Frankreich: Ein hängender Garten von Patrick Blanc sowie kokonartige Kabinen aus heller Eiche und zart beleuchteten Papierwänden, entworfen von Pierre David, machen es zu einer Oase mitten in der Stadt, deren Bilder in Echtzeit an eine Wand projiziert werden.

Fin 2009, Six Senses a inauguré son premier Spa en France à l'hôtel The Westin de Paris : un mur végétal de Patrick Blanc et des cabines-cocons en chêne clair tapissées de panneaux de papier rétro-éclairés, conçues par Pierre David, le transforment en une oasis au cœur de la capitale. Celle-ci est toujours présente : des images du ciel de Paris sont projetées en temps réel sur des écrans disposés sur un pan du mur.

The Westin Paris
3, Rue de Castiglione
75001 Paris
France
Tel. +33 1 44 77 11 11
Fax +33 1 44 77 14 60
reservation.01729@westin.com
www.thewestinparis.com

Six Senses Spa
Tel. +33 1 43 16 10 10
Fax +33 1 43 16 10 11
reservations-castiglione-spa@
sixsenses.com
www.sixsenses.com

LOCATION
Close to Place Vendôme and the Tuileries, 19 miles south-west of Charles de Gaulle airport.

ROOMS
360 rooms and 80 suites.

FOOD
The spa offers a refreshing signature ginger tea; the hotel restaurant "Le First", designed by Jacques Garcia, also serves spa cuisine.

SPA FACILITIES
2,600 sq ft with 6 treatment rooms.

SIGNATURE TREATMENT
The "Opéra de Paris" facial with honey from beehives on the opera house roof.

BOOK TO PACK
"Hunting and Gathering" by Anna Gavalda.

LAGE
Nahe der Place Vendôme und der Tuilerien gelegen, 30 km südwestlich des Flughafens Charles de Gaulle.

ZIMMER
360 Zimmer und 80 Suiten.

KÜCHE
Im Spa erfrischt der Signature-Ingwertee; das von Jacques Garcia designte Hotelrestaurant »Le First« serviert außerdem Spa-Cuisine.

SPAAUSSTATTUNG
240 qm mit 6 Behandlungsräumen.

SIGNATURE TREATMENT
Das »Opéra de Paris«-Facial mit Honig von den Bienenstöcken auf dem Operndach.

BUCHTIPP
»Weil nichts bleibt, wie es ist« von Laurence Tardieu.

SITUATION
À proximité de la Place Vendôme et des Tuileries, à 30 km au sud-ouest de l'aéroport Charles-de-Gaulle.

CHAMBRES
360 chambres et 80 suites.

RESTAURATION
Un thé au gingembre rafraîchissant est proposé au spa ; l'hôtel-restaurant « Le First », dont le design est signé Jacques Garcia, propose la spa cuisine.

SERVICES DU SPA
240 mètres carrés avec 6 cabines de soins.

SOIN SIGNATURE
Le soin du visage « Opéra de Paris », à base de miel provenant des ruches placées sur le toit de l'opéra.

LIVRE À EMPORTER
« Puisque rien ne dure » de Laurence Tardieu.

SIX SENSES

Spa Vinothérapie Caudalie

at Les Étangs de Corot

Ville-d'Avray has been a refuge for artists since the 19th century, with painter Jean-Baptiste-Camille Corot (1796–1875) among the many who have sought inspiration here. Now the colours of his landscapes have, in turn, inspired the decor of this beautiful hotel. Seven of its vinotherapy spa's eight treatment rooms have views of the ponds ("étangs") depicted by Corot.

Ville-d'Avray ist seit dem 19. Jahrhundert ein Refugium der Künstler. Hier ließ sich auch der Landschaftsmaler Jean-Baptiste-Camille Corot (1796–1875) inspirieren. Das Interieur dieses bezaubernden Hotels ist in den Farben seiner Werke gehalten, und aus sieben der acht Behandlungsräumen des Vinotherapie-Spas blickt man direkt auf die Weiher (étangs), die Corot auf Leinwand verewigte.

De nombreux artistes ont cherché refuge à Ville-d'Avray depuis le 19e siècle – le peintre Jean-Baptiste-Camille Corot (1796–1875) y trouvait souvent l'inspiration. Les espaces intérieurs de cet hôtel adorable évoquent les couleurs de ses tableaux, et sur les huit cabines de soins du Spa-vinothérapie, sept donnent sur les étangs que Corot a immortalisés sur la toile.

Les Étangs de Corot
55, Rue de Versailles
92410 Ville-d'Avray
France
Tel. +33 1 41 15 37 00
Fax +33 1 41 15 37 99
contact@etangs-corot.com
www.etangs-corot.com

Spa Vinothérapie Caudalie
Tel. +33 1 41 15 37 70
spa@etangs-corot.com

LOCATION
West of Paris, 10 miles from the city centre.

ROOMS
40 rooms and 3 suites, all individually designed and named after artists.

FOOD
"Le Corot" serves innovative gourmet cuisine; "Le Café des Artistes" offers bistro meals and tapas.

SPA FACILITIES
7,535 sq ft with 8 treatment rooms, steam bath and outdoor jacuzzi.

SIGNATURE TREATMENT
"Caudalie Vinotherapy" using grape and vine extracts.

BOOK TO PACK
"The Flowers of Evil" by Charles Baudelaire (another visitor to Ville-d'Avray and a Corot devotee).

LAGE
Westlich von Paris gelegen; 16 km vom Stadtzentrum entfernt.

ZIMMER
40 Zimmer und 3 Suiten, die alle individuell designt und nach Künstlern benannt worden sind.

KÜCHE
»Le Corot« serviert innovative Gourmetmenüs, »Le Café des Artistes« Bistrogerichte und Tapas.

SPAAUSSTATTUNG
700 qm mit 8 Behandlungsräumen, Dampfbad, Outdoor-Jacuzzi.

SIGNATURE TREATMENT
Die »Caudalie-Vinotherapie« mit Extrakten aus Weintrauben.

BUCHTIPP
»Die Blumen des Bösen« von Charles Baudelaire (ebenfalls Gast in Ville-d'Avray und Anhänger Corots).

SITUATION
À l'ouest de Paris ; à 16 km du centre-ville.

CHAMBRES
40 chambres et 3 suites offrant toutes un décor individuel et portant des noms d'artistes.

RESTAURATION
« Le Corot » propose des menus gastronomiques innovants, « Le Café des Artistes » des plats de bistro et des tapas.

SERVICES DU SPA
700 mètres carrés avec 8 cabines de soins, bain de vapeur, jacuzzi en plein air.

SOIN SIGNATURE
La « Vinothérapie Caudalie » aux extraits de vigne et de raisin.

LIVRE À EMPORTER
« Les Fleurs du mal » de Charles Baudelaire (il a séjourné lui aussi à Ville-d'Avray et admirait Corot).

Buddha-Bar Spa

at the Hilton Évian-les-Bains

Buddha-Bar founder Raymond Visan opened the brand's first spa in March 2007, bringing an eclectic interpretation of the "East meets West" idea to Évian-les-Bains. Against a backdrop of Buddha statues, refined lighting and turquoise- and red-hued walls, guests can enjoy ancient Tibetan and Indian therapies with a modern twist.

Buddha-Bar-Gründer Raymond Visan eröffnete das erste Spa seiner Marke im März 2007 – und brachte mit ihm eine eklektische Version des »East meets West«-Gedankens nach Évian-les-Bains. Vor einer Kulisse aus Buddha-Statuen, raffinierten Lichtquellen und in Türkis- und Rottönen gestrichenen Wänden bekommen hier alte Therapien aus Tibet und Indien einen modernen Touch.

Raymond Visan, le fondateur du Buddha-Bar, a inauguré son premier spa en mars 2007, apportant à Évian-les-Bains son idée éclectique de la rencontre entre l'Orient et l'Occident. Au milieu de statues de Bouddha, de sources d'éclairage raffinées et de murs peints en teintes rouge et turquoise, les anciennes thérapies tibétaines et indiennes ont ici un accent moderne.

Hilton Évian-les-Bains
Quai Paul Léger
74500 Évian-les-Bains
France
Tel. +33 4 50 84 60 00
Fax +33 4 50 84 60 50
info.hiltonevianlesbains@hilton.com
www.evianlesbains.hilton.com

Buddha-Bar Spa
Tel. +33 4 50 84 60 40
Fax +33 4 50 84 60 41
buddhabarspa-evian@buddhabar.com
www.buddhabar.com

LOCATION
On the southern shores of Lake Geneva, 37 miles north-east of Geneva airport.

ROOMS
136 rooms and 34 suites.

FOOD
The spa has its own tea and juice bar; the hotel restaurant offers an international menu.

SPA FACILITIES
16,100 sq ft with 6 treatment rooms, 2 rooms for Oriental scrubs, spa suite, 2 plunge pools, outdoor and indoor pool, Finnish sauna, hammam, fitness studio, yoga, Pilates and qigong rooms and meditation garden.

SIGNATURE TREATMENT
"Buddhattitude" massage with warm oils.

BOOK TO PACK
"Buddha Da" by Anne Donovan.

LAGE
Am Südufer des Genfer Sees gelegen, 60 km nordöstlich des Flughafens Genf.

ZIMMER
136 Zimmer und 34 Suiten.

KÜCHE
Das Spa besitzt eine Tee- und Saftbar, das Hotel ein Restaurant mit internationaler Karte.

SPAAUSSTATTUNG
1.500 qm mit 6 Behandlungsräumen, 2 Räumen für orientalische Peelings, Spa-Suite, 2 Tauchbecken, Außen- und Innenpool, finnischer Sauna, Hamam, Fitnessstudio, Räumen für Yoga, Pilates und Qigong, Meditationsgarten.

SIGNATURE TREATMENT
Die »Buddhattitude«-Massage mit warmen Ölen.

BUCHTIPP
»Einmal Buddha und zurück« von Anne Donovan.

SITUATION
Sur la rive sud du lac Léman, à 60 km au nord-est de l'aéroport de Genève.

CHAMBRES
136 chambres et 34 suites.

RESTAURATION
Le spa possède un bar à jus de fruits et infusions, le restaurant de l'hôtel propose une cuisine internationale.

SERVICES DU SPA
1500 mètres carrés avec 6 cabines de soins, 2 salles pour les gommages orientaux, suite spa, 2 bassins d'eau froide, piscine intérieure et extérieure, sauna finlandais, hammam, studio de remise en forme, des salles de yoga, pilates et qi gong, jardin de méditation.

SOIN SIGNATURE
Le massage « Buddhattitude » aux huiles tièdes.

LIVRE À EMPORTER
« Moi, Bouddha » de José Frèches.

Spa Vinothérapie Caudalie

at Les Sources de Caudalie

The world's first vinotherapy spa opened in 1999 on the 14th-century Château Smith Haut Lafitte estate. Its treatments, developed in conjunction with the pharmaceutics department at the University of Bordeaux, combine warm spring water from an 1,800-foot-deep source with grapeseed and vine extracts that help the skin to combat ageing.

Auf dem Grundstück des Château Smith Haut Lafitte aus dem 14. Jahrhundert wurde 1999 das erste Vinotherapie-Spa der Welt eröffnet. Die Anwendungen – entwickelt mithilfe der pharmazeutischen Fakultät der Universität Bordeaux – kombinieren warmes Mineralwasser aus einer 540 Meter tiefen Quelle mit Extrakten aus Weinranken und Traubenkernen, die der Hautalterung entgegenwirken.

Le premier spa de vinothérapie du monde a ouvert ses portes en 1999 sur la propriété du Château Smith Haut Lafitte, un domaine datant du 14e siècle. Mis au point avec la faculté de pharmacie de Bordeaux, les traitements proposés contre le vieillissement cutané combinent l'eau minérale tiède d'une source située à 540 mètres de profondeur avec des extraits de sarments de vigne et de pépins de raisin.

Les Sources de Caudalie
Chemin de Smith Haut Lafitte
33650 Bordeaux – Martillac
France
Tel. +33 5 57 83 83 83
Fax +33 5 57 83 83 84
sources@sources-caudalie.com
www.sources-caudalie.com

Spa Vinothérapie Caudalie
Tel. +33 5 57 83 82 82
Fax +33 5 57 83 82 81
vino@caudalie.com

LOCATION
In the vineyards of Graves, 16 miles south of Bordeaux-Mérignac airport.

ROOMS
40 rooms and 9 suites in 5 separate buildings. The suite "Île aux Oiseaux" was designed in 2010 by Maison Martin Margiela.

FOOD
The head chef at "La Grand' Vigne" serves perfectly balanced cuisine and also shares his recipe secrets in cooking courses.

SPA FACILITIES
28,000 sq ft with 18 treatment rooms, indoor and outdoor pool and steam bath.

SIGNATURE TREATMENTS
Vinotherapy treatments such as the wine-barrel bath.

BOOK TO PACK
"Essays" by Michel de Montaigne.

LAGE
In den Weinbergen von Graves gelegen, 25 km südlich des Flughafens Bordeaux-Mérignac.

ZIMMER
40 Zimmer und 9 Suiten in 5 Gebäuden. Die Suite »Île aux Oiseaux« wurde 2010 von Maison Martin Margiela designt.

KÜCHE
Der Chefkoch des »La Grand' Vigne« serviert perfekt ausbalancierte Menüs und verrät seine Rezepte bei Kochkursen.

SPAAUSSTATTUNG
2.600 qm mit 18 Behandlungsräumen, Innen- und Außenpool, Dampfbad.

SIGNATURE TREATMENTS
Die Vinotherapie-Anwendungen, wie das Bad im Weinfass.

BUCHTIPP
»Die Essais« von Michel de Montaigne.

SITUATION
Au cœur des vignobles de Graves, à 25 km au sud de l'aéroport de Bordeaux-Mérignac.

CHAMBRES
40 chambres et 9 suites dans 5 bâtiments. La suite « Île aux Oiseaux » a été dessinée en 2010 par la Maison Martin Margiela.

RESTAURATION
Le chef cuisinier de « La Grand' Vigne » propose des menus parfaitement équilibrés et livre ses secrets dans des cours de cuisine.

SERVICES DU SPA
2600 mètres carrés avec 18 cabines de soins, piscine intérieure et extérieure, bain de vapeur.

SOINS SIGNATURE
Les traitements de vinothérapie ; par exemple le bain barrique à l'eau de source enrichie de marc de raisin.

LIVRE À EMPORTER
« Les Essais » de Michel de Montaigne.

CAUDALIE

Kami Spa

The façade of this townhouse may still be Roman, but the entrance bears Thai Lanna carvings while beyond lies an Oriental day spa created by art collectors Raffaella and Stefano Sciarretta with Pure Design from Thailand. Inside, guests can admire copies of stone Khmer sculptures, plus contemporary Balinese woodwork, and enjoy treatments from the Far East.

Nur noch die Fassade dieses Stadthauses ist römisch: Bereits die Pforte zieren thailändische Lanna-Schnitzereien, und dahinter öffnet sich ein asiatisches Day Spa, das die Kunstsammler Raffaella und Stefano Sciarretta mit Pure Design aus Thailand entworfen haben. Hier bewundert man Kopien von Steinskulpturen der Khmer sowie zeitgenössische balinesische Holzarbeiten und genießt Anwendungen aus Fernost.

Seule la façade de la maison est romaine ; des sculptures Lanna thaïlandaises décorent le portail du spa de jour asiatique conçu par les collectionneurs d'art Raffaella et Stefano Sciaretta avec Pure Design de Thaïlande. On y admire des copies de statues khmères et des bois sculptés balinais contemporains en faisant l'expérience de soins venus d'Extrême-Orient.

Kami Spa
Via degli Avignonesi 11/12
00187 Rome
Italy
Tel. +39 06 42 01 00 39
Fax +39 06 42 01 64 81
info@kamispa.com
www.kamispa.com
Open Sunday to Thursday from 10am to 10pm, Friday and Saturday from 10am to midnight

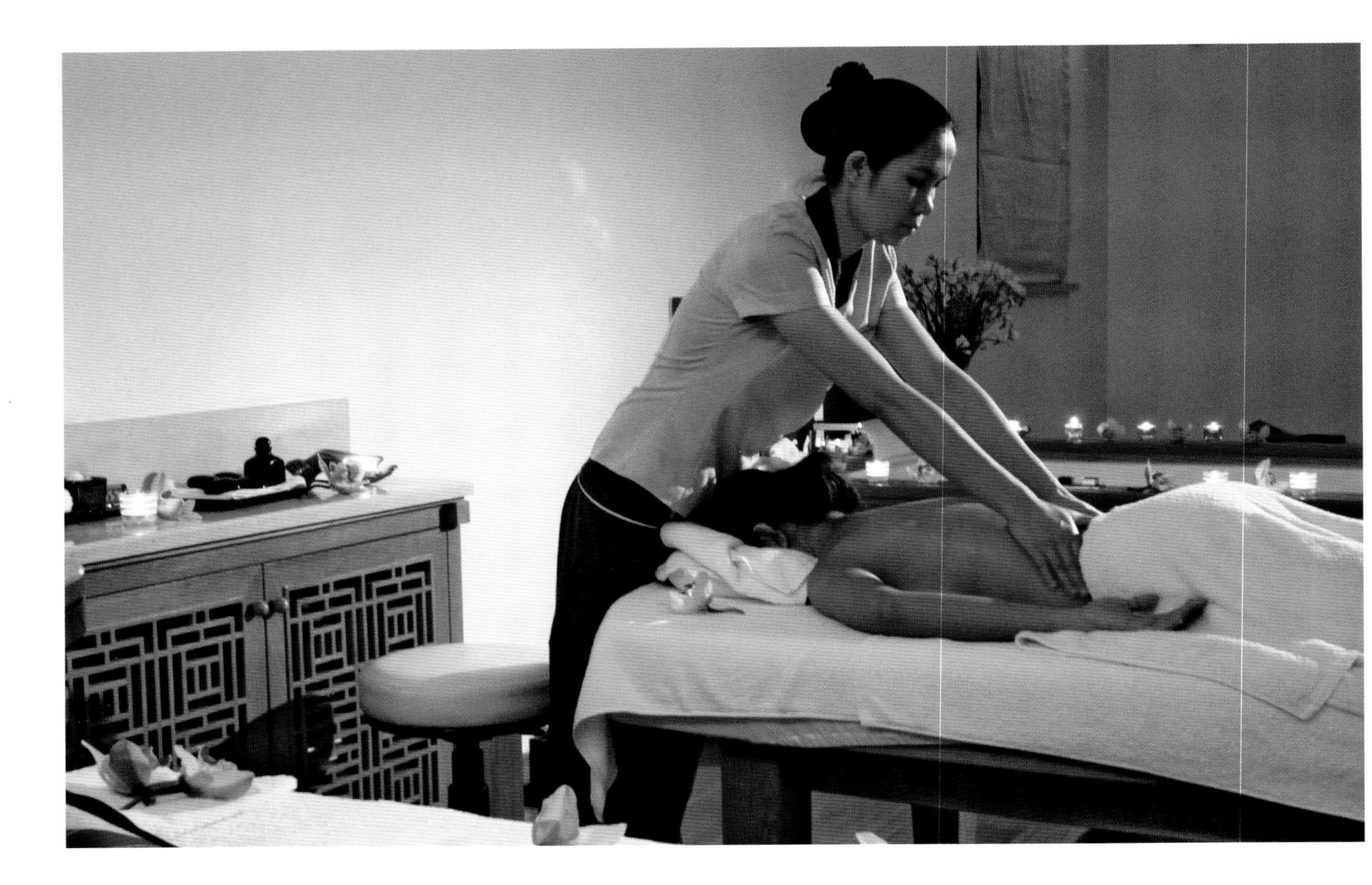

LOCATION
Central Rome, 26 miles north-east of Fiumicino airport, 5 min from the Trevi Fountain.

ROOMS
The spa doesn't have rooms of its own but can recommend accommodation in the local area.

FOOD
No restaurant of its own, but dried fruits and tea are served after treatments.

SPA FACILITIES
16,100 sq ft with 11 treatment rooms and 5 spa suites, indoor Japanese onsen pool, area for outdoor treatments and beauty salon.

SIGNATURE TREATMENTS
The four-handed hot-stone massage and the "AyurLomi" massage combining Ayurvedic and Lomi Lomi techniques.

BOOK TO PACK
"Roman Tales" by Alberto Moravia.

LAGE
42 km nordöstlich des Flughafens Fiumicino im Zentrum Roms gelegen, 5 min vom Trevi-Brunnen entfernt.

ZIMMER
Das Spa bietet keine Zimmer, empfiehlt aber gerne nahe Unterkünfte.

KÜCHE
Kein eigenes Restaurant; nach den Behandlungen werden aber getrocknete Früchte und Tee serviert.

SPAAUSSTATTUNG
1.500 qm mit 11 Behandlungsräumen und 5 Spa-Suiten, japanischer Onsen-Innenpool, Bereich für Outdoor-Treatments, Beautysalon.

SIGNATURE TREATMENTS
Die vierhändige »Hot Stones«-Massage sowie die »AyurLomi«-Massage, die Ayurveda- und Lomi-Lomi-Techniken verbindet.

BUCHTIPP
»Römische Erzählungen« von Alberto Moravia.

SITUATION
À 42 km au nord-est de l'aéroport de Fiumicino au centre de Rome, la fontaine de Trevi est à 5 min.

CHAMBRES
Pas de chambres, le spa fournit volontiers des adresses d'hébergements proches.

RESTAURATION
Pas de restaurant, mais des fruits secs et des infusions sont proposés après les soins.

SERVICES DU SPA
1500 mètres carrés avec 11 cabines de soins et 5 suites spa, piscine onsen japonaise couverte, espace pour les traitements en extérieur, salon de beauté.

SOINS SIGNATURE
Le massage « Hot Stones » à quatre mains et le massage « AyurLomi » qui associe les techniques Ayurvéda et Lomi Lomi.

LIVRE À EMPORTER
« Nouvelles romaines » d'Alberto Moravia.

Six Senses Spa

at Hotel Arts Barcelona

With its 44 storeys, this Bruce Graham-designed glass-and-steel hotel ower is the tallest building in Barcelona, and indeed in the whole of Spain. Near the top, on the 42nd and 43rd floors, is a spa that affords fantas-ic views across Barcelona and the Mediterranean. Treatments such as moisturising body wraps and chromotherapy are inspired by water and sunlight.

Mit 44 Etagen ist dieser von Bruce Graham aus Glas und Stahl entwor-ene Hotelturm das höchste Gebäude in Barcelona und sogar in Spanien. Das fast ganz oben im 42. und 43. Stock gelegene Spa eröffnet einen fan-astischen Blick über Barcelona und das Mittelmeer. Viele Anwendungen greifen die Elemente Wasser und Sonnenlicht auf – wie feuchtigkeitsspen-dende Körperwickel und die Farbtherapien.

Cet hôtel, une tour de 44 étages de verre et d'acier conçue par Bruce Graham, est le plus haut bâtiment de Barcelone et même d'Espagne. Au 42e et au 43e étage, le spa offre un panorama fantastique sur Barcelone et la Méditerranée. De nombreux soins ont recours à l'eau et à la lumière du soleil, ainsi les enveloppements hydratants et les chromothérapies.

Hotel Arts Barcelona
Carrer de la Marina 19–21
08005 Barcelona
Spain
Tel. +34 93 221 10 00
Fax +34 93 221 10 70
artsreservations@
ritzcarlton.com
www.hotelartsbarcelona.com

Six Senses Spa
reservations-arts-spa@
sixsenses.com
www.sixsenses.com
Closed in August

LOCATION
In the Olympic Village, 330 ft from the beach and 7 miles north-east of the airport.

ROOMS
397 rooms, 58 suites and 28 apartments.

FOOD
The restaurants "Enoteca" and "Arola" serve fine Mediterranean dishes.

SPA FACILITIES
9,700 sq ft with 8 treatment rooms; women's and men's areas with separate saunas, chromotherapy steam baths, vitality pools, ice fountain; fitness area with yoga, tai chi and Pilates rooms.

SIGNATURE TREATMENT
"Rescue Breathe Easy" aromatherapy treatment involving the inhalation of eucalyptus, tea tree and pine essences.

BOOK TO PACK
"O'Clock" by Quim Monzó.

LAGE
Im olympischen Dorf gelegen, 100 m vom Strand entfernt und 11 km nordöstlich des Flughafens.

ZIMMER
397 Zimmer, 58 Suiten und 28 Apartments.

KÜCHE
Feine mediterrane Gerichte servieren die »Enoteca« und das »Arola«.

SPAAUSSTATTUNG
900 qm mit 8 Behandlungsräumen; Damen- und Herrenbereichen mit eigenen Saunen, Farbtherapie-Dampfbädern, Vitality-Pools, Eisbrunnen; Fitnessbereich mit Räumen für Yoga, Tai-Chi und Pilates.

SIGNATURE TREATMENT
Die Aromatherapie »Rescue Breathe Easy«, bei der man Eukalyptus-, Teebaum- und Pinienessenzen einatmet.

BUCHTIPP
»Die beste aller Welten« von Quim Monzó.

SITUATION
Au cœur du village olympique, à 100 m de la plage et 11 km au nord-est de l'aéroport.

CHAMBRES
397 chambres, 58 suites et 28 appartements.

RESTAURATION
L'« Enoteca » et l'« Arola » proposent des saveurs méditeranéennes.

SERVICES DU SPA
900 mètres carrés avec 8 cabines de soins ; espace mixte avec saunas, bains de vapeur avec chromothérapie, piscines Vitalité, fontaine de glace ; espace de remise en forme avec salle de yoga, salle de tai chi et salle de Pilates.

SOIN SIGNATURE
L'aromathérapie « Rescue Breathe Easy », pendant laquelle on respire des essences d'eucalyptus, d'arbre à thé et de pin.

LIVRE À EMPORTER
« Le Meilleur des mondes » de Quim Monzó.

Spaciomm

at Hotel Omm

With their clean lines, refined lighting and natural materials such as wood, stone, linen and silk, the elegant Spaciomm interiors by Sandra Tarruella and Isabel López owe a clear debt to modern Oriental design. The Far Eastern influence is evident in the spa menu too, which includes Thai and tuina massages as well as shiatsu and Ayurvedic treatments.

Klare Linien, raffinierte Beleuchtung und natürliche Materialien wie Holz, Stein, Leinen oder Seide – bei der Gestaltung des eleganten Spaciomm ließen sich Sandra Tarruella und Isabel López von modernem asiatischem Design inspirieren. Fernöstliche Einflüsse bestimmen auch das Spa-Menü: Es umfasst Thai- und Tuina-Massagen sowie Shiatsu- und Ayurveda-Anwendungen.

Des lignes claires, un éclairage raffiné et des matières naturelles comme le bois, la pierre, le lin ou la soie – Sandra Tarruella et Isabel López se sont inspirées du design asiatique moderne pour décorer l'élégant Spaciomm. L'Extrême-Orient est aussi au rendez-vous sur la carte spa qui propose des massages thaïlandais ou Tuina ainsi que des soins Shiatsu ou Ayurveda.

Hotel Omm
Rosselló 265
08008 Barcelona
Spain
Tel. +34 93 445 40 00
Fax +34 93 445 40 04
reservas@hotelomm.es
www.hotelomm.es

Spaciomm
spaciomm@hotelomm.es

LOCATION
Near Paseo de Gracia, 11 miles north-east of El Prat airport.

ROOMS
74 rooms and 17 suites.

FOOD
The spa has an honesty bar with tea and juices; the hotel restaurant "Moo" serves modern Catalan cuisine.

SPA FACILITIES
4,300 sq ft with 8 treatment rooms, indoor pool, hammam, hydromassage tub, hot tub, zero-gravity loungers (with chromotherapy), Pilates studio and hair salon.

SIGNATURE TREATMENTS
The "Rituals", performed on a heated marble lounger, include a dry brush massage, body scrub, mud wrap, reflexology massage and hydromassage.

BOOK TO PACK
"The Shadow of the Wind" by Carlos Ruiz Zafón.

LAGE
Nahe der Paseo de Gracia gelegen, 18 km nordöstlich des Flughafens El Prat.

ZIMMER
74 Zimmer und 17 Suiten.

KÜCHE
Die Honesty-Bar des Spas bietet Tee und Säfte an und das Hotelrestaurant »Moo« serviert moderne katalanische Menüs.

SPAAUSSTATTUNG
400 qm mit 8 Behandlungsräumen, Innenpool, Hamam, Hydromassage-Wanne, Heißbecken, Gravitationsliegen (mit Farblichttherapie), Pilatesstudio, Friseursalon.

SIGNATURE TREATMENTS
Die »Rituale« auf einer warmen Marmorliege beinhalten Bürstenmassage, Körperpeeling, Schlammpackung mit Reflexzonenmassage und Hydromassage.

BUCHTIPP
»Der Schatten des Windes« von Carlos Ruiz Zafón.

SITUATION
À proximité du Paseo de Gracia, à 18 km au nord-est de l'aéroport El Prat.

CHAMBRES
74 chambres et 17 suites.

RESTAURATION
L'Honesty Bar du spa sert thés et jus de fruits, l'hôtel-restaurant « Moo » propose une cuisine catalane moderne.

SERVICES DU SPA
400 mètres carrés avec 8 cabines de soins, piscine intérieure, hammam, bassin d'hydromassage, bassin d'eau chaude, lits gravitationnels (avec chromothérapie), studio Pilates, salon de coiffure.

SOINS SIGNATURE
Les rituels : sur une table de massage en marbre chaud, brossage du corps avec des fibres végétales, gommage, enveloppement de boue avec réflexologie plantaire et hydromassage.

LIVRE À EMPORTER
« L'Ombre du vent » de Carlos Ruiz Zafón.

Spa Vinothérapie Caudalie

at Marqués de Riscal

Opened in 2006 in Spain's Rioja region, this hotel is dedicated to all things wine: the Frank O. Gehry-designed building is topped with a sweeping rosé, silver and gold titanium roof representing a stylised vine. The red-hued interior recalls the colour of the local wine and the spa offers vinotherapy treatments that rejuvenate the skin using grape extracts.

Dieses in der Rioja-Region gelegene und 2006 eröffnete Hotel hat sich ganz dem Wein verschrieben: Frank O. Gehry hat die Architektur mit einem geschwungenen Titandach in Rosé, Silber und Gold gekrönt, das eine stilisierte Rebe darstellt. Im Inneren greifen Rottöne die Farben des Weines auf, und das Spa bietet Vinotherapien an, welche die Haut mit Traubenextrakten verjüngen.

Ouvert en 2006, cet hôtel situé dans la région viticole de la Rioja est voué au produit de la vigne : Frank O. Gehry a couronné la construction d'un toit ondoyant de titane rose, argent et or évoquant les vrilles de la vigne ; à l'intérieur les tons rouges du vin dominent et le spa propose des cures de vinothérapie à base d'extraits de raisin aux effets rajeunissants.

Marqués de Riscal
A Luxury Collection Hotel
Calle Torrea 1
01340 Elciego
Spain
Tel. +34 945 18 08 80
Fax +34 945 18 08 81
reservations.marquesderiscal@luxurycollection.com
www.hotel-marquesderiscal.com

Spa Vinothérapie Caudalie
Tel. +34 945 18 08 70
Fax +34 945 18 08 71

LOCATION
Elciego is situated in the Basque Country, 84 miles south of Bilbao airport.

ROOMS
33 rooms and 10 suites.

FOOD
"Bistro 1860" serves a modern, creative interpretation of Basque cuisine made using fresh market ingredients.

SPA FACILITIES
14,000 sq ft with 14 treatment rooms, indoor pool, steam bath, jacuzzi, wine barrel for special bath treatments, vitality shower and fitness area.

SIGNATURE TREATMENT
The "Crushed Cabernet Scrub".

BOOK TO PACK
"Obabakoak" by Bernardo Atxaga.

LAGE
Elciego liegt im Baskenland, 135 km südlich des Flughafens von Bilbao.

ZIMMER
33 Zimmer und 10 Suiten.

KÜCHE
Frische Marktküche serviert das »Bistro 1860«, hier stehen kreative, moderne Menüs des Baskenlandes auf der Karte.

SPAAUSSTATTUNG
1.300 qm mit 14 Behandlungsräumen, Innenpool, Dampfbad, Jacuzzi, Weinfass für Spezialbäder, Vitaldusche, Fitness-bereich.

SIGNATURE TREATMENT
Das Körperpeeling »Crushed Cabernet Scrub«.

BUCHTIPP
»Obabakoak« von Bernardo Atxaga.

SITUATION
Au Pays Basque, à 135 km au sud de l'aéroport de Bilbao.

CHAMBRES
33 chambres et 10 suites.

RESTAURATION
Le « Bistro 1860 » propose une cuisine du marché. Au menu, des plats modernes de la gastronomie basque.

SERVICES DU SPA
1300 mètres carrés avec 14 cabines de soins, piscine intérieure, bain de vapeur, jacuzzi, barrique pour les bains spéciaux, douche vitalisante, espace de remise en forme.

SOIN SIGNATURE
Le gommage corporel « Crushed Cabernet Scrub ».

LIVRE À EMPORTER
« Obabakoak : Les gens d'Obaba » de Bernardo Atxaga.

Aquapura Spa

at Aquapura Douro Valley

This 19th-century estate was converted into a luxury hotel by Luís Rebelo de Andrade and Nini Andrade Silva. It harmoniously combines historic architecture and minimalist contemporary design – the spa rooms with private plunge pools are particularly stylish, as is the spa itself, in which guests can enjoy holistic treatments from the ancient Orient.

Diese Quinta aus dem 19. Jahrhundert wurde von Luís Rebelo de Andrade und Nini Andrade Silva in ein Luxushotel verwandelt. Historische Architektur und modern-minimalistisches Design spielen hier harmonisch zusammen. Besonders stilvoll sind die Spa-Zimmer mit privatem Tauchpool sowie das Spa selbst, in dem ganzheitliche traditionelle Anwendungen aus Asien verwöhnen.

Ce manoir du 19ᵉ siècle a été transformé par Luís Rebelo de Andrade et Nini Andrade Silva en un hôtel de luxe. L'architecture historique fait ici bon ménage avec le design moderne minimaliste. Les chambres avec spa disposant d'un bassin privé sont particulièrement élégantes ainsi que le spa lui-même, qui propose des traitements holistiques de l'Asie ancienne.

Aquapura Spa
at Aquapura Douro Valley
Quinta do Vale Abraão
5100-758 Lamego
Douro
Portugal
Tel. +351 254 66 06 00
Fax +351 254 66 06 61
aquapuradouro@
aquapuradouro.com
www.aquapurahotels.com

LOCATION
Surrounded by vineyards and overlooking Douro Valley, the hotel is situated in the valley of the same name, 65 miles east of Porto.

ROOMS
50 rooms plus 21 villas designed by Giano Gonçalves.

FOOD
2 restaurants serving fresh Portuguese-Mediterranean fusion cuisine.

SPA FACILITIES
23,700 sq ft with 10 treatment rooms, indoor pool, saunas, laconium, steam bath, herbal bath, tropical showers and fitness area.

SIGNATURE TREATMENT
The four-handed "Ytsara Sabaijai" massage with hot lemon-and-herb compresses.

BOOK TO PACK
"Journey to Portugal" by José Saramago.

LAGE
Das Hotel liegt im Douro-Tal 104 km östlich von Porto und überblickt die Weinberge sowie den Fluss.

ZIMMER
50 Zimmer. Außerdem 21 Villen, die von Giano Gonçalves designt wurden.

KÜCHE
2 Restaurants servieren frische portugiesisch-mediterrane Fusion Cuisine.

SPAAUSSTATTUNG
2.200 qm mit 10 Behandlungsräumen, Innenpool, Saunen, Laconium, Dampfbad, Kräuterbad, Tropenduschen, Fitnessbereich.

SIGNATURE TREATMENT
Die vierhändige Massage »Ytsara Sabaijai« mit heißen Zitronen-Kräuter-Kompressen.

BUCHTIPP
»Die portugiesische Reise« von José Saramago.

SITUATION
Dans la vallée du Douro, à 104 km à l'est de Porto, surplombant les vignobles et le fleuve.

CHAMBRES
50 chambres et 21 villas dont le design est signé Giano Gonçalves.

RESTAURATION
2 restaurants proposent une cuisine à base de produits frais qui marie influences portugaises et méditerranéennes.

SERVICES DU SPA
2200 mètres carrés avec 10 cabines de soins, piscine intérieure, sauna, laconium, bain de vapeur, bain aromatique, douches tropicales, espace de remise en forme.

SOIN SIGNATURE
Le massage à quatre mains « Ytsara Sabaijai » avec des compresses chaudes aux extraits de citron et de plantes.

LIVRE À EMPORTER
« Pérégrinations portugaises » de José Saramago.

Six Senses Spa

at Evason Ma'In Hot Springs

Water from the Ma'In thermal springs cascades straight into the main pool of this luxurious eco-hotel's spa, which also uses mineral-rich salt and mud from the Dead Sea, as well as Jordanian olives and olive oil. Guests can even enjoy treatments in their own room, by booking one of the spa suites that include a treatment room.

Ein Wasserfall der Thermalquellen von Ma'In rauscht direkt in den Hauptpool dieses Spas, das zudem mit mineralhaltigem Salz und Schlamm aus dem Toten Meer sowie Oliven und Olivenöl aus Jordanien pflegt. Gäste des luxuriösen Öko-Hotels, welche die Anwendungen privat im Zimmer genießen möchten, buchen eine der schönen Spa-Suiten mit eigenem Wellnessraum.

Une chute d'eau des sources thermales de Ma'In alimente le bassin principal de ce spa dont les traitements incluent aussi le sel riche en minéraux et la boue de la mer Morte ainsi que les olives et l'huile d'olive de Jordanie. Les hôtes de cet éco-hôtel luxueux désirant recevoir ces soins dans leur chambre réservent une suite spa avec salle de bien-être individuelle.

Six Senses Spa
at Evason Ma'In Hot Springs
P.O. Box 801 Madaba
11117 Ma'In
Jordan
Tel. +962 5 324 55 00
Fax +962 5 324 55 50
reservations-main@
sixsenses.com
www.sixsenses.com

LOCATION
866 ft below sea level, 19 miles southwest of Madaba. The resort is 30 min from the Dead Sea and 60 min from Amman Queen Alia Airport.

ROOMS
78 rooms and 19 suites.

FOOD
The "At the Springs" restaurant has its own juice bar; all food is freshly prepared at live cooking counters.

SPA FACILITIES
13,000 sq ft with 10 treatment rooms, 2 with steam bath and jacuzzi, 2 outdoor pools beneath waterfalls, natural cave sauna and 2 hammams.

SIGNATURE TREATMENT
The "Hammam Ma'In Signature Journey" full-body massage.

BOOK TO PACK
"Seven Pillars of Wisdom" by T. E. Lawrence.

LAGE
264 m unter dem Meeresspiegel gelegen, 30 km südwestlich von Madaba. Das Tote Meer ist 30 min entfernt, der Amman Queen Alia Airport 60 min.

ZIMMER
78 Zimmer und 19 Suiten.

KÜCHE
Im Restaurant »At the Springs« mit Saftbar wird alles frisch an Live-Kochstationen zubereitet.

SPAAUSSTATTUNG
1.200 qm mit 10 Behandlungsräumen, 2 davon mit Dampfbad und Jacuzzi, 2 Außenpools unter Wasserfällen, Naturhöhlensauna, 2 Hamams.

SIGNATURE TREATMENT
Die Ganzkörpermassage »Hammam Ma'In Signature Journey«.

BUCHTIPP
»Die sieben Säulen der Weisheit« von T. E. Lawrence.

SITUATION
264 m sous le niveau de la mer, à 30 km au sud-ouest de Madaba. La mer Morte est à 30 min, l'Amman Queen Alia Airport à 60 min.

CHAMBRES
78 chambres et 19 suites.

RESTAURATION
Au restaurant « At the Springs » qui dispose d'un bar à jus de fruits, tout est préparé directement avec des produits frais sur des comptoirs de cuisine.

SERVICES DU SPA
1200 mètres carrés avec 10 cabines de soins dont 2 avec bains de vapeur et jacuzzi, 2 piscines extérieures sous des cascades, sauna dans une grotte naturelle, 2 hammams.

SOIN SIGNATURE
Le massage complet « Hammam Ma'In Signature Journey ».

LIVRE À EMPORTER
« Les Sept piliers de la sagesse » de T. E. Lawrence.

- 200 m
BELOW
SEA LEVEL

SIX SENSES SPA
Balancing Senses

Six Senses Spa

at Sharq Village

This fairy-tale hotel takes its name from the surrounding area, which is known as "Sharq" (Orient). It was designed in the mould of a traditional Qatari village, with buildings linked by paths and courtyards, and is centred around a bazaar-style Six Senses spa where guests can enjoy Middle Eastern treatments such as a Cleopatra bath and conventional massages.

Dieses märchenhafte Hotel erhielt seinen Namen von der Gegend, in der es liegt: Sie ist als »Sharq« (Orient) bekannt. Gestaltet wurde es wie eine traditionelle Siedlung Katars, deren Gebäude durch Pfade und Innenhöfe verbunden sind. Herzstück ist das im Stil eines Bazars designte Six Senses Spa, das mit arabischen Anwendungen wie dem Kleopatrabad sowie klassischen Massagen verwöhnt.

Cet hôtel féerique tient son nom de la région dans laquelle il se trouve, « sharq », l'Orient. Conçu comme un village traditionnel qatari dont les bâtiments sont reliés par des sentiers et des cours intérieures, le cœur du complexe est le Six Senses Spa dont le style évoque un souk, offrant à ses hôtes des soins arabes comme le bain de Cléopâtre ainsi que des massages classiques.

Sharq Village
P.O. Box 26662
Doha
Qatar
Tel. +974 425 66 66
Fax +974 425 66 60
rc.dohsq.leads@ritzcarlton.com
www.sharqvillage.com

Six Senses Spa
Tel. +974 425 69 99
Tel. +974 425 69 96
reservations-sharq-spa@
sixsenses.com
www.sixsenses.com

LOCATION
Situated on a 1,100 ft stretch of private coastline on the Persian Gulf, 5 min north-west of Doha International Airport.

ROOMS
149 rooms, 24 suites and 1 villa.

FOOD
4 restaurants, plus the idyllic "Al Wanis Shisha Terrace", where meze dishes are served.

SPA FACILITIES
4 separate "Spa Villages"; 70,000 sq ft with 23 treatment rooms; main area with saunas, steam baths, plunge pools, fitness centre and rooms for yoga, Pilates, tai chi and meditation; women's area with fitness area and beauty salon; 2 outdoor pools, 2 hammams and prayer rooms.

SIGNATURE TREATMENT
The "Sensory Spa Journey", a facial and body treatment performed by 2 therapists in unison.

BOOK TO PACK
"Cities of Salt" by Abdelrahman Munif.

LAGE
An einem 350 m langen Privatstrand am Persischen Golf gelegen, 5 min nordwestlich des Doha International Airport.

ZIMMER
149 Zimmer, 24 Suiten und 1 Villa.

KÜCHE
4 Restaurants und die »Al Wanis Shisha Terrace«, auf der Mezze serviert werden.

SPAAUSSTATTUNG
4 separate »Spa Villages«. Insgesamt 6.500 qm mit 23 Behandlungsräumen; Hauptbereich mit Saunen, Dampfbädern, Tauchbecken, Fitnesscenter, Räumen für Yoga, Pilates, Tai-Chi und Meditation; Damenbereich mit Fitnessbereich und Beautysalon; 2 Außenpools, 2 Hamams, Gebetsräume.

SIGNATURE TREATMENT
Die »Sensory Spa Journey«, eine Gesichts- und Körperbehandlung simultan ausgeführt von 2 Therapeuten.

BUCHTIPP
»Reise zwischen Nacht und Morgen« von Rafik Schami.

SITUATION
Sur une plage privée de 350 m de long dans le golfe Persique, à 5 min au nord-ouest du Doha International Airport.

CHAMBRES
149 chambres, 24 suites et 1 villa.

RESTAURATION
4 restaurants et l'idyllique « Al Wanis Shisha Terrace » quelle propose un mezzé.

SERVICES DU SPA
4 « Spa Villages » distincts. 6500 mètres carrés avec 23 cabines de soins ; espace principal avec saunas, bains de vapeur, bassin d'eau froide, centre de remise en forme, salles de yoga, Pilates, tai chi et méditation ; espace dames avec zone de remise en forme et salon de beauté ; 2 piscines extérieures, 2 hammams, salles de prière.

SOIN SIGNATURE
Le « Sensory Spa Journey », un soin du visage et du corps exécuté simultanément par 2 thérapeutes.

LIVRE À EMPORTER
« Une Poignée d'étoiles » de Rafik Schami.

Anantara Spa

at the Emirates Palace

114 domes grace the roof of this Arabian Nights-style palace. One of the most beautiful is the bright blue dome spanning the Anantara Spa's fairy-tale hammam. Besides the opulent atmosphere, guests here can enjoy exotic treatments on marble loungers, the refreshing ice room and herbal tea to finish, in the Moroccan tradition.

114 Kuppeln krönen diesen Palast aus Tausendundeiner Nacht. Eine der schönsten, leuchtend blau gefärbten Kuppeln überspannt den märchenhaften Hamam im Anantara Spa. In opulentem Ambiente lässt man sich hier nach marokkanischer Tradition pflegen und genießt die Behandlung auf der Marmorliege, den erfrischenden Eisraum sowie den Kräutertee zum Abschluss.

114 coupoles surmontent ce palais des Mille et Une Nuits et l'une des plus belles, d'un bleu éclatant, coiffe le hammam féerique du spa Anantara. Ici on peut goûter dans le calme et l'opulence les soins de la tradition marocaine, le traitement sur un lit de massage en marbre, la fraîcheur du frigidarium et l'infusion offerte à la fin.

Emirates Palace
P.O. Box 39999
West End Corniche
Abu Dhabi
United Arab Emirates
Tel. +971 2 690 90 00
Fax +971 2 690 99 99
info.emiratespalace@
kempinski.com
www.emiratespalace.com

Anantara Spa
anantaraspa.emiratespalace@
kempinski.com

LOCATION
On a nearly mile-long private beach, 24 miles from Abu Dhabi airport.

ROOMS
302 rooms and 92 suites.

FOOD
8 excellent restaurants, including "Las Brisas", which serves fresh salads, and "Sayad", specialising in fine seafood.

SPA FACILITIES
10,800 sq ft with 7 Moroccan-style spa suites with oversize tubs and Vichy showers, hammam, ice room, 2 steam baths and 2 jacuzzis.

SIGNATURE TREATMENT
The "Gateway to Arabia" hammam treatment with traditional washing and massage by the therapist.

BOOK TO PACK
"The Emirates of Yesteryear" by Ronald Codrai.

LAGE
An einem 1,3 km langen Privatstrand gelegen, 38 km vom Flughafen Abu Dhabi entfernt.

ZIMMER
302 Zimmer und 92 Suiten.

KÜCHE
8 exzellente Restaurants – darunter das »Las Brisas« mit frischen Salaten und das »Sayad« mit Fischspezialitäten.

SPAAUSSTATTUNG
1.000 qm mit 7 Spa-Suiten im marokkanischen Stil mit Oversize-Wanne und Vichydusche, Hamam, Eisraum, 2 Dampfbädern, 2 Jacuzzis.

SIGNATURE TREATMENT
Die Hamam-Behandlung »Gateway to Arabia«, bei der man sich traditionell vom Bademeister waschen und massieren lässt.

BUCHTIPPS
»Der Spiegel« von Muna Abdul Qader Al Ali und »The Emirates of Yesteryear« von Ronald Codrai.

SITUATION
Sur une plage privée de 1,3 km de long, à 38 km de l'aéroport d'Abu Dhabi.

CHAMBRES
302 chambres et 92 suites.

RESTAURATION
8 restaurants excellents dont le « Las Brisas » qui propose des salades rafraîchissantes et le « Sayad » qui sert des spécialités de poisson.

SERVICES DU SPA
1000 mètres carrés avec 7 suites spa de style marocain abritant une baignoire over-size et une douche Vichy, hammam, frigidarium, 2 bains de vapeur, 2 jacuzzis.

SOIN SIGNATURE
Le soin en hammam « Gateway to Arabia », avec savonnage et massage traditionnels.

LIVRES À EMPORTER
« Poèmes d'amour » de Dhabya Khamis et « The Emirates of Yesteryear » de Ronald Codrai.

Maia Spa

at the Maia Luxury Resort

The Maia was named after the most beautiful of Atlas's seven daughters and is, in fact, one of the most stunning refuges in the Seychelles – not to mention one of the most exclusive. In open-air spa pavilions, Bali-trained therapists pamper guests with luxurious La Prairie beauty products and specially devised treatments featuring coconut, banana and vanilla.

Benannt nach der schönsten der sieben Töchter des Atlas, ist das Maia auch wirklich eines der schönsten und exklusivsten Refugien auf den Seychellen. In Spa-Pavillons verwöhnen auf Bali ausgebildete Therapeuten unter freiem Himmel mit luxuriösen Beauty-Anwendungen von La Prairie sowie Treatments, die speziell für das Maia kreiert wurden mit Produkten aus Kokos, Banane oder Vanille.

Le Maia, qui porte le nom de l'aînée des sept filles du titan Atlas, est l'un des plus beaux refuges des Seychelles et aussi l'un des plus exclusifs : dans des pavillons de plein air, des thérapeutes formés à Bali entourent les hôtes de soins en utilisant des produits de luxe La Prairie ainsi que des traitements à base d'extraits de noix de coco, de banane ou de vanille, créés spécialement pour le Maia.

Maia Spa
at the Maia Luxury Resort
P.O. Box 722
Anse Louis
Mahé
Seychelles
Tel. +248 39 00 00
Fax +248 35 54 76
reservations@southernsun.sc
www.maia.com.sc

LOCATION
Situated on a private, densely forested peninsula in Anse Louis Bay, 25 min from Mahé airport.

ROOMS
30 villas, each with private pool, butler and spa minibar stocked with La Prairie products.

FOOD
The Mediterranean-Creole restaurant "Tec Tec" offers low-calorie options.

SPA FACILITIES
3 pavilions of 800–1,100 sq ft each, pavilion for yoga, shiatsu and qigong, outdoor pool and fitness area.

SIGNATURE TREATMENTS
The "Maia Signature Massage" and the "Maia Signature Bath" with essences of ylang-ylang, sandalwood and bergamot.

BOOK TO PACK
"Treasure Island" by Robert Louis Stevenson.

LAGE
Auf einer privaten, dicht bewachsenen Halbinsel an der Bucht Anse Louis gelegen, 25 min vom Flughafen Mahé entfernt.

ZIMMER
30 Villen mit Privatpool, Butler und »Spa-Minibar« mit La-Prairie-Produkten.

KÜCHE
Das mediterran-kreolische Restaurant »Tec Tec« bietet auch Diät-Menüs an.

SPAAUSSTATTUNG
3 Pavillons à 75–100 qm, Pavillon für Yoga, Shiatsu und Qigong, Außenpool, Fitnessbereich.

SIGNATURE TREATMENTS
Die »Maia Signature Massage« und das »Maia Signature Bath« mit Essenzen aus Ylang-Ylang, Sandelholz und Bergamotte.

BUCHTIPP
»Die Schatzinsel« von Robert Louis Stevenson.

SITUATION
Sur la côte sud-ouest de Mahé, un lieu luxuriant dans la baie d'Anse Louis, à 25 min de l'aéroport de Mahé.

CHAMBRES
30 villas avec piscine privée, majordome et « minibar spa » contenant des produits La Prairie.

RESTAURATION
Le restaurant « Tec Tec », aux influences méditerranéennes et créoles, propose aussi des menus de régime.

SERVICES DU SPA
3 pavillons de 75 à 100 mètres carrés, pavillon pour les cours de yoga, shiatsu et qi gong, piscine extérieure, espace de remise en forme.

SOINS SIGNATURE
Le « Maia Signature Massage » et le « Maia Signature Bath » aux essences de ylang-ylang, bois de santal et bergamote.

LIVRE À EMPORTER
« L'Île au trésor » de Robert Louis Stevenson.

Le Spa de Constance

at the Constance Ephelia Resort

According to local legend, Port Launay was once home to the goddess Ephelia, whose skin was so clear that it reflected the sunlight dancing on the sea. The spa villas and the 53,800-square-foot spa of this Mahé resort, which opened in 2010, pay tribute to her beauty with heavenly treatments featuring natural Seychelles ingredients such as lemongrass and coconut.

Der Sage nach lebte hier einst die Göttin Ephelia – ihre Haut war so klar, dass sie das Glitzern des Meeres und das Strahlen der Sonne widerspiegelte. Eine Hommage an ihre Schönheit sind die Spa-Villen sowie das 5.000 Quadratmeter große Spa dieses 2010 eröffneten Resorts. Hier erlebt man wahrhaft göttliche Therapien mit Naturprodukten der Seychellen wie Zitronengras oder Kokosnuss.

La légende veut que la déesse Ephelia ait autrefois vécu ici – sa peau était si claire qu'elle reflétait le scintillement des vagues et les rayons du soleil. Les villas avec spa et le spa de 5000 mètres carrés de ce resort ouvert en 2010 sont un hommage à sa beauté – les soins à base de produits naturels des Seychelles, tels la citronnelle et la noix de coco, sont divins.

Constance Ephelia Resort
Port Launay
Mahé
Seychelles
Tel. +248 39 50 00
Fax +248 39 50 01
resa@constancehotels.com
www.epheliaresort.com

Le Spa de Constance
Tel. +248 39 50 02
spa@epheliaresort.com

LOCATION
On the west coast of Mahé, 40 min from the airport.

ROOMS
224 suites and 43 pool villas, including 10 spa villas.

FOOD
5 restaurants; "Cyann" serves the resort's light signature cuisine, which combines French, Creole and Oriental influences.

SPA FACILITIES
53,800 sq ft with 14 treatment rooms, 3 Shiseido cosmetics rooms, manicure room, outdoor and thermal pools, sauna, whirlpool, yoga pavilion, fitness area and hair salon.

SIGNATURE TREATMENT
The four-handed "Ephelia Signature Massage" with orange and mandarin oils.

BOOK TO PACK
"On Beauty" by Zadie Smith.

LAGE
An der Westküste von Mahé gelegen, 40 min vom Flughafen entfernt.

ZIMMER
224 Suiten und 43 Poolvillen, darunter 10 Spa-Villen.

KÜCHE
5 Restaurants; das »Cyann« serviert die leichte »Ephelia Signature Cuisine« mit französischen, kreolischen und asiatischen Einflüssen.

SPAAUSSTATTUNG
5.000 qm mit 14 Behandlungsräumen, 3 Shiseido-Kosmetikräumen, Raum für Maniküren, Außen- und Thermalpools, Sauna, Whirlpool, Yogapavillon, Fitnessbereich, Friseursalon.

SIGNATURE TREATMENT
Die vierhändige »Ephelia Signature Massage« mit Orangen- und Mandarinenöl.

BUCHTIPP
»Von der Schönheit« von Zadie Smith.

SITUATION
Sur la côte occidentale de Mahé, à 40 min de l'aéroport.

CHAMBRES
224 suites et 43 villas avec piscine, dont 10 villas avec spa.

RESTAURATION
5 restaurants ; le « Cyann » propose la légère « Ephelia Signature Cuisine » aux accents français, créoles et asiatiques.

SERVICES DU SPA
5000 mètres carrés avec 14 cabines de soins, 3 salles de soins Shiseido, salle de manucure, piscine extérieure et piscine thermale, sauna, bain à remous, pavillon de yoga, espace de remise en forme, salon de coiffure.

SOIN SIGNATURE
Le « Ephelia Signature Massage » à quatre mains, aux huiles essentielles d'orange et de mandarine.

LIVRE À EMPORTER
« De la beauté » de Zadie Smith.

SHISEIDO
SHISEIDO

SHISEIDO
SHISEIDO

Aman Spa

at the Aman New Delhi

Designed by Kerry Hill and opened in 2009, this hotel is the perfect place to unwind in pulsating New Delhi. Its spa boasts minimalist interiors and a bamboo garden that calm both body and soul. It also offers extras such as yoga classes in the nearby Lodhi Gardens, amidst ruined 15th-century tombs and where guests can admire over 100 exotic tree species.

Im ständig pulsierenden Neu-Delhi ist dieses von Kerry Hill entworfene und 2009 eröffnete Hotel der perfekte Ort zum Durchatmen. Sein Spa lässt in minimalistisch designten Räumen sowie im Bambusgarten Körper und Seele zur Ruhe kommen. Es bietet auch Extras wie Yoga in den nahen Lodhi-Gärten an, wo man Grabruinen aus dem 15. Jahrhundert und mehr als 100 exotische Baumsorten bewundern kann.

Conçu par Kerry Hill, cet hôtel qui a ouvert ses portes en 2009 est l'endroit idéal pour décompresser dans la métropole palpitante. Le corps et l'esprit s'apaisent dans les espaces aux lignes épurées du spa et de la bambouseraie. Le spa propose aussi des extras comme des cours de yoga dans les jardins Lodhi tout proches, où l'on peut admirer des ruines funéraires du 15e siècle et plus de 100 arbres exotiques.

Aman Spa
at the Aman New Delhi
Lodhi Road
New Delhi 110003
India
Tel. +91 11 43 63 33 33
Fax +91 11 43 63 33 35
amannewdelhi@
amanresorts.com
www.amannewdelhi.com

LOCATION
In the heart of New Delhi; 22 miles north-east of Indira Gandhi International Airport.

ROOMS
31 rooms and 8 suites in the main building; 28 suites in the annex.

FOOD
"Aman" serves fine French-Asian fusion food, while the "Tapas Lounge" offers authentic Spanish cuisine.

SPA FACILITIES
32,292 sq ft with 8 treatment rooms, 2 hammams, 50-m outdoor pool, beauty salon and fitness centre with Pilates studio.

SIGNATURE TREATMENT
The "Khidmat Massage" with sandalwood, sesame and pomegranate essences and a combination of Swedish, Thai, deep-tissue, Reiki and shiatsu massage techniques.

BOOK TO PACK
"The White Tiger" by Aravind Adiga.

LAGE
Im Herzen Neu-Delhis gelegen; 35 km nordöstlich des Indira Gandhi International Airports.

ZIMMER
31 Zimmer und 8 Suiten im Haupthaus; 28 Suiten im Nebengebäude.

KÜCHE
Das »Aman« serviert u.a. feine asiatisch-französische Fusion Cuisine und die »Tapas Lounge« spanische Spezialitäten.

SPAAUSSTATTUNG
3.000 qm mit 8 Behandlungsräumen, 2 Hamams, 50-m-Außenpool, Beautysalon, Fitnesscenter mit Pilatesstudio.

SIGNATURE TREATMENT
Die »Khidmat Massage« mit Ölessenzen aus Sandelholz, Sesam und Granatapfel, die 5 Techniken kombiniert: schwedisch, Thai, Deep-Tissue, Reiki und Shiatsu.

BUCHTIPP
»Der weiße Tiger« von Aravind Adiga.

SITUATION
Au cœur de New Delhi ; à 35 km au nord-est de l'Indira Gandhi International Airport.

CHAMBRES
31 chambres et 8 suites dans le bâtiment principal ; 28 suites dans l'annexe.

RESTAURATION
L'« Aman » propose entre autres une cuisine fusion, mariage franco-asiatique raffiné, et le « Tapas Lounge » des spécialités espagnoles.

SERVICES DU SPA
3000 mètres carrés avec 8 cabines de soins, 2 hammams, une piscine extérieure de 50 m, un salon de beauté, un centre de remise en forme avec studio Pilates.

SOINS SIGNATURE
Le « Khidmat Massage » aux huiles essentielles de santal, de sésame et de grenade qui combine 5 techniques : suédoise, thaï, Deep Tissue, reiki et shiatsu.

LIVRE À EMPORTER
« Le tigre blanc » d'Aravind Adiga.

1.20 M

Ananda Spa

at Ananda – In the Himalayas

This palace with views over the Ganges Valley, Rishikesh and the Himalayan foothills was built in 1895 for the maharaja of Tehri Garhwal. Since 2000, the estate has been home to one of the world's best spas. Here, guests can enjoy a fairy-tale atmosphere and achieve harmony in body and soul with individually devised Ayurvedic treatments, yoga and meditation.

1895 wurde dieser Palast mit Blick über das Gangestal, Rishikesh und die Vorberge des Himalaya für den Maharadscha von Tehri Garhwal erbaut. Seit 2000 residiert hier eines der besten Spas der Welt: In märchenhaftem, fast magischem Ambiente sorgen individuell zusammengestellte Ayurveda-Anwendungen, Yoga sowie Meditation dafür, dass jeder Gast vollkommene Harmonie von Körper und Seele erfährt.

Ce palais avec vue sur la vallée du Gange, Rishikesh et les contreforts de l'Himalaya a été édifié en 1895. Depuis l'an 2000, un des meilleurs spas du monde réside dans cette propriété. Dans une atmosphère magique, les hôtes sont traités individuellement par l'Ayurveda et suivent des cours de yoga et de méditation, ce qui génère une harmonie parfaite du corps et de l'âme.

Ananda Spa
at Ananda – In the Himalayas
The Palace Estate
Narendra Nagar
Tehri Garhwal
Uttarakhand 249175
India
Tel. +91 1378 22 75 00
Fax +91 1378 22 75 50
sales@anandaspa.com
www.anandaspa.com

LOCATION
In Uttarakhand, 162 miles north-east of Delhi; 6–7 h by car, or domestic flight to Dehradun, then 1 h drive.

ROOMS
70 rooms, 5 suites and 3 pool villas.

FOOD
"The Restaurant" serves the Ananda Spa Cuisine featuring ingredients from the hotel's organic garden.

SPA FACILITIES
24,000 sq ft with 24 treatment rooms, couples suite, beauty salon, hydro-therapy centre with sauna and steam bath, outdoor pool, meditation room and fitness room, plus 5 yoga areas.

SIGNATURE TREATMENTS
The individually tailored "Ananda Fusion" massages.

BOOK TO PACK
"A Fine Balance" by Rohinton Mistry.

LAGE
In Uttarakhand gelegen, 260 km nord-östlich von Delhi; mit dem Auto fährt man 6–7 h. Alternative: Inlandsflug nach Dehradun und 1 h Transfer.

ZIMMER
70 Zimmer, 5 Suiten und 3 Poolvillen.

KÜCHE
Die Ananda Spa Cuisine mit Zutaten aus dem hoteleigenen Biogarten wird im »The Restaurant« serviert.

SPAAUSSTATTUNG
2.230 qm mit 24 Behandlungsräumen, Paar-Suite, Beautysalon, Hydrotherapie-Zentrum mit Sauna und Dampfbad, Außenpool, Meditationsraum, Fitness-raum, 5 Yogabereiche.

SIGNATURE TREATMENTS
Die individuell gestaltbaren »Ananda Fusion«-Massagen.

BUCHTIPP
»Das Gleichgewicht der Welt« von Rohinton Mistry.

SITUATION
Dans l'État d'Uttarakhand, à 260 km au nord-est de Delhi. 6 à 7 h de voiture ou vol à destination de Dehradun, puis transfert d'1 h.

CHAMBRES
70 chambres, 5 suites et 3 villas avec piscine.

RESTAURATION
« The Restaurant » sert l'Ananda Spa Cuisine avec des produits du jardin bio.

SERVICES DU SPA
2230 mètres carrés avec 24 cabines de soins, suite pour couple, salon de beauté, centre d'hydrothérapie avec sauna et bain de vapeur, piscine extérieure, salle de méditation, espace de remise en forme, 5 zones de yoga.

SOINS SIGNATURE
Les massages « Ananda Fusion » à la carte.

LIVRE À EMPORTER
« L'Équilibre du monde » de Rohinton Mistry.

Aman Spa

at Amankora

Bhutan, the "Land of the Thunder Dragon", is one of the planet's most fascinating destinations, and the five lodges at Amankora enable guests to experience its nature and culture at close quarters. All five boast spectacular locations, combine traditional and modern design and feature intimate spas that offer treatments using local herbs and cedarwood.

Bhutan, das »Land des Donnerdrachens«, ist eines der faszinierendsten Ziele der Erde, und seine Natur und Kultur erlebt man in den fünf Lodges von Amankora ganz unmittelbar. Alle Häuser sind herrlich gelegen, verbinden traditionelles mit modernem Design und besitzen intime Spas, in denen lokale Kräuter sowie Anwendungen mit Zedernholz pflegen.

Bhoutan, le « royaume du Dragon tonnerre », est l'une des destinations les plus fascinantes de la planète et un séjour à Amankora permet de découvrir la nature et la culture du pays. Magnifiquement situés, les cinq lodges marient la tradition au design moderne et abritent des spas garantissant l'intimité et proposant des soins à base de plantes de la région et de bois de cèdre.

Aman Spa
at Amankora
P.O. Box 831
Thimphu
Bhutan
Tel. +975 2 33 13 33
Fax +975 2 33 19 99
amankora@amanresorts.com
www.amankora.com

LOCATION
Paro, Bhutan's only airport, is within easy reach of Bangkok (3 h 20 min); the transfer to Amankora Paro lodge takes 30 min; journeys on to Thimphu, Gangtey, Punakha and Bumthang lodges are arranged from there.

ROOMS
72 suites in 5 lodges (24 in Paro, 16 each in Thimphu and Bumthang, 8 each in Punakha and Gangtey).

FOOD
The lodges' dining rooms offer refined Bhutanese cuisine.

SPA FACILITIES
Separate spa per lodge with 2–5 treatment rooms and, in some cases, a sauna, steam bath and yoga room.

SIGNATURE TREATMENT
The hot-stone herbal bath in which hot stones are placed beneath the tub.

BOOK TO PACK
"Lost Horizon" by James Hilton.

LAGE
Bhutans einziger Flughafen Paro ist gut ab Bangkok zu erreichen (3 h 20 min); der Transfer zur Lodge Amankora Paro dauert 30 min. Von dort aus wird die Fahrt zu den Lodges Thimphu, Gangtey, Punakha und Bumthang organisiert.

ZIMMER
72 Suiten in 5 Lodges (Paro 24, Thimphu und Bumthang je 16, Punakha und Gangtey je 8).

KÜCHE
In den Speisesälen der Lodges genießt man verfeinerte bhutanische Speisen.

SPAAUSSTATTUNG
Pro Lodge ein Spa mit 2–5 Behandlungsräumen, z.T. auch Sauna, Dampfbad sowie Yogaraum.

SIGNATURE TREATMENT
Das Hot-Stone-Kräuterbad, bei dem heiße Steine unter der Wanne liegen.

BUCHTIPP
»Der verlorene Horizont« von James Hilton.

SITUATION
Paro, le seul aéroport du Bhoutan, est facile à joindre de Bangkok (3 h 20 min) ; le trajet jusqu'au lodge Amankora Paro dure 30 min. Le transfert vers les lodges Thimphu, Gangtey, Punakha et Bumthang est organisé à partir d'ici.

CHAMBRES
72 suites dans 5 lodges (Paro 24, Thimphu et Bumthang 16, Punakha et Gangtey 8).

RESTAURATION
Les plats aux riches saveurs de la cuisine bhoutanaise sont servis dans les salles de repas.

SERVICES DU SPA
Un spa par lodge avec 2–5 cabines de soins et en partie aussi sauna, bain de vapeur et salle de yoga.

SOIN SIGNATURE
Le bain aux plantes « Hot Stone », dans lequel des pierres chaudes sont placées sous la baignoire.

LIVRE À EMPORTER
« Horizon perdu » de James Hilton.

Como Shambhala Urban Escape

at the Metropolitan Bangkok

Shambhala means "place of bliss" in Sanskrit, and the Metropolitan aims to combine the energy of Bangkok with an oasis-like calm. For the hotel and spa interiors, designer Kathryn Kng has created a highly sophisticated blend of contemporary Western and Far Eastern influences. The treatments, too, are a successful mix of Oriental and modern European techniques.

Shambhala bedeutet »Ort des Friedens« auf Sanskrit. Energie von Bangkok mit der Ruhe einer Oase zu verbinden, ist das Thema des Metropolitan. Kathryn Kng kombiniert im Hotel sowie im Spa sehr sophisticated modernes Design aus Ost und West. Dem Designkonzept entspricht auch die gelungene Mischung der Wellnessanwendungen aus Ost und West.

En sanskrit, Shambhala signifie « source de bonheur » et le concept du Metropolitan consiste à marier l'énergie de Bangkok au calme d'une oasis. Dans l'hôtel et le spa, Kathryn Kng marie les designs contemporains très sophistiqués de l'Orient et de l'Occident, et les soins sont eux aussi un mélange réussi d'anciennes techniques asiatiques et de méthodes occidentales modernes.

Metropolitan Bangkok
27 South Sathorn Road
Tungmahamek
Sathorn
Bangkok 10120
Thailand
Tel. +66 2 625 33 33
Fax +66 2 625 33 00
info.bkk@metropolitan.como.bz
www.metropolitan.bangkok.como.bz

Como Shambhala Urban Escape
metropolitan.bkk@comoshambhala.bz

LOCATION
In the central business district, 40 min from Suvarnabhumi International Airport.

ROOMS
158 rooms and 13 suites.

FOOD
Situated next door to the spa, "Glow" offers enzyme-, vitamin- and mineral-rich dishes made from organic ingredients.

SPA FACILITIES
13,000 sq ft with 10 treatment rooms, 20-m outdoor pool, hydropools, seperate men's and women's steam baths, yoga studio, hair salon and fitness studio.

SIGNATURE TREATMENT
The relaxing "Como Shambhala Bath", including salt scrub, bath and massage.

BOOK TO PACK
"Venom" by Saneh Sangsuk.

LAGE
Im Central Business District gelegen, 40 min vom Suvarnabhumi International Airport entfernt.

ZIMMER
158 Zimmer und 13 Suiten.

KÜCHE
Direkt neben dem Spa serviert das Restaurant »Glow« enzym-, vitamin- und mineralreiche Gerichte aus organischen Zutaten.

SPAAUSSTATTUNG
1.200 qm mit 10 Behandlungsräumen, 20-m-Außenpool, Hydropools und getrennte Dampfbädern für Herren und Damen, Yogastudio, Friseursalon, Fitnessstudio.

SIGNATURE TREATMENT
Das entspannende »Como Shambhala Bath« inklusive Salzpeeling, Bad und Massage.

BUCHTIPP
»Der Traum des Puppenspielers« von Saneh Sangsuk.

SITUATION
Dans le Central Business District, à 40 min du Suvarnabhumi International Airport.

CHAMBRES
158 chambres et 13 suites.

RESTAURATION
Juste à côté du spa, le restaurant « Glow » propose des plats riches en enzymes, en vitamines et sels minéraux, à base de produits bio.

SERVICES DU SPA
1200 mètres carrés avec 10 cabines de soins, piscine extérieure de 20 m, bassins Hydropool et bains de vapeur pour dames et messieurs, salle de yoga, salon de coiffure, studio de remise en forme.

SOIN SIGNATURE
Le relaxant « Como Shambhala Bath » incluant gommage au sel, bain et massage.

LIVRE À EMPORTER
« L'Ombre blanche : Portrait de l'artiste en jeune vaurien » de Saneh Sangsuk.

Six Senses Spa

at Soneva Kiri

For modern Robinson Crusoes: guests reach the remote island of Koh Kood by private plane and boat, are welcomed by their own personal "Mr or Ms Friday" butler, then take up residence in their own eco-villa and relax beneath the palm trees or in the Six Senses Spa. The herbs and fruits for the excellent Thai treatments are organically grown in the hotel garden.

So sehen moderne Robinsonaden aus: Wer die abgelegene Insel Koh Kood per Privatflugzeug und Boot erreicht hat, wird am Strand von seinem persönlichen Butler Herrn oder Frau Freitag begrüßt und kommt in edlen Öko-Villen sowie im Six Senses Spa unter Palmen zur Ruhe. Die Kräuter und Früchte für die exzellenten Thai-Anwendungen werden im Hotelgarten angebaut.

Une robinsonnade moderne : celui qui a atteint l'île de Koh Kood après un voyage en avion privé et en bateau, est accueilli par son majordome personnel, monsieur ou madame Vendredi, et peut se reposer sous les palmiers dans d'élégantes éco-villas et dans le spa Six Senses. Les plantes et fruits à la base des excellents soins thaïlandais sont cultivés dans le jardin de l'hôtel.

Six Senses Spa
at Soneva Kiri
110 Moo 4
Koh Kood District
Trat 23000
Thailand
Tel. +66 39 61 98 00
Fax +66 39 61 98 08
reservations-kiri@sixsenses.com
www.sixsenses.com

LOCATION
Koh Kood lies to the south-east of Bangkok, a 1 h flight away. Guests are taken in the hotel's private plane to the Soneva Kiri airfield. From there it is a 1-mile boat trip to the hotel.

ROOMS
29 pool villas, 5 with their own spa area.

FOOD
The spa has a juice bar; the hotel restaurants serve organic Thai cuisine.

SPA FACILITIES
19,900 sq ft with 15 treatment rooms, Watsu pool, sauna, steam baths, yoga and meditation pavilion and fitness area.

SIGNATURE TREATMENTS
"Slow Life Spa Journeys", for example the "Siam Journey" with mint and lime bath, herbal scrub and Thai massage.

BOOK TO PACK
"The Beach" by Alex Garland.

LAGE
Koh Kood liegt 1 Flugstunde südöstlich von Bangkok. Man fliegt im Privatflugzeug des Hotels zum Soneva Kiri Flughafen, von dort fährt man mit dem Boot zum 2 km entfernten Hotel.

ZIMMER
29 Poolvillen, 5 davon mit eigenem Spa-Bereich.

KÜCHE
Das Spa besitzt eine Saftbar. Die Hotelrestaurants servieren organische Thai-Menüs.

SPAAUSSTATTUNG
1.850 qm mit 15 Behandlungsräumen, Watsu-Pool, Sauna, Dampfbäder, Pavillon für Yoga und Meditation, Fitnessbereich.

SIGNATURE TREATMENTS
Die »Slow Life Spa Journeys«, etwa nach Siam – mit Minz-Limetten-Bad, Kräuterpeeling und Thai-Massage.

BUCHTIPP
»Der Strand« von Alex Garland.

SITUATION
Koh Kood est à 1 h d'avion au sud-est de Bangkok. L'avion privé de l'hôtel transporte les hôtes au aérodrome Soneva Kiri, à 2 km en bateau de l'hôtel.

CHAMBRES
29 villas avec piscine dont 5 avec espace spa individuel.

RESTAURATION
Le spa abrite un bar à jus de fruits. Les restaurants de l'hôtel proposent des menus thaïlandais aux produits bio.

SERVICES DU SPA
1850 mètres carrés avec 15 cabines de soins, bassin watsu, sauna, bains de vapeur, pavillon de yoga et de méditation, espace de remise en forme.

SOINS SIGNATURE
Les « Slow Life Spa Journeys », par exemple au Siam – avec bain à la menthe et au citron kaffir, gommage aux plantes et massage thaïlandais.

LIVRE À EMPORTER
« La Plage » d'Alex Garland.

Six Senses Spa

at the Six Senses Hideaway Samui

Tucked away at the northern tip of Koh Samui, this hotel affords perhaps the finest vistas on the entire island. From its romantic multi-level villas, restaurants and holistic Thai spa, the views stretch far across the Gulf of Siam, while the headland location means guests can admire both sunset and sunrise!

Auf einer Landzunge an der nördlichsten Spitze von Koh Samui versteckt, eröffnet dieses Hotel die wohl schönsten Panoramen der Insel. Von den romantischen Villen mit mehreren Ebenen, den Restaurants sowie dem ganzheitlichen Thai-Spa blickt man weit über den Golf von Siam. Die exponierte Lage macht es sogar möglich, Sonnenaufgang und Sonnenuntergang zu bewundern!

Dominant l'extrémité nord de la pointe de Koh Samui, cet hôtel offre les plus beaux panoramas de l'île. Des villas romantiques à plusieurs niveaux, des restaurants et du spa thaïlandais proposant des soins holistiques, on a une vue imprenable sur le golfe de Siam. L'emplacement privilégié permet d'admirer aussi bien le lever que le coucher du soleil !

Six Senses Spa
at the Six Senses Hideaway Samui
9/10 Moo 5, Baan Plai Laem,
Bophut
Koh Samui
Surat Thani 84320
Thailand
Tel. +66 77 24 56 78
Fax +66 77 24 56 71
reservations-samui@
sixsenses.com
www.sixsenses.com

LOCATION
4 miles from Koh Samui airport, a 45-min flight south of Bangkok.

ROOMS
66 villas, 52 with private pool.

FOOD
The "Dining on the Hill" restaurant serves balanced, healthy meals; "Dining on the Rocks" gives traditional Thai recipes a modern twist and boasts 270-degree panoramic views.

SPA FACILITIES
7 indoor and 4 outdoor treatment rooms, steam bath, sauna, room for yoga, Pilates and tai chi, fitness area and beauty salon.

SIGNATURE TREATMENT
"Secret La Stone 4 Hands", a four-handed massage with hot basalt stones.

BOOK TO PACK
"Sightseeing" by Rattawut Lapcharoensap.

LAGE
6 km vom Flughafen Koh Samui entfernt, 45 Flugminuten südlich von Bangkok.

ZIMMER
66 Villen, davon 52 mit Privatpool.

KÜCHE
Das »Dining on the Hill« serviert gesunde, ausbalancierte Gerichte; das »Dining on the Rocks« mit 270-Grad-Panoramablick interpretiert alte Thai-Rezepte modern.

SPAAUSSTATTUNG
7 Innen-, 4 Außenbehandlungsräume, Dampfbad, Sauna, Raum für Yoga, Pilates und Tai-Chi, Fitnessbereich, Beautysalon.

SIGNATURE TREATMENT
»Secret La Stone 4 Hands«, eine vierhändige Massage mit warmen Basaltsteinen.

BUCHTIPP
»Sightseeing« von Rattawut Lapcharoensap.

SITUATION
À 6 km de aérodrome de Koh Samui, à 45 min en avion au sud de Bangkok.

CHAMBRES
66 villas, dont 52 avec piscine privée.

RESTAURATION
Le « Dining on the Hill » propose des plats légers, équilibrés ; le « Dining on the Rocks » avec sa vue à 270 degrés sur la mer, offre une version moderne d'anciennes recettes thaïlandaises.

SERVICES DU SPA
7 cabines de soins à l'intérieur, 4 à l'extérieur, bain de vapeur, sauna, salles de yoga, Pilates et tai chi, espace de remise en forme, salon de beauté.

SOIN SIGNATURE
« Secret La Stone 4 Hands », un massage à quatre mains avec des pierres de basalte chaudes.

LIVRE À EMPORTER
« Café Lovely » de Rattawut Lapcharoensap.

SALA
TARN COUR
RECEPTION

Espa

at Phulay Bay

With their sumptuous indoor and outdoor bathing facilities, the villas and pavilions of this hotel paradise could pass as private spas in their own right. What's more, the actual Espa spa is just as delightful. Interior designers IA49 and architect Lek Bunnag used glass walls, terraces and outdoor rain showers to blur the boundary between architecture and nature.

Schon die Villen und Pavillons dieses Paradieses könnten dank sinnlicher Innen- und Außenbäder als private Spas gelten. Hier verdoppelt das Espa Spa das Glück: Designer IA49 und Architekt Lek Bunnag lassen Architektur und Natur mithilfe von Glaswänden, Terrassen und Outdoor-Regenduschen ineinanderübergehen.

Synonymes de détente et de volupté, les bassins intérieurs et extérieurs transforment en spas privés les villas et pavillons de ce paradis – le spa Espa, c'est deux fois plus de bonheur. Le designer IA49 et l'architecte Lek Bunnag marient l'architecture et l'environnement à l'aide de murs en verre, de terrasses et de douches d'eau de pluie extérieures.

Espa
at Phulay Bay
A Ritz Carlton Reserve
111 Moo 3 Nongthalay, Muang
Krabi 81000
Thailand
Tel. +66 75 62 81 11
kbvrz.leads@ritzcarlton.com
www.phulaybay.com

LOCATION
On the Andaman coast in south-west Thailand, 40 min to the west of Krabi International Airport.

ROOMS
30 villas and 24 pavilions.

FOOD
The spa café "Raw" has exotic fruit and vegetables, as well as juices and herbal teas.

SPA FACILITIES
21,528 sq ft spread across 3 Thai pavilions with 11 treatment rooms, 2 of which are spa suites with aroma steam baths, VIP treatment area with separate entrance, sauna, aroma steam bath, seperate men's and women's vitality pools, out-door rain showers and wellness studio.

SIGNATURE TREATMENT
The "Thai Herbal Infusion Ritual", a head massage with prai oil.

BOOK TO PACK
"Platform" by Michel Houellebecq.

LAGE
An der Südwestküste Thailands an der Andamanensee gelegen, 40 min westlich des Krabi International Airport.

ZIMMER
30 Villen und 24 Pavillons.

KÜCHE
Im Spa-Café »Raw« gibt es exotische Früchte und Gemüse, Säfte und Kräutertees.

SPAAUSSTATTUNG
3 Thai-Pavillons mit insgesamt 2.000 qm mit 11 Behandlungsräumen, davon 2 Spa-Suiten mit Aroma-Dampfbädern, VIP-Behandlungsbereich mit separatem Eingang, Sauna, Aroma-Dampfbad, getrennte Vitality-Pools für Damen und Herren, Outdoor-Regenduschen, Wellnessstudio.

SIGNATURE TREATMENT
Das »Thai Herbal Infusion Ritual«, eine Kopfmassage mit Prai-Öl.

BUCHTIPP
»Plattform« von Michel Houellebecq.

SITUATION
Dans le sud-ouest de la Thaïlande, sur la côte Andamane, à 40 min à l'ouest du Krabi International Airport.

CHAMBRES
30 villas et 24 pavillons.

RESTAURATION
Le café « Raw » propose des fruits et des légumes de la région, des jus frais pressés et des infusions.

SERVICES DU SPA
3 pavillons thaï sur 2000 mètres carrés avec 11 cabines de soins, dont 2 suites spa avec bains de vapeur aromatiques, espace de soin VIP avec entrée séparée, sauna, bain de vapeur aromatique, piscines Vitalité pour dames et messieurs, douches d'eau de pluie extérieures, studio de bien-être.

SOIN SIGNATURE
Le « Thai Herbal Infusion Ritual », un massage de la tête à l'huile de prai.

LIVRE À EMPORTER
« Plateforme » de Michel Houellebecq.

Como Shambhala Retreat

on Cocoa Island

"Treatment rooms" hardly seems the right word for the enchanting spaces of this spa, whose straw-roof beach houses open up to the Indian Ocean and feature simple interiors by Cheong Yew Kuan. Here, guests can enjoy first-rate Ayurveda treatments from nearby southern India as well as free daily yoga courses.

»Behandlungsräume« wäre wirklich der falsche Begriff für die zauberhaften Räumlichkeiten dieses Spas: Es besteht aus strohgedeckten Strandhäuschen, die weit zum Indischen Ozean geöffnet sind und von Cheong Yew Kuan geradlinig designt wurden. Die hier buchbaren Ayurveda-Behandlungen aus dem nahen Südindien sind ausgezeichnet. Die täglichen Yogakurse sind kostenfrei.

« Cabines de soins » n'est vraiment pas le terme adéquat pour désigner les espaces enchanteurs que proposent ce spa composé de huttes de plage coiffées de paille et ouvertes largement sur l'océan Indien, qui ont été dessinées sans fioritures par Cheong Yew Kuan. Les soins Ayurveda de l'Inde du Sud toute proche prodigués ici sont remarquables et des cours de yoga gratuits sont dispensés tous les jours.

Cocoa Island
Makunufushi
South Malé Atoll
Maldives
Tel. +960 664 18 18
Fax +960 664 19 19
res@cocoaisland.como.bz
www.cocoaisland.como.bz

Como Shambhala Retreat
cocoaisland@comoshambhala.bz

LOCATION
On a private island in the South Malé Atoll, 40 min by boat from Malé International Airport.

ROOMS
17 suites and 16 villas.

FOOD
"Ufaa" offers dishes inspired by the flavours of the Indian Malabar Coast and also serves Como Shambhala's spa cuisine.

SPA FACILITIES
3 single and 1 double massage pavilion, yoga pavilion, outdoor pool, steam baths, meditation area and fitness studio.

SIGNATURE TREATMENT
The calming and rejuvenating "Como Shambhala Massage".

BOOK TO PACK
"The Moor's Last Sigh" by Salman Rushdie.

LAGE
Auf einer Privatinsel im Süd-Malé-Atoll gelegen, 40 min mit dem Boot vom Malé International Airport entfernt.

ZIMMER
17 Suiten und 16 Villen.

KÜCHE
Das Restaurant »Ufaa« – inspiriert von den Aromen der indischen Malabarküste – serviert auch die Spa-Cuisine von Como Shambhala.

SPAAUSSTATTUNG
3 Einzel- und 1 Doppel-Massagepavillon, Yogapavillon, Außenpool, Dampfbäder, Meditationsbereich, Fitnessstudio.

SIGNATURE TREATMENT
Die »Como Shambhala Massage«, die beruhigt und zugleich die Haut verjüngt.

BUCHTIPP
»Des Mauren letzter Seufzer« von Salman Rushdie.

SITUATION
Sur une île privée de l'atoll de Malé-Sud, à 40 min en bateau du Malé International Airport.

CHAMBRES
17 suites et 16 villas.

RESTAURATION
Le restaurant « Ufaa » dont la cuisine est inspirée des arômes de la côte de Malabar propose aussi la spa cuisine de Como Shambhala.

SERVICES DU SPA
3 pavillons de massage simples et 1 double, pavillon de yoga, piscine extérieure, bains de vapeur, espace de méditation, salle de remise en forme.

SOIN SIGNATURE
Le « Como Shambhala Massage » aux propriétés relaxantes et régénérantes.

LIVRE À EMPORTER
« Le dernier soupir du Maure » de Salman Rushdie.

CB-115

The Nam Hai Resort & Spa

Architect Reda Amalou and designer Jaya Ibrahim have created eight beautiful villas for The Nam Hai's holistic spa. The treatments here are all based on ancient Eastern healing traditions. Guests can experience Balinese bathing rituals, discover the secrets of Indian Ayurvedic teachings and relax with a hot-stone massage from the Himalayas.

Acht wunderschöne Villen haben Architekt Reda Amalou und Designer Jaya Ibrahim dem ganzheitlichen Spa des The Nam Hai gewidmet. Hier basieren alle Anwendungen auf alten Heiltraditionen des Ostens. Man zelebriert balinesische Baderituale, lässt sich in die Geheimnisse der indischen Ayurveda-Lehre einweihen oder entspannt bei einer Hot-Stone-Massage aus dem Himalaya.

L'architecte Reda Amalou et le designer Jaya Ibrahim ont conçu huit magnifiques villas pour le spa holistique du The Nam Hai. Tous les soins prodigués ici sont basés sur la tradition asiatique. On célèbre des rituels de bain balinais, on se laisse initier aux mystères de l'Ayurveda indien ou on se détend pendant un massage aux pierres chaudes himalayen.

The Nam Hai Resort & Spa
Hoi An
Hamlet 1
Dien Duong Village,
Dien Ban District
Quang Nam Province
Vietnam
Tel. +84 510 394 00 00
Fax +84 510 394 09 99
afomre@thenamhai.com
www.thenamhai.com

LOCATION
On China Beach close to Hoi An; 30 min south of Danang airport.

ROOMS
60 villas and 40 pool villas.

FOOD
"The Dining Room" serves light Vietnamese cuisine; "The Beach Restaurant" offers seafood and salads.

SPA FACILITIES
80,800 sq ft spread across 8 villas. 4 single and 4 double treatment rooms, each with steam bath and shower room. The sauna and pool are in the nearby Health Club.

SIGNATURE TREATMENT
The "Chedi Jade Massage" performed by two therapists in unison.

BOOK TO PACK
"A Taste of Earth" by Thich Nhat Hanh.

LAGE
Am China Beach nahe von Hoi An gelegen; 30 min südlich des Flughafens Danang.

ZIMMER
60 Villen und 40 Poolvillen.

KÜCHE
»The Dining Room« serviert leichte vietnamesische Menüs, »The Beach Restaurant« Seafood und Salate.

SPAAUSSTATTUNG
7.500 qm verteilt auf 8 Villen. 4 Einzel-, 4 Doppelbehandlungsräume, alle mit Dampfbad und Duschraum. Sauna und Pool liegten im nahen Health Club.

SIGNATURE TREATMENT
Die »Chedi Jade Massage«, die 2 Therapeuten synchron durchführen.

BUCHTIPP
»Drachenprinz und Göttervogel« von Thich Nhat Hanh.

SITUATION
Sur la China Beach à côté de Hoi An ; à 30 min au sud de l'aéroport de Danang.

CHAMBRES
60 villas et 40 villas avec piscine.

RESTAURATION
« The Dining Room » propose des plats vietnamiens frais et légers, « The Beach Restaurant » du poisson, des fruits de mer et des salades.

SERVICES DU SPA
7500 mètres carrés répartis dans 8 villas, 4 cabines de soins simples, 4 doubles, toutes avec bains de vapeur et douche. Sauna et piscine au Health Club tout proche.

SOIN SIGNATURE
Le « Chedi Jade Massage », effectué simultanément par deux thérapeutes.

LIVRE À EMPORTER
« Le Prince dragon – Contes et récits du Viêt Nam » de Thich Nhat Hanh.

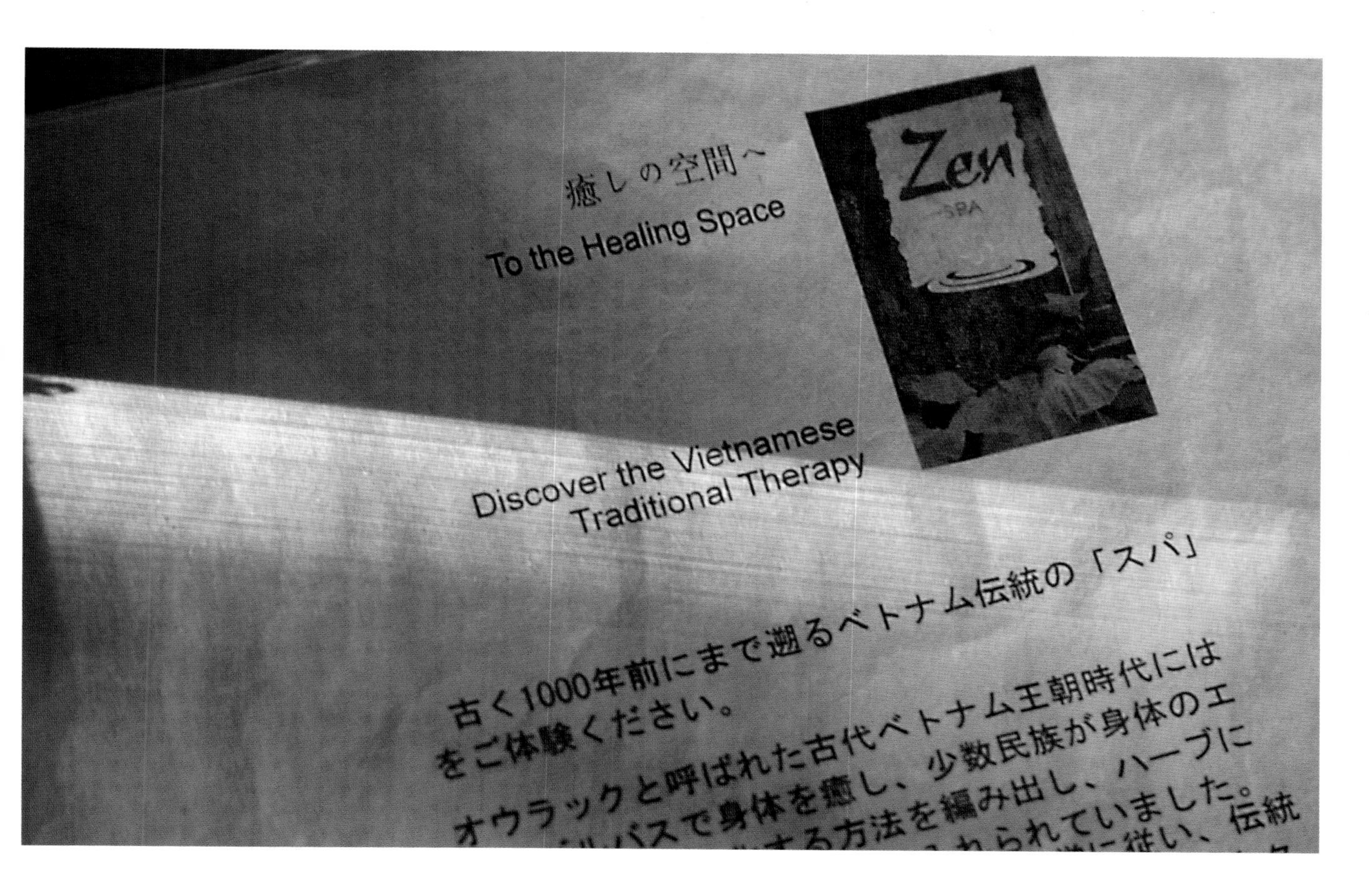

Zen Spa Red River

The secrets of Vietnamese herbal therapies are handed down from generation to generation. Lang-Huong Nguyen has applied the knowledge acquired from her own mother and grandmother at her Hanoi day spa. No modern techniques are used within its bamboo huts, which resemble an idyllic village, the therapists relying solely on the healing power of their hands and the plants cultivated in the spa's own bonsai garden.

Die vietnamesische Kräuterkunde wird von Generation zu Generation weitergegeben – auch Lang-Huong Nguyen erwarb ihr Wissen von ihrer Großmutter und Mutter. In den Bambushütten, die wie ein idyllisches Dorf wirken, verzichten die Therapeuten auf moderne Technik; hier wirken nur die Kraft von Händen und von den im Bonsai-Garten kultivierten Pflanzen.

Depuis toujours au Viêt-Nam, le nom des plantes qui guérissent est transmis de génération en génération – Lang-Huong Nguyen tient son savoir de sa grand-mère et de sa mère. Dans les cabanes de bambou qui forment un village idyllique, les thérapeutes renoncent aux techniques modernes ; seules comptent la force des mains et les vertus des plantes cultivées dans le jardin de bonsaïs.

Zen Spa Red River
310 Nghi Tam Alley
Tay Ho District
Hanoi
Vietnam
Tel. +84 4 37 19 98 89
Fax +84 4 37 19 12 69
info@zenspa.com.vn
www.zenspa.com.vn
Open daily from 9am to 9pm

LOCATION
By West Lake in Hanoi's Tay Ho district, 40 min south of the airport.

ROOMS
The spa doesn't have rooms of its own but can recommend accommodation in the local area.

FOOD
Guests are offered tea and "Zen food": light meals made with organically grown ingredients plus Vietnamese soups and noodle dishes.

SPA FACILITIES
4 double and 2 single treatment rooms, each with steam bath and wooden tub for petal baths, plus a small outdoor pool.

SIGNATURE TREATMENTS
"The Five Elements", 5 different treatments named after the elements metal, wood, water, fire and earth and featuring Vietnamese healing rituals such as herbal body wraps and inhalations.

BOOK TO PACK
"When Heaven and Earth Changed Places" by Le Ly Hayslip.

LAGE
Am West Lake im Distrikt Tay Ho von Hanoi gelegen, 40 min südlich des Flughafens.

ZIMMER
Das Spa bietet keine Zimmer, empfiehlt aber gerne nahe Unterkünfte.

KÜCHE
Man erhält Tee und »Zen Food«: leichte organische Gerichte sowie vietnamesische Suppen und Nudelgerichte.

SPAAUSSTATTUNG
4 Doppel- und 2 Einzelbehandlungsräume mit Dampfbad und Holzzuber für Blumenbäder, kleiner Außenpool.

SIGNATURE TREATMENTS
»The Five Elements«: 5 Anwendungen, die nach den Elementen Metall, Holz, Wasser, Feuer und Erde benannt sind und vietnamesische Heilrituale wie Kräuterwickel und Kräuterinhalationen umfassen.

BUCHTIPP
»Geboren in Vietnam« von Le Ly Hayslip.

SITUATION
Au bord du lac de l'Ouest dans le quartier Tay Ho d'Hanoi, à 40 min au sud de l'aéroport.

CHAMBRES
Pas de chambres, le spa fournit volontiers des adresses d'hébergement proches.

RESTAURATION
Infusions et « Zen Food » : de légers repas à base de produits bio ainsi que des soupes et des plats de nouilles vietnamiens.

SERVICES DU SPA
4 cabines de soins doubles, 2 individuelles avec bain de vapeur et baquet de bois pour les bains aux fleurs, petite piscine extérieure.

SOINS SIGNATURE
« The Five Elements »: 5 soins nommés d'après les éléments métal, bois, eau, feu, terre et comprenant des rituels thérapeutiques vietnamiens comme les enveloppements et les inhalations aux plantes.

LIVRE À EMPORTER
« Entre le ciel et la terre » de Le Ly Hayslip.

ZEN
Foot Rest

FRANÇAISE
1909
1900
REPUBLIQUE
POIDS 27 GR

The Oriental Spa

at The Landmark Mandarin Oriental

In Hong Kong, where the first-ever Mandarin Oriental was opened, in 1963, the group has added another luxury hotel to its portfolio: The Landmark. Adam D. Tihany designed its stylish restaurants; Peter Remedios the spa and the rooms, which feature a plethora of technical refinements. Guests enjoy holistic treatments in maximum privacy.

In Hongkong, wo 1963 das erste Mandarin Oriental eröffnet wurde, steht ein weiteres Hotel der Gruppe: The Landmark. Die stilvollen Restaurants richtete Adam D. Tihany ein; Peter Remedios entwarf die mit allen technischen Raffinessen ausgestatteten Zimmer sowie das Spa. Dieses verwöhnt mit holistischen Anwendungen und höchster Privatsphäre.

À Hong Kong, où le premier Mandarin Oriental a ouvert ses portes en 1963, se trouve maintenant un autre hôtel du groupe : The Landmark. Les restaurants ont été aménagés avec goût par Adam D. Tihany ; Peter Remedios a conçu les chambres dotées des équipements dernier cri ainsi que le spa. Offrant une approche holistique du bien-être, celui-ci respecte au plus haut point la vie privée de ses hôtes.

The Landmark Mandarin Oriental
15 Queen's Road Central
The Landmark, Central
Hong Kong
China
Tel. +852 21 32 01 88
Fax +852 21 32 01 99
lmhkg-enquiry@mohg.com
www.mandarinoriental.com

The Oriental Spa
Tel. +852 21 32 00 11
Fax +852 31 72 80 11
lmhkg-spa@mohg.com

LOCATION
In Central, 40 min east of Hong Kong's airport.

ROOMS
101 rooms and 12 suites.

FOOD
The spa's café serves teas, juices, smoothies and dishes based on the ancient Cretan diet.

SPA FACILITIES
25,000 sq ft with 14 treatment rooms, spa suite, 18-m indoor pool; mixed area with vitality pools, tepidarium chairs and ice fountain; women's area with laconium, steam bath and rasul; men's area with Finnish sauna, tropical rain sauna and hammam; fitness centre, yoga studio and Pilates studio.

SIGNATURE TREATMENTS
The "Time Rituals" – guests book time, which is then filled with treatments tailored to their individual needs.

BOOK TO PACK
"The World of Suzie Wong" by Richard Mason.

LAGE
Im Distrikt Central gelegen, 40 min östlich des Flughafens.

ZIMMER
101 Zimmer und 12 Suiten.

KÜCHE
Das Spa-Café serviert Tees, Säfte, Smoothies und Gerichte auf Basis der Kreta-Diät.

SPAAUSSTATTUNG
2.322 qm mit 14 Behandlungsräumen, Spa-Suite, 18-m-Innenpool; Bereich für Damen und Herren mit Vitality-Pools, Tepidarium-Stühlen und Eisbrunnen, Bereich für Damen mit Laconium, Dampfbad und Rasul; Bereich für Herren mit finnischer Sauna, tropischer Regensauna und Hamam; Fitnesscenter, Yogastudio, Pilatesstudio.

SIGNATURE TREATMENTS
Die »Time Rituals«, bei denen man Zeit bucht und diese mit maßgeschneiderten Anwendungen füllt.

BUCHTIPP
»Suzie Wong« von Richard Mason.

SITUATION
Dans le quartier de Central, à 40 min à l'est de l'aéroport de Hong Kong.

CHAMBRES
101 chambres et 12 suites.

RESTAURATION
Le café du spa sert infusions, jus de fruits, smoothies et plats basés sur le régime crétois.

SERVICES DU SPA
2322 mètres carrés avec 14 cabines de soins, suite spa, piscine intérieure de 18 m; espace mixte avec avec piscines Vitalité, tepidarium, fontaine de glace ; espace dames avec laconium, bain de vapeur, soin au rassou ; espace messieurs avec sauna finlandais, sauna forêt tropicale, hammam ; centre de remise en forme, studios de yoga et de Pilates.

SOINS SIGNATURE
Les « Time Rituals » – vous réservez du temps employé aux soins individuels.

BUCHTIPP
« Le Monde de Suzie Wong » de Richard Mason.

Aman Spa

at Amanfayun

Surrounded by tea bushes, bamboo groves and magnolia trees, this enchanting spa offers ancient Chinese therapies inspired by the seasons. They include a detoxifying green-tea wrap in spring, invigorating bamboo massages on summer days, a relaxing bath of gui hua petals (sweet osmanthus) in the autumn and, to beat the winter chill, Chinese ginger.

Umgeben von Teesträuchern, Bambushainen und Magnolienbäumen bietet dieses zauberhafte Spa alte chinesische Heiltherapien an, welche von den vier Jahreszeiten inspiriert sind. Im Frühling entschlackt beispielsweise ein Wickel mit grünem Tee, an Sommertagen belebt eine Bambusmassage, im Herbst entspannt man im Gui-Hua-Blütenbad (Süßer Osmanthus), und bei Winterkälte wärmt Jiang, chinesischer Ingwer.

Entouré de champs de thé, de bambouseraies et de magnolias, ce spa enchanteur offre des thérapies chinoises ancestrales inspirées des quatre saisons : un enveloppement au thé vert désintoxique au printemps, un massage au bambou tonifie en été, un bain aux fleurs de gui hua (osmanthus suavis) relaxe en automne, et le jiang, gingembre, réchauffe en hiver.

Aman Spa
at Amanfayun
22 Fayun Nong
Xihujiedao
Xihufengjingmingsheng District
310013 Hangzhou
China
Tel. +86 571 87 32 99 99
Fax +86 571 87 32 99 00
amanfayun@amanresorts.com
www.amanfayun.com

LOCATION
50 min from Hangzhou airport. Alternatively, Shanghai airport further east is 1 h 20 min away by train or 3 h by car.

ROOMS
16 rooms, 21 suites and 5 villas.

FOOD
4 restaurants; "Hangzhou House" and "Steam House" both serve fine Chinese cuisine.

SPA FACILITIES
12,900 sq ft in 5 buildings: reception with room for reflexology massages, bathhouse with 3 rooms featuring wood tubs and steam bath, fitness centre with tai chi, yoga, Pilates and meditation rooms, beauty salon and spa house with 5 treatment rooms.

SIGNATURE TREATMENTS
Massages with warm bamboo rolls or freshly mixed herbs.

BOOK TO PACK
"Brothers" by Yu Hua.

LAGE
50 min vom Flughafen Hangzhou entfernt. Alternativ reist man über das östlich gelegene Shanghai an: 1 h 20 min mit dem Zug, 3 h mit dem Auto.

ZIMMER
16 Zimmer, 21 Suiten und 5 Villen.

KÜCHE
4 Restaurants; feine chinesische Gerichte servieren das »Hangzhou House« und das »Steam House«.

SPAAUSSTATTUNG
1.198 qm in 5 Häusern: Rezeption mit Raum für Reflexzonenmassagen, Badehaus mit 3 Räumen mit Holzzuber und Dampfbad, Fitnesscenter mit Räumen für Tai-Chi, Yoga, Pilates und Meditation, Beautysalon, Spa-Haus mit 5 Behandlungsräumen.

SIGNATURE TREATMENTS
Die Massagen mit warmen Bambusrollen oder frisch angerührten Kräutern.

BUCHTIPP
»Brüder« von Yu Hua.

SITUATION
À 50 min de l'aéroport de Hangzhou. On peut aussi passer par Shanghai situé à l'est : 1 h 20 min en train, 3 h en voiture.

CHAMBRES
16 chambres, 21 suites et 5 villas.

RESTAURATION
4 restaurants ; La « Hangzhou House » et la « Steam House » proposent des spécialités chinoises raffinées.

SERVICES DU SPA
1198 mètres carrés dans 5 bâtiments : réception avec salle de réflexologie plantaire, maison de bains avec 3 salles abritant un baquet de bois et un bain de vapeur, centre de remise en forme avec espaces réservés au tai chi, au yoga, au Pilates et à la méditation, salon de beauté, maison spa avec 5 cabines de soins.

SOINS SIGNATURE
Les massages à l'aide de tiges de bambous tièdes ou de mélanges frais de plantes.

LIVRE À EMPORTER
« Brothers » de Yu Hua.

Ginzan Hot Spring Fujiya Inn

Perhaps the most stylish place to relax in all Japan, this modern masterpiece was created out of an old guest house. Designed by architect Kengo Kuma, it features wooden screens, bamboo parasols and glass panels symbolising various levels of space and time, something guests can reflect upon while enjoying a soothing and pain-relieving natural hot-spring bath – whose water has a temperature of 140.5 degrees Fahrenheit.

Stilvoller als hier kann man in Japan kaum entspannen. Kengo Kuma verwandelte dieses alte Gasthaus in ein modernes Meisterwerk, in dem Holzparavents, Bambusschirme und Glasflächen verschiedene Raum- und Zeitebenen symbolisieren. Die 60,3 Grad Celsius heißen natürlichen Quellbäder wirken beruhigend und schmerzlindernd.

Impossible de se relaxer avec plus de classe au Japon : Kengo Kuma a transformé cette ancienne auberge en un chef-d'œuvre moderne dans lequel paravents de bois, écrans de bambou et murs de verre symbolisent divers plans de l'espace et du temps. On peut philosopher dans les bains alimentés par la source thermale chaude (60,3 degrés Celsius) aux propriétés calmantes et antalgiques.

Ginzan Hot Spring Fujiya Inn
443 Shinpata Oaza Ginzan
Obanazawa
Yamagata 999-4333
Japan
Tel. +81 237 28 21 41
Fax +81 237 28 21 40
info@fujiya-ginzan.com
www.fujiya-ginzan.com

LOCATION
On the Ginzan River in the town of the same name, 22 miles north of Yamagata airport, a 1 h flight from Tokyo.

ROOMS
8 rooms with 2–3 beds.

FOOD
In addition to Western-style coffee and cake, the inn's café also serves fine traditional Japanese cuisine, featuring light dishes made with fresh ingredients.

SPA FACILITIES
4 indoor baths and 1 open-air bath on the top floor.

SIGNATURE TREATMENTS
Traditional hot-spring baths. The waters can also be drunk to relieve high blood pressure, anaemia, diabetes and gastric disorders.

BOOK TO PACK
"Shirobamba" by Yasushi Inoue.

LAGE
Am Fluss Ginzan im gleichnamigen Ort gelegen, 35 km nördlich des Flughafens von Yamagata, 1 h Flugzeit ab Tokio.

ZIMMER
8 Zimmer mit 2–3 Betten.

KÜCHE
Das hauseigene Café serviert neben westlich inspiriertem Kaffee und Kuchen klassische japanische Spezialitäten, die leicht, sehr fein und immer ganz frisch sind.

SPAAUSSTATTUNG
4 Innenbäder und 1 Außenbad in der obersten Etage.

SIGNATURE TREATMENTS
Heiße traditionelle Heilbäder, inklusive Trinkkuren, die gegen Bluthochdruck, Anämie, Diabetes und Magen-Darm-Probleme helfen.

BUCHTIPP
»Shirobamba« von Yasushi Inoue.

SITUATION
Sur la rivière Ginzan dans le village du même nom, à 35 km au nord de l'aéroport de Yamagata, à 1 h d'avion de Tokyo.

ZIMMER
8 chambres à 2–3 lits.

RESTAURATION
À côté du café et de la pâtisserie d'inspiration occidentale, le café de la maison propose des spécialités japonaises classiques et légères, très fines et d'une grande fraîcheur.

SERVICES DU SPA
4 bassins intérieurs et 1 bassin extérieur au dernier étage.

SOINS SIGNATURE
Bains chauds traditionnels, cure d'eau minérale inclue, pour soigner la tension artérielle, l'anémie, le diabète et les problèmes gastro-entérologiques.

LIVRE À EMPORTER
« Shirobamba » de Yasushi Inoué.

Mayflower Inn & Spa

In 1992, art dealer and former banker Robert Mnuchin turned a run-down country house into this luxurious New England retreat. Today, the Mayflower Inn is a Relais & Châteaux hotel whose guests often include famous faces and whose stylish spa offers custom fitness and wellness programmes devised by personal advisors.

Ein renovierungsbedürftiges Landhaus verwandelte der Galerist und ehemalige Banker Robert Mnuchin 1992 in dieses Hotel im luxuriösen Countrystil Neu Englands. Heute ist das Mayflower Inn Mitglied bei Relais & Châteaux und verwöhnt seine oft prominenten Gäste im stilvollen Spa. Persönliche Berater sorgen dafür, dass alle Fitness- und Wellnessprogramme maßgeschneidert sind.

Le galeriste et ex-banquier Robert Mnuchin a transformé en 1992 une maison de campagne délabrée en un hôtel montrant le style campagnard luxueux de la Nouvelle-Angleterre. Aujourd'hui, le Mayflower Inn est membre de Relais & Châteaux et ses hôtes souvent éminents sont choyés dans le spa élégant où des conseillers personnels veillent à ce que les programmes de remise en forme et de bien-être soient taillés sur mesure.

Mayflower Inn & Spa
118 Woodbury Road
Route 47
Washington, CT 06793
USA
Tel. +1 860 868 9466
Fax +1 860 868 1497
www.mayflowerinn.com

LOCATION
In the small town of Washington, Connecticut; 95 miles north-east of New York City.

ROOMS
19 rooms and 11 suites in 4 buildings.

FOOD
The spa offers healthy snacks; the Mayflower Spa Cuisine is served in the hotel restaurant.

SPA FACILITIES
20,000 sq ft with 8 treatment rooms, spa suite, 3 fitness studios, Pilates studio, indoor pool, whirlpool, thermal area, beauty salon and yoga and meditation garden.

SIGNATURE TREATMENTS
The "Mayflower Massage" combining various rhythmic massage techniques and the "Mayflower Stonecrop and Rose Facial" with organic herbs and fruits.

BOOK TO PACK
"The Poetry of Robert Frost" by Robert Frost.

LAGE
Im Städtchen Washington in Connecticut gelegen; 150 km nordöstlich von New York City.

ZIMMER
19 Zimmer und 11 Suiten in 4 Gebäuden.

KÜCHE
Im Spa werden gesunde Snacks bereitgehalten; das Restaurant serviert die Mayflower Spa Cuisine.

SPAAUSSTATTUNG
1.858 qm mit 8 Behandlungsräumen, Spa-Suite, 3 Fitnessstudios, Pilatesstudio, Innenpool, Whirlpool, Thermalbereich, Beautysalon, Yoga- und Meditationsgarten.

SIGNATURE TREATMENTS
Die »Mayflower Massage«, die verschiedene rhythmische Techniken kombiniert, und das »Mayflower Stonecrop and Rose Facial« mit Früchten und Kräutern aus organischem Anbau.

BUCHTIPP
»Promises to keep« von Robert Frost.

SITUATION
Dans la petite ville de Washington au Connecticut ; à 150 km au nord-est de New York.

CHAMBRES
19 chambres et 11 suites dans 4 bâtiments.

RESTAURATION
Le spa propose des collations légères ; le restaurant offre les plats de la Mayflower Spa Cuisine.

SERVICES DU SPA
1858 mètres carrés avec 8 cabines de soins, suite spa, 3 studios de remise en forme, studio Pilates, piscine intérieure, bain à remous, espace thermal, salon de beauté, jardin de yoga et de méditation.

SOINS SIGNATURE
Le « Mayflower Massage », qui combine des techniques rythmiques, le soin du visage « Mayflower Stonecrop and Rose Facial » à base de fruits et de plantes.

LIVRE À EMPORTER
« Une Âme en incandescence » d'Emily Dickinson.

EXIT

The Spa

at the Mandarin Oriental New York

Although located in the heart of Manhattan, this spa is far removed from the urban bustle. Its designers Hirsch Bedner Associates have created a peaceful refuge whose bamboo floors, stone walls, rice-paper curtains and artistic carvings lend a refined Oriental touch. The first-class treatments from the West and Far East are tailored to each individual guest.

Dieses Spa liegt mitten in Manhattan – und doch weit entfernt von der hektischen Metropole: Hirsch Bedner Associates haben es als ruhiges Refugium gestaltet. Bambusböden, Wände aus Naturstein, Vorhänge aus Reispapier und kunstvolle Schnitzereien verleihen ihm eine edle asiatische Anmutung. Die exzellenten Behandlungen aus Ost und West werden auf jeden Gast individuell abgestimmt.

Situé au cœur de Manhattan, ce spa est pourtant loin de la métropole trépidante : Hirsch Bedner Associates ont conçu un refuge paisible auquel parquets de bambou, murs en pierre naturelle, rideaux en papier de riz et bois sculptés donnent un élégant accent asiatique. Les soins excellents sont issus d'Orient et d'Occident, chaque hôte profite d'un traitement individuel.

Mandarin Oriental New York
80 Columbus Circle at
60th Street
New York, NY 10023
USA
Tel. +1 212 805 8800
Fax +1 212 805 8888
monyc-reservations@mohg.com
www.mandarinoriental.com

The Spa
Tel. +1 212 805 8880
monyc-spa@mohg.com

LOCATION
The hotel is situated 16 miles north-west of John F. Kennedy Airport on floors 35–54 of the Time Warner Center and has spectacular views of Central Park and the Hudson River.

ROOMS
202 rooms and 46 suites.

FOOD
The spa has an Oriental tea lounge.

SPA FACILITIES
14,500 sq ft with 6 treatment rooms, Thai yoga suite, VIP spa suite, manicure and pedicure room, indoor pool, men's and women's vitality pools, steam bath and fitness centre.

SIGNATURE TREATMENTS
The "Mandarin Oriental Signature Spa Therapies", body massages based on the principles of aromatherapy and traditional Chinese medicine.

BOOK TO PACK
"What I Loved" by Siri Hustvedt.

LAGE
Das Hotel liegt 25 km nordwestlich des Flughafens John F. Kennedy in den Etagen 35–54 des Time Warner Center mit Traumblick auf den Central Park und den Hudson.

ZIMMER
202 Zimmer und 46 Suiten.

KÜCHE
Zum Spa gehört eine orientalische Tee-Lounge.

SPAAUSSTATTUNG
1.350 qm mit 6 Behandlungsräumen, Thai-Yoga-Suite, VIP-Spa-Suite, Raum für Maniküre und Pediküre, Innenpool, Vitality-Pools für Damen und Herren, Dampfbad, Fitnesscenter.

SIGNATURE TREATMENTS
Die »Mandarin Oriental Signature Spa Therapies« nach Grundsätzen der Aromatherapie und der traditionellen chinesischen Medizin kreierte Körpermassagen.

BUCHTIPP
»Was ich liebte« von Siri Hustvedt.

SITUATION
À 25 km au nord-ouest de l'aéroport John F. Kennedy, aux étages 35–54 du Time Warner Center offrant une vue de rêve sur Central Park et l'Hudson.

CHAMBRES
202 chambres et 46 suites.

RESTAURATION
Le spa possède un salon de thé oriental.

SERVICES DU SPA
1350 mètres carrés avec 6 cabines de soins, suite Thaï Yoga, suite VIP Spa, salle pour manucure et pédicure, piscine intérieure, piscines Vitalité pour dames et messieurs, bain de vapeur, centre de remise en forme.

SOINS SIGNATURE
Les « Mandarin Oriental Signature Spa Therapies », basées sur les principes de la médecine chinoise traditionnelle et des massages corporels avec aromathérapie.

LIVRE À EMPORTER
« Tout ce que j'aimais » de Siri Hustvedt.

FEET 6INCHES DEEP
3FEET 6INCHES DEEP

Shibui Spa

at The Greenwich Hotel

The centrepiece of the Shibui Spa in Robert De Niro's atmospheric Greenwich Hotel is an original, 250-year-old wood-and-bamboo Japanese farmhouse, inside which a lantern-illuminated pool has been installed. There are also first-rate therapists on hand to relax spa guests with traditional and modern treatments from Japan, China and Malaysia.

Herzstück des Shibui Spas in Robert De Niros atmosphärischem Greenwich Hotel ist ein originales, 250 Jahre altes japanisches Bauernhaus aus Holz und Bambus, in dem ein mit Laternen beleuchteter Pool eingerichtet wurde. Zudem verwöhnen hier hervorragende Therapeuten mit traditionellen und modernen Wellnessanwendungen aus Japan, China sowie Malaysia.

Dans le si douillet Greenwich Hotel de Robert De Niro, le cœur du Shibui Spa est une authentique ferme japonaise de 250 ans, en bois et bambou, dans laquelle on a aménagé une piscine éclairée par des lanternes. Des thérapeutes remarquables veillent ici sur les hôtes, combinant des soins de bien-être traditionnels et modernes, originaires du Japon, de Chine ou de Malaisie.

Shibui Spa
at The Greenwich Hotel
377 Greenwich Street
New York, NY 10013
USA
Tel. +1 212 941 8900
Fax +1 212 941 8600
info@thegreenwichhotel.com
www.thegreenwichhotel.com

LOCATION
In Manhattan's Tribeca district, 20 miles west of John F. Kennedy Airport.

ROOMS
75 rooms, 12 suites and 1 penthouse, all with interiors by Grayling Design.

FOOD
"Locanda Verde" offers first-rate Italian taverna-style cooking.

SPA FACILITIES
6,000 sq ft with separate rooms for Japanese baths and massages, shiatsu, scrubs and wraps, plus 2 massage rooms, indoor pool, yoga area and fitness room.

SIGNATURE TREATMENT
The "Sake Ki" massage with soothing ginger and black pepper ointment.

BOOK TO PACK
"The Godfather" by Mario Puzo.

LAGE
Im Viertel Tribeca in Manhattan gelegen, 32 km westlich des Flughafens John F. Kennedy.

ZIMMER
75 Zimmer, 12 Suiten und 1 Penthouse, alle gestaltet von Grayling Design.

KÜCHE
In der »Locanda Verde« werden beste italienische Spezialitäten zubereitet.

SPAAUSSTATTUNG
560 qm mit Räumen für Shiatsu, japanische Bäder und Massagen, Peelings und Wickel, 2 Massageräumen, Innenpool, Yogabereich, Fitnessraum.

SIGNATURE TREATMENT
Die »Sake Ki«-Massage mit einer Heilcreme aus Ingwer und schwarzem Pfeffer.

BUCHTIPP
»Der Pate« von Mario Puzo.

SITUATION
Dans le quartier de Tribeca à Manhattan situé à 32 km à l'ouest de l'aéroport John F. Kennedy.

CHAMBRES
75 chambres, 12 suites et 1 penthouse ; le design est signé Grayling Design.

RESTAURATION
La « Locanda Verde » propose les meilleures spécialités italiennes faites maison.

SERVICES DU SPA
560 mètres carrés avec salle de shiatsu, espace bains japonais et massages, espace gommage et enveloppements, 2 salles de massage, piscine intérieure, salle de yoga, centre de remise en forme.

SOIN SIGNATURE
Le massage « Sake Ki » avec une crème de soins à base de gingembre et de poivre noir.

LIVRE À EMPORTER
« Le Parrain » de Mario Puzo.

The Standard Spa

at The Standard Miami Beach

For the Romans, Turks and Russians, baths were not just somewhere to wash and cleanse; they were also important meeting places. This idea inspired André Balazs for his modernisation of the former Lido Spa Hotel. Guests now relax together under the Roman waterfall, the hammam or the sauna and take part in yoga and meditation courses.

Für die Römer, Türken und Russen waren Bäder nicht nur Orte der Körperpflege, sondern auch soziale Treffpunkte. Diese Idee inspirierte André Balazs, als er das ehemalige Lido Spa Hotel neu eröffnete. Seine Gäste entspannen gemeinsam unterm römischen Wasserfall, im Hamam oder in der Sauna sowie bei Yoga- und Meditationskursen.

Pour les Romains, les Turcs et les Russes, les bains publics n'étaient pas seulement un lieu où l'on prodiguait des soins du corps, ils avaient aussi une fonction sociale. André Balazs s'en est souvenu lorsqu'il a rouvert les portes de l'ancien Lido Spa Hotel. Ses hôtes se détendent ensemble sous la cascade romaine, au hammam ou dans le sauna ainsi qu'en prenant des cours de yoga et de méditation.

The Standard Miami Beach
40 Island Avenue
Miami Beach, FL 33139
USA
Tel. +1 305 673 1717
Fax +1 305 673 8181
miami@standardhotel.com
www.standardhotels.com

The Standard Spa
Tel. +1 305 704 3945

LOCATION
On Belle Isle in the Bay of Biscayne, 12 miles east of Miami airport.

ROOMS
105 rooms.

FOOD
The menu at "The Lido Restaurant" features healthy Mediterranean cuisine made with organic ingredients.

SPA FACILITIES
Indoor baths: hammam, aroma steam bath, cedar sauna, sound and rain showers, mud lounge, scrub room and 7 treatment rooms; outdoor baths: Roman waterfall, Arctic plunge pool and underwater music pool; yoga centre and fitness room.

SIGNATURE TREATMENT
Hammam body treatment, including moisturising coconut milk bath and scrub.

BOOK TO PACK
"Islands in the Stream" by Ernest Hemingway.

LAGE
Auf der Belle Isle in der Biscayne-Bucht gelegen, 20 km östlich des Flughafens Miami.

ZIMMER
105 Zimmer.

KÜCHE
Die Karte des »The Lido Restaurant« basiert auf gesunder Mittelmeerküche aus organischen Zutaten.

SPAAUSSTATTUNG
Innenbäder: Hamam, Aroma-Dampfbad, Zedernsauna, Sound- und Regendusche, Lounge für Schlammbäder, Raum für Peelings, 7 Behandlungsräume; Außenbäder: Römischer Wasserfall, arktischer Tauchpool, Pool mit Unterwassermusik; Yogacenter, Fitnessraum.

SIGNATURE TREATMENT
Die Ganzkörperpflege im Hamam inklusive feuchtigkeitsspendendem Kokosmilchbad und Peeling.

BUCHTIPP
»Inseln im Strom« von Ernest Hemingway.

SITUATION
Sur la Belle Isle dans la baie de Biscayne, à 20 km à l'est de l'aéroport de Miami.

CHAMBRES
105 chambres.

RESTAURATION
Les plats que propose « The Lido Restaurant » sont axés sur la cuisine méditerranéenne réalisée avec des produits bio.

SERVICES DU SPA
À l'intérieur : hammam, bain de vapeur aromatique, sauna en bois de cèdre, douche musicale et douche d'eau de pluie, espace bains de boue, salle de gommage, 7 cabines de soins. À l'extérieur : chute d'eau romaine, bassin arctique, piscine avec musique subaquatique ; centre de yoga, salle de remise en forme.

SOIN SIGNATURE
Le soin complet au hammam, bain de lait de coco hydratant et gommage inclus.

LIVRE À EMPORTER
« Îles à la dérive » d'Ernest Hemingway.

Japanese Spa

at Ten Thousand Waves

Since 1981, there's been a small corner of Japan in the woods of Santa Fe. Modelled on an onsen, a Japanese bathhouse, this spa offers traditional communal and private bathing in water heated to approximately 104 degrees Fahrenheit, Oriental massages and a ryokan, a Japanese inn. Advance booking is recommended for these!

Seit 1981 liegt ein Stück Japans in den Wäldern von Santa Fe. Dieses Spa ist einem Onsen, einem japanischen Badehaus, nachempfunden. Nach alter Tradition bietet es Gemeinschafts- und Privatbäder mit rund 40 Grad Celsius warmem Wasser, asiatische Massagen sowie ein japanisches Gasthaus, ein sogenannter Ryokan. Hier muss man rechtzeitig reservieren!

Depuis 1981, on trouve un coin de Japon dans les forêts de Santa Fe : inspiré d'un onsen, maison de bain traditionnelle, ce spa propose des bains communs ou privés dans de l'eau chauffée à 40 degrés Celsius, des massages asiatiques ainsi qu'un ryokan, une auberge japonaise. Il faut réserver à temps !

Ten Thousand Waves
3451 Hyde Park Road
Santa Fe, NM 87501
USA
Tel. +1 505 992 5003
www.tenthousandwaves.com

Japanese Spa
Tel. +1 505 982 9304

LOCATION
North-east of Santa Fe, 19 miles from the city's airport with daily services to and from Dallas.

ROOMS
13 "Houses of the Moon" almost all of which have the word "moon" in their name.

FOOD
Snacks such as sushi are available in the lobby; there's also tea and lemon and cucumber-scented water.

SPA FACILITIES
2 public baths (1 for women only) plus 6 private baths, some with saunas.

SIGNATURE TREATMENT
Japanese baths.

BOOK TO PACK
"The Wind-Up Bird Chronicle" by Haruki Murakami.

LAGE
Nordöstlich von Santa Fe gelegen, 30 km vom Flughafen der Stadt entfernt, von wo es täglich Verbindungen nach Dallas gibt.

ZIMMER
13 »Houses of the Moon«, die fast alle das Wort »Mond« im Namen tragen.

KÜCHE
In der Lobby sind Snacks wie Sushi erhältlich; zudem Tee und Wasser mit Zitronen- und Gurkenaroma.

SPAAUSSTATTUNG
2 öffentliche Bäder (1 davon für Damen), 6 private Bäder, z.T. mit Sauna.

SIGNATURE TREATMENT
Japanische Bäder.

BUCHTIPP
»Mister Aufziehvogel« von Haruki Murakami.

SITUATION
Au nord-est de Santa Fe, à 30 km de l'aéroport de la ville avec liaisons quotidiennes à partir ou à destination de Dallas.

CHAMBRES
13 « Houses of the Moon », la lune est presque partout présente dans leur nom.

RESTAURATION
Des en-cas, par exemple des sushis, sont proposés dans le hall de l'hôtel ainsi que du thé et de l'eau aromatisée au citron et au concombre.

SERVICES DU SPA
2 bains publics (1 réservé aux dames), 6 bains privés, en partie avec sauna.

SOIN SIGNATURE
Bains japonais.

LIVRE À EMPORTER
« Chroniques de l'oiseau à ressort » de Haruki Murakami.

滝

Please report offensive
behavior immediately
to front desk
Speak softly
Sauna
CALL
FRONT
DESK

Mii Amo Destination Spa

at the Enchantment Resort

Mii amo, meaning "one's path", takes its guests on a spiritual and sensual journey into the world of Arizona's Native Americans. The spa was built in 2001 in a reputedly sacred canyon, with architecture inspired by Anasazi dwellings. Its treatments are based on Native American healing techniques and use natural products such as orange, cedar and bay laurel oils.

Mii amo bedeutet »Weg« oder »Passage« und ein Urlaub dort ist eine so sinnliche wie spirituelle Reise ins Reich der Indianer von Arizona. Das Spa entstand 2001 in einem Canyon, der als heiliger Ort gilt, und ließ sich von der Architektur der Anasazi inspirieren. Alle Anwendungen basieren auf indianischen Heiltechniken sowie natürlichen Pflegeprodukten wie Ölen aus Orange, Zeder und Lorbeer.

Mii Amo signifie « chemin » ou « passage » et un séjour ici est un voyage aussi sensuel que spirituel au pays des Indiens d'Arizona. Le spa a ouvert ses portes en 2001 dans un canyon considéré comme un lieu sacré, et son architecture est inspirée de celle des Anasazi. Tous les soins sont basés sur des techniques amérindiennes ainsi que sur des produits naturels, telle l'huile essentielle d'orange, de cèdre ou de laurier.

Mii Amo Destination Spa
at the Enchantment Resort
525 Boynton Canyon Road
Sedona, AZ 86336
USA
Tel. +1 928 203 8500
info@miiamo.com
www.miiamo.com

LOCATION
At the Enchantment Resort near Sedona, 4,500 ft above sea level; 190 miles north of Phoenix airport.

ROOMS
14 spa rooms and 2 spa suites.

FOOD
The "Mii Amo Café" has a juice bar and serves organic spa dishes.

SPA FACILITIES
24,000 sq ft with 20 indoor and 5 outdoor treatment rooms, Crystal Grotto (central meditation area), indoor and outdoor pool, whirlpool and fitness studio.

SIGNATURE TREATMENT
"Journey Spa Treatment" with individual spiritual guidance plus treatment session.

BOOK TO PACK
"The Lone Ranger and Tonto Fistfight in Heaven" by Sherman Alexie.

LAGE
Auf dem Gelände des Enchantment Resorts bei Sedona auf 1.400 m Höhe gelegen, 177 km nördlich des Flughafens Phoenix.

ZIMMER
14 Spa-Zimmer und 2 Spa-Suiten.

KÜCHE
Das »Mii Amo Café« mit Saftbar serviert organische Spa-Gerichte.

SPAAUSSTATTUNG
2.230 qm mit 20 Innen- und 5 Außenbehandlungsräumen, Crystal Grotto (zentraler Meditationsbereich), Innen- und Außenpool, Whirlpool, Fitnessstudio.

SIGNATURE TREATMENT
»Journey Spa Treatment« mit einer individuellen spirituellen Beratung und anschließender Behandlung.

BUCHTIPP
»Regenmacher« von Sherman Alexie.

SITUATION
Dans la propriété de l'Enchantment Resorts près de Sedona, à 1400 m d'altitude ; à 177 km au nord de l'aéroport de Phoenix.

CHAMBRES
14 chambres avec spa et 2 suites avec spa.

RESTAURATION
Le « Mii Amo Café », qui possède un bar à jus de fruits, propose des plats spa bio.

SERVICES DU SPA
2230 mètres carrés avec 20 cabines de soins intérieures et 5 extérieures, Crystal Grotto (la zone de méditation), piscine intérieure et extérieure, bain à remous, studio de remise en forme.

SOIN SIGNATURE
« Journey Spa Treatment » avec encadrement spirituel personnalisé avant le traitement.

LIVRE À EMPORTER
« Indian Blues » de Sherman Alexie.

Aman Spa

at Amangiri

The spa at Amangiri, built by architects Marwan Al-Sayed, Wendell Burnette and Rick Joy in the southern Utah desert, is a homage to ancient Navajo healing rituals. Its holistic treatments include the use of cedar smoke, clay and hot stones and are aimed at enhancing "hozho", a person's beauty, harmony, balance and health.

Das Spa des Amangiri, das die Architekten Marwan Al-Sayed, Wendell Burnette und Rick Joy in der Wüste Süd-Utahs erbaut haben, ist eine Hommage an alte Heilrituale der Navajo. Bei den holistischen Anwendungen werden etwa Zedernrauch, Bleicherde oder heiße Steine verwendet. Sie sollen das »Hozho« stärken, das die Schönheit, Harmonie, Balance sowie Gesundheit des Menschen bezeichnet.

Construit dans le désert de l'Utah par les architectes Marwan Al-Sayed, Wendell Burnette et Rick Joy, le spa de l'Amangiri est un hommage aux anciens rituels curatifs Navajo. Les soins holistiques prévoient entre autres l'utilisation de fumée de cèdre, d'argile ou de pierres chaudes censées fortifier le « Hozho » qui caractérise la beauté, l'harmonie, l'équilibre et la santé de l'être humain.

Aman Spa
at Amangiri
1 Kayenta Road
Canyon Point, UT 84741-285
USA
Tel. +1 435 675 3999
Fax +1 435 675 8999
amangiri@amanresorts.com
www.amangiri.com

LOCATION
In the Four Corners region, where Utah, Colorado, New Mexico and Arizona meet; 20 min north of Page airport.

ROOMS
34 suites.

FOOD
The "Dining Room" serves local cuisine.

SPA FACILITIES
25,000 sq ft with 5 treatment rooms, each with steam shower, outdoor pool, water pavilion with steam bath, sauna and plunge pool; floatation pavilion with hot plunge pool, yoga pavilion, fitness centre and beauty salon.

SIGNATURE TREATMENTS
The journey "White East Silver Dawn", which includes a body scrub, a full-body massage and an aroma facial compress and massage.

BOOK TO PACK
"The Border Trilogy" by Cormac McCarthy.

LAGE
Im Gebiet der Four Corners gelegen, wo Utah, Colorado, New Mexico und Arizona zusammentreffen; 20 min nördlich des Flughafens Page.

ZIMMER
34 Suiten.

KÜCHE
Der »Dining Room« serviert lokale Menüs.

SPAAUSSTATTUNG
2.322 qm mit 5 Behandlungsräumen jeweils mit Dampfdusche, Außenpool, Wasserpavillon mit Dampfbad, Sauna und Tauchbecken, Floatation-Pavillon mit heißem Tauchbecken, Yogapavillon, Fitnesscenter, Beautysalon.

SIGNATURE TREATMENTS
Die Zeitreise »White East Silver Dawn«: mit Körperpeeling, Ganzkörpermassage und Aroma-Gesichtskompresse und -massage.

BUCHTIPP
»Die Border-Trilogie« von Cormac McCarthy.

SITUATION
Dans la région des Four Corners, là où se rencontrent l'Utah, le Colorado, le Nouveau-Mexique et l'Arizona ; à 20 min au nord de l'aéroport de Page.

CHAMBRES
34 suites.

RESTAURATION
Le « Dining Room » sert une cuisine locale.

SERVICES DU SPA
2322 mètres carrés 5 cabines ; de soins une douche à vapeur, piscine extérieure, pavillon aquatique avec bain de vapeur, sauna et bassin d'eau froide, pavillon de flottaison avec bassin d'eau chaude, salle de yoga, centre de remise en forme, salon de beauté.

SOINS SIGNATURE
Le voyage dans le temps « White East Silver Dawn » avec gom-mage corporel, massage complet, compresse et massage aromatiques du visage.

LIVRE À EMPORTER
« La trilogie des confins » de Cormac McCarthy.

Osmosis Day Spa Sanctuary

The Osmosis is the only day spa in the United States that specialises in Japanese cedar enzyme baths. Opened in 1985, it offers guests the chance to enjoy enchanting bamboo and bonsai gardens while relaxing in a wooden tub of ground cedar, rice bran and plant enzymes. This warm mixture detoxifies the body and stimulates the metabolism.

Das Osmosis hat sich als einziges Day Spa der USA auf das japanische Zedern-Enzymbad spezialisiert. Seit 1985 entspannt man hier inmitten zauberhafter Bambus- und Bonsaigärten in Holzwannen, die mit einer warmen Mischung aus geriebenem Zedernholz, Reiskleie und Pflanzenenzymen gefüllt sind. So wird der Stoffwechsel angeregt und der Körper entschlackt.

L'Osmosis est le seul spa de jour des États-Unis à proposer un bain de cèdre aux enzymes japonais. Depuis 1985, on se relaxe ici au milieu de jardins enchanteurs plantés de bambous et de bonsaïs, dans des baignoires en bois remplies d'un mélange tiède de bois de cèdre moulu, de son de riz et d'enzymes végétaux – le métabolisme est stimulé, l'organisme désintoxiqué.

Osmosis Day Spa Sanctuary
209 Bohemian Highway
Freestone, CA 95472
USA
Tel. +1 707 823 8231
Fax +1 707 874 3788
www.osmosis.com
Open daily from 9am to 8pm

LOCATION
In Sonoma County, 61 miles north of San Francisco.

ROOMS
The spa doesn't have rooms of its own but can recommend accommodation in the local area.

FOOD
Organic herbal tea with enzymes from 25 different plants is served before every bath.

SPA FACILITIES
5-acre site with 2 enzyme bath areas for up to 6 guests, 8 massage rooms, 3 rooms for facials, 2 rooms for body wraps and 4 outdoor pagodas.

SIGNATURE TREATMENT
The Japanese enzyme bath plus special massage featuring Thai or shiatsu methods or an aromatherapy facial with rosemary, camphor, lavender and thyme.

BOOK TO PACK
"The Pastures of Heaven" by John Steinbeck.

LAGE
In Sonoma County gelegen, 98 km nördlich von San Francisco.

ZIMMER
Das Spa bietet keine Zimmer, empfiehlt aber gerne nahe Unterkünfte.

KÜCHE
Vor jedem Bad wird organischer Kräutertee mit Enzymen aus 25 Pflanzen serviert.

SPAAUSSTATTUNG
2 ha großes Grundstück mit 2 Enzymbad-Bereichen für bis zu 6 Gäste, 8 Massageräumen, 3 Räumen für Facials, 2 Räumen für Körperwickel, 4 Außenpagoden.

SIGNATURE TREATMENT
Das japanische Enzymbad, ergänzt durch eine »Specialty Massage« mit Thai- oder Shiatsu-Elementen oder ein Aromatherapie-Facial mit Rosmarin, Kampfer, Lavendel und Thymian.

BUCHTIPP
»Das Tal des Himmels« von John Steinbeck.

SITUATION
À Sonoma County, à 98 km au nord de San Francisco.

CHAMBRES
Pas de chambres, le spa fournit volontiers des adresses d'hébergements proches.

RESTAURATION
Une infusion bio aux enzymes de 25 plantes est servie avant chaque bain.

SERVICES DU SPA
Propriété de 2 ha avec 2 espaces de bains aux enzymes pour jusqu'à 6 personnes, 8 salles de massage, 3 salles pour soins du visage, 2 salles pour enveloppements, 4 pavillons extérieurs.

SOIN SIGNATURE
Le bain aux enzymes japonais enrichi d'un « Specialty Massage » comportant des éléments du massage thaïlandais ou shiatsu, ou un soin du visage par l'aromathérapie avec du romarin, du camphre, de la lavande et du thym.

LIVRE À EMPORTER
« Les Pâturages du ciel » de John Steinbeck.

Verana Day Spa

at Verana

Following on from their successful Jungle Spa, which is for hotel Verana guests only, Veronique Lievre and Heinz Legler decided to add an idyllic day spa for up to 16 visitors per day. Opened in late 2008, it offers a relaxing body-temperature Watsu pool and treatments featuring extracts of papaya, avocado or coconut sourced from the nearby jungle.

Nach dem Erfolg des Jungle Spa – exklusiv für Gäste ihres Hotels Verana – haben Veronique Lievre und Heinz Legler Ende 2008 dieses idyllische Day Spa für Tagesgäste eröffnet. Maximal 16 Besucher pro Tag entspannen hier im Watsu-Pool mit körperwarmem Wasser sowie bei Pflegeritualen mit Extrakten aus Papayas, Avocados oder Kokosnüssen, die im nahen Dschungel wachsen.

Voyant le succès du Jungle Spa – proposé exclusivement aux hôtes de leur Hotel Verana –, Veronique Lievre et Heinz Legler ont ouvert fin 2008 ce Day Spa idyllique. 16 visiteurs par jour maximum se relaxent ici dans un bassin watsu rempli d'eau à température du corps ou savourent les rituels de soins à base d'extraits de papaye, d'avocat et de noix de coco, qui poussent dans la jungle toute proche.

Verana
Calle Zaragoza #499,
Colonia Centro
48304 Puerto Vallarta, Jalisco
Mexico
Tel. +52 322 222 08 78
www.verana.com
Open from early November
to early June

Verana Day Spa
dayspa@verana.com
www.dayspa.verana.com
Open daily from 9.30am to 5pm

LOCATION
Perched on the cliffs of Yelapa; accessible by boat in 30 min from Boca de Tomatlán, daily transfers at 9.30am and 5pm.

ROOMS
The nearby hotel Verana has 8 houses for 2–4 guests and the "V House" for up to 6 guests.

FOOD
The spa restaurant serves organic lunch options and smoothies.

SPA FACILITIES
2 treatment rooms, waiting room with Vichy shower, steam bath, Watsu pool and meditation pool.

SIGNATURE TREATMENT
The "Organic Signature Facial" using Ilike products.

BOOK TO PACK
"Frida" by Bárbara Mujica.

LAGE
Auf den Klippen von Yelapa gelegen; ab Boca de Tomatlán in 30 min per Boot erreichbar, täglicher Transfer um 9:30 und 17 Uhr.

ZIMMER
Das nahe Verana bietet 8 Häuser für jeweils 2–4 Gäste und das »V House« für bis zu 6 Gäste.

KÜCHE
Das Spa-Restaurant serviert organische Lunchmenüs und Smoothies.

SPAAUSSTATTUNG
2 Behandlungsräume, Warteraum mit Vichydusche, Dampfbad, Watsu-Pool, Meditations-Pool.

SIGNATURE TREATMENT
Das »Organic Signature«-Facial mit Produkten von Ilike.

BUCHTIPP
»Meine Schwester Frida« von Bárbara Mujica.

SITUATION
Sur les falaises de Yelapa ; accessible uniquement par bateau de Boca de Tomatlán en 30 min ; transferts quotidiens vers 9h30 et 17h.

CHAMBRES
Verana toute proche offre 8 maisons pour 2–4 personnes et la « V House » pour max. 6 personnes.

RESTAURATION
Le restaurant du spa propose des smoothies et des déjeuners préparés avec des produits bio.

SERVICES DU SPA
2 cabines de soins, salle d'attente avec douche Vichy, bain de vapeur, bassin watsu, bassin de méditation.

SOIN SIGNATURE
Les soins du visage « Organic Signature » avec des produits d'Ilike.

LIVRE À EMPORTER
« Loin, très loin de la maison de ma mère » de Bárbara Mujica.

El Silencio Lodge & Spa

This eco-lodge is the perfect place to experience the Costa Rican rainforest up close. Its wood, bamboo and glass buildings, designed by architect Ronald Zürcher, are seamlessly integrated into their surroundings, while the spa treatments feature local volcanic mud, coffee, vanilla or honey to the sound of bird song, rushing water and wind in the trees.

Wer den Regenwald von Costa Rica ganz unmittelbar erleben möchte, ist in dieser Öko-Lodge an der besten Adresse: Ronald Zürcher lässt die Architektur aus Holz, Bambus und Glas mit der Natur verschmelzen. Im Spa hört man überall das Rascheln der Bäume, plätscherndes Wasser sowie Vogelgesang. Pflegen lässt man sich mit lokalem Vulkanschlamm, Kaffee, Vanille oder Honig.

Si vous voulez voir de près la forêt pluviale du Costa Rica, cet écolodge est le top : Ronald Zürcher laisse son architecture de bois, de bambou et de verre fusionner avec l'environnement. Et dans le spa on entend aussi le bruissement des branches, le clapotis de l'eau et les chants d'oiseaux tout en se laissant soigner avec de la boue volcanique locale, du café, de la vanille et du miel.

El Silencio Lodge & Spa
Bajos del Toro
Alajuela
Costa Rica
Tel. +506 2 761 03 01
Fax +506 2 761 03 02
info@elsilenciolodge.com
www.elsilenciolodge.com

LOCATION
Between Juan Castro Blanco and Poás Volcano national parks, 60 min north of San José's Juan Santamaría International Airport.

ROOMS
16 cottage suites, all with outdoor whirlpools.

FOOD
Regional cuisine with a modern twist, made with fruit, vegetables and herbs from the lodge's own organic garden.

SPA FACILITIES
3,800 sq ft with 5 treatment rooms and yoga deck.

SIGNATURE TREATMENT
The "El Silencio Purifying Ritual", a Swedish massage with aromatic oils and organic herbs, combined with Thai stretching techniques.

BOOK TO PACK
"Calypso" by Tatiana Lobo.

LAGE
Zwischen dem Nationalpark Juan Castro Blanco und dem Nationalpark Poás Volcano gelegen, 60 min nördlich des Juan Santamaría International Airport von San José.

ZIMMER
16 Cottage-Suiten, alle mit Außen-Whirlpool.

KÜCHE
Obst, Gemüse und Kräuter für die regionalen Menüs mit modernem Touch, stammen aus dem eigenen Biogarten.

SPAAUSSTATTUNG
350 qm mit 5 Behandlungsräumen und Yogadeck.

SIGNATURE TREATMENT
Das »El Silencio Purifying Ritual«, eine schwedische Massage mit Aromaölen und organischen Kräutern; ergänzt durch Thai-Stretchingtechniken.

BUCHTIPP
»Hahnenbräute« von Tatiana Lobo.

SITUATION
Entre le parc national Juan Castro Blanco et le parc national Poás Volcano, à 60 min au nord du Juan Santamaría International Airport de San José.

CHAMBRES
16 suites-bungalows avec bain à remous extérieur.

RESTAURATION
Les fruits, légumes et fines herbes qui entrent dans la composition de la cuisine régionale revisitée sont de culture biologique et proviennent du jardin de l'hôtel.

SERVICES DU SPA
350 mètres carrés avec 5 cabines de soins et pavillon de yoga.

SOIN SIGNATURE
L'« El Silencio Purifying Ritual », un massage suédois aux huiles aromatiques et aux extraits de plantes bio complété par des techniques de stretching thaïlandaises.

LIVRE À EMPORTER
« Le Paradis assiégé » de Tatiana Lobo.

Le Spa Natura

at Hotel Santa Teresa

This Relais & Châteaux hotel, once a coffee-plantation mansion, has an elegant ethnic theme that combines tropical wood, banana plant and coconut fibres with furniture by Brazilian designers such as Sergio Rodrigues. The spa, too, pays homage to Brazil's culture and flora, with treatments using cocoa butter, Brazil nut butter and andiroba oil from the Amazon.

Aus dem einstigen Herrenhaus einer Kaffeeplantage wurde ein Relais-&-Châteaux-Hotel, das Tropenhölzer, Bananen- und Kokosfasern mit Mobiliar brasilianischer Designer wie Sergio Rodrigues zu einem eleganten Ethno-Stil verbindet. Auch das Spa ist eine Hommage an die Natur und Kultur Brasiliens: Hier pflegen Andirobaöl aus dem Amazonasgebiet, Kakao- und Paranussbutter.

L'ancienne maison de maître d'une plantation de café est devenue cet hôtel Relais & Châteaux où bois tropicaux, fibres de bananier et de palmier sont associés aux meubles de designers brésiliens comme Sergio Rodrigues, pour obtenir un style ethno-chic. Le spa rend hommage à la nature et à la culture du pays : les soins sont à base d'huile d'andiroba amazonienne, de noix du Brésil et de beurre de cacao.

Hotel Santa Teresa
Rua Almirante Alexandrino 660
Santa Teresa
Rio de Janeiro-RJ
20241-260
Brazil
Tel. +55 21 33 80 02 00
reservas@santateresahotel.com
www.santa-teresa-hotel.com

Le Spa Natura
Tel. +55 21 33 80 02 10
le-spa@santateresahotel.com

LOCATION
On a hill in the upmarket Santa Teresa district, 12 miles from Galeão International Airport.

ROOMS
28 rooms and 12 suites.

FOOD
The excellent "Térèze" restaurant combines fine French cuisine with Brazilian flavours.

SPA FACILITIES
1,500 sq ft with 5 treatment rooms, outdoor pool and sauna.

SIGNATURE TREATMENT
The three-dimensional anti-stress treatment, a combination of massotherapy, lymph drainage and energy therapy.

BOOK TO PACK
"Brazil" by John Updike.

LAGE
Auf einem Hügel im noblen Viertel Santa Teresa gelegen, 20 km von Galeão International Airport entfernt.

ZIMMER
28 Zimmer und 12 Suiten.

KÜCHE
Das ausgezeichnete Restaurant »Térèze« verbindet feine französische Küche und brasilianische Aromen.

SPAAUSSTATTUNG
140 qm mit 5 Behandlungsräumen, Außenpool, Sauna.

SIGNATURE TREATMENT
Die dreidimensionale Anti-Stress-Behandlung, eine Kombination aus Massotherapie, Lymphdrainage, energetischer Therapie.

BUCHTIPP
»Brasilien« von John Updike.

SITUATION
Sur une colline, dans le quartier résidentiel de Santa Teresa, à 20 km de Galeão International Airport.

CHAMBRES
28 chambres et 12 suites.

RESTAURATION
L'excellent restaurant « Térèze » marie le raffinement de la cuisine française aux arômes brésiliens.

SERVICES DU SPA
140 mètres carrés avec 5 cabines de soin, piscine extérieure, sauna.

SOINS SIGNATURE
Le traitement antistress tridimensionnel, une combinaison de massothérapie, de drainage lymphatique et de thérapie énergétique.

LIVRE À EMPORTER
« Brésil » de John Updike.

Glossary

Acupressure (also shiatsu) A massage technique employed in traditional Chinese medicine whereby the practitioner uses hands, elbows or knees to apply pressure, often forcefully and even painfully, to the body's acupressure points. The aim is to counter disruptions in the flow of life energy, "qi". The gentler Japanese version is called shiatsu. When performed as a body treatment, shiatsu is mostly administered with the patient lying on a floor mat and wearing light, comfortable clothing.

Acupuncture In this treatment method from traditional Chinese medicine, ultra-thin needles are used to target special acupoints linked to the organs via energy pathways (meridians). The most common application of acupuncture is for pain relief, but it is also used, for example, to treat sleep disorders.

Algae bath (also algae wrap) Treatments using marine algae, which are rich in minerals, trace elements and vitamins, can help to cleanse and tone the skin. Algae baths and wraps are used in thalassotherapy.

Algae wrap → Algae bath

Aromatherapy A branch of herbal medicine in which essential oils are used to stimulate body and mind – with baths or massages, for example. The underlying assumption is that aroma can enhance one's well-being through the brain's olfactory centre and limbic system. In addition, essential oils can have a positive effect on the body when absorbed via a massage.

Ayurveda Sanskrit for "science of life", Ayurveda derives from India and is one of the world's most ancient healing systems – it is estimated to be around 5,000 years old. Rather than simply looking at the symptoms of an illness, it also considers the causes and aims to restore the balance between an individual's three elemental forces, or "doshas": "vata" (movement, breathing and nervous system), "pitta" (body temperature, metabolism and digestion) and "kapha" (bodily fluids and immune system). Ayurveda sees mind, body and soul as one, and thus encompasses massages, yoga and meditation as well as its own dietary philosophy.

Caldarium Originally one of the rooms in a Roman bathhouse, this steam bath has a temperature of 40–50 degrees Fahrenheit, for a gentler effect on the circulation, and a humidity of over 90 per cent. Aromatic or herbal essences are often added to the steam to benefit the respiratory system.

Chromotherapy → Colour therapy

Cleopatra bath Named after the Egyptian queen Cleopatra, who regularly bathed in mare's and donkey's milk. Nowadays, the body is usually wrapped in towels or sheeting soaked in milk and essential oils, or immersed in bath-water enriched with milk and oils. It's a treatment that moisturises and softens the skin.

Colour therapy (also chromotherapy) Colours can have a positive effect on mental phenomena such as mood swings as well as on ailments such as skin disorders. Chromotherapy involves training special lamps on the body. The beams of light penetrate the skin to different degrees, depending on their wavelength, and have different effects according to their colour. Red, in chromotherapy, is seen as energising, green as harmonising, blue as calming and yellow as cheering.

Compress Compresses are a traditional means of treating wounds – gauze compresses can staunch the flow of blood, cold compresses can reduce swelling and hot compresses can ease muscle tension. In spas, the basic compress tends to be used as part of a more elaborate treatment, such as a massage therapy featuring herb-filled compresses.

Crystal therapy → Gemstone therapy

Deep-tissue massage This type of massage focuses primarily on the deeper layers of muscle tissue. The techniques used are firm strokes along the muscle, concentration on pressure points and friction across the grain of the muscle.

Detox therapy → Detox treatment

Detox treatment (also detox therapy) Detox is short for "detoxification" and denotes the removal of toxins from the body. Detox treatments include drinking medicinal waters, dietary regimes, saunas and massages as well as movement therapies such as yoga.

Facial Generic term for cosmetic treatments applied to the face. A facial can include cleansing with a scrub or with steam, massages, masks and make-up.

Fango A relaxing treatment originally from Italy, in which mineral-rich volcanic mud with a temperature of 113–122 degrees Fahrenheit is applied to the skin. Fango packs stimulate the metabolism and circulation and are recommended for back pain and rheumatism as well as skin conditions such as dermatitis.

Finnish sauna Usually a spruce or fir-panelled sauna with a temperature of 176–212 degrees Fahrenheit, in which water is regularly poured over stones heated via logs. In traditional Finnish saunas, it's the custom for guests to massage their skin using a bunch of beech twigs, a "vihta" or "vasta", and to cool off afterwards in the fresh air and in ice-cold water.

Flotation pool (also flotation tank) A pool or tank – often in the shape of a mussel and with a closable lid – containing body-temperature water with a high salt content, in which the body is able to float effortlessly. Often used in conjunction with light therapy in wellness areas, flotation pools and tanks have a deeply relaxing, meditative effect.

Flotation tank → Flotation pool

F. X. Mayr therapy A fasting method named after the Austrian doctor Franz Xaver Mayr (1875–1965). It focuses on detoxifying the intestines, which he considered to be the key organ in a person's health. The therapy involves cleansing the intestines with Epsom salts, then adhering to a diet that consists primarily of milk (which can occasionally be replaced by yoghurt, soya or almond milk) and stale rolls.

Gemstone therapy (also crystal therapy, lithotherapy) This alternative therapy is based on the assumption that the colours and vibrations of gemstones have a beneficial effect on health. Stones such as rose quartz, lapis lazuli and amethyst are worn on the body or placed on reflexology zones or acupoints in order to release energy.

Hammam (also Turkish bath, Oriental bath) Oriental baths mostly have marble-clad walls and traditionally consist of several rooms kept at various temperatures: a domed room with a warm navel stone in the centre and washbasins, a steam bath and a quiet room at the side. Hammams traditionally have separate areas for men and women. Dressed in a "pestemal" (waist cloth), guests wash themselves at the basins in warm and cold water, then lie down on the navel stone to relax the muscles and warm up. After the steam bath, they then exfoliate using a "kese" (exfoliation glove) or recline on marble beds while the "tellak" (attendant) provides a body scrub, foam wash and massage. The ritual is followed by a cooling-off period in a quiet room, where freshly brewed tea is served.

Hay bath A treatment in which the body is immersed in a bath of moist, warm hay with a temperature of 104–108 degrees Fahrenheit. The body begins to sweat and detoxify, while the essential oils have a beneficial effect on the respiratory passages. Hay baths can also help to ease conditions such as rheumatism and sciatica.

Herbal bath A bath in which fresh or dried herbs or herbal oils are added to water with a temperature of 97–100 degrees Fahrenheit. The bath can be either relaxing, stimulating or refreshing, depending on the choice of herbs.

Hot-stone massage In this massage treatment traditionally practised in Asia, the Americas and the Pacific region, gentle pressure is applied to the body with stones – often polished ovals of black lava or basalt – that have been heated to 122–140 degrees Fahrenheit. The combination of warmth and motion helps to relax the muscles.

Hydromassage (also underwater massage) This treatment is performed either in a thermal pool equipped with massage jets or in a special bath with a perforated floor, in which air is pumped through the holes. Hydromassages often feature as part of thalassotherapy.

Ice fountain → Ice shower

Ice grotto → Ice shower

Ice shower (also ice fountain, ice grotto) Cooling off after a sauna with the help of flakes or lumps of ice or a cold shower or pool stimulates the circulation, firms the skin and strengthens the immune system.

Jacuzzi → Whirlpool

Japanese enzyme bath For this warming bath, the body is immersed in a tub filled with ground wood, rice bran and plant enzymes. No artificial heat is applied to the mixture, which heats up naturally via fermentation. The enzyme bath stimulates the circulation and has a detoxifying effect.

Kneipp pool The most widely known of the Kneipp treatments, a therapy system developed by Bavarian priest Sebastian Kneipp (1821–1897). These foot pools are filled with knee-high cold and hot water. The Kneipp water-stepping technique involves wading stork-like through the various pools, with the change in temperature between the pools stimulating the circulation.

Laconium This mild steam bath takes its name from the region of Laconia in southern Greece. It is slowly heated to 122–140 degrees Fahrenheit, gently stimulating the circulation while cleansing and detoxifying the body.

Lifestyle shower A shower with a variety of individually adjustable jets, both overhead and at the sides; often used in conjunction with aroma or colours.

Lithotherapy → Gemstone therapy

Lomi lomi massage Part of the natural healing traditions of Hawaii, lomi is a relaxing massage ritual featuring Hawaiian music and fragrances, in which the entire body is covered in kukui nut oil and massaged using broad sweeps of the underarm, with the practitioner alternating between fast and slow strokes and gentle and firm pressure. Often also offered as a four-handed massage performed by two practitioners.

Lymph drainage This therapy activates the body's lymphatic system, unblocking and draining areas of swelling. Performed by specially trained masseurs or physiotherapists, it involves the use of pressure or manual manipulation to shift cell fluid from the tissue and into the lymph vessels. Lymph drainage is often used after operations to relieve pain.

Manicure Derived from the Latin word "manus", meaning hand, the term manicure is used to describe a comprehensive treatment in which the hands are bathed, the nails cut and filed, and the cuticles pushed back, with the option of also having the nails varnished. Manicures are often combined with a scrub, a skin-care mask and a hand-and-arm massage.

Massage Generic term for skin, tissue or muscle treatments involving stretching, twisting, pulling or the application of pressure.

Medical wellness Generic term for combinations of Western medicine and wellness practices aimed at enhancing the effectiveness of treatments. Medical wellness focuses not only on medically based wellness treatments, but also on preventative measures and on generally promoting a healthy lifestyle.

Meditation Generic term for a spiritual discipline that forms an integral part of many religions and cultures. The purpose of meditation is to attain a state of mental calm and collectedness; some forms of meditation also aim to achieve a higher state of consciousness.

Onsen A Japanese public bathhouse fed by a natural hot spring – traditionally a volcanic spring. Thanks to its high mineral content, the water has a therapeutic effect on the skin and is particularly relaxing. Traditionally, men and women bathe together; many onsens now offer separate baths for each sex, however.

Oriental bath → Hammam

Pedicure Derived from the Latin word "pes" for foot, the term pedicure denotes a comprehensive treatment in which the feet are bathed, calloused skin removed, the nails cut and filed, and the cuticles pushed back, with the option of also having the nails varnished. Usually offered in combination with a foot massage.

Petal bath A treatment in which dried or fresh petals are added to a bath of body-temperature water (97–100 degrees Fahrenheit). The warm water and the scent of the petals have a relaxing effect, while the petals' natural oils nourish the skin. Rose and lavender petals are particularly widely used.

Pilates A gentle, holistic physical-fitness system developed by the German gymnast Joseph Hubert Pilates (1883–1967). The exercises focus primarily on the deep abdominal and pelvic floor muscles, with the aim of promoting a correct and healthy posture, a taut figure and natural movements.

Qigong A therapy from traditional Chinese medicine that aims to strengthen a person's life energy, "qi". Qigong takes a holistic approach and includes movement, breathing and meditation techniques that can also be used to support healing processes for ailments such as rheumatism and asthma.

Rain shower (also tropical shower) A shower with an extra-large head that ensures the water falls more gently, exerting less pressure on the body.

Rasul In this detoxifying Oriental skin-care ritual, the body is covered in mud consisting of healing clay, chalk or algae, which is then heated in a herbal steam bath and massaged into the skin. After showering off, the rasul is often followed with a gentle, relaxing oil massage.

Reflexology massage An alternative therapy in which the soles of the feet or the palms of the hands are massaged – the reflexology zones located there are associated with particular organs and muscle groups within the body. By massaging these areas, the practitioner aims to stimulate or relieve pain in the associated muscle group or organ, thereby enhancing physical and mental well-being.

Reiki The meaning of Reiki is "life energy". It is an alternative therapy developed in the early 20th century by the Japanese doctor Mikao Usui (1865–1926). The Reiki therapist acts as a kind of medium, placing his or her palms on the patient in order to channel universal energy into the body and thereby enhance its ability to heal itself.

Salt-water bath (also salt-water grotto) A bath to which sea salt or table salt has been added and which therefore has very high mineral levels, with a salt content of up to 6 per cent. Salt-water baths are used as a complementary treatment for combatting skin conditions such as dermatitis, allergies, digestive problems and metabolic or sleep disorders.

Salt-water grotto → Salt-water bath

Sanarium → Saunarium

Sauna Generic term for a usually wood-panelled sweat room with a temperature of between 122 and 266 degrees Fahrenheit. Cleanses and detoxifies the body and strengthens the immune system. Traditionally, a sweat in the sauna is followed by a cooling-off period and a rest phase.

Saunarium (also sanarium, soft sauna) A mild type of sauna that stimulates the circulation more gently, with temperatures of around 50 degrees Fahrenheit and a humidity of 40–50 per cent. Often, saunaria use the slow evaporation of essential oils rather than the traditional pouring of water over hot sauna stones. Can be combined with sound and light therapies.

Scrub Cosmetic or dermatological exfoliation using natural products such as salt grains or ground coffee beans, chemical substances such as acids or laser devices. Gentle scrubs exfoliate only the outermost layer of skin; more intensive scrubs can also have an effect on the layers below.

Shiatsu → Acupressure

Soft sauna → Saunarium

Spa suite → Treatment room

Steam bath Generic term for saunas kept at lower temperatures (40–50 degrees Fahrenheit) and higher humidity levels (80–100 per cent). Examples include Roman caldaria, Turkish hammams, Russian banyas and Mexican temazcals.

Swedish massage At a time when there had long been a lack of interest in massage in Europe, the Swede Pehr Henrik Ling (1776–1839) developed a form of massage in which the five classic massage techniques of gliding, kneading, friction, tapping and vibration are performed in a particular order. This massage, also known as classic massage, can be performed on the back or the whole body and aims primarily to loosen the muscles.

Tai chi Also known as Chinese shadow boxing, Tai chi is a type of internal martial art that comprises flowing, almost slow-motion movements, breathing exercises and meditation. Closely connected to the concept of yin and yang, and the need for equilibrium between the two, tai chi aims to have a holistic effect on a person's mind and body, to relax their muscles, enhance their posture and improve their perception of their own body.

TCM → Traditional Chinese medecine

Tepidarium Originally a room in a Roman bathhouse, tepidaria are heated to 100–104 degrees Fahrenheit, i.e. just above body temperature. They gently stimulate the immune system and can help to heal minor infections.

Thai massage In Thailand itself, this massage is known as "nuad phaen boran", which means "ancient healing touch". Its practitioners manipulate ten selected energy lines in the body via gentle stretching and the rhythmic application of pressure by the thumb and palm of the hand, as well as the knees, elbows and feet. Many of the stretches and positions in Thai massage are similar to those in yoga; as a result, it is also known as passive yoga. The aim of Thai massage, for which light, comfortable clothing is worn, is to remove the energy blockages that cause illness.

Thalassotherapy Taking its name from the Greek word "thalassa" for sea, thalassotherapy comprises treatments featuring sea water, sea air, algae, silt, sand and sun. A genuine thalassotherapy spa is thus always by the sea. The English physician Richard Russell (1687–1759), who in 1750 described the healing powers of sea water on infectious illnesses in his PhD dissertation, is considered to be the father of thalassotherapy. Today, thalassotherapy is used as a complementary treatment for respiratory, skin and joint ailments, as well as for general relaxation.

Traditional Chinese medicine (also TCM) A millennia-old healing system from China developed against the background of Taoist teachings. It involves special medicinal therapies using mainly plant ingredients, its own dietary science, acupuncture, tuina massage and qigong movement therapy. The core principle of traditional Chinese medicine is life energy "qi" and the importance of keeping it in balance.

Treatment room (also spa suite) This private area is where most of a spa's treatments take place. Simpler treatment rooms are equipped with a massage bed and/or treatment chair. Those at more upmarket spas have extras such as a separate shower, a bath/whirlpool and a steam bath or sauna. The luxury version of a treatment room is the spa suite, which is available to the guest for a given period, rather than merely for the duration of their treatments. All come as either single or double rooms, while there are also luxury versions for a family or group.

Tropical shower → Rain shower

Tuina massage In traditional Chinese medicine, tuina is a massage during which the practitioner aims to stimulate the body's acupoints and energy lines (meridians) by gripping or pressing. It has a regulating and harmonising effect and is used to relieve pain as well as to counter sleep and digestive disorders.

Turkish bath → Hammam

Underwater massage → Hydromassage

Vichy shower This horizontal shower originates from the French spa town of Vichy. It is fixed above a wet table – a waterproof bed with special drainage facilities – and has several horizontally laid out jets that spray the body with water, sometimes alternating between hot and cold water. Vichy showers are used in thalassotherapy.

Vinotherapy A therapy based on the use of vine and grape extracts, in particular the seeds of the grape, whose polyphenols protect the skin against free radicals and hence offer anti-ageing benefits. Vinotherapy treatments stimulate the metabolism and promote the formation of new skin cells.

Vitality pool A particularly luxurious whirlpool with bubble jets and massage jets – and often featuring special areas (seats/beds) for leg, back or neck massages.

Watsu pool Watsu is a contraction of the words "water" and "shiatsu". This complementary hydrotherapy treatment relaxes the entire body with gentle twisting and stretching in body-temperature water.

Whey bath A bath in which whey powder is added to 35–40 degree Fahrenheit water. Rich in minerals, trace elements, vitamins and proteins, whey moisturises the skin, aids in healing eczema and dermititis and, with its lactic acid, helps the skin's acid mantle to regenerate.

Whirlpool (also jacuzzi) In these indoor or outdoor pools, water jets of different intensities can be used to massage the body, the relaxing effect of which is enhanced by the warm water.

Yoga Sanskrit for "union" or "conjunction", Yoga is an Indian philosophy combining physical and mental disciplines with the aim of achieving harmony in body, mind and soul, as well as inner calm and composure. There are various branches of yoga – outside India, the best-known is hatha yoga, which includes physical exercises (asanas), breathing control and meditation.

Glossar

Akupressur (auch Shiatsu) Eine in der traditionellen chinesischen Medizin angewandte Massage, bei der der Therapeut mit Händen, Ellbogen oder Knien zum Teil sehr kräftigen und manchmal sogar schmerzhaften Druck auf die Akupressurpunkte des Körpers ausübt. Dadurch sollen Störungen im Fluss der Lebensenergie (Qi) aufgehoben werden. Die japanische und sanftere Variante ist Shiatsu. Shiatsu als Ganzkörperbehandlung wird in leichter und bequemer Kleidung und meistens auf einer Bodenmatte durchgeführt.

Akupunktur Bei dieser Behandlungsmethode aus der traditionellen chinesischen Medizin werden spezielle Stellen des Körpers, die über Energiebahnen (Meridiane) mit den Organen verbunden sind, mit hauchdünnen Nadeln punktiert. Akupunktur wird vor allem zur Schmerztherapie eingesetzt, aber z.B. auch zur Behandlung von Schlafstörungen.

Algenbad (auch Algenwickel) Behandlung mit Meeresalgen, die reich an Mineralstoffen, Spurenelementen und Vitaminen sind, wirkt entschlackend und haustraffend. Algenbäder und -wickel sind Bestandteil der Thalassotherapie.

Algenwickel → Algenbad

Aromatherapie Die Aromatherapie ist Teil der Pflanzenheilkunde und stimuliert mit ätherischen Ölen Psyche und Körper, z.B. bei einem Bad oder einer Massage. Dabei geht man davon aus, dass die Düfte das Wohlbefinden des Menschen über das Riechzentrum und limbische System im Gehirn beeinflussen. Darüber hinaus entfalten ätherische Öle, nachdem sie bei einer Massage über die Haut aufgenommen wurden, ihre Wirkung im Körper.

Ayurveda Das indische Ayurveda (Sanskrit für »Wissen vom Leben«) ist eine der ältesten Gesundheitslehren der Welt. Man schätzt, dass sie vor etwa 5.000 Jahren entstanden ist. Sie betrachtet nicht nur die Symptome einer Krankheit, sondern forscht auch nach den Ursachen und zielt darauf, die Lebensenergie jedes Menschen, die drei »Doshas« »Vata« (Bewegung, Atmung und Nerventätigkeit), »Pitta« (Wärmehaushalt, Stoffwechsel und Verdauung) und »Kapha« (Flüssigkeitshaushalt und Immunsystem), ins Gleichgewicht zu bringen. Ayurveda betrachtet Körper, Geist und Seele als Einheit und umfasst daher Massagen, Yoga und Meditation sowie eine eigene Ernährungslehre.

Behandlungsraum (auch Spa-Suite) In diesem privaten Bereich finden die meisten individuellen Anwendungen statt. Einfache Behandlungsräume sind mit einer Massageliege und/oder einem Behandlungsstuhl ausgestattet. Räume gehobener Kategorie verfügen über Extras wie eine eigene Dusche, eine Badewanne oder einen Whirlpool, ein Dampfbad oder eine Sauna. Die Luxusvariante des Behandlungsraums ist die Spa-Suite, die dem Gast auch über die Behandlungen hinaus für einen bestimmten Zeitraum zur Verfügung steht. Alle Varianten der Behandlungsräume gibt es für Einzelpersonen und Paare, die Spa-Suite auch für Familien bzw. kleine Gruppen.

Biosauna → Softsauna

Blütenbad Bei diesem Vollbad wird das 36–38 Grad Celsius warme Wasser mit getrockneten oder frischen Blüten angereichert. Wärme und Duft entspannen, zudem pflegen die Blütenöle die Haut. Besonders häufig werden Rosen- und Lavendelblüten verwendet.

Caldarium Ursprünglich war dieses milde und kreislaufschonende Dampfbad mit einer Temperatur von 40–50 Grad Celsius und einer Luftfeuchtigkeit von über 90 Prozent Teil der römischen Thermen. Die Luft im Caldarium wird häufig mit Duft- und Kräuteressenzen angereichert, die wohltuend auf die Atemwege wirken.

Dampfbad Überbegriff für eine Saunavariante mit niedrigerer Temperatur (40–50 Grad Celsius) und höherer Luftfeuchtigkeit (80–100 Prozent). Zu den Dampfbädern zählen z.B. das römische Caldarium, der türkische Hamam, die russische Banja und das mexikanische Temazcal.

Deep-Tissue-Massage Diese Massage zielt hauptsächlich auf eine Wirkung in den tiefen Schichten der Muskulatur. Sie verwendet als Techniken feste Streichungen entlang der Muskelstränge, kräftige Druckpunktarbeit sowie Friktionen (Reibungen) quer zu den Muskelfasern.

Detox-Behandlung (auch Detox-Kur) Detox ist die Abkürzung für »Detoxification« und bezeichnet das Entschlacken und Entgiften des Körpers. Detox-Behandlungen können Trinkkuren und Diäten umfassen, Saunagänge und Massagen sowie Bewegungstherapien wie Yoga.

Detox-Kur → Detox-Behandlung

Edelsteintherapie (auch Kristall- oder Lithotherapie) Diese alternative Heiltherapie geht davon aus, dass Farben und Schwingungen von Edelsteinen gesundheitsfördernde Wirkung haben. Steine wie Rosenquarz, Lapislazuli oder Amethyst werden am Körper getragen oder auf Reflexzonen oder Akupunkturpunkte gelegt, um Energien freizusetzen.

Eisbrunnen → Eisdusche

Eisdusche (auch Eisgrotte, Eisbrunnen) Die Abkühlung unter der kalten Dusche, im kalten Becken oder mit Eisflocken bzw. Eisstückchen nach dem Saunagang oder dem Besuch eines Dampfbades regt den Kreislauf an, strafft die Haut und stärkt das Immunsystem.

Eisgrotte → Eisdusche

Erlebnisdusche (auch Lifestyledusche) Eine Dusche mit unterschiedlichen Düsen an Decke und Wänden, die individuell eingestellt werden können, oft in Verbindung mit Düften und Farben.

Facial Überbegriff für eine kosmetische Gesichtsbehandlung. Ein Facial kann z.B. eine Reinigung mit einem Peeling oder Wasserdampf beinhalten, Massagen, Masken sowie ein Make-up.

Fango Eine aus Italien stammende Anwendung mit mineralhaltigem Vulkanschlamm, der 45–50 Grad Celsius warm auf die Haut aufgetragen wird, Stoffwechsel sowie Durchblutung anregt und entspannt. Fangopackungen werden z.B. bei Rückenschmerzen und Rheuma empfohlen sowie bei Hauterkrankungen wie Neurodermitis.

Farblichttherapie → Farbtherapie

Farbtherapie (auch Farblichttherapie) Farben können sowohl auf die Psyche wirken, etwa bei Stimmungsschwankungen, als auch auf den Körper, z.B. bei Hauterkrankungen. Bei der Farbtherapie wird der Körper mit Speziallampen bestrahlt. Je nach ihrer Wellenlänge dringen die Farben unterschiedlich tief in die Haut ein und haben unterschiedliche Wirkungen: Rot gilt in der Farbtherapie als vitalisierend, Grün als ausgleichend, Blau als beruhigend, Gelb als ermunternd.

Finnische Sauna Eine meist mit Fichten- oder Tannenholz verkleidete Sauna mit 80–100 Grad Celsius heißer Luft. Über Holzscheite erhitzte Steine dienen als Wärmequelle und werden für regelmäßige Aufgüsse genutzt. In der traditionellen finnischen Sauna massieren die Gäste ihre Haut mit zusammengebundenen Birkenzweigen (Vihta bzw. Vasta) und kühlen sich nach dem Schwitzen an der frischen Luft und mit eiskaltem Wasser ab.

Floatation-Pool (auch Floatation-Tank) Ein mit hochprozentigem Salzwasser gefüllter Pool oder Tank – oft in Form einer Muschel, die geschlossen werden kann –, in dessen körperwarmen Wasser der Körper ohne eigene Anstrengung schwebt. Das Bad wird im Wellnessbereich häufig durch eine Lichttherapie ergänzt und wirkt meditativ-tiefenentspannend.

Floatation-Tank → Floatation-Pool

F. X.-Mayr-Kur Eine Heilfasten-Methode, benannt nach dem österreichischen Arzt Franz Xaver Mayr (1875–1965). Sie konzentriert sich auf eine Entgiftung und Entschlackung des Darms, der hier als zentrales Organ für die Gesundheit des Menschen angesehen wird. Er wird mithilfe von Bittersalz gereinigt, anschließend ernährt man sich in erster Linie von Milch (manchmal ersetzt durch Joghurt, Soja- oder Mandelmilch) und altbackenen Brötchen – daher ist die Methode auch als »Milch-Semmel-Kur« bekannt.

Hamam (auch türkisches Bad, orientalisches Bad) Das orientalische Bad ist meistens mit Marmor ausgekleidet und besteht ursprünglich aus mehreren Räumen mit unterschiedlichen Temperaturen: Kuppelraum mit warmem Nabelstein in der Mitte und seitlichen Waschbecken, Dampfbad und Ruheraum. Traditionell gibt es getrennte Bereiche für Männer und Frauen. Mit einem Pestemal

(Stofftuch) bekleidet wäscht man sich an den Becken mit warmem und kaltem Wasser und legt sich zur Muskelentspannung und zum Aufwärmen auf den warmen Nabelstein. Nach einem Aufenthalt im Dampfbad peelt man sich mit dem Kese (Peelinghandschuh) selbst oder lässt sich vom Tellak (Bademeister) auf Marmorliegen peelen, mit Seifenschaum waschen und massieren. Zum Abschluss des Rituals folgt eine Abkühlphase im Ruheraum, wo frisch gebrühter Tee serviert wird.

Heubad Beim Heubad liegt der Körper in feuchtem, 40–42 Grad Celsius warmem Heu, beginnt zu schwitzen und entschlackt. Die ätherischen Öle wirken wohltuend auf die Atemwege; zudem können im Heubad Beschwerden wie Rheuma und Ischias gelindert werden.

Hot-Stone-Massage Bei dieser Anwendung, deren Ursprünge sowohl im asiatischen als auch im pazifischen und amerikanischen Raum liegen, wird der Körper mit 50–60 Grad Celsius warmen Steinen mit leichtem bis mittlerem Druck massiert. Häufig werden oval geschliffene, schwarze Lava- und Basaltsteine verwendet. Durch die Tiefenwärme und Bewegung entspannen sich die Muskeln.

Hydromassage (auch Unterwassermassage) Diese Behandlung wird entweder in einem mit Massagedüsen ausgestatteten Thermalbecken ausgeführt oder in einer Spezialwanne mit perforierter Liegefläche, durch deren Löcher Luft gepumpt wird. Hydromassagen werden oft im Rahmen einer Thalassotherapie angeboten.

Jacuzzi → Whirlpool

Japanisches Enzymbad Bei diesem Bad liegt der Körper in einer Holzwanne, die mit Holzspänen, Reiskleie und Pflanzenenzymen gefüllt ist. Diese Mischung wird nicht künstlich erwärmt, sondern heizt sich durch Gärprozesse auf natürlichen Weg auf. Das Enzymbad regt den Kreislauf an und wirkt entschlackend.

Kleopatrabad Benannt nach der ägyptischen Königin Kleopatra, die regelmäßig in Stuten- und Eselsmilch badete. Heute wird der Körper entweder in mit Milch und ätherischen Ölen getränkte Tücher oder Folien gewickelt oder man liegt in mit Milch und Ölen angereichertem Badewasser. Die Haut wird so mit Feuchtigkeit versorgt und sehr zart.

Kneippbecken Die bekannteste Form der nach dem Pfarrer Sebastian Kneipp (1821–1897) benannten Kneippkur. Die Fußbecken sind mit kniehohem kaltem und warmem Wasser gefüllt. Beim Kneippgang durchwatet man im Storchenschritt die unterschiedlich temperierten Becken. Durch den Temperaturwechsel wird der Kreislauf angeregt und die Durchblutung gefördert.

Kompresse Ursprünglich dienen Kompressen der Wundversorgung – so können Mullkompressen Blut stillen, Kaltkompressen Schwellungen lindern und Warmkompressen Verspannungen lösen. Im Spa wird diese Basisform verfeinert, z.B. durch Kompressen, die mit Kräutern gefüllt sind, als Teil einer Massage.

Kräuterbad Ein Vollbad mit einer Temperatur von 36–38 Grad Celsius, dessen Wasser mit frischen oder getrockneten Kräutern oder Kräuterölen versetzt wird. Das Bad kann entspannen, anregen oder erfrischen, je nach Auswahl der Kräuter.

Kristalltherapie → Edelsteintherapie

Laconium Seinen Namen erhielt dieses sanfte Schwitzbad vom südgriechischen Volk der Lakonier. Es wird langsam auf 50–60 Grad Celsius erhitzt, sodass der Kreislauf schonend angeregt und der Körper entschlackt und entgiftet wird.

Lifestyledusche → Erlebnisdusche

Lithotherapie → Edelsteintherapie

Lomi-Lomi-Massage Ursprünglich aus der traditionellen Naturheilkunde Hawaiis stammend, ist die Lomi ein Massageritual, bei dem hawaiianische Musik und Düfte entspannen und der ganze Körper mit dem Öl der Kukui-Nuss abwechselnd schnell und langsam, leicht und kräftig und vor allem großflächig mit dem Unterarm massiert wird. Oft wird diese Anwendung auch als vierhändige Massage mit zwei Therapeuten angeboten.

Lymphdrainage Diese Therapieform aktiviert das Lymphsystem des Körpers – sie entstaut und entwässert geschwollene Körperpartien. Dabei transportieren speziell ausgebildete Masseure oder Physiotherapeuten Zellflüssigkeit aus dem Gewebe mittels Druck- und Verschiebetechniken in das Lymphgefäßsystem. Die Lymphdrainage wird häufig nach Operationen und zur Schmerzlinderung angewandt.

Maniküre Abgeleitet vom lateinischen Wort manus (Hand), bezeichnet die Maniküre eine umfassende Behandlung der Hände. Sie besteht aus einem Handbad, dem Kürzen und Feilen der Nägel, dem Zurückschieben der Nagelhaut und auf Wunsch dem Lackieren der Nägel. Häufig wird die Maniküre auch durch ein Peeling, eine Pflegemaske und eine Hand- und Armmassage ergänzt.

Massage Überbegriff für eine Körperbehandlung, die auf Haut, Gewebe oder Muskulatur mittels Dehnen, Drücken, Drehen oder Ziehen wirkt.

Medical Wellness Überbegriff für Synergien oder Kooperationen von westlicher Medizin und Wellness, die durch diese Kombination einen höheren Effekt erzielen. Medical Wellness konzentriert sich nicht nur auf medizinisch basierte Wellness-Anwendungen, sondern auch auf Präventionsmaßnahmen und eine generelle Motivation für einen gesunden Lebensstil.

Meditation Überbegriff für eine in vielen Religionen und Kulturen verankerte spirituelle Disziplin. Durch Meditation soll sich der Geist beruhigen und sammeln – manche Meditationen zielen auch auf eine Bewusstseinserweiterung.

Molkebad Ein 35–40 Grad Celsius warmes Bad, in dessen Wasser Molkepulver gegeben wird. Molke ist reich an Mineralstoffen, Spurenelementen, Vitaminen und Proteinen – sie regeneriert mithilfe von Milchsäure den Säureschutzmantel der Haut, spendet Feuchtigkeit und unterstützt Heilungsprozesse von Hautkrankheiten wie Ekzemen oder Neurodermitis.

Onsen Ein japanisches öffentliches Bad, das von einer heißen natürlichen Quelle – traditionell von einer Vulkanquelle – gespeist wird. Dank des hohen Mineralgehalts wirkt das Wasser wohltuend auf die Haut und entspannt. Traditionell baden Männer und Frauen gemeinsam, mittlerweile sind aber viele Bäder nach Geschlechtern getrennt.

Orientalisches Bad → Hamam

Pediküre Der Begriff stammt vom lateinischen Wort pes (Fuß). Die Pediküre ist eine Behandlung der Füße und umfasst ein Fußbad, das Entfernen von Hornhaut, das Kürzen und Feilen der Nägel und das Zurückschieben der Nagelhaut. Meist erhält man auch eine Fußmassage und kann sich die Nägel lackieren lassen.

Peeling Eine kosmetische oder dermatologische Schälkur der Haut mit Naturprodukten wie Salzkörnern oder zerstoßenen Kaffeebohnen, chemischen Produkten wie Säuren oder mit Lasergeräten. Leichte Peelings wirken nur auf die Hornhaut, intensivere Kuren auch auf darunterliegende Hautschichten.

Pilates Ein nach dem deutschen Sportler Joseph Hubert Pilates (1883–1967) benanntes ganzheitliches und sanftes Körpertraining, das sich besonders auf die Tiefenmuskulatur im Becken und in der Taille konzentriert. Ziele sind eine gesunde, korrekte Körperhaltung, eine gestraffte Silhouette und natürliche Bewegungsabläufe.

Qigong Ein Teil der traditionellen chinesischen Medizin, welche die Lebensenergie des Menschen (Qi) stärken soll. Qigong hat einen ganzheitlichen Ansatz und umfasst Bewegungs-, Atem- und Meditationstechniken, die auch zur Unterstützung von Heilungsprozessen eingesetzt werden können, z.B. bei Krankheiten wie Rheuma oder Asthma.

Rasul Bei diesem orientalischen, entschlackenden Pflegeritual wird der Körper mit Pflegeschlamm aus Heilerde, Kreide oder Algen eingerieben, der im Kräuter-Dampfbad erwärmt und in die Haut einmassiert wird. Nach dem Abduschen kann eine leichte, entspannende Ölmassage folgen.

Reflexzonenmassage Eine alternative Massage der Fußsohlen oder Handflächen. Die dort gelegenen Reflexzonen sind den einzelnen Organen und Muskelgruppen des Körpers zugeordnet, sodass die Massage dieser Stellen diese stimulieren und unterstützend bei Schmerztherapien wirken kann. Körperliches und geistiges Wohlbefinden wird gefördert.

Regendusche (auch Tropendusche) Eine Dusche mit extragroßem Duschkopf, sodass das Wasser mit nicht zu hohem Druck wie ein Regenschauer weich auf den Körper fällt.

Reiki Der Begriff Reiki bedeutet »universelle Lebensenergie« und bezeichnet eine alternative Behandlungsmethode, die Anfang des 20. Jahrhunderts vom Japaner Dr. Mikao Usui (1865–1926) entwickelt wurde. Der Therapeut fungiert dabei als eine Art Medium und lässt die universelle Energie mittels Handauflegen in den Körper des Patienten fließen, damit dessen Selbstheilungskräfte gestärkt werden.

Sanarium → Softsauna

Sauna Überbegriff für einen meist holzverkleideten Schwitzraum mit 50–130 Grad Celsius hoher Temperatur zur Entschlackung und Entgiftung des Körpers sowie zur Stärkung des Immunsystems. Ein klassischer Saunagang besteht aus einer Schwitz-, einer Abkühl- und einer Ruhephase.

Schwedische Massage Nachdem es in Europa lange kein Interesse an Massagen gab, entwickelte der Schwede Pehr Henrik Ling (1776–1839) eine Form von Massage, der in einer bestimmten Abfolge die fünf klassischen Techniken Streichen, Kneten, Reiben, Klopfen und Vibrieren zugrunde liegen. Diese Massage, bei uns als klassische Massage bekannt, kann als Rücken- oder Ganzkörpermassage durchgeführt werden und zielt vor allem auf die Lockerung der Muskulatur.

Shiatsu → Akupressur

Softsauna (auch Sanarium, Biosauna) Eine milde, kreislaufschonende Saunavariante mit Temperaturen um 50 Grad Celsius und einer Luftfeuchtigkeit von 40–50 Prozent. In vielen Softsaunen werden Aufgüsse ersetzt durch milde Vernebelung mit sanften ätherischen Öle; zudem können ergänzende Licht- und Klangtherapien eingesetzt werden.

Solebad (auch Solegrotte) Ein mit Meer- oder Kochsalz angereichertes und damit sehr mineralhaltiges Bad; der Salzgehalt beträgt bis zu sechs Prozent. Das Solebad wird als ergänzende Therapie z.B. bei Hauterkrankungen wie Neurodermitis, bei Allergien, Verdauungsbeschwerden, Stoffwechsel- und Schlafstörungen angewandt.

Solegrotte → Solebad

Spa-Suite → Behandlungsraum

Tai-Chi Eine Form der inneren Kampfkunst, auch chinesisches Schattenboxen genannt, die wie in Zeitlupe ausgeführte, fließende Bewegungen, Atem- und Meditationsübungen umfasst. Tai-Chi ist eng mit dem Prinzip von Yin & Yang verbunden, deren Gleichgewicht ganzheitlich auf Körper und Geist wirken, die Muskulatur entspannen und stärken sowie die Körperhaltung und -wahrnehmung verbessern soll.

TCM → Traditionelle chinesische Medizin

Tepidarium Ein aus der römischen Badekultur stammender Wärmeraum, dessen Temperatur mit 38–40 Grad Celsius knapp über der Körpertemperatur liegt. Hier wird das Immunsystem sanft angeregt, und die Heilung leichter Infektionen kann unterstützt werden.

Thai-Massage In Thailand selbst heißt diese Massage »Nuad Phaen Boran«, was uralte heilsame Berührung bedeutet. Bei dieser Anwendung werden zehn ausgewählte Energielinien des Körpers durch sanfte Dehnung und mit dem rhythmischen Druck von Handballen, Daumen, Knien, Ellbogen und Füßen bearbeitet. Viele Dehnungen und Positionen ähneln Yoga, sodass diese Behandlung auch als passives Yoga bezeichnet wird. Ziel ist es, Energieblockaden, die die Ursache von Krankheiten sind, zu lösen. Bei der Thai-Massage trägt man leichte, bequeme Kleidung.

Thalasso (auch Thalassotherapie) »Thalassa« ist das griechische Wort für Meer – Thalasso bezeichnet Behandlungen mit Meerwasser, Meeresluft, Algen, Schlick, Sand und Sonne. Ein echtes Thalasso-Spa muss daher direkt am Meer liegen. Als Vater der Thalassotherapie gilt der englische Arzt Richard Russell (1687–1759), der in seiner Doktorarbeit 1750 von der heilenden Wirkung des Meerwassers bei Infektionskrankheiten berichtete. Heute wird die Thalassotherapie z.B. zur unterstützenden Behandlung bei Haut-, Atemwegs- und Gelenkerkrankungen eingesetzt sowie zur allgemeinen Entspannung.

Thalassotherapie → Thalasso

Traditionelle chinesische Medizin (auch TCM) Ein jahrtausendealtes Heilkundesystem aus China, das vor dem Hintergrund der daoistischen Lehre entstand. Es umfasst eine spezielle Arzneitherapie, die vor allem pflanzliche Rohstoffe verwendet, eine eigene Diätetik, Akupunktur, die Tuina-Massage und die Qigong-Bewegungstherapie. Im Mittelpunkt der traditionellen chinesischen Medizin stehen das Qi, die (Lebens-) Energie, und ihr Gleichgewicht.

Tropendusche → Regendusche

Tuina-Massage Eine Massage der traditionellen chinesischen Medizin, die durch Massagegriffe und Druckausübung die Akupunkturpunkte sowie Energiebahnen des Körpers (Meridiane) stimuliert. Sie wirkt regulierend und harmonisierend und wird zur Schmerztherapie und bei Schlaf- sowie Verdauungsstörungen eingesetzt.

Türkisches Bad → Hamam

Vichydusche Diese Liegedusche stammt aus dem französischen Kurort Vichy. Sie ist über einem Wet Table, einer wasserfesten Liege mit speziellen Ablaufvorrichtungen, angebracht und sprüht aus mehreren, horizontal angebrachten Düsen Wasser auf den Körper, das wechselwarm sein kann. Die Vichydusche ist Teil der Thalassotherapie.

Vinotherapie Die Vinotherapie arbeitet mit Extrakten aus Weinranken und Weintrauben. Vor allem die in den Traubenkernen enthaltenen Polyphenole schützen vor freien Radikalen, welche die Haut altern lassen. Vinotherapie-Anwendungen aktivieren den Stoffwechsel und fördern die Neubildung von Hautzellen.

Unterwassermassage → Hydromassage

Vitality-Pool Ein besonders hochwertig ausgestatteter Whirlpool mit Luftsprudel- und Massagedüsen – häufig bietet er verschiedene Bereiche (Sitze, Liegen) speziell für Bein-, Rücken- oder Nackenmassagen.

Watsu-Pool Watsu setzt sich aus den Worten »water« und »shiatsu« zusammen und ist eine alternative hydrotherapeutische Behandlung: eine leichte, den Organismus entspannende Dreh- und Dehnbehandlung des Körpers in einem Becken mit körperwarmem Wasser.

Whirlpool (auch Jacuzzi) In diesem Innen- oder Außenbecken erzeugen Jetdüsen unterschiedlich starke Wasserstrahlen, die zur Massage genutzt werden können. Unterstützt wird der entspannende Effekt durch das warme Wasser.

Yoga Der Begriff Yoga steht in Sanskrit für »Vereinigung« oder »Integration«. Er bezeichnet eine indische philosophische Lehre, die körperliche und geistige Disziplinen verbindet und nach Harmonie von Körper, Geist und Seele, innerer Ruhe und Gelassenheit strebt. Es gibt verschiedene Yoga-Richtungen – außerhalb Indiens ist das Hatha-Yoga am bekanntesten, das körperliche Übungen (Asanas), Atemtraining und Meditation umfasst.

Glossaire

Acupressure (ou shiatsu) En usage dans la médecine traditionnelle chinoise. Le masseur exerce avec ses mains, ses coudes ou ses genoux une pression parfois très forte, et qui peut même être douloureuse, sur les points méridiens du corps. Il s'agit de neutraliser les perturbations dans le flux de l'énergie vitale (chi). Le shiatsu est la version japonaise, plus douce, de l'acupressure. Lorsque le corps dans son ensemble est traité, le shiatsu demande des vêtements légers et confortables et est le plus souvent pratiqué sur une natte à même le sol.

Acupuncture Cette méthode fait partie de la médecine traditionnelle chinoise. Des aiguilles très fines sont enfoncées dans des points spécifiques reliés aux organes par des lignes où circule l'énergie (méridiens). L'acupuncture est surtout utilisée pour lutter contre la douleur, mais aussi pour traiter, par exemple, les troubles du sommeil.

Aromathérapie L'aromathérapie fait partie de la phytothérapie et stimule le corps et l'esprit à l'aide d'huiles essentielles de plantes utilisées, par exemple, dans un bain ou une huile de massage. On part du principe que les arômes influencent le bien-être par l'intermédiaire du centre olfactif et du système limbique. En usage externe, les huiles essentielles diluées sont absorbées par la peau et exercent leur influence à l'intérieur du corps.

Ayurveda Originaire de l'Inde, la médecine ayurvédique (Ayurveda = « science de la vie » en sanskrit) est l'une des plus anciennes au monde – on estime qu'elle est apparue il y a environ 5000 ans. Elle n'étudie pas seulement les symptômes d'une maladie, mais en recherche les causes et vise l'équilibre des trois énergies vitales ou doshas que sont « Vata » (mobilité, respiration, activité nerveuse), « Pitta » (chaleur, métabolisme et digestion) et « Kapha » (humidité et système immunitaire). Pour les médecins ayurvédiques, le corps, l'esprit et l'âme ne font qu'un et cette thérapie inclue donc des massages, du yoga, de la méditation ainsi qu'un régime alimentaire particulier.

Bain à l'eau salée (ou grotte à l'eau salée) Un bain enrichi d'eau de mer ou de sel, donc très riche en minéraux avec une teneur en sel pouvant atteindre 6 pour cent. Il est utilisé en thérapie d'appoint, par exemple pour soigner les maladies de peau comme la névrodermite, les allergies, les problèmes digestifs, les troubles métaboliques ou du sommeil.

Bain à remous (ou jacuzzi) Dans ce bassin intérieur ou extérieur, des buses diffusent des jets d'eau de pression variable qui viennent masser le corps et détendre les muscles. L'utilisation d'eau chaude renforce l'effet relaxant.

Bain au petit-lait Un bain d'une température de 35–40° Celsius dans une eau enrichie de poudre de petit-lait. Celui-ci est riche en minéraux, en oligo-éléments, en vitamines et en protéines – l'acide lactique qu'il contient rétablit le pH de la peau, hydrate celle-ci et favorise le processus de guérison de maladies de peau comme l'eczéma et la névrodermite.

Bain aux algues (ou enveloppement aux algues) Soins aux algues riches en minéraux, en oligo-éléments et en vitamines. Ils désintoxiquent l'organisme et raffermissent l'épiderme. Les bains et les applications d'algues font partie de la thalassothérapie.

Bain aux huiles essentielles Un bain d'une température de 36–38 degrés Celsius dont l'eau est enrichie d'huiles essentielles de plantes ou de plantes fraîches ou sèches. Il a des vertus relaxantes, stimulantes ou rafraîchissantes, selon les plantes choisies.

Bain de Cléopâtre Il porte le nom de la célèbre reine d'Égypte qui se baignait régulièrement dans du lait de jument ou d'ânesse. De nos jours, le corps est enveloppé dans des tissus ou des films plastiques imbibés de lait et d'huiles essentielles ou il est allongé dans un bain au lait ou enrichi d'huiles. La peau ainsi hydratée et nourrie devient très douce.

Bain de fleurs Un bain d'une température de 36–38 degrés Celsius dont l'eau est enrichie de fleurs fraîches et sèches. La chaleur et le parfum ont des vertus relaxantes, et les huiles essentielles de fleurs soignent la peau. La rose et la lavande sont utilisées particulièrement souvent.

Bain de foin Le corps enveloppé dans du foin humide dont la température est de 40–42 degrés Celsius, commence à transpirer, ce qui élimine les toxines. Les huiles essentielles ont des effets bienfaisants sur les voies respiratoires ; en outre, le bain de foin peut soulager les rhumatismes et les sciatiques.

Bain de vapeur Terme général désignant un type de sauna à faible température (40–50 degrés Celsius), dont l'air est saturé de vapeur d'eau (80–100 pour cent). Le caldarium romain, le hammam turc, le banja russe et le temazcal mexicain sont, par exemple, des bains de vapeur.

Bain japonais aux enzymes Le corps est allongé dans une baignoire en bois remplie de sciure, de son de riz et d'enzymes végétales. Ce mélange chauffe tout seul grâce à une fermentation naturelle. Le bain aux enzymes stimule la circulation du sang et détoxique l'organisme.

Bain oriental → Hammam

Bain turc → Hammam

Bassin Kneipp La forme la plus connue de la cure Kneipp qui doit son nom à un prêtre, Sebastian Kneipp (1821–1897). Les bassins sont remplis jusqu'à hauteur du genou d'eau froide et d'eau chaude. On traverse ces bassins de température différente en marchant à la manière des cigognes. Le changement de température stimule le système vasculaire et favorise la circulation du sang.

Bassin Watsu Le Watsu est, comme son nom l'indique – « water » et « shiatsu » –, une technique de shiatsu adaptée à l'eau : des torsions et des étirements légers du corps, qui détendent l'organisme, sont pratiqués dans un bassin rempli d'eau chaude.

Cabine de soins (ou suite spa) La plupart des soins individuels sont administrés dans cet espace privé. Les cabines de soins simples sont équipées d'une table de massage et/ou d'un fauteuil de soins. Les cabines haut de gamme disposent d'extras comme une douche, une baignoire/un bain à remous, un bain de vapeur ou un sauna. La version luxueuse de la cabine de soins est la suite spa qui, au-delà des soins reçus, est à la disposition du client durant un temps défini. Il existe des cabines de soins individuelles, pour couple, la version luxe est également proposée aux familles et aux petits groupes.

Caldarium À l'origine, il s'agissait de la partie des thermes romains où l'on pouvait prendre des bains de vapeur d'une température de 40–50 degrés Celsius. L'air – son humidité atteint plus de 90 pour cent – y est souvent enrichi d'essences aromatiques et d'extraits de plantes qui exercent une action bienfaisante sur les voies respiratoires.

Chromothérapie Les couleurs ont un effet aussi bien sur l'état psychologique et émotionnel que sur le corps, par exemple sur les maladies de peau. Le corps est ici soumis au rayonnement de lampes spéciales. Selon leur longueur d'ondes, les couleurs pénètrent plus ou moins profondément dans la peau et ont des effets différents : le rouge est vitalisant, le vert équilibrant, le bleu est apaisant et le jaune chasse la déprime.

Cocon de flottaison Un bassin, ou une capsule qui a souvent la forme d'un coquillage et peut être fermée, rempli d'eau tiède à forte teneur en sel – le corps peut y flotter en apesanteur. Dans l'espace Bien-être, le bain est souvent complété par une luminothérapie et ses effets favorisent la méditation et la relaxation en profondeur.

Compresses Initialement utilisées pour traiter les plaies – les compresses de gaze peuvent étancher le sang qui coule, les compresses froides réduisent les enflures, les compresses chaudes ont une action spasmolytique. Ce principe est plus élaboré dans le spa où des compresses remplies de plantes sont utilisées durant les massages.

Cristalothérapie → Thérapie aux pierres précieuses

Cure détox → Soin détoxifiant

Cure F. X. Mayr Une méthode de jeûne thérapeutique qui porte le nom du médecin autrichien Franz Xaver Mayr (1875–1965) et vise en premier lieu la désintoxication et la purification de l'intestin. Considéré ici comme l'organe central pour la santé de l'être humain, il est nettoyé à l'aide de sel d'Epsom, ensuite on se nourrit surtout de lait (qui peut être remplacé par du yaourt, du lait de soja ou du lait d'amande) et de pain blanc rassis, raison pour laquelle cette cure est aussi nommée « cure pain-lait ».

Douche lifestyle (ou douche sensorielle) Une cabine de douche équipée de diverses buses réparties sur le plafond et les parois, réglables individuellement, souvent en combinaison avec des parfums et des couleurs.

Douche pluie tropicale (ou douche tropicale) Une douche dotée d'une pomme surdimensionnée, ce qui fait que l'eau tombe sur le corps avec peu de pression, douce comme une pluie d'été.

Douche sensorielle → Douche lifestyle

Douche tropicale → Douche pluie tropicale

Douche Vichy Elle a été créée dans la ville thermale de Vichy. Plusieurs buses placées sur une rampe au-dessus d'une table de massage résistant à l'eau et dotée de systèmes d'écoulement spéciaux, diffusent sur le corps des jets d'eau dont la température peut varier. La douche Vichy est un élément de la thalassothérapie.

Drainage lymphatique Cette méthode stimule le système lymphatique, en drainant la lymphe accumulée dans les tissus qui sont ainsi désengorgés. Des masseurs ou des physiothérapeutes ayant reçu une formation particulière effectuent des pressions et des glissements sur les tissus, ce qui permet à la lymphe de retourner dans les veines. Le drainage lymphatique est souvent utilisé après les opérations et pour soulager la douleur.

Enveloppement aux algues → Bain aux algues

Fangothérapie Un traitement originaire d'Italie à base de boue volcanique riche en minéraux et chauffée à une température de 45–50 degrés Celsius et qui est appliquée sur la peau. Le métabolisme et la circulation sanguine sont stimulés, le corps se détend. Les applications de fango sont recommandées en cas de douleurs dorsales et de rhumatismes ainsi que lors de certaines maladies de peau comme la névrodermite.

Fontaine de glace Prendre une douche froide, plonger dans le bassin d'eau froide ou se frotter avec des flocons ou des cristaux de glace après le sauna ou le bain de vapeur stimule la circulation sanguine, raffermit l'épiderme et active le système immunitaire.

Gommage (ou peeling) Une exfoliation cosmétique ou dermatologique de la peau pratiquée à l'aide de produits naturels (grains de sel ou café moulu), de produits chimiques (acides) ou au laser. Un gommage doux n'élimine que les cellules mortes de la peau, un peeling plus intense agit sur les couches superficielles.

Grotte à l'eau salée → Bain à l'eau salée

Hammam (ou bain turc, bain oriental) Pratiqué dans un établissement le plus souvent tapissé de marbre et comportant à l'origine plusieurs salles aux températures différentes : une salle sous coupole avec une dalle centrale chaude et des bassins de lavage latéraux, bain de vapeur et salle de repos. Traditionnellement, des espaces sont réservés aux hommes, d'autres aux femmes. Drapé dans un « pestemal » (une serviette de bain) on se lave dans le bassin avec de l'eau chaude et froide et on s'allonge pour détendre ses muscles ou se réchauffer sur la dalle chaude. Après un séjour dans le bain de vapeur, on se frotte le corps avec une « kassa » (un gant de toilette granuleux) pour exfolier sa peau ou on se laisse gommer le corps, savonner et masser sur une table de marbre par un « tellak ». Le rituel est suivi d'une phase de refroidissement et s'achève par la dégustation d'une tasse de thé.

Hydromassage (ou massage subaquatique) Ce traitement est pratiqué dans un bassin thermal équipé de buses de massages ou dans une baignoire spéciale dotée d'un matelas perforé laissant passer des bulles d'air. Les massages subaquatiques sont souvent proposés dans le cadre d'une thalassothérapie.

Jacuzzi → Bain à remous

Laconium Ce bain de sudation doux et sec tient son nom du peuple antique des Laconiens, qui vivaient dans le sud de la Grèce. La pièce est chauffée jusqu'à 50–60 degrés Celsius, ce qui fait que la circulation sanguine est stimulée et l'élimination des toxines favorisée.

Lithothérapie → Thérapie aux pierres précieuses

Manucure Comme son nom l'indique – du latin manus qui signifie main –, elle est consacrée aux soins des mains. Elle commence par un bain à l'eau tiède, ensuite les ongles sont raccourcis, limés, les cuticules repoussées et un vernis à ongle est appliqué sur demande. La manucure est souvent complétée par un gommage, un masque nourrissant et un massage des mains et des bras.

Massage Terme général désignant une technique manuelle qui agit sur la peau, les tissus ou la musculature par l'intermédiaire d'élongations, de pressions, de torsions ou d'étirements.

Massage aux pierres chaudes Dans ce traitement originaire de l'espace asiatique mais aussi pacifique et américain, le corps est massé avec des galets chauffés à 50–60 degrés Celsius, la pression exercée étant légère ou moyenne. Des pierres volcaniques (basalte) polies en ovale sont souvent utilisées. Les muscles se décontractent sous l'effet du mouvement et de la chaleur qui pénètre en profondeur.

Massage Lomi-Lomi Issu des thérapies naturelles ancestrales d'Hawaii, le Lomi est un rituel de massage au cours duquel la musique et les arômes hawaiiens favorisent la détente tandis que le corps est massé à l'huile de noix de kukui à l'aide des avant-bras, en alternant les mouvements lents et rapides, légers et puissants mais toujours amples. Ce soin est souvent proposé aussi à quatre mains avec deux masseurs.

Massage profond des tissus Ce massage recherche surtout une action sur les couches musculaires profondes. Les techniques utilisées prévoient des frottements vigoureux le long des faisceaux musculaires, de fortes pressions sur certains points ainsi que des frictions transversalement aux fibres musculaires.

Massage subaquatique → Hydromassage

Massage suédois Alors que pendant longtemps plus personne ne s'intéressait au massage en Europe, le Suédois Pehr Henrik Ling (1776–1839) a élaboré une forme de massage basé sur un enchaînement des cinq techniques classiques, qui consistent à effleurer, pétrir, frotter, tapoter et vibrer. Ce massage, classique sous nos latitudes, peut être pratiqué sur le dos ou l'ensemble du corps et vise surtout à décontracter les muscles.

Massage thaïlandais On l'appelle en Thaïlande Nuad Phaen Boran, ce qui signifie « l'ancien toucher qui guérit ». Le masseur traite dix lignes énergétiques du corps par étirements doux et la pression rythmique des paumes, des pouces, des genoux, des coudes et des pieds. De nombreux étirements et positions évoquent le yoga, si bien que cette méthode est parfois appelée « yoga passif ». Pratiqué par-dessus des vêtements légers et confortables, il vise à dénouer les blocages d'énergie qui sont la cause des maladies.

Massage Tui Na Une des branches de la médecine traditionnelle chinoise qui stimule les points d'acupuncture et les lignes énergétiques du corps (méridiens) par des manipulations et des pressions. Il a un effet régulateur et harmonisant et est utilisé pour soulager la douleur et en cas de troubles du sommeil et de la digestion.

Médecine traditionnelle chinoise (ou MTC) Né il y a quelques milliers d'années en Chine sur fond d'enseignement taoïste, ce système comprend une pharmacopée surtout basée sur des herbes médicinales chinoises, une diététique particulière, l'acupuncture, le massage Tui Na et les exercices énergétiques du qi gong. Le Qi (l'énergie vitale) et son équilibre sont au cœur de la médecine traditionnelle chinoise.

Medical Wellness Terme général désignant l'action coordonnée de la médecine occidentale et des pratiques visant le bien-être, celles-ci gagnant en intensité grâce à leurs effets conjugués. Le Medical Wellness ne se concentre pas seulement sur des soins de bien-être basés sur la médecine, mais aussi sur des mesures de prévention et, en général, la recherche d'un mode de vie plus sain.

Méditation Terme général désignant une discipline spirituelle ancrée dans de nombreuses religions et cultures. Grâce à elle, l'esprit s'apaise et s'absorbe – certaines pratiques visent aussi à élargir le champ de la conscience.

MTC → **Médecine traditionnelle chinoise**

Onsen Bain public japonais alimenté par une source naturelle chaude – traditionnellement volcanique. Grâce à sa teneur élevée en minéraux, l'eau a un effet bienfaisant sur la peau et favorise la détente. L'usage veut que les hommes et les femmes se baignent ensemble, mais aujourd'hui de nombreux établissements pratiquent la séparation des sexes.

Pédicurie Son nom vient du mot latin pes (pied) – les soins de pédicurie comprennent un bain de pieds tiède avant la suppression par abrasion des peaux mortes et des callosités ; ensuite, les ongles sont coupés et fraisés, les cuticules repoussées. Elle s'achève le plus souvent par un massage des pieds et l'application de vernis si souhaité.

Peeling → **Gommage**

Pilates (Méthode) Un entraînement physique global et doux qui porte le nom du sportif allemand Joseph Hubert Pilates (1883-1967). Centré sur la musculature profonde du bassin et de la taille, il vise une position correcte de la colonne vertébrale, un bon maintien, une silhouette amincie et des mouvements naturels.

Piscine Vitalité Un bain à remous haut de gamme avec buses à pression pour faire bouillonner l'eau et pour masser – il offre souvent diverses zones spécifiques (sièges, couchettes) pour le massage des jambes, du dos ou de la nuque.

Qi gong Un des piliers de la médecine traditionnelle chinoise, il doit renforcer l'énergie vitale de l'être humain. Le qi gong se place dans une approche globale et comprend des techniques de mouvement, de respiration et de méditation qui peuvent aussi être utilisées pour favoriser les processus de guérison, par exemple en cas de maladies comme les rhumatismes et l'asthme.

Réflexologie plantaire ou palmaire Une technique non conventionnelle de massage de la plante des pieds ou de la paume des mains. Les zones réflexes situées ici correspondent à des organes ou des groupes de muscles, si bien que masser ces zones stimule ceux-ci et peut aider à soulager la douleur. Le bien-être physique et spirituel est amélioré.

Reiki Le reiki (énergie vitale universelle) est une méthode de traitement non conventionnelle, élaborée au début du 20e siècle par le médecin japonais Mikao Usui (1865–1926). Le thérapeute agit comme une sorte de médium et, en imposant les mains, il laisse le flux d'énergie vitale s'écouler dans le corps du patient, ce qui vise à renforcer les facultés d'autoguérison de celui-ci.

Sanarium → **Sauna soft**

Sauna Terme général désignant une cabine, le plus souvent en bois, dont l'air est chauffé entre 50 et 130 degrés Celsius. La transpiration génère l'élimination des toxines et le renforcement du système immunitaire. Une visite au sauna classique comporte une phase de sudation, une phase de refroidissement et une phase de repos.

Sauna bio → **Sauna soft**

Sauna finlandais Une cabine revêtue de bois de sapin et d'épicéa, la température de l'air est d'environ 80–100 degrés Celsius. Des pierres chauffées au bois servent de source de chaleur, et on peut verser de l'eau dessus pour obtenir des bouffées de vapeur régulières. Dans le sauna finlandais classique, les visiteurs se fouettent légèrement la peau à l'aide de bouquets de rameaux de bouleau (« vihta » ou « vasta ») et refroidissent leur corps après la sudation à l'air frais et dans l'eau glacée.

Sauna soft (ou sanarium, sauna bio) La version soft du sauna régule doucement la circulation sanguine avec des températures de l'ordre de 50 degrés Celsius et une humidité de 40–50 pour cent. Ici, l'arrosage des pierres brûlantes est souvent remplacé par la diffusion d'huiles essentielles à l'effet plus doux ; les vertus thérapeutiques de la lumière et des sons peuvent aussi être utilisées.

Shiatsu → **Acupressure**

Soin détoxifiant (ou cure détox) Detox est l'abréviation de « détoxication » et désigne l'élimination des toxines présentes dans le corps. Les traitements Detox peuvent comprendre des cures liquides et des régimes spéciaux, des passages au sauna et des massages ainsi que des thérapies par le mouvement, comme le yoga.

Soin au rassoul Ce rituel de soin purifiant originaire d'Orient consiste à appliquer sur le corps du rassoul (ou ghassoul), une argile naturelle, à laquelle on peut ajouter des algues, réchauffée dans un bain de vapeur aux huiles essentielles et à frictionner la peau. Il peut être suivi, après la douche, d'un léger massage à l'huile relaxant.

Soin du visage Terme général désignant un soin cosmétique du visage. Il peut comprendre, par exemple, un nettoyage avec gommage ou vapeur d'eau, un massage, un masque ainsi qu'un maquillage.

Suite spa → **Cabine de soins**

Tai chi Le tai chi est une discipline dérivée des arts martiaux mais tournée vers l'intérieur, qui comprend des mouvements fluides s'enchaînant comme au ralenti, des exercices respiratoires et de méditation. Étroitement lié au principe du Yin & Yang et de leur équilibre, le tai chi doit agir à la fois sur le corps et l'esprit, détendre et affermir les muscles et améliorer le maintien et la perception que l'on a de son corps.

Tepidarium Une zone tiède – sa température de 38–40 degrés Celsius voisine de celle du corps – que l'on trouve déjà dans les thermes romains. Le système immunitaire y est doucement stimulé et les petites infections peuvent guérir plus facilement.

Thalasso (ou Thalassothérapie) Thalassa est le nom de la mer en grec – la thalassothérapie combine les bienfaits de l'eau de mer, de l'air marin, des algues, des boues marines, du sable et du soleil. Une spa thalasso authentique doit donc être au bord de la mer. Le médecin anglais Richard Russell (1687–1759) est considéré comme le père de la thalassothérapie – dans sa thèse de doctorat de 1750, il évoque les effets thérapeutiques de l'eau de mer en cas de maladies infectieuses. Elle est aujourd'hui utilisée en traitement de soutien des maladies de la peau, des voies respiratoires et des articulations, ou tout simplement pour se détendre.

Thalassothérapie → **Thalasso**

Thérapie aux pierres précieuses (ou Cristalothérapie, Lithothérapie) Cette thérapie non conventionnelle part du principe que les couleurs et les vibrations des pierres précieuses exercent une influence bienfaisante sur le corps et l'esprit. Des pierres comme le quartz rose, le lapis-lazuli ou l'améthyste sont portées à même le corps ou placées sur des zones réflexes ou des points d'acupuncture afin de libérer des énergies.

Vinothérapie Elle exploite les propriétés des extraits de vigne et de grains de raisin. Ce sont surtout les polyphénols contenus dans les graines du raisin qui protègent des radicaux libres, cause du vieillissement de la peau. Les soins activent le métabolisme et favorisent la formation de nouvelles cellules de la peau.

Yoga Son nom vient du sanskrit qui signifie union, intégration. Le yoga est un enseignement philosophique indien qui marie les disciplines physiques et spirituelles et vise l'harmonie du corps, de l'esprit et de l'âme, le calme intérieur et la sérénité. Il existe diverses écoles de yoga – hors de l'Inde, le hatha-yoga est la plus connue, qui comprend des exercices physiques (asanas) visant la maîtrise de à la respiration et à la méditation.

Photo Credits / Fotonachweis Crédits photographiques

Europe

Pädaste Spa
at Pädaste Manor
p. 12–21 supplied by the hotel

Espa
at The Ritz-Carlton Moscow
p. 22–27 supplied by the hotel

Espa
at The Ritz-Carlton Powerscourt
p. 28–33 supplied by the hotel

Grand Spa Resort
at A-Rosa Sylt
p. 34–39 supplied by the hotel

Heiligendamm Spa
at the Grand Hotel Heiligendamm
p. 40–45 supplied by the hotel

Brune Balance Med & Spa
at Gut Klostermühle Alt Madlitz
p. 46–53 supplied by the hotel

Adlon Day Spa
at Hotel Adlon
p. 54–57 supplied by the hotel

Gräflicher Park Hotel & Spa
p. 58–63 supplied by the hotel

Aiyasha Spa
p. 64–67 supplied by the spa

Grand Spa Resort
at A-Rosa Kitzbühel
p. 68–73 supplied by the hotel

Balance Center & Spa
at the Mavida Balance Hotel
p. 74–81 supplied by the hotel

Susanne Kaufmann Spa
at Hotel Post
p. 82–89 Alexander Gnädinger, supplied by the hotel

Aurelio Spa
at Aurelio Lech
p. 90–97 supplied by Aurelio Lech

Dolder Grand Spa
at The Dolder Grand
p. 98–105 supplied by the hotel (p. 98–99, 102–105 by Peter Hebeisen, p. 100, 101 top by Stefan Schmidlin, p. 101 bottom by Heinz Unger)

Delight Spa & Beauty
at Waldhaus Flims
p. 106–109 supplied by the hotel

Therme Vals
p. 110–115 supplied by the hotel

Kronenhof Spa
at the Grand Hotel Kronenhof
p. 116–121 supplied by the hotel

Six Senses Spa
at The Westin Paris
p. 122–129 Eric Laignel, supplied by Six Senses Resorts & Spas

Spa Vinothérapie Caudalie
at Les Étangs de Corot
p. 130–137 supplied by the hotel

Buddha-Bar Spa
at the Hilton Évian-les-Bains
p. 138–147 supplied by the hotel

Spa Vinothérapie Caudalie
at Les Sources de Caudalie
p. 148–155 supplied by the hotel

Kami Spa
p. 156–159 Massimo Grassi, supplied by the spa

Six Senses Spa
at Hotel Arts Barcelona
p. 160, 162 Pep Escoda/TASCHEN GmbH
www.pepescoda.com
p. 161, 163 supplied by Six Senses Resorts & Spas

Spaciomm
at Hotel Omm
p. 164, 169 Pep Escoda/TASCHEN GmbH
www.pepescoda.com
p. 165–168 Olga Planas, supplied by the hotel

Spa Vinothérapie Caudalie
at Marqués de Riscal
p. 170–172, 174–175 supplied by the hotel
p. 173 supplied by the spa

Aquapura Spa
at Aquapura Douro Valley
p. 176-181 supplied by the hotel (p. 176 top, 179 top right by Miguel Costa, p. 176 bottom, 177, 180 bottom, 181 bottom by Dan Kuhlberg, p. 179 top left, bottom right & left, 181 top by Carlos Cézanne)

Africa & the Middle East

Six Senses Spa
at Evason Ma'In Hot Springs
p. 182–189 supplied by Six Senses Resorts & Spas

Six Senses Spa
at Sharq Village
p. 190–195 supplied by Six Senses Resorts & Spas

Anantara Spa
at the Emirates Palace
p. 196–199 supplied by the hotel

Maia Spa
at the Maia Luxury Resort
p. 200–209 supplied by the hotel

Le Spa de Constance
at the Constance Ephelia Resort
p. 210–217 supplied by the hotel

Asia

Aman Spa
at the Aman New Delhi
p. 218–227 supplied by Amanresorts

Ananda Spa
at Ananda – In the Himalayas
p. 228–235 supplied by the hotel

Aman Spa
at Amankora
p. 236–245 supplied by Amanresorts

Como Shambhala Urban Escape
at the Metropolitan Bangkok
p. 246–253 supplied by the Metropolitan Bangkok

Six Senses Spa
at Soneva Kiri
p. 254–261 supplied by Six Senses Resorts & Spas

Six Senses Spa
at the Six Senses Hideaway Samui
p. 262–267 supplied by Six Senses Resorts & Spas

Espa
at Phulay Bay
p. 268–275 supplied by the hotel

Como Shambhala Retreat
on Cocoa Island
p. 276–285 supplied by the hotel

The Nam Hai Resort & Spa
p. 286–293 Mirjam Bleeker
www.mirjambleeker.nl

Zen Spa Red River
p. 294–301 Mirjam Bleeker
www.mirjambleeker.nl

The Oriental Spa
at The Landmark Mandarin Oriental
p. 302–307 supplied by the hotel

Aman Spa
at Amanfayun
p. 308–317 supplied by Amanresorts

Ginzan Hot Spring Fujiya Inn
p. 318–319, 322 bottom supplied by the hotel
p. 320–321, 322 top, 323 Jimmy Cohrssen
www.jimmycohrssen.com

North America

Mayflower Inn & Spa
p. 324–329 Poul Ober/TASCHEN GmbH
www.poulober.com

The Spa
at the Mandarin Oriental New York
p. 330–333 Poul Ober/TASCHEN GmbH
www.poulober.com
p. 334–337 supplied by the hotel

Shibui Spa
at The Greenwich Hotel
p. 338–343 Poul Ober/TASCHEN GmbH
www.poulober.com

The Standard Spa
at The Standard Miami Beach
p. 344–351 supplied by the hotel (p. 344–346, 348–351 by Nikolas Koenig, p. 347 by Ken Hayden)

Japanese Spa
at Ten Thousand Waves
p. 352–359 Don Freeman/TASCHEN GmbH
www.donfreemanphoto.com

Mii Amo Destination Spa
at Enchantment Resort
p. 360–363 supplied by the hotel

Aman Spa
at Amangiri
p. 364–369 supplied by Amanresorts

Osmosis Day Spa Sanctuary
p. 370–375 supplied by the spa

Latin America

Verana Day Spa
at Verana
p. 376–387 Jae Feinberg, supplied by the hotel

El Silencio Lodge & Spa
p. 388–393 supplied by the hotel (p. 388 top, 389, 390, 392 bottom, 393 by Sergio Pucci, p. 388 bottom, 391, 392 top by Brendan Austin/BAARK)

Le Spa Natura
at Hotel Santa Teresa
p. 394–403 supplied by the hotel

Imprint

Hohenzollernring 53, D-50672 Köln
www.taschen.com

To stay informed about upcoming TASCHEN titles, please request our magazine at www.taschen.com/magazine or write to TASCHEN, Hohenzollernring 53, D-50672 Cologne, Germany; contact@taschen.com; Fax: +49-221-254919. We will be happy to send you a free copy of our magazine, which is filled with information about all of our books.

Compiled, Edited & Layout
Angelika Taschen, Berlin

General Project Manager
Stephanie Paas, Cologne

Editorial Assistant
Nina Schumacher, Cologne

Texts
Christiane Reiter, Hamburg

English Translation
Iain Reynolds, Berlin

French Translation
Michèle Schreyer, Cologne

Design
Daniel Siciliano Bretas, Cologne

Lithograph Manager
Thomas Grell, Cologne

Endpapers
Verana Day Spa
at Verana
Photo: Jae Feinberg
supplied by the hotel

Page 2
Ananda Spa
at Ananda – In the Himalayas
Photo: supplied by the hotel

Page 8
Pädaste Spa
at Pädaste Manor
Photo: supplied by the hotel

Page 413
Aman Spa
at Amangiri
Photo: supplied by Amanresorts

Printed in Italy
ISBN 978-3-8365-1955-7